D1647853

Advances in

COMPUTERS

VOLUME 76

Advances in
COMPUTERS

Social Networking and The Web

EDITED BY

MARVIN V. ZELKOWITZ

Department of Computer Science
University of Maryland
College Park, Maryland

VOLUME 76

AMSTERDAM • BOSTON • HEIDELBERG • LONDON • NEW YORK • OXFORD
PARIS • SAN DIEGO • SAN FRANCISCO • SINGAPORE • SYDNEY • TOKYO
Academic Press is an imprint of Elsevier

ELSEVIER

ACADEMIC
PRESS

Academic Press is an imprint of Elsevier
30 Corporate Drive, Suite 400, Burlington, MA 01803, USA
84 Theobald's Road, London WC1X 8RR, UK
Radarweg 29, PO Box 211, 1000 AE Amsterdam, The Netherlands
525 B Street, Suite 1900, San Diego, CA 92101-4495, USA

First edition 2009

Library of Congress Cataloging-in-Publication Data
A catalog record for this book is available from the Library of Congress

British Library Cataloguing in Publication Data
A catalogue record for this book is available from the British Library

ISBN: 978-0-12-374811-9

ISSN: 0065-2458

For information on all Academic Press publications
visit our web site at books.elsevier.com

Printed and bound in USA

09 10 11 12   10 9 8 7 6 5 4 3 2 1

Contents

Information Sharing and Social Computing: Why, What, and Where?

Oded Nov

Social Network Sites: Users and Uses

Mike Thelwall

Highly Interactive Scalable Online Worlds

Graham Morgan

The Future of Social Web Sites: Sharing Data and Trusted Applications with Semantics

Sheila Kinsella, Alexandre Passant, John G. Breslin, Stefan Decker and Ajit Jaokar

Semantic Web Services Architecture with Lightweight Descriptions of Services

Tomas Vitvar, Jacek Kopecky, Jana Viskova, Adrian Mocan, Mick Kerrigan and Dieter Fensel

Issues and Approaches for Web 2.0 Client Access to Enterprise Data

Avraham Leff and James T. Rayfield

Web Content Filtering

José María Gómez Hidalgo, Enrique Puertas Sanz, Francisco Carrero García and Manuel De Buenaga Rodríguez

Contributors

Dr. John Breslin is currently a lecturer at the Department of Electronic Engineering in the National University of Ireland, Galway. He is also an associate researcher and leader of the Social Software Unit at the Digital Enterprise Research Institute at NUI Galway, researching semantically-enabled social networks and community portals. He is the founder of the SIOC project, which aims to semantically-interlink online communities. He has received a number of awards for website design, including two Net Visionary awards from the Irish Internet Association for the Irish community website boards; that is, which he co-founded in 2000. Dr. Breslin is a member of the IEI, IET, and IEEE.

Dr. Manuel de Buenaga is a full-time professor in the Department of Information Systems at the Universidad Europea de Madrid (UEM). He received a Ph.D. in Physics from Universidad Complutense de Madrid, where he was a researcher and lecturer from 1990 to 1997. He currently leads research projects at UEM in the areas of Natural Language Processing and Text Mining with applications in the Biomedical Domain and Content Filtering with academic and industrial partners. He has supervised several Ph.D. students and is co-author of more than 60 conferences, book chapters, and journal papers in these areas.

Dr. Francisco Carrero is Professor of Computer Science at Universidad Europea de Madrid (UEM), in Spain. His main research interest is Natural Language Processing (NLP) and Machine Learning (ML), with special emphasis on its application to Information Retrieval in biomedicine and Web Content Filtering. He has taken part in almost 10 research projects that have produced a number of research papers centered on these topics.

Prof. Stefan Decker is a professor at the National University of Ireland, Galway, and is the director of the Digital Enterprise Research Institute. Previously, he worked at ISI in the University of Southern California for two years as a research assistant professor and computer scientist, at Stanford University's Computer Science Department (Database Group) for three years as a postdoctoral researcher and research associate, and at Institute AIFB in the University of Karlsruhe for four years as a Ph.D. student and junior researcher. He is one of the most widely-cited Semantic Web scientists, and his current research interests include semantics in collaborative systems, Web 2.0, and distributed systems.

Dr. Dieter Fenselis is the scientific director of the Semantic Technology Institute in Innsbruck, Austria. His research interests are the Semantic Web, Semantic Web services, and semantically enabled service-oriented architectures. He obtained his Ph.D. in economic science from the University of Karlsruhe. He is a member of the IEEE Intelligent Systems advisory board. He could be reached at dieter.fensel@sti2.at

Dr. José María Gómez holds a Ph.D. in Mathematics, and has been a lecturer and researcher at the Universidad Complutense de Madrid (UCM) and the Universidad Europea de Madrid (UEM), for 10 years, where he has been the Head of the Department of Computer Science. Currently, he is R&D Director at the security firm Optenet. His main research interests include Natural Language Processing (NLP) and Machine Learning (ML), with applications to Information Access in newspapers and biomedicine, and Adversarial Information Retrieval with applications to spam filtering and pornography detection on the Web. He has taken part in around 10 research projects, heading some of them. José María has co-authored a number of research papers in the topics above, which can be accessed at his home page. He is Program Committee member for CEAS 2007, the spam Symposium 2007 and other conferences, and he has reviewed papers for JASIST, ECIR, and others. He has also reviewed research project proposals for the European Commission.

Ajit Jaokar is the founder of the London-based publishing company Futuretext focused on emerging Web and Mobile technologies. His thinking is widely followed in the industry and his blog, the OpenGardensBlog, was recently rated a top 20 wireless blog worldwide by readers of "Fierce Wireless." Currently, he plays an advisory role to a number of mobile start-ups in the UK and Scandinavia. Ajit believes in a pragmatic but open mobile data industry. He is also a member of the Web 2.0 workgroup.

Dr. Mick Kerrigan is a Ph.D. researcher in the Semantic Technology Institute (STI) located in the University of Innsbruck, Austria. Originally from Dublin, Ireland, Mick holds a B.Sc. from the University College Dublin and an M.Sc. from the National University of Ireland Galway, both in Computer Science. Mick's main area of interest is in the Software Life Cycle of Semantic Web Services and particularly in supporting the developer throughout the Semantic Web Service Development Cycle. The primary output of his work has been the Web Service Modeling Toolkit

(WSMT), an Integrated Development Environment for Semantic Web Services, focusing on tools for creating and managing WSMO descriptions. Mick contributes to the WSMO, WSML, and WSMX working groups and has been involved in a number of EU funded projects, namely DIP, Knowledge Web, SEEMP, and SHAPE. Mick is also a contributor to and the secretary of the OASIS Semantic Execution Environment Technical Committee (SEE-TC). He could reached at mick. kerrigan@sti2.at

Sheila Kinsella received a B.E. degree with first class honors from the National University of Ireland, Galway, in 2006. She is currently a graduate researcher with the Digital Enterprise Research Institute, the world's largest Semantic Web research group. Her research interests include semantic social networks, mapping ontology usage on the Semantic Web, and tag usages on the Web. In 2008, she was a visiting researcher at the Ecole Polytechnique Fédérale de Lausanne (EPFL) in Switzerland. She is also an associate researcher with IBM's Centre for Advanced Studies in Dublin.

Dr. Jacek Kopecký is a Ph.D. researcher at the Semantic Technologies Institute (STI) located at the University of Innsbruck, Austria. He holds a Master's degree from Palacky University, Czech Republic. His research interests cluster around Web technologies, with particular focus on Semantic Web Services, especially for automation supported by lightweight semantic descriptions. Since 2001, Kopecký has been contributing to Web services standardization especially at the W3C, and he chaired the W3C SAWSDL working group. He has also been involved in EU research projects DIP, TripCom, and SOA4All. He could be reached at jacek.kopecky@sti2.at

Dr. Avraham Leff is a research staff member in the Enterprise Collaboration Technologies department. He joined IBM in 1991. His research interests include distributed components and distributed application development. He received a B.A. in Computer Science and Mathematical Statistics from the Columbia University in 1984, and an M.S. and Ph.D. in Computer Science from the Columbia University in 1985 and 1992, respectively. Dr. Leff has been issued 6 patents and has 11 patents pending.

Dr. Adrian Mocan was a researcher at the Semantic Technology Institute Innsbruck (STI Innsbruck) and a member of the Service Web Intelligence and Semantic Execution Environment (SEE) groups while contributing to this book. Adrian started his work in the area of Semantic technologies in 2004 at the Digital Enterprise Research Institute, Galway, Ireland and he has completed his doctoral studies in 2008 at the National University of Ireland, Galway in the area of Data Interoperability. Currently, Dr. Adrian Mocan is a researcher at the SAP Research Center in Dresden and he is working in the area of Data Management and Analytics. He could be reached at adrian.mocan@sap.com

Dr. Graham Morgan earned his Ph.D. from Newcastle University in the area of distributed systems middleware, creating the NewTOP group communication service. Dr. Graham is a faculty member at the Newcastle University and continues to work in this area while applying knowledge and skills learnt from distributed systems research in the domain of online gaming. Working in the industry, Graham creates university courses, research projects, and software tools in an effort to ease computer game development of the future. After completing this chapter Graham is visiting George Mason University for a year to help lead their initiative in computer games research and teaching.

Dr. Oded Nov is an assistant professor at the Polytechnic Institute of New York University. He received his Ph.D. from the Cambridge University, UK. His research focuses on behavioral and social aspects of information systems and social media. In particular, his research deals with motivational and network structure aspects of contribution to Web 2.0 systems, such as Wikipedia, Flickr, and open source software projects.

Dr. Alexandre Passant is currently a postdoctoral researcher at the Digital Enterprise Research Institute, National University of Ireland, Galway. His research activities focus around the Semantic Web and Social Software: in particular, how these fields can interact with and benefit from each other in order to provide a socially-enabled machine-readable Web. He is the co-author of SIOC, a model to represent the activities of online communities on the Semantic Web, the author of MOAT, a framework to let people tag their content using Semantic Web technologies, and is also involved in various related applications. Prior to joining DERI, he was a Ph.D. student at the Université Paris-Sorbonne and carried out applied research work on "Enterprise 2.0" at Electricité De France.

Dr. Enrique Puertas (www.enriquepuertas.com) is Professor of Computing Science at Universidad Europea de Madrid, Spain. His research interests are broad and include topics like Artificial Intelligence, Adversarial Information Retrieval, Content Filtering, Usability and User Interface Designs. He has co-authored many research papers in those topics and has participated in several research projects in the field of AI.

Dr. James T. Rayfield is a research staff member in the Enterprise Collaboration Technologies department. He joined IBM in 1989. His research interests include transaction-processing systems and database systems. He received a B.Sc. in 1983, an M.Sc. in 1985, and a Ph.D. in 1988, all in Electrical Engineering from the Brown University. Dr. Rayfield has 9 patents issued and 12 patents pending.

Dr. Mike Thelwall is Professor of School of Computing and Leader of the Statistical Cybermetrics Research Group at the University of Wolverhampton, UK. He is a visiting fellow of the Amsterdam Virtual Knowledge Studio, a Docent at Åbo Akademi University Department of Information Studies, and a research associate at the Oxford Internet Institute. He has developed tools for analyzing web sites, blogs and social networking sites, including the web crawler SocSciBot, and software for statistical and topological analyses of site structures and content. He sits on nine editorial boards and has published 141 refereed journal articles and the book *Link Analysis: An Information Science Approach.*

Dr. Jana Viskova is a Ph.D. researcher at the department of information networks and faculty of informatics and management at the University of Zilina, Slovakia. She has received a masters degree from the same university, faculty of electrical engineering, department of telecommunications. Her research interests are in the next generation telecommunication networks and semantic web. She could be reached at viskova@fri.utc.sk

Dr. Tomas Vitvaris a senior researcher at the Semantic Technologies Institute in Innsbruck, Austria. He received his Ph.D. in computer science from the Czech Technical University. His research interests are in distributed systems and applications, including service-oriented computing, Semantic Web services, and enterprise computing. He is a member of the IEEE and of the working groups in the World Wide Web Consortium and the Organization for the Advancement of Structured Information Standards. He could be reached at tomas@vitvar.com

Preface

This is volume 76 of the *Advances in Computers*. Since 1960, annual volumes are produced containing chapters by some of the leading experts in the field of computers today. For almost 50 years these volumes present ideas and developments that are radically changing our society. This volume is no different. One of the most important ideas sweeping through the society today is the social networking website. Names like Wikipedia, Flickr, Second Life, Twitter, Facebook, Meetup, MySpace, LinkedIn, among others, are becoming common parlance as the youth, and a growing segment of the adult population, now view such websites as alternatives to the corner convenience store or coffee shop and critically important avenues for social interactions. In this volume, we explore this phenomenon to describe the development of some of these ideas as well as developments in web technology that enable this to occur.

This volume contains seven chapters divided into two parts. The first four chapters describe the social networking phenomenon and provide insights into the technology and its influences on our culture. The last four chapters provide details of the underlying technology that allows the web to expand to include these social networking sites, as well as other new applications, for information dissemination, accessing, and sharing.

Chapter 1 by Oded Nov, "Information Sharing and Social Computing: Why, What, and Where?" provides insights into the social networking phenomenon. Why have such sites been created, what are the motivations that encourage users to join, and what sort of information is shared? The chapter uses Wikipedia and Flickr as example models of social interaction websites.

"Social Network Sites: Users and Uses" by Mike Thelwell (Chapter 2) covers similar ground as Nov, but from a different perspective. He gives a more inclusive survey of social networking websites as well as more in-depth discussion of the variety of such sites, characteristics of the users of these sites, and technical concerns such as security and privacy issues that have been raised by users of such sites. Although he discusses many such sites, he provides a more complete survey of the characteristics of the MySpace domain.

Another form of social interaction website is the massively multiplayer online role-playing game or MMORPG. Games (i.e., websites) for some of these, such as World of Warcraft, can have up to 10 million subscribers each paying around US $14 per month to join. At US $140 million per month in revenue, there is some serious money being spent on these. In Chapter 3, Graham Morgan in "Highly Interactive Scalable Online Worlds" discusses the virtual world phenomenon. How does one develop such a game where users are distributed across large geographical areas across many networked machines? One critical problem is to ensure that temporal properties are preserved. That is, if two players, hosted on different computers are viewing the same action, what are the technical problems to solve to ensure that they see the same interactions?

Sheila Kinsella, Alexandre Passant, John G. Breslin, Stefan Decker, and Ajit Jaokar's (Chapter 4) "The Future of Social Websites: Sharing Data and Trusted Applications with Semantics" discusses the role of the web and semantic nets and their impact on the development of social networking websites. What are wikis and blogs, and how do we add semantics to these? Most social websites create groups or communities of users and their goal is to share information among the users within each community. Each social website has its own method of sharing this information tailored to the set of users it is trying to attract. How do we implement this sharing using the underlying technology of the web?

"Semantic Web Services Architecture with Lightweight Descriptions of Services" by Tomas Vitvar, Jacek Kopecky, Jana Viskova, Adrian Mocan, Mick Kerrigan, and Dieter Fensel (Chapter 5) continues some of the ideas on the semantic web from Chapter 4. The World Wide Web Consortium (W3C) has developed several standards for implementing semantic services including WSDL (Web Service Description Language) using XML as the underlying language and SOAP (Service Oriented Architecture Protocol). In this chapter the authors describe their Semantic Web Services (SWS) architecture using a lightweight description of such services.

A major impetus for the development of social networking has been the developing of an enhanced web-based set of interaction services called Web 2.0. In Chapter 6, "Issues and Approaches for Web 2.0 Client Access to Enterprise Data" by Avraham Leff and James T. Raymond, the authors describe the major issues involved by organizations using these Web 2.0 services. What services have been developed and how do programs utilize them for enhanced web applications?

In the final chapter, José María Gómez Hidalgo, Enrique Puertas Sanz, Francisco Carrero García, and Manuel de Buenaga Rodríguez in "Web Content Filtering" look at the problem of filtering certain web content. Issues such as spam, malware, visiting undesired websites, pornography, web surfing on company computers, and other related issues concern many system administrators. What are the issues involved with and what technologies can be employed to deal with appropriate use of the web?

I hope that you find these chapters of use to you in your work. If you have any topics you would like to see in these volumes or if you would like to write a chapter for a forthcoming volume, please let me know. I can be reached at mvz@cs.umd.edu.

Marvin Zelkowitz
College Park, Maryland

Information Sharing and Social Computing: Why, What, and Where?

ODED NOV

Department of Management, Polytechnic Institute of New York University, Brooklyn, New York 11201

Abstract

Why do people share content, metainformation, and programming knowledge with people they don't know, in return for no money? In a series of studies, the different drivers for information sharing in social computing systems are identified, and the effect of these drivers on actual levels of sharing is estimated, using a combination of survey and system data from Wikipedia, Flickr and a number of open source software projects. This way, we gain deeper understanding of why people share information, what types of information they share, and what are the venues used for the different types of sharing.

ADVANCES IN COMPUTERS, VOL. 76
ISSN: 0065-2458/DOI: 10.1016/S0065-2458(09)01001-8

1

1. Introduction

In recent years, social computing systems gained much popularity [24, 32]. Some of the most known social computing systems include Web sites such as Wikipedia, Flickr, YouTube, social networks such as MySpace and Facebook, and social bookmarking services such as del.icio.us [24, 32]. Such systems are characterized by online community formation and user content contribution [33]. Sustained participation and content contribution from individual members are critical for the viability of online communities [7, 11, 19], and this is particularly the case with social computing systems, where content is created by users.

In this chapter, I focus on social computing as a medium for information sharing. In particular, the focus is on three types of questions as a general framework (see Fig. 1):

1. Why people share information?
2. What type of information do they share?
3. What are the venues used for the different types of sharing?

Addressing the *Why* question, the research presented in this chapter focuses on a number of factors, primarily individual motivations (e.g., intrinsic/extrinsic motivations) and network structure properties (e.g., position in a network). Addressing the *What* and *Where* questions, the focus is on the different types of information and the venues in which they are shared. Examples include code (e.g., open source software), factual content (e.g., Wikipedia), metainformation (e.g., tags), and photos

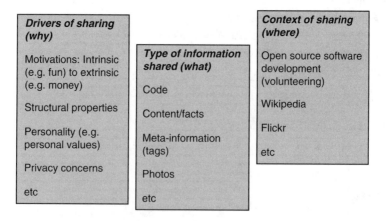

FIG. 1. Information sharing framework.

(shared on systems such as Flickr). These questions are interrelated, and often various connections exist between drivers of sharing, the type of information shared, and the venues used for sharing. While some of these questions have been studied in isolation, an integrative group of studies addressing social computing and information sharing in a unified way is useful for those working on collaborative systems, peer production, and community-based initiatives. The results of these studies are presented in what follows.

2. Information Sharing: Wikipedia

Wiki technology enables users to create and edit a Web page [13, 23]. A prominent example of a large-scale use of wiki technology is Wikipedia, a Web-based user-created encyclopedia [26]. In recent years, Wikipedia has become one of the most popular sites on the Web [6, 26], with more than 2.4 million entries written in English alone.

Wikis represent an approach—often referred to as the community-based model or peer production—that changes the way in which knowledge and knowledge bases are created and maintained. Evans and Wolf [15] describe the decentralized and social approach to knowledge accumulation, which draws on the open source movement, as a revolutionary approach to the delivery of information goods [3]. Wikipedia is also referred to as an example of open content or open source content project [31, 39]).

Why, then, do people share vast amounts of information with people they don't know in return for no monetary incentive? This question can be framed using the *Why/What/Where* framework (see Fig. 2).

Addressing this question, Nov [26] used the volunteering motivational categories identified by Clary et al. [12] to identify what motivates such contributions. These include:

- *Values.* Volunteering gives volunteers an opportunity to express values related to altruistic and humanitarian concerns for others.

- *Social.* Volunteering provides for volunteers the opportunities to be with their friends or to engage in activities viewed favorably by important others.

- *Understanding.* Through volunteering, individuals may have an opportunity to learn new things and exercise their knowledge, skills, and abilities.

- *Career.* Volunteering may provide an opportunity to achieve career-related benefits such as preparing for a new career or maintaining career-relevant skills.

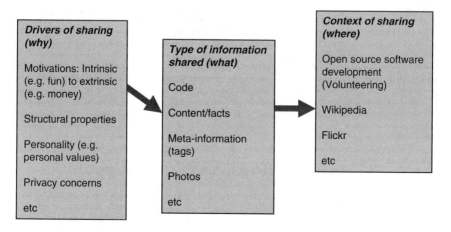

FIG. 2. Information sharing: Wikipedia.

- *Protective*. It involves protecting the ego from negative features of the self, reduces guilt over being more fortunate than others, or addresses one's own personal problems.
- *Enhancement*. This is category somewhat related to the Protective category; however, in contrast to the latter's concern with eliminating negative aspects related the ego, Enhancement involves positive strivings of the ego.

Wikipedia relies on the open source model [18, 31] where people contribute their time and knowledge to create publicly available products. Therefore, in addition to the general volunteering motivations, two other motivations used extensively in research on open source software development were used in the Wikipedia study: fun and ideology [17] and [41], respectively.

Using a survey method, Nov [26] found that the weekly average level of contribution was 8.3 h. The top motivations for contribution were Fun and Ideology, whereas Social, Career, and Protective were not found to be strong motivations for contributions (see Table I). It was found that the levels of each of the motivations Fun, Values, Understanding, Enhancement, Protective, and Career were positively correlated with contribution level (also in Table I). However, unexpectedly, contribution level was not correlated significantly with the Ideology and Social motivations.

Why weren't some of the motivations associated with increased contribution? The Ideology case was particularly puzzling: while people stated that ideology is high on their list of reasons to contribute, it was found that being more ideologically motivated does not necessarily translate into increased contribution. The effect of social desirability [10] as a possible explanation was ruled out as social desirability

TABLE I
MOTIVATION LEVELS AND CORRELATIONS WITH CONTRIBUTION LEVELS

Motivation	Mean
Fun	6.10 (1.15) [0.322**]
Ideology	5.59 (1.71) [0.110]
Values	3.96 (1.55) [0.175*]
Understanding	3.92 (1.48) [0.296**]
Enhancement	2.97 (1.39) [0.313**]
Protective	1.97 (1.05) [0.306**]
Career	1.67 (0.94) [0.185*]
Social	1.51 (0.92) [0.027]

* significant at 0.05 level;
** significant at 0.001 level.
Standard deviations in parentheses ( ) and Pearson correlation coefficient in square brackets [ ]. *Source*: Nov [26].

was controlled for in the data analysis. An explanation the author suggests is a case of "talk is cheap": while people have strong opinions about ideology, these do not translate into actual behavior. Yet another possible explanation might be that contributors who are motivated by ideology may also contribute to other ideology-related projects, such as open source software projects, and would therefore have less time to contribute in each project.

In a related study, Schroer and Hertel [39] studied the determinants of Wikipedia contributors' satisfaction and actual contribution. Their findings indicate that contributors' level of contribution is determined by the contributors' tolerance for opportunity costs and the experienced characteristics of their tasks, the latter effect being partially mediated by intrinsic motivation. The most relevant task characteristics for contribution were autonomy, task significance, and skill variety. Additional motives reported by Wikipedia contributors suggest the importance of the generativity motive, manifest in the opportunity to create a heritage for children, and help collect knowledge. In addition, Schroer and Hertel found that contributors' satisfaction was determined by perceived benefits, identification with the Wikipedia community, and task characteristics. In this case as well, the most relevant task characteristics for contributors' satisfaction were autonomy, task significance, and skill variety.

Wikipedia aggregates information from a large and diverse author base, where authors are free to modify any article. What, then, leads to content quality of these contributions? Addressing this question, Arazy et al. [3] developed and tested empirically a model of the factors that determine Wikipedia's articles' quality.

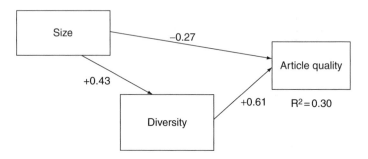

FIG. 3. PLS results: Wikipedia article quality.

Their findings (see Fig. 3, which presents the model and the path coefficients found) indicate a positive effect of size on diversity and a positive impact of group diversity on content quality (path coefficients are 0.43 and 0.61, respectfully, both significant at 0.05). Overall, the Arazy et al.'s [3] model explains more than 30% of the variance in article content quality. These findings are important, as they highlights other aspects—in addition to those covered in motivation studies—of Wikipedia contribution.

2.1 Motivations: Wikipedia Versus Open Source

Research on the motivations of community-based model contributors (such as Wikipedia or open source software) has, for the most part, focused on either software or content. However, recently the question of whether there are differences in motivations between contributors in these two different contexts has been addressed until. In their comparative study of open source software and Wikipedia contributors, Oreg and Nov [31] suggested that the salience of contribution motivations may differ across contexts. Oreg and Nov examined whether certain motivations are more prominent in the case of software contributors whereas others are be more prominent in the case of Wikipedia contributors (see Fig. 4).

Oreg and Nov [31] focused on three motivations that have been well established in the open source software literature: reputation building, learning, and altruism. These motivations represent three different positions on the continuum of extrinsic to intrinsic motivations: extrinsic motivations are instrumental in nature and represent cases with a focus on extrinsic rewards. Intrinsic motivations, on the other hand, tend to be terminal in the sense that they emphasize inherent satisfaction rather than the action's consequence [36].

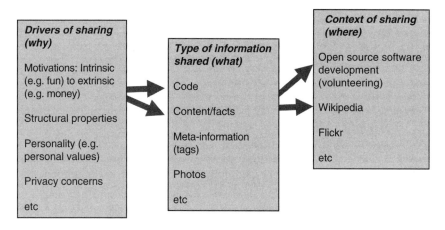

FIG. 4. Information sharing: content versus software.

Using a survey method, Oreg and Nov found that contributors to open source software projects rated the reputation building and learning motivations significantly higher than Wikipedia contributors' ratings of these motivations [$(F_{(1,293)} = 9.20, p < 0.01$) in the case of reputation building and ($F_{(1,295)} = 7.62, p < 0.01$) in the case of self-development]. On the other hand, survey respondents from Wikipedia gave significantly higher ratings to altruistic motivations ($F_{(1,296)} = 14.71, p < 0.001$). These findings offer a view that emphasizes the unique nature of contribution contexts. Furthermore, the findings provide insights into the different incentives that can be used in different contexts: in the case of open source software initiatives, project organizers should highlight aspects of learning and recognition as experts in their efforts to recruit contributors, whereas in content-based projects such as Wikipedia, organizers need to highlight aspects of reciprocity and altruism, such as the benefit to the community.

2.2   The Sustainability of Wikipedia: The Role Justice

Is the community-based model that underlies open source software and content projects such as Wikipedia, sustainable? The sustainability of the open source model has often been questioned (e.g., [4, 5, 14]). This is because open source projects, like other collective action efforts, are susceptible to free-riding [42]. The literature on collective action emphasizes the importance of recruiting and motivating contributors [42] to mitigate against the effect of free-riding. Thus, to examine the sustainability potential of the open source model, it is important to understand the relationship between contribution motivations and the threat of external appropriation—a case of free-riding whereby the results of open source contributors' efforts (e.g., source code, content) are monetized by a third party that did not contribute to the project and does not share the proceeds from commercializing it with the project's contributors.

Nov and Kuk [27] explored the impact of external appropriation on intended efforts in Wikipedia by asking what determines Wikipedia contributors' response to expected external appropriation. Justice perceptions have been associated with behavioral reactions such as counterproductive behavior [9]. Since in the Wikipedia environment contributors have limited opportunities to react counterproductively, a counterproductive reaction may be effort withdrawal—a decrease in the level of contribution as a response to perceived unjust behavior. Nov and Kuk [27] examined whether there is a negative correlation between justice perception of external appropriation, and expected effort withdrawal. Furthermore, Nov and Kuk looked at the relationship between extrinsic and intrinsic motivations and effort withdrawal intentions.

Participants in Nov and Kuk's [27] two-stage study were presented with the following external appropriation scenario. First, they were informed that under the GNU Free Documentation License, which is the license under which Wikipedia operates, anyone (including corporations or people who did not contribute to Wikipedia) can copy and redistribute content commercially, without sharing the profits with the people who were part of the project. Then, participants were presented with a scenario in which a corporation, which does not contribute to Wikipedia in any way, will take the content they have helped create, start distributing and charging money for it, and not share the profits with those who created it. In the second stage of the questionnaire, following the presentation of the scenario, participants were asked again, using the same set of items presented in the first stage, about their intention to reduce their contribution in the next 6 months.

Justice was measured using a four-item scale comprising of both two distributive and two procedural justice items adapted from Colquitt et al. [9]. The scale included items such as "How fair will be the outcome of such profit sharing?" and "How fair is the procedure used to distribute future profits?" The motivations measured were the same motivations used by Nov [26] to study Wikipedians' motivations, and were presented earlier. This time, the motivations were grouped into extrinsic motivations and intrinsic motivations. In their review of open source motivations, Rossi and Bonaccorsi [35] classified monetary rewards, reputation among peers, future career benefits and learning as extrinsic motivations, and creative pleasure, altruism, sense of belonging to the community and fight against proprietary software as intrinsic motivations. Thus, the motivations of Career,

Enhancement, Social, Protective, and Understanding were classified as extrinsic, while Values, Ideology, and Fun were classified as intrinsic. Effort withdrawal was measured as the difference between intention to contribute less to the project before and after the external appropriation scenario was presented. Hence, a negative difference score indicates effort retention, whereas a positive difference score indicates effort withdrawal. As a manipulation check, the mean difference before (mean = 4.73, SD = 1.55) and after (mean = 4.47, SD = 1.66) the external appropriation scenario were compared. The pair-samples T-test was significant, indicating that the reported mean of intention to withdraw effort was significantly higher after the appropriation manipulation.

Effort withdrawal was found to be negatively and significantly correlated with perceived justice and intrinsic motivation, whereas effort withdrawal was found not to be significantly correlated with intrinsic motivation. Moreover, it was found that perceived justice moderates the effect of intrinsic motivations on effort withdrawal, such that the effect of intrinsic motivations on effort withdrawal is stronger for people who are low in perceived justice and weaker for individuals high in perceived justice. This supports the view that contributors who score high on justice (i.e., believe that the licensing terms upon which external appropriation is based are just) would be less sensitive to external appropriation, and therefore, for them, the difference between those high on intrinsic motivations and those low in intrinsic motivations would be less pronounced than for those who score low on justice.

Reflecting the findings of the study, organizers of community-based content projects who seek to recruit and retain content contributors are recommended to inform potential and actual contributors about the open source model and its license terms. Furthermore, it is recommended that the aspects of contribution that may appeal to intrinsic motivations—such as the fun associated with contribution—be highlighted. This way, contributors might be less inclined to withdraw efforts as a result of future external appropriation. Another issue is the importance of license terms: different open source licenses may reflect different stances toward the possibility of external appropriation. This may help organizers of open source content projects to make informed decisions about the license to be adopted.

3. Photo Sharing: Flickr

What motivates people to share photos online? Like other forms of social computing services such as Wikipedia, photo sharing communities rely on contributions of users. However, according to Nov and Ye [28], photo sharing differs from other forms of content contribution in that the act of contributing in the case of photos is separate from the act of content creation. Photographers have been taking photos regardless of whether they can share it or not. In contrast, not many people would be willing to invest the time and effort in writing an encyclopedia entry, without the goal of publishing it. This difference may have implications as far as motivations for contribution go. On the one hand, the "second act" of contributing photos online is an optional action separated from the "first act" of photo taking; on the other hand, once photos have been created, uploading them for sharing is a fairly easy step and requires little mental effort. The studies on online information sharing and social computing have mainly focused on services where creation is coupled with sharing, and there has been no study that investigates drivers of contribution that is decupled from creation. This gap was addressed by Nov and Ye [28] who studied what drives photo sharing by taking into consideration the effects of two sets of factors: individual motivations on the one hand and network structure factors on the other hand (see Fig. 5).

3.1   Background on Flickr

With more than 15 million users, who have uploaded more than a billion photos, Flickr is a prominent example a Web 2.0 image sharing, whose content is created by its users. A Flickr user can upload images, and image tagging is done by annotating them with tags, or unstructured textual labels, mostly by the user who uploaded the

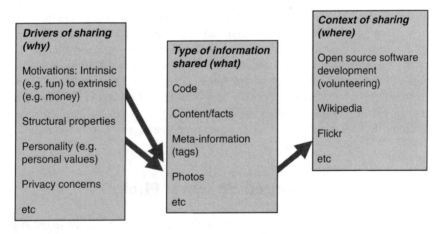

Fig. 5. Information sharing: photos.

photos [24]. A Flickr user can belong and post photos to multiple user groups, which are normally formed around a common subject of interest (e.g., Birds, Boston). In addition, a Flickr user can designate other users as "contacts," people whose photos the user follows (contacts are often reciprocal). When a user joins a group or adds people to his contact list, the user implicitly accepts that his images will be exposed to members of the group or the user's contacts.

3.2   Individual Motivations

Nov and Ye [28] followed the motivational categories for knowledge sharing in open source communities outlined by Lakhani and Wolf [20]:

1. Enjoyment-based intrinsic motivations
2. Obligation/community-based intrinsic motivations
3. Extrinsic motivations

In addition to individual motivations, Nov and Ye [28] considered structural properties, and in particular, structural embeddedness. The structural embeddedness of an actor in a network can manifest in the actor's degree of centrality. Prior research has found a positive effect of individuals' structural embeddedness on their knowledge contribution [11, 43]. Thus, a positive relationship between structural embeddedness of actors and their level of sharing is expected. In addition, Nov and Ye used as a control variable the users' tenure in the community.

A Web-based survey was administered to Flickr users, using a combination of survey responses and independent system data of the actual image uploading behavior of the user. System data for each user who took the survey were extractable via the Flickr API (application programming interface). The Flickr API allows third-party Web sites to communicate with Flickr and exchange information. Respondents were asked, at the end of the Web-based survey, to log in via the survey Web site to their Flickr account. This way, data about the respondents' activities were automatically extracted using and recorded together with the respondents' responses to the questionnaire.

Table II summarizes Nov and Ye's [28] results.

The results demonstrate that users with higher commitment to the community and higher network centrality tend to share more photos. Enjoyment, however, was not related to the level of contribution. This lack of correlation may be attributed to the particular characteristics of photo sharing in that unlike social computing systems such as Wikipedia, in the case of photo sharing, content creation and content are two separate steps, and users may be motivated more by the "fun" in content *creation*, and not by the enjoyment of *sharing*. The negative relation found between the self-development motivation and the level of photo sharing may be explained by the

TABLE II
REGRESSION RESULTS

		Step 2		
	Independent variables	β	t	p
Results of predictors	Constant	–	13.432	0.000
	Log (years)	0.269	5.872	0.000
	Log (contacts)	0.249	5.258	0.000
	Self-development	−0.126	−2.705	0.007
	Enjoyment	−0.007	−0.153	0.879
	Commitment	0.170	3.496	0.001
Results of the overall model	R^2	0.238		
	Adjusted R^2	0.229		
	F	27.32 (df $= 5, p < 0.001$)		

view that the more a user is motivated by self-development, the more this user will focus on the *quality* (rather than the quantity) of the photos shared, at the expense of the quantity.

Overall, the results of this study suggest that user contribution in photo-sharing systems is primarily socially motivated. Therefore, opportunities for social interaction need to be an essential part of such systems' design, and by encouraging users to use existing social interaction avenues.

4. Metainformation Sharing: Tags

4.1 Background

Advances in computer technologies, and social computing in particular, have led to the creation of large-scale information available to users [30]. Information repositories are often characterized by heterogeneity of information sources and large volume of information pieces deposited [38]. Metainformation, or "the description of additional information about pieces of data stored in a database or knowledge base" [38], plays a crucial role in such information repositories, by facilitating the organization and retrieval of information [25, 38]. User-contributed annotation in the form of tags is a form of metainformation that can improve the discovery, retrieval, and understanding of information from large-scale repositories [38]. Tags are keywords (e.g., "lighthouse," "California") used to annotate various types of content, including images, bookmarks, blogs, and videos [34, 40], and the rise of social computing has been supported an increase in user-contributed tags [8, 16, 24, 34]. The popularity of tagging is attributed to the benefits users gain from effectively organizing and sharing very large amounts of information [2, 8]. In the case of photos, tagging represents an important change in the way images are organized and shared photography [40].

Sharing metainformation in the form tags represents another form of sharing facilitated by social computing. With the goal of understanding why people add tags, to their photos, thus sharing metainformation, Nov et al. [29] studied Flickr tagging (see Fig. 6).

Nov et al. examined what drivers tagging by users, and what effects do the different drivers have on actual tagging behavior. Users' motivations for tagging were explored qualitatively by Ames and Naaman [2] who studied Flickr users. In their study, Ames and Naaman drew the distinction between motivations stemming from three categories of the tags' *target audience*. These categories include *Self*, *Family & Friends*, and the general *Public* of Flickr users. Within each category, the researchers identified two functional dimensions for tagging, representing the tag's intended use: *Organization* and *Communication*. *Organization* is tied to categorization and future retrieval of photos, and *Communication* focuses on providing additional context to viewers of the photo. For example, in the *Self* category, the *Organization* function is intended to facilitate future search and retrieval by the user, and the *Communication* function involves adding context to the image for the user's own future recall or understanding (e.g., "where did I take this photo?"). In the *Public*

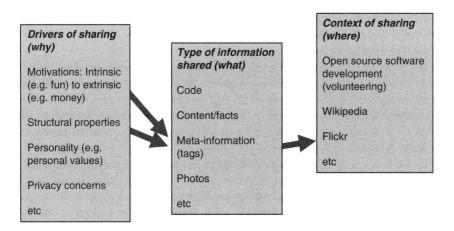

Fig. 6. Metainformation sharing: tags.

and *Family & Friends* categories, the *Organization* function is intended to facilitate future search and retrieval by others in the Flickr community.

In addition to the Ames and Naaman framework, Nov et al. [29] suggested that *social presence* may play a role in tagging behavior. According to social psychology research, behavior is affected by presence—actual, imagined, or implied—of others [1]. The effect of perceived social presence was found to exist even when such presence was computer mediated (e.g., [22, 37]). Perceived social presence was also found to have a positive effect on tagging in del.icio.us, a system used for collaborative sharing and management of bookmarks [21]. According to Nov et al. [29], the *Public* and *Family & Friends* motivations would not exist without the user's awareness of other people in the community who might be viewing his photos. On Flickr, there are multiple ways in which a user perceives social presence, such as *groups* and *contacts*. By marking certain contacts as "friends" or "family," a user may provide his contacts with a special access for to his semiprivate photos. When a user joins a group or adds people to his contact list, the user implicitly accepts that his images will be exposed to members of the group or the user's contacts, thereby leading to a perception of social presence.

4.2   The Empirical Study

Nov et al. [29] carried out a study of tagging on Flickr, using both survey data and system data. To measure the effects of different tagging motivations, they developed a scale based on Ames and Naaman's qualitative work, which includes three constructs, representing the three categories of intended users of the tags: *Self*, *Family & Friends*, and *Public*. For each construct, they included questionnaire items representing both the communication and the organization functions. After validation in a pilot study, the final scale consisted of four, six, and six questionnaire items for *Self*, *Family & Friends*, and *Public*, respectively.

The analysis of the data received revealed that the model, consisting of stated motivations, social presence indicator, and control variables explained 57.1% of the variance in user tagging behavior (see Fig. 7). The levels of the *Self* and *Public* motivations, as well as the social presence indicators and the number of photos, were positively correlated with tagging level. The *Family & Friends* motivation, however, was not correlated with tagging level.

The absence of significant relationship between the *Family & Friends* motivation and tagging level was suggested to be explained in a number of ways: one was that Ames and Naaman [2] suggested that for the *Family & Friends* target of tagging, the Organization function was a relatively weak motivation; the stronger motivation stems from the Communication function. Since the Communication function on Flickr is served by other ways in addition to tagging (e.g., titles, captions, and sets),

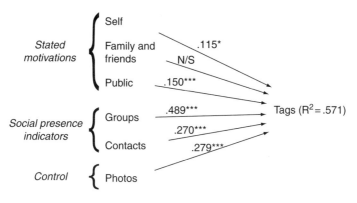

FIG. 7. Regression results ($N = 237$) (*significant at 0.05 level; **significant at 0.01 level; and ***significant at 0.001 level). Numbers next to arrows represent standardized path coefficients.

the need in tagging for this purpose is reduced. In addition, users may communicate information about the photos to their friends and family in other ways, such as email and thus explain the lack of correlation found.

The findings indicate that tagging is essentially a social activity, driven by social participation and perceptions. Therefore, just like in the case of photo sharing, organizers of social computing systems seeking to increase tagging activity should focus their communication and marketing efforts on public- and social-driven motivations, maximizing the opportunities for social interaction, and exposing users to the benefits of such interactions.

5.   Conclusion

Future research related to social computing and information sharing can follow a number of paths. First, the study of additional drivers and forms of contribution, within and outside the *Why/What/Where* framework is needed. For example, studying the role of privacy perceptions in information sharing seems important, as more and more concerns about privacy issues related to social computing are raised. Second, better understanding of the different venues for information, including the similarities and differences between them, may focus on a comparative study of different sharing venues, using similar survey instruments and system data. Third, further studies may focus on other outcomes of social computing information sharing. For example, it would be useful to know what drives *quality* and/or *popularity* of the information shared. Overall, information sharing and social computing require further study—work that will hopefully lead to better understanding of this increasingly popular and important trend.

REFERENCES

[1] Allport G., 1968. The historical background of modern social psychology. In *The Handbook of Social Psychology*, (G. Lindzey and E. Aronson, eds.), 2nd edn, vol. 1, pp. 1–80. Addison-Wesley, Reading, MA.

[2] Ames M., and Naaman M., 2007. Why we tag: Motivations for annotation in mobile and online media. In *Proceedings of CHI*. ACM Press, San Jose, CA.

[3] Arazy O., Morgan W., and Patterson R., 2006. Wisdom of the Crowds: Decentralized Knowledge Construction in Wikipedia. In *Proceeding of the 16th Workshop on Information Technologies & Systems* (WITS06), December 2006.

[4] Benkler Y., 2000. The battle over institutional ecosystem in the digital environment. *Communications of the ACM*, **44**(2): 84–90.

[5] Bonaccorsi A., and Rossi C., 2003. Why Open Source software can succeed. *Research Policy*, **32**(7): 1243–1258.

[6] Bryant S. L., Forte A., and Bruckman A., 2005. Becoming Wikipedian: Transformation of participation in a collaborative online encyclopedia. *Proceedings of the 2005 international ACM SIGGROUP*.

[7] Butler B., 2001. Membership size, communication activity, and sustainability: A resource-based model of online social structures. *Information Systems Research*, **12**(4): 346–362.

[8] Cattuto C., Loreto V., and Pietronero L., 2007. Semiotic dynamics and collaborative tagging. *Proceedings of the National Academy of Sciences of the United States of America*, **104**: 1461–1464.

[9] Colquitt J., Scott B., Judge T., and Shaw J., 2006. Justice and personality: Using integrative theories to derive moderators of justice effects. *Organizational Behaviour and Human Decision Processes*, **100**(1): 110–127.

[10] Crowne D., and Marlowe C., 1960. A new scale of social desirability independent of psychopathology. *Journal of consulting psychology*, **24**, 349–354.

[11] Chiu C., Hsu M., and Wang E., 2006. Understanding knowledge sharing in virtual communities: An integration of social capital and social cognitive theories. *Decision Support Systems*, **42**(3): 1872–1888.

[12] Clary E., Snyder M., Ridge R., Copeland J., Stukas A., Haugen J., and Miene P., 1998. Understanding and assessing the motivations of volunteers: A functional approach. *Journal of Personality and Social Psychology*, **74**, 1516–1530.

[13] Denning P., Horning J., Parnas D., and Weinstein L., 2005. Inside risks: Wikipedia risks. *Communications of the ACM*, **48**(12): 152.

[14] Economist, 2006. Open, but not as usual–Open-source business. *The Economist*, March 18, (378:8469), 74.

[15] Evans P., and Wolf B., 2005. Collaboration rules. *Harvard Business Review*, **83**(7/8): 96–104.

[16] Golder S., and Huberman B., 2006. Usage patterns of collaborative tagging systems. *Journal of Information Science*, **32**(2): 198–208.

[17] Hars A., and Ou S., 2002. Working for Free? Motivations of participating in Open Source projects. *International Journal of Electronic Commerce*, **6**(3): 25–39.

[18] Hendry D., Jenkins J., and McCarthy J., 2006. Collaborative bibiliography. *Information Processing and Management*, **42**(3): 805–825.

[19] Koh J., Kim Y., Butler B., and Bock G., 2007. Encouraging participation in virtual communities. *Communications of the ACM*, **50**(2): 68–73.

[20] Lakhani K., and Wolf R., 2005. Why hackers do what they do: Understanding motivation and effort in free/open source software projects. In *Perspectives in Free and Open Source Software*, (J. Feller, B. Fitzgerald, S. Hissam, and K. Lakhani, eds.), MIT Press, Cambridge, MA.

[21] Lee K., 2006. What goes around comes around: An analysis of del.icio.us as social space. In *Proceedings of CSCW 2006*. ACM Press, New York, NY.

[22] Ling K., Beenen G., Ludford P., Wang X., Chang K., Li X., Cosley D., Frankowski D., Terveen L., Rashid A., Resnick P., and Kraut R., 2005. Using social psychology to motivate contributions to online communities. *Journal of Computer-Mediated Communication*, **10**(4).

[23] Leuf B, and Cunningham W., 2001. The wiki way: Quick collaboration on the web. Addison Wesley, Boston.

[24] Marlow C., Naaman M., Davis M., and Boyd D., 2006. Tagging paper, taxonomy, Flickr, academic article. In *Proceedings of Hypertext*.

[25] Michalski R., and Radermacher F. J., 1993. Challenges for information systems: Representation, modeling, and metaknowledge. In *Recent Developments in Decision Support Systems* (NATO ASI Series/Computer and Systems Sciences).

[26] Nov O., 2007. What motivates Wikipedians. *Communications of the ACM*, **50**(11): 60–64.

[27] Nov O., and Kuk G., 2008. Open content contributors' response to free riding: The roles of motivations and perceived justice. *Computers in Human Behavior*, **24**(6): 2848–2861.

[28] Nov O., and Ye C., 2008. Community photo sharing: Motivational and structural antecedents. In *Proceedings of the 29th International Conference on Information Systems (ICIS)*, Paris, France, December 2008.

[29] Nov O., Ye C., and Kumar N., 2008. Why do people contribute meta-knowledge? A social capital perspective. In *Annual Meeting of the Academy of Management*, Anaheim, CA, August 2008.

[30] OECD, 2007. Participative Web: User-Created Content Working Party on the Information Economy. Directorate for Science, Technology and Industry.

[31] Oreg S., and Nov O., 2008. Exploring motivations for contributing to open source initiatives: The roles of contribution context and personal values. *Computers in Human Behavior*, **24**(5): 2055–2073.

[32] Parameswaran M., and Whinston A., 2007. Research issues in social computing. *Journal of the Association for Information Systems*, **8**(6): 336.

[33] Parameswaran M., and Whinston A., 2007. Social computing: An overview. *Communications of the Association for Information Systems*, **19**: 762–780.

[34] Rattenbury T., Good N., and Naaman M., 2007. Social networks: Towards extracting Flickr tag semantics. In *Proceedings of the 16th International Conference on World Wide Web*, Banff, Alberta, Canada.

[35] Rossi C., and Bonaccorsi A., 2006. Intrinsic vs. Extrinsic Incentives in Profit-Oriented Firms Supplying Open Source Products and Services. *First Monday*, **10**.

[36] Ryan, R. M., and Deci, E. L. (2000). Intrinsic and extrinsic motivations: Classic definitions and new directions. *Contemporary Educational Psychology*, **25**, 54–67.

[37] Savicki V., Kelley M., and Oesterreich E., 1999. Judgments of gender in computer-mediated communication. *Computers in Human Behavior*, **15**(2): 185–194.

[38] Schueler B., Sizov S., and Staab S., 2007. Management of meta-knowledge for RDF repositories. In *International Conference on Semantic Computing*, pp. 543–550.

[39] Schroer J., and Hertel G., 2009. Voluntary engagemnt in an open web-based encyclopedia: Wiki-pedians, and why they do it. *Media Psycology*, **12**, 1–25.

[40] Shneiderman B., Bederson B. B., and Drucker S., 2006. Find that photo! Interface strategies to annotate, browse, and share. *Communications of the ACM*, **49**(4): 69–71.

[41] Stewart K. S., and Gosain S., 2006. The impact of ideology on effectiveness in open source software development teams. *MIS Quarterly*, **30**(2): 291–314.

[42] von Hippel E., and von Krogh G., 2003. Open Source Software and the Private-Collective Innova-tion Model: Issues for Organization Science. *Organization Science*, **14**(2): 208–223.

[43] Wasko M. M., and Faraj S., 2005. Why should I share? Examining knowledge contribution in electronic networks of practice. *MIS Quarterly*, **29**(1): 1–23.

Social Network Sites: Users and Uses

MIKE THELWALL

School of Computing, Statistical Cybermetrics Research Group, University of Wolverhampton, United Kingdom

Abstract

Social network sites (SNSs) have rapidly become very popular, challenging even the major portals and search engines in terms of usage and commercial value. This chapter introduces key SNS issues and reviews relevant academic research from sociology, communication science, computer science, and information science. The chapter introduces a broad classification of SNS friendship and demonstrates the range of types of SNS, each with its own unique combination of functionalities and objectives. The users and uses for SNSs are also varied, both in terms of the broad range of reasons for using a site and also, at the microlevel, in terms of the understanding of the core concept of friending. The commonly discussed issues of privacy and security are reviewed, including the extent to which they are taken seriously by users and SNS designers. New forms of electronic communication seem to always generate their own new language varieties and SNS language is briefly discussed. The chapter is supported by a series of MySpace investigations to illustrate key points and give additional information. Finally, the potential for programmers to create small applications to run within SNSs or with SNS data is discussed and speculations made about future developments.

ADVANCES IN COMPUTERS, VOL. 76
ISSN: 0065-2458/DOI: 10.1016/S0065-2458(09)01002-X

19

1. Introduction

Social network sites (SNSs) like Facebook, MySpace, and Bebo developed mass user bases during the middle of the first decade of the twenty-first century, but who are their users, how are they used and are SNSs a passing fad or will they be a relatively permanent feature of the Internet? At the same time, a number of specialist sites have emerged that incorporate social networking features, including digg.com (news filtering), YouTube (video sharing), and Flickr (picture sharing): Are these the future in the sense that social networking will become embedded into other applications rather than maintaining a relatively independent existence?

SNSs have attracted significant media interest because of their rapid rise and wide user base, especially amongst younger people, and because of various scares such as the posting of inappropriate material by minors and the potential SNS use in identity fraud. There is also an understandable concern from parents about their children spending a significant amount of time in an unknown online environment. But there is little systematic research into SNSs to examine the prevalence of desirable and undesirable features and to get concrete evidence of patterns of users and uses. This chapter reviews such research and many qualitative and mixed-method investigations into specific aspects of SNS use or into specific groups of users. One of the problems with gathering data about SNSs is that they are profit-making enterprises and information about aspects such as user demographics and usage patterns are commercial secrets. In addition to the implementation of privacy policies to protect members' information, this makes systematic analyses difficult. MySpace is a partial exception, however, and this chapter takes advantage of that to present several investigations of MySpace users to complement the literature reviews.

This chapter is structured as follows. First, a definition of SNSs is given, along with a brief history and an overview of the different kinds of Web site that use social networking features. Second, characteristics of SNS members are reviewed, for sites with available data. This includes examinations of the international spread, age, and gender of members. This is followed by a survey of how the different sites are used and why. Next, the core concept of friendship is discussed to assess its meaning in different sites and for different user groups. Language in SNSs is then explored with reference to patterns of language use for other forms of computer-mediated communication (CMC). The issues of privacy and security are discussed in a separate section. The penultimate section discusses how programmers can build their own applications to be embedded in one or more SNSs. Several of the sections are complemented with small-scale MySpace investigations using new data. The conclusion summarizes the key issues and speculates about the future of social networking technology. Finally, note that this chapter is aimed at a general audience, but with a focus on computer science. As such, it gives only a surface description of many of the topics reviewed. Readers wishing to gain a more in-depth understanding are urged to consult the primary sources to engage with the theoretical underpinnings of the studies reviewed.

2. Definition, History, and Typology

In their editorial introduction to a journal special issue on social networks, boyd and Ellison [17] define SNSs as: "Web-based services that allow individuals to (1) construct a public or semipublic profile within a bounded system, (2) articulate a list of other users with whom they share a connection, and (3) view and traverse their list of connections and those made by others within the system." The term *social network* site was preferred to the more common *social networking* site in recognition that the most popular sites seem to be used for socializing amongst existing friends (i.e., social networks) rather than *networking* in the sense of seeking new friendships or interacting with acquaintances or friends of friends (see Section 5). This definition and terminology has been criticized by Beer [8] as being too broad because it includes sites like YouTube for which friendship is not the main focus. Although YouTube matches the definition above, it is primarily neither for social *networking* nor for social activity within existing social (friendship) networks. Confusingly, however, it could be viewed as a SNS in the sense of *navigating* social networks: users can find YouTube videos by browsing selected video posters and their friends. In this chapter, the broad Boyd and Ellison definition above is used but a typology is introduced below to differentiate between different types of SNS.

The current (2008) most popular SNSs, like Facebook, MySpace, Cyworld, and Bebo, are free to join with members having a profile page containing a photograph, some personal information, a list of pictures of registered friends, a list of comments recorded by friends (often called a guestbook, wall, or comment list). In addition, the profile page includes links to the member's blog/diary/journal, pictures, and videos (if any). The profile page *may* also contain other customized features, such as music, videos, a personalized layout, and extra content, such as a self-administered personality questionnaire. Although each of these four sites has the same core set of social networking features, they have different emphases and capabilities. For example, Facebook profile pages often have sets of selected applications, such as a map of where in the world the user has been, or a quiz game. In contrast, MySpace has a particular emphasis on music and Cyworld stresses that each user's "minihompy" is a virtual social space by including a prominent animated diagram of the user and others living in an imaginary room.

From the perspective of the computer science of social network applications, relatively little is in the public domain because the owning companies have not announced their methods in academic publications. Some key issues are known, however. From a technical perspective, one of the challenges is storing and efficiently coping with the huge quantities of interrelated data, such as friend connections and comment data. Profile pages need to be constructed in real time in order to reflect the most recent new friend connections and comments and hence need to be dynamic rather than static. Serving large numbers of complex dynamic pages is clearly nontrivial. This apparently caused critical problems to Friendster in the US [13]. The founder of Bebo.com, Michael Birch, has described the key hurdle for a new SNS as being the attraction of the initial critical mass of users. Once there are enough users in the system, then they can derive pleasure from interacting with each other but before this point, users tend to be quite isolated and so the system has to be designed to be engaging even for these isolated users [10]. Hence, human–computer interaction and design issues seem to be critical in the early stages. Facebook seems to be an exception to this rule because its early incarnations had little functionality for lone users. Presumably, it was able to spread rapidly enough in college networks through novelty and rapid word-of-mouth communication to offset this problem.

2.1   Brief History

According to boyd and Ellison [17], social networking features arose from relatively unsuccessful experiments, like sixdegrees.com, as well as the dating-oriented and community-based sites, like AsianAve (US), BlackPlanet (US), and MiGente (US) around the turn of the century. Sixdegrees.com began in 1997 and was a full-scale SNS from 1998. It was designed to help people connect and communicate with each other. It seems to have failed because too few people were online at the time for friend networks to be established and the site did not offer enough to do other than connect and communicate in simple ways [17]. Launched in 1999 (without full social network support), BlackPlanet's mission was to connect people and to strengthen the Black community, partly by encouraging more to use the Internet [23]. At the time, most successful sites were attempting instead to deliver useful content to Internet users. BlackPlanet therefore reflected an emerging shift to a new way of thinking about Web use, which later matured with additional technology—particularly the publicly visible friend lists. AsianAve (formed 1997) predated BlackPlanet and had a similar emphasis on community identity and connecting people. It may have been the success of these sites for specific groups that encouraged others to attempt to build larger-scale projects.

In some ways, the Korean Cyworld can claim to have been in 2001 the first successful general-purpose SNS, since it did not focus on a particular community or activity but aimed at a mass user base. Friendster, launched in 2002, was for a time the most popular of the US sites but faded due to technology issues related to its rapid growth [13]. It subsequently re-emerged as a major SNS in the Asia–Pacific area, according to comScore [35]. Friendster's initial promise in the US was fulfilled by MySpace, which launched in 2003 and in many ways replaced it [13]. MySpace was better able to cope with large numbers of members and also had a musical orientation. Hi5 launched in 2003 and Orkut at the start of 2004 [17].

From 2003 onwards, a range of new services with social network features were released, including LinkedIn (2003, business networking), Last.FM (2003, music), Flickr (2004, photographs), and IMEEM (2004, all media types). The success of these services demonstrated that social network features could be useful in a wider context than pure socializing. New SNSs have been released regularly since 2004, either with a new twist on the genre or aimed at a different user base. SNSs have also appeared in different languages and for different communities around the world (e.g., Cloob (Iran)—2004; Mixi (Japan)—2004; and Ultra Egypt—2007). Some important milestones are Facebook (2005 as a college network, 2006 for everyone), Bebo (2005 as a social network) Windows Live Spaces (2006, mainly for its blog), and Twitter (2006, fast microblogging).

2.2   Typology

In addition to the relatively general-purpose Web sites like MySpace and Facebook, which are primarily social environments, many other sites have social networking capabilities to support a different purpose. Sites like digg.com (news), Flickr (pictures) and YouTube (video) are clearly different from general SNSs. These all have social network capabilities but their primary purpose is not social in the sense of interpersonal communication. Instead, they are tools for collaborative filtering because they help users navigate content through friendship patterns [64]. For instance a digg.com user may ignore the main news stories of the day but read those posted or recommended by their friends sharing the same interests (e.g., computer software, soccer, Barack Obama). Similarly, a Flickr user may only look at the family pictures of their relatives, or the photographs taken by ''friends'' chosen for similar artistic taste or subject matter interests. An underlying difference is the *type* of friends sought and displayed by users. These can be existing offline friends, new friends/contacts/acquaintances, or ''friends'' as an information seeking device (see below).

A slightly different and more convenient distinction is between the *purposes* for which friendship connections are made: socializing in the sense of interpersonal communication for recreational purposes, as an end in itself; networking in the sense of interpersonal communication for reasons other than socializing; and navigation in the sense of using the connection as a device to help locate information or resources. These three purposes are characterized below as socializing, networking, and social navigation:

- *Socializing SNSs* are designed for recreational social communication between members. Friend connections are normally (but not always) used for finding and displaying lists of existing offline friends. Examples include MySpace, Hi5, Bebo, Facebook, and Cyworld. Gaia Online is an unusual example—it is a social environment (see below) but one in which members may be anonymous and hence friend connections may be rarely offline friends, even though the purpose of the SNS is purely recreational.

- *Networking SNSs* are primarily designed for nonsocial interpersonal communication. Friend connections are used for finding new contacts. Friend lists probably include a substantial proportion of acquaintances and previously unknown people. LinkedIn is a good example: members are expected to make new contacts by examining friends' contacts.

- *(Social) navigation SNSs* have social network features but use them primarily as a way to help users find a particular type of information or resource. Friend connections are used for finding and displaying lists of people as a device to access the information or resources associated with those people. Many social navigation SNSs are sites in which social navigation is not the primary purpose, just the main purpose of the SNS feature. For instance, digg.com members (see below) can choose to read the widely recommended news stories on the front page or to use social navigation by reading the stories posted or recommended by their friends.

The classification above is fluid and concerns the intention of a site or the practices of its members more than its actual features. For instance, LiveJournal can be categorized as navigation SNS: it has long been a blog with social network features and since it is oriented on the contents of its blogs, it is expected that members friend those with blogs of interest [17]. Nevertheless, many of these blogs are quite personal and so friending on the basis of a personal blog is likely to lead to an online friendship, and in this sense LiveJournal also supports socializing but it can also support networking through professional blogs. Another predominantly blogging site is Live Spaces: although it has all of the essential social network features and members could use it as a socializing SNS, the blogging element is emphasized, that is, the production of relatively permanent textual content that is intended for a wider readership than personal friends. BlackPlanet is another example: although it can be used as a socializing SNS, it also supports dating via its BlackPlanetLove facility and this is essentially a form of networking, using the above definition.

A second important feature of SNSs is the extent to which their SNS functionality is core to their use. YouTube is an example of a Web site with SNS features but which can probably survive very well without them. In contrast, MySpace appears to be totally dependant upon SNS connections, even though its music element is important [16]. Figure 1 contains a representation of where a range of sites might sit in respect to the three classifications.

Web sites with social network features but focusing on content sharing are important examples of Web 2.0 applications. Web 2.0 is a term coined for Web sites driven by content created by users rather than by Web designers [76]. It encompasses all SNSs but is especially significant to those that focus on the production of content or information for a wider audience than just personal friends. Social network features are not essential to Web 2.0 because Wikipedia is a prominent example of a successful Web 2.0 site that does not (currently in 2008) incorporate the core social network features.

A feature common to many resource-oriented Web 2.0 sites that is not essential to social networking is folksonomy tagging: the user assignment of tags to resources in a system to aid the future retrieval of relevant information [37]. For example, a YouTube video might be tagged "funny" and a Flickr picture tagged "geranium." Visitors can use the tags to navigate, perhaps by clicking on tags associated with a

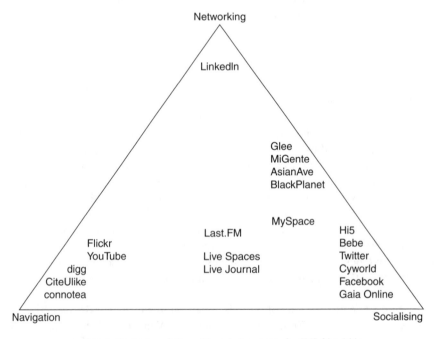

Fig. 1. Examples of sites with varied purposes for SNS friendship.

resource they are currently viewing or by selecting a tag from a tag cloud generated by a keyword search. Although a folksonomy is a collaborative endeavor it is not a social network because the navigation is by tags rather than by the tagger. Often, however, both types of navigation are supported, as in Flickr and YouTube. Tagging can interact with friending in practice because users can make their videos findable to friends by giving them cryptic tags that only their friends know about (e.g., their user name) or that they know that a circle of acquaintances might search for (e.g., the name of a club that they are all members of) [59].

2.3   Popular Social Network Sites

Table I lists the world's most popular sites with social networking features, according to Alexa's traffic analysis, as reported in May 2008. The Alexa statistics are derived from users of its toolbar and are probably not a representative sample of Internet users since they rely upon people wanting to download and install the toolbar. Nevertheless, they are useful to help identify an international collection of popular Web sites with social networking features. The rankings listed concern Web sites of all types, and so the table indicates that SNSs are amongst the highest traffic Web sites. This list includes some that are likely to be unfamiliar to many native English speakers, including Russian, French, Spanish, Japanese, Spanish, and Taiwanese sites. There is only one social navigation SNS, suggesting that this type is less popular than the others or that there is not any single dominant social navigation SNS.

Tables II and III list the top 10 US and UK SNSs according to Nielsen online/ HitWise, and all sites with SNS features that are in the top 100 visited US or UK sites, according to Alexa, with data taken from similar time periods. There are significant differences between the Nielsen and Alexa rankings and it seems likely that the Nielsen/HitWise statistics are more reliable, since they are based upon data from Internet service providers rather than self-selected users. The longer Alexa list is useful, however, because it illustrates a greater variety of Web sites.

Figure 2 uses Google search term frequencies (as a proxy for exact figures on the number of users) to illustrate the rapid rise of three popular sites with social network features in comparison to the established site Yahoo!. Whilst Yahoo! exhibited a steady rise, MySpace grew spectacularly from mid-2005, although leveling out in 2007. YouTube grew even more rapidly from early 2006, overtaking MySpace by 2007 and not yet having peaked by mid-2008. Facebook grew more slowly from mid-2006 but overtook MySpace in the first half of 2008 (this is corroborated by Alexa site traffic statistics).

Table I
Social Network Sites in the Top 100 Internet Sites, According to Alexa (May, 2008)

Alexa global	Global Alexa rank[a]	Comments
YouTube	3	Video sharing SNS
MySpace	6	Socializing SNS
Facebook	8	Socializing SNS
Orkut	11	Socializing SNS (Google)
Hi5	19	Socializing SNS
VKontakte	30	Russian socializing SNS
Flickr	39	Image sharing navigational SNS
Friendster	40	Socializing SNS
Skyrock	41	French socializing SNS
Одноклассники.ru	44	Russian classmates socializing SNS
LiveJournal	56	Blog sharing social navigation SNS
Fotolog	57	Photoblog sharing social navigation SNS
Mixi	62	Japanese socializing SNS
PerfSpot	76	Business networking social navigation SNS
DeviantArt	77	Art sharing social navigation SNS
metroFLOG	84	Spanish photoblog sharing social navigation SNS
Wretch	100	Taiwanese photo album and blog sharing social navigation SNS

[a] Combined page views and unique users metric over 3 months (http://www.alexa.com/site/ds/top_500).

2.4 Examples of SNSs with Different Features

This section describes a few SNSs to illustrate a range of different successful approaches. Note that all descriptions were current in 2008 but the sites may have subsequently changed.

2.4.1 LinkedIn

LinkedIn, a business networking SNS, allows members to enter information about themselves, centering on their career and educational history, and tries to help them connect online with people that they know or that might be helpful to them at work. In contrast to most other popular SNSs, LinkedIn actively promotes the creation of new contacts (i.e., friends) by prompting members with information about new people registering from their university or workplace, and information about existing contacts adding new contacts. LinkedIn emphasizes networking through friends of friends and includes both free and paid services, such as advertising and job seeking. Members may contact each other via their normal email accounts rather than through an internal LinkedIn messaging system.

TABLE II

TOP US SOCIAL NETWORKING SITES ACCORDING TO NIELSEN ONLINE AND/OR ALEXA

Name	Nielsen US SNS rank (February 2008)[a]	Alexa US rank (May 2008)[b]	Comments
MySpace	1	3	Socializing SNS
Facebook	2	5	Socializing SNS
Classmates online	3		School-centered SNS
Windows Live Spaces	4	(6)	Blog sharing SNS
LinkedIn	5	54	Business networking
AOL Hometown	6	(10)	Socializing SNS
Club Penguin	7		Socializing SNS for young children
Reunion.com	8		School-centered socializing SNS
AOL Community	9	(10)	Socializing SNS
Flixster	10		Movie review sharing social navigation SNS
YouTube	–	4	Video sharing social navigation SNS
Flickr	–	20	Image sharing social navigation SNS
LiveJournal	–	31	Blog sharing social navigation SNS
Digg	–	32	News-based social navigation SNS
DeviantArt	–	42	Art-based site with SNS-like features
Orkut	–	52	Socializing SNS
IMEEM	13	57	Media-sharing social navigation SNS
Hi5	–	75	Socializing SNS
Gaia Online	–	87	Community role-playing site with SNS features

[a] Unique audience data from Nielsen online (http://mashable.com/2008/03/13/social-networking-statistics-2/).

[b] Combined page views and unique users metric over 3 months; bracketed numbers indicate the rank of a parent site (http://www.alexa.com/site/ds/top_500).

2.4.2 Facebook

Facebook, at least as of mid-2008, offered basic SNS features and did not have a particular focus on any additional service. It seems to have been successful because it was a simple and effective platform for online socializing with friends. A typical

TABLE III

TOP UK SOCIAL NETWORK SITES ACCORDING TO HITWISE AND/OR ALEXA

Name	HitWise UK SNS rank (November 2007)[a]	Alexa UK rank (May 2008)[b]	Comments
Facebook	1	6	Socializing SNS
Bebo	2	12	Socializing SNS
MySpace	3	10	Socializing SNS
Faceparty	4		Socializing SNS for under 35s
Windows Live Spaces	5	(3)	Blog sharing social navigation SNS
BBC h2g2	6		Collaborative online encyclopedia with SNS features
StumbleUpon	7		Resource discovery social navigation SNS
Club Penguin	8		Socializing SNS for young children
Friends Reunited UK	9		School reunion socializing SNS
Yahoo! Groups	10	(2)	Group discussion—not SNS
YouTube	–	5	Video sharing social navigation SNS
Flickr	–	18	Image sharing social navigation SNS
Orkut	21	25	Socializing SNS
Hi5	16	52	Socializing SNS
LiveJournal	14	56	Blog sharing social navigation SNS
Digg	–	64	News-based social navigation SNS
DeviantArt	–	79	Art sharing social navigation SNS

[a] Total Internet visits (http://www.hitwise.co.uk/).

[b] Combined page views and unique users metric over 3 months; bracketed numbers indicate the rank of a parent site (http://www.alexa.com/site/ds/top_500).

social network profile is dominated by a photograph of the owner at the top, together with some personal information (name, gender, birthday, hometown, politics, and relationship status). Immediately underneath this is a set of six friends' pictures, chosen by a Facebook algorithm from all the user's friends, and a "mini-feed" listing a few of the recent activities of the profile owner. This tells the visitor (normally a friend of the owner) something about who they are and what they have been doing. There are also some links to view "photos of me" and photos of "my friends." Facebook hosts photos (which seems to be popular [82]) and allows

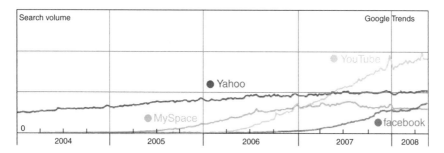

Fɪɢ. 2. Google search volumes for four terms from 2004 to mid-2008.

them to be tagged with Facebook identities, and hosts videos (via its own and third-party "applications"). It has a form of blog, called Facebook notes, but this does not seem to be widely used. It also allows members to form groups which can be serious or "Pointless—just for fun" (e.g., "Official Petition to Bring Back Whose Line is it Anyway!," over 500 groups containing "flash mob," and "If Wikipedia Says It, It Must Be True"). In terms of communication, a profile visitor can click a link to send a private message, or scroll down to the "wall" to post a public message. Members can also be "poked," which means that they will be sent a message telling them who poked them. The significance of poking is deliberately obscure: members can infer or agree on its meaning, although in British English there is a bawdy connotation: a male poking a female is having sex with her. Facebook gifts are pictures that can be sent to other users, for a price, and will then appear in the recipient's profile. Members can set their own status, which their friends can easily see, and this can be used to describe current activities (e.g., *Mike is editing his chapter*) or send a comic message (e.g., *Kim is updating his status*). Facebook users seem to spend time writing funny messages to each other, and perhaps also looking for new friends (e.g., [82]). Facebook has an online marketplace where members can advertise to sell goods, and also has an Events feature that members can use to organize offline or online meetings. In March 2007, Facebook began to allow developers to create small programs to embed in user profiles, presumably as a way of giving Facebook a more varied feature set. These applications seem to have been predominantly fun communication rather than practical tools (e.g., games, gift exchanges, and play fights) and could not be used to customize the overall appearance of a profile.

2.4.3 MySpace

MySpace has a similar set of features overall to Facebook but with some significant differences. First, MySpace profiles have an embedded music player and in most cases if a member hears a song on a friend's profile or a musician's profile, they can add it to their own profile with a few simple mouse clicks. This makes MySpace very music-friendly which is important for young members as "music is cultural glue among youth" [16]. A second key difference is that MySpace allows members to freely customize the appearance of their profile, including the whole color scheme and by adding a background picture. This allows users to creatively express themselves through their profile appearance, although it seems that a minority take advantage: including inactive users, only about 22% have customized profiles, with a higher proportion of younger users [78]. Although the process of changing the appearance of profiles is quite technical, it is widely achieved by members who are able to cut and paste from examples or specialist sites [80]. MySpace does not allow pokes and does not have a status that users can set but it does give brief user information and a photograph, as well as a list of friends' comments. MySpaces have fairly prominent blogs, but not all MySpace users employ its blog feature and it seems that it is often used by those who are less socially integrated and who seek an online mechanism to cope with social stress [7]. Members can upload pictures and videos, as well as commenting on friends' pictures, videos, blog postings, and profiles. MySpace friends can communicate through private messages as well as public comments. In summary, MySpace emphasizes personal expression through content production and customization more than Facebook, which is more focused on direct communication.

2.4.4 Cyworld

Cyworld, of Korean origin, is a socializing SNS that is dominant in South Korea. Like MySpace, it has customization as a major theme, but, unlike MySpace, this is embedded into its environment as an essential part of its business strategy. The member "lives" as an avatar in a virtual room (miniroom) pictured on the home page (minihompy), on their own or with friends and can buy coverings and contents for their room to decorate and customize the environment in which they live. This purchase is made in the virtual "acorns" currency which must be traded for real money (a significant source of income for the owning company, SK Telecom). This means that Cyworld is not dependant upon advertising for its revenue—an approach seen by some as being an alternative Asian business model for supporting online communication [65]. Members can also post blog (diary) entries, interact in chatrooms, upload and customize pictures, upload videos, customize their minihompy with standard skins, add background music, and leave comments in friends' guestbooks [42]. Cyworld members seem to often see it as a venue for personal reflection and for sharing their inner thoughts [54], suggesting a very personal nature to the contents of this SNS. Perhaps related to this, Cyworld users seem rarely to meet in person new friends met online, possibly regarding online friends as acquaintances [22].

Sharing digital photographs is one of the most popular Cyworld activities, as is the exchange of decorative virtual gifts [22]. Mobile phone connections are also important, both for uploading photographs and for communicating with friends [42].

2.4.5   BlackPlanet

BlackPlanet is a US-based SNS aimed mainly at black Americans. It includes a range of standard socializing SNS features, like a blog, instant messaging, chatrooms, groups, forums (e.g., "Who should Obama choose as his V.P. running mate?"), and quizzes (e.g., "Which brother in the movie are you? The funny guy, the love interest or the guy who gets killed in the first 5 minutes of the film? Take our quiz and find out"). It has several additional features, including a free dating service, style and "rate me" areas, job searches, and searches for professionals. Dating features quite prominently on the site, perhaps because it added dating at an early stage in its development [23]. As part of this, members can have a separate dating profile with additional information. Dating connections can be made through networking (friends of friends) or by geography, gender, age, and sexual orientation. BlackPlanet awards Member Points for certain activities, which can be exchanged for "premium services," such as virtual gifts for friends or an enhanced dating listing. Some other US SNSs also aim at particular sections of the community, including AsianAve, MiGente (Latinos), Glee ("gay, lesbian, bisexual, transgender, or everyone else" www.glee.com, accessed 30 June 2008), all owned by the same (nonethnic) company, Community Connect, Inc., that owns BlackPlanet [19] and these sites seem to have more intrusive advertising than most other mainstream SNSs. Discussion forums seem to be active and political in BlackPlanet (as with AsianAve and MiGente), with a strong sense of ethnic identity, which Byrne [20] argues is valuable for its users as a counterweight to racism within society.

2.4.6   Gaia Online

Gaia Online provides an interesting contrast to the sites discussed above (although it has features in common with Cyworld) because it has its own anime (Japanese animation) theme encompassing the whole service. The site is aimed at children aged at least 13 and contains safety and other information for parents. One key element of the site is its forums, which may include role playing, and have the open nature of chatrooms. In forums, members are likely to meet people that they do not know offline. This is also likely to occur in the virtual events staged by the company. One such, a prom in April 2008 modeled on US high school proms, was claimed by the developers to have attracted 500,000 members and to have hosted four million "dance sessions" (http://www.gaiaonline.com/prom, accessed 8 June 2008; see also http://themoment.blogs.nytimes.com/2008/05/16/hot-prom-mess/). Members do not upload a personal picture but have a cartoon avatar instead that they can customize (the avatar idea is also used by Club Penguin). Members can navigate a virtual world and can organize together into Guilds. Another important element is social game playing, with members being rewarded with virtual gold for playing collaborative or competitive games (e.g., fishing, jigsaw, rally). Gold can be spent in shops selling virtual items for use within the system, although real money can also be used to purchase the same items. Gaia Online contrasts with the hugely popular online role-playing game World of Warcraft in that it is not three-dimensional and war is not an element of the games, although a war game was set to be added in mid-2008. As with Cyworld, members have a home that they live in and can buy items with which to decorate or furnish their home (see Fig. 3). Gaia Online is similar to the popular virtual world Second Life [6], but with social networking features and with a two-dimensional cartoon interface instead of the three-dimensional navigation and more realistic appearance of Second Life.

Fig. 3. A Gaia Online member in their (sparsely furnished) virtual room.

2.4.7 Digg

Digg is "a place for people to discover and share content from anywhere on the Web" (http://digg.com/about, 4 May 2008). Digg works by members submitting the URLs of news stories (typically from major news Web sites) and other interesting Web pages. Other members may then digg these stories—registering their interest or approval. Digg's home page contains current lists of the most "dugg" (i.e., popular) of the submitted stories. The stories can also be viewed by category, and there is a separate page listing upcoming stories that have been recently submitted and may or may not subsequently receive enough diggs to appear on the home page. It is also possible to browse the news stories submitted by individual members and so it can be useful for someone to browse the stories of members with similar interests or who are known to be quick to identify interesting relevant stories. Statistically, friends tend to digg similar stories to each other and to digg friends' submitted stories [64]. Although social networking is possibly not essential to digg, members can register other members as friends. Presumably, friends are mainly selected on the basis of having an interest in similar story types. Other sites with similar goals include del. icio.us (sharing bookmarks, members can add others to their networks and can "subscribe to" tags to identify new content of interest) and StumbleUpon (uses collaborative filtering to help find sites "that you might like"). CiteULike and Connotea use the same principle applied to academic publications rather than Web pages. Figure 4 is a network diagram illustrating links from Digg and StumbleUpon to other SNSs. Both send their links mainly to content-oriented SNS, with the exception of the two very large sites MySpace and Facebook. Figure 4 shows links from digg and StumbleUpon to the SNSs in Tables I–III. Both popular sites and content-based sites tend to attract the most links.

2.4.8 YouTube

YouTube is primarily a video hosting and sharing site but has additional social network capabilities. The site can be freely browsed by nonmembers but users must join to post content, comment on others' videos, save favorites, and create groups of videos. YouTube members receive a profile page with a picture, some viewing frequency data and information about their posted videos and favorites. In addition, they are allowed to add other users as friends, presumably if they think their videos worth watching [59], although there is a separate option to "subscribe" to a person's videos, which is different from the friendship status. Friending in YouTube, like DeviantArt, Flickr, Xanga, and LiveJournal, seems to be more of a navigation aid than social friendship, although there are undoubtedly some users for both purposes.

Fig. 4. Links from Digg and StumbleUpon to other popular SNSs. Circle areas are proportional to the number of site pages indexed by Yahoo! and arrow widths are proportional to the number of intersite links reported by Yahoo! (May 2008).

A similar site is IMEEM, which encompasses a range of media types, including music, video, and photos, and allows users to post their own content.

2.4.9 Last.FM

Last.FM is a music-based site that primarily attempts to help members listen to music that they like. Unlike YouTube, the music is not mainly uploaded by members but seems chiefly to be copyright material played with the permission of record companies. Although similar to MySpace in this respect, Last.FM is much more music focused. Last.FM actively helps people to find (and perhaps befriend) others with similar music tastes. This might be for social friendship or as a navigation aid:

to investigate the music liked by others with overlaps in taste. Last.FM seems to attract revenue through advertising online music shops: when listening to a track on Last.FM, links are provided to buy it online. Restrictions are placed on playing music within Last.FM so that there is an incentive to purchase tracks in order to have full control over when they can be played. Last.FM's AudioScrobbler database tracks the music tastes of people and uses this to guess music that they might enjoy. Similar to Last.FM is iLike, which launched in 2007. iLike grew rapidly based upon a Facebook application, although it also has its own separate Web site. MOG is another similar site.

2.4.10   DeviantArt

DeviantArt is a site for artists to exhibit their work and connect to other artists that they like. It is similar to Flickr in that it hosts images, but is different in that its target audience is restricted: practicing artists. It is thus surprising that it has a significant membership but it presumably plays a useful role in giving artists a virtual space in which to show their work as well as a knowledgeable and interested audience. It can also be useful in education, which must help it to gain new members [98].

In addition to the sites reviewed so far, there are many more specialist initiatives (http://blogs.zdnet.com/social/?p=492), including Fuzzster (SNS for pets), Nurse-LinkUp (professional site for nurses throughout the world), Yub (''meet, hang, shop...'' shopaholics), Model Mayhem (connecting professional photographers and aspiring models), gather.com (''Make lasting connections, read thought-provoking articles, publish your own thoughts & images'' standard SNS but with more text content, apparently aimed at older users), and Meetup (enabling geographically close strangers to meet for shared interests). These show the potential for niche sites to thrive based upon satisfying specific needs. Indeed the site Ning allows users to set up their own social network for any purpose, including fan groups and political groups. Finally, one feature not mentioned for any of the above sites is present in the Japanese SNS mixi: an area where members can share product reviews.

3.   User Characteristics

In the West, the popular perception of social network users is probably of youth and students, predominantly in the richer, networked nations, and with richer people being disproportionately represented. But to what extent is this true?

3.1   Where Are SNS Users Located?

The most reliable data on the international spread of social networking may be those of comScore (comScore.com), an online information company. They gather data on Internet usage through a panel of about two million volunteers across the globe. Although comScore attempts to gather a representative sample of volunteers, its self-selected nature is not ideal but it seems to be reasonable for reporting a comparison of the extent to which SNSs are used internationally. The comScore data, which split the world into five large zones, suggest that the most frequent SNS usage comes from the Asia–Pacific area, which accounts for 25% more uses than either Europe or North America. Latin America accounts for about a third as much usage as North America, and Africa and the Middle east account for half as much again [35]. The apparent domination of the Asia–Pacific area in these gross figures is due to the huge population concerned: on a per-capita basis (using population data from http://www.internetworldstats.com/stats.htm), North America has the highest proportion of users (37%), with Europe second (16%), Latin America third (7%), the Asia–Pacific area fourth (4%), and Africa/Middle East last (2%). In summary, although the Asia–Pacific region has the most users, they are spread thinly and are probably concentrated mainly in technologically advanced countries and areas, such as Japan, Taiwan, Korea, and Australia. The take-up of SNSs by different countries is also quite varied [17, 89]. For example, although Bebo's relative popularity in the UK compared to the US could be related to the UK origins of its US-based founders, the popularity of Google's Orkut in Brazil does not seem to have any linguistic or marketing cause.

There seems to be only one detailed study of SNS geography: An empirical analysis of US MySpace profiles addressed issues of geography within a single country by comparing rural to urban users, finding that urban users had a much higher level of almost all types of online MySpace activity [36]. Another study has shown how geographic factors might be investigated by using Google Maps to plot the geographic location of friends in order to explore the spread of friendship networks [32].

3.2   Who Are the Typical Social Network Users?

There is not a typical SNS user because different general SNSs with similar features can have widely different audiences. In some cases this is understandable, as in the tendency for Facebook users to be more educated than MySpace users [14], presumably because of Facebook's educational origins. The most widely studied potential social network users are probably US teens, due to the Pew Internet & American Life project. About half of US teens had a SNS space in October–November, 2006 [62], in comparison to about 14% of adults (or 20% of adult Internet users) [70].

This confirms that in the US social networking has been especially relevant to teens even though the majority of social network users are adults. It seems likely that this would not be true in other countries where computers are less available at home and school. Presumably, in such nations children would have few opportunities to use any Internet facilities regularly. In the UK in 2007, a survey of Internet usage found that students were the social group most likely to have an SNS profile, with almost no pensioners having one [29]. Perhaps surprisingly, men were more likely to report having a profile than women.

A study of over 1000 first-year students from an ethnically diverse US urban public research university has investigated student SNS membership of Bebo, Facebook, Friendster, MySpace, Orkut, and Xanga in early 2007 [43]. The majority used Facebook (79%) and MySpace (55%) and although most had heard of Xanga, only 6% used it; the others were less well known and less used. There were differences in usage based upon gender and ethnicity. Women were slightly more likely than average (for the students surveyed) to use MySpace (and Friendster), Hispanics were overrepresented in MySpace, and Asian Americans/Asians were underrepresented in MySpace (and overrepresented in Xanga and Friendster). Students with more educated parents were overrepresented on Facebook (and Xanga and Friendster) whereas students with less educated parents were overrepresented on MySpace (see also [14]). The study also examined a range of factors that might influence whether a student uses an SNS, finding that these factors vary by service [43]. For example, students living at home were less likely to use Facebook than students living at college, but this factor did not seem to affect MySpace use. Hargittai [43] cautioned that differences between SNSs mean that research into one service cannot necessarily be generalized to other similar services and that research aggregating multiple SNSs may hide significant individual differences. This is particularly noteworthy because the study did not include any specific ethnic SNS, although Friendster, Orkut, and Xanga may have substantial user bases outside the US that affect their uptake within the US.

3.3   MySpace Investigation

This section reports the results of a study of the profiles of two samples of MySpace users: 40,000 members who joined on 10 March 2007 and a systematic sample of 40,000 profiles from all MySpace users. The profile pages of the former were downloaded on 10–11 March 2008 and the profile pages of the latter sample were downloaded on 3–4 March 2008. The March 10 "yearlings" sample was chosen to compare the activities of members who joined on the same date whereas the other sample, "all members," was chosen to reveal differences in members over time. The samples were gathered using MySpace's member ID feature.

Each MySpace member has a unique member number and inserting this into an appropriate URL gives the URL of their home page. Since member IDs are allocated consecutively, it is possible to work out a person's joining date from their ID and it is also possible to take random and systematic samples of members through the ID feature. The all members sample included 40,000 IDs from about 51,000 (exact figure hidden for privacy reasons) in steps of 5193 (excluding the very earliest members) and the yearlings sample included 40,000 IDs from about 166,846,000 in steps of 54. In the remainder of this chapter, the data reported are the March 10 data set, unless otherwise stated.

After downloading the profile pages for each sample and extracting their data, former members' profiles were eliminated. Registered musicians, comedians, and film makers also were removed because these may not operate as individuals but may behave with a commercial motive. Members with no friends or one friend were also removed because these are typically inactive—the one friend is normally the system help agent Tom. Members with private profiles were excluded from analyses except those of gender, age, and last login date (i.e., the publicly available information). The procedures described so far mainly echo those of a previous study that processed earlier data, except that all analyses here exclude all members with fewer than two friends [90]. The final number of profiles analyzed were yearlings—16,364 (9823 private, 6541 public); all members—16,977 (8185 private, 8792 public).

Figure 5 illustrates the range or reported ages for MySpace members, excluding the 10% of members reporting ages above 36. There is a clear trend for younger members to be female. The yearlings data set, which contains more recent members (on average), contains a much higher proportion of younger members than the other data set. This is unsurprising because the all members' data are significantly older, with 82% of its members joining before 10 March 2007. For members aged above 17, the proportion of male and females is very similar overall.

4. Usage

4.1   Why Do We Use Social Network Sites?

Why have SNSs become popular so quickly? Are they a passing fad or do they have significant staying power? The answer seems to be that they satisfy a deep human need which implies that they are unlikely to disappear unless they are replaced by something more powerful addressing the same need. This need is the desire to investigate and gossip about human relationships [26, 96]. Donath and Tufekci noted that from the evolutionary psychology perspective of Dunbar [28], this desire may have evolved from social grooming by primates, which itself seems

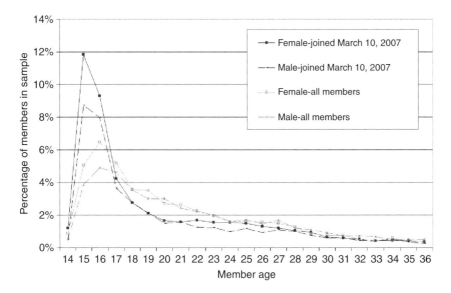

Fɪɢ. 5. Ages of MySpace members in the two data sets, as tested in March 2008.

to be an evolutionary method to help bond together large enough groups of primates to be able to survive in a hostile environment. In particular, primates within a large group may form friendships/alliances through mutual grooming and these help promote their interests within the larger group [28]. Examples of this local ape politics include female solidarity against overzealous dominant males ([28], pp. 20–21), and dominant male coalitions to protect against other males ([28], p. 27). From similar observations, such alliances are not formed in response to threats but are developed prior to times of need through patterns of grooming. Dunbar argues that language may have mainly evolved, via women, through an evolutionary drive for more effective intragroup politics (in the larger groups needed for survival in increasingly hostile environments) and that gossiping about relationships (e.g., hierarchies, alliances, and trustworthiness) would have been the key part of this. As Dunbar claims, this would explain the widespread love of gossip, whether between friends or in newspapers (including the ''serous'' press), magazines, and fiction (in the sense that stories are often about relationships). Irrespective of whether this evolutionary theory is accepted, scientists have long recognized the importance of apparently trivial conversation, or ''phatic communion,'' in human interaction (e.g., [71]). Dunbar's social grooming theory of language has been independently picked up by Donath and Tufekci as the key to explaining the popularity of SNSs.

Donath [26] argues that much of the information provided by SNSs is about relationships (who are friends; how these friends communicate) and about the attributes of friends and acquaintances (how many friends they have; what they have been doing; where they live, what jobs they have). She claims that SNS "social supernets" are very efficient at transmitting the kind of information that would have previously been obtained through gossip, in addition to SNS use as an interface for gossip (e.g., via private or public messages). As a consequence, Donath sees SNSs as allowing us to "increase the scale of [our] social world" (p. 231) through their efficiency. This is also an argument for the longevity of SNSs: presumably, we will not want to lose track of our social supernets and will only abandon SNSs if something more powerful emerges that can preserve our enhanced social ability. Tufekci [96] tested the hypothesis that social grooming is an important component of social network use through a statistical analysis of a survey of 713 US college students, finding that people who did not value "social grooming (gossip, small-talk and generalized, nonfunctional people-curiosity)" were significantly less likely to use SNSs (and other online forms of social communication). This is useful evidence of the validity of the social grooming hypothesis. The same survey also found evidence in support of Donath's social supernets idea, in the sense that SNS users were able to keep in regular contact with more people than were nonusers.

A study of specific motivations for using Facebook found seven different types from a factor analysis of the responses from an online survey of 137 members [53]. The main motivation was social connection: the desire to connect and communicate with others. The other factors were shared identities (mainly joining groups or events), photographs (viewing, posting, tagging), content (applications, quizzes, games), social investigation (people watching, finding, and meeting new people), social network surfing (viewing profiles of nonfriends), and status updates (viewing or updating). This survey both confirms the importance of the purely social aspects of Facebook and illustrates that it is flexible enough to be used for very different purposes. Note that all of these reasons could be viewed as social grooming motivations because even the games tend to be social.

Different types of people can benefit from SNS membership. A study of Facebook users found that it could be most useful for people with low self-esteem and low levels of happiness [31]. People operating in heterogeneous networks (i.e., with high "bridging social capital") were found to be particularly likely to be active Facebook users.

Some other suggestions have been made about reasons for SNS use. Tufekci's [96] survey found a motivation for students not using SNSs: concerns about privacy. Other reasons for avoiding SNS use include lack of Internet access (or parental restrictions) and those who object on principle, seeing SNSs as being "stupid," or corporate controlled [16]. Finally, one negative result is significant: SNS use does not seem to be associated with people with more (or less) close friends [96].

4.2   How Do We Use Social Network Sites?

What do people do in SNSs? Much information about how SNSs are used can be inferred from the above section or is implicit in the findings elsewhere in this chapter. For instance, the SNSs discussed here are all highly successful and so most of their services are presumably valuable to some members (e.g., music, forums, blogs, comment space, photo, and video posting) or they would have been removed. This section covers the key issue of identity expression and a few studies that give additional insights into SNS uses.

A Pew Internet & American Life project has dealt with the issue of the *online activities of youth* in late 2006, some of which is relevant to SNS uses. A majority of US teens had posted online content, including Web pages, blogs, pictures, and videos. Much of this content is likely to be either in SNSs—either general sites like MySpace (which allows blogging and the posting of pictures and videos) or specialist sites like Flickr and YouTube. The majority of all content types were posted by girls, with the exception of video [62].

A study of *messaging* within Facebook found that most pairs of friends did not exchange messages: in other words, a small proportion of Facebook friends are also online communication partners [38]. This supports the notion that friendship in Facebook is seen as a relatively trivial, although it is possible that these pairs of friends communicate offline or online via other mechanisms (e.g., email or chatrooms) instead. Messages tended to be exchanged between friends at the same college rather than between distant friends, suggesting that it was not primarily used to overcome geographic distance problems (see also [57]). Nevertheless, an increase in messages during holiday times indicated that overcoming geographic distance was sometimes useful.

Some SNSs encourage *communication between nonfriends*. For example, the forums in BlackPlanet, MiGente, AsianAve, Glee and Gaia Online, and the groups in Facebook allow nonfriend users to interact around specific topics. A few research findings about SNS forums have been published. A study of BlackPlanet forums found that Black community issues were a common theme but there was no evidence that typical online discussions translated into offline activism [19]. Within open discussions in the "ethnic" sites BlackPlanet, AsianAve, and MiGente, there seem to be discussions around ethnicity definitions and they seem to sometimes strengthen cultural identities and perform a useful social support function [20].

4.2.1   Identity Expression or Performance

With an emphasis on teenage users of MySpace, boyd [12] sees SNS profiles as digital blank slates that members use to "write themselves into being." She argues that SNS profiles can be seen as identity performances, much in the same way as choices of clothes are often a conscious part of portraying a desired image to others. Identities can be expressed in various ways, with profile appearance customization (in some SNSs), the content of profile pages, and music, video, and picture selection. In addition, following trends can be an important part of identity projection, such as through the use of deliberately incorrect spellings [15]. The choice of friends is another important aspect of online identity [27]. Young people may also customize MySpace and add content to it to entertain their visitors and because they have time to do it rather than to accurately reflect their identity or as part of a self-reflexive process, however [18]. Customizing MySpace profiles may be of particular interest to younger members: older teenagers seem to prefer to express their identity through connections rather than customization [69].

4.3　When Do We Use Social Network Sites?

There is apparently only one detailed study of the usage patterns of a SNS [38]. It analyzed Facebook when it was predominantly a college network and used log files provided by the owning company to track the activities of members between February 2004 and March 2006. The data revealed that students tended to access the site at times when they were likely to be studying. This suggests that the students saw social networking as something that occurred as a natural part of computer use, and perhaps also integrated into studying routines, rather than seeing it as a separate activity that they would switch their computer on for. Facebook members were most active just before midnight, except on Friday and Saturday, and were least active on Saturday, suggesting that Facebook had not replaced the key social activities of going out on a Friday and Saturday night for most students. A similar usage analysis of the corporate networks within Facebook found a completely different pattern of use, with peaks during office hours and very little usage in the evening, at night and at weekends [38].

4.4　MySpace Investigation

Figure 6 gives a gender breakdown of the declared reason(s) for using MySpace. Although the most common reason is friendship alone, this is more frequently the main reason for women than for men. All other combinations (except "Networking, Friends" and Networking, Serious Relationships, which differ by 1 in gender frequency) are more common for men than women. Although this is a minority goal, men are significantly more likely to be interested in—or prepared to declare an interest in—dating, serious relationships, and networking.

Figure 7 shows the distribution of numbers of days since the last logon of the yearlings. About a third did not log on again a week after they had first joined and

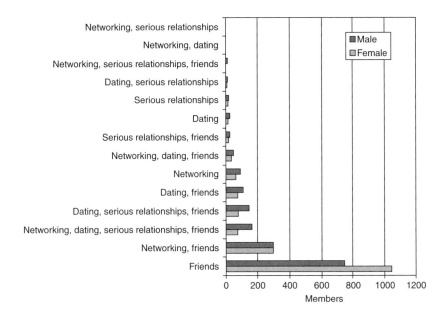

F_{IG}. 6. Declared purpose for using MySpace, broken down by gender.

about a third had logged on in the previous week. This shows that some members regularly check their MySpace, and other members probably did not find a use for MySpace, forgot their logon information, or only joined to see what it was like. In the middle are members that either ceased using MySpace or only log on occasionally. Recall that members with fewer than two friends were excluded from the data, so the graph represents people who have used MySpace to the extent of making at least one friend.

Figure 8 shows that the number of comments received by MySpace members follows a typical power law (see below for more about power laws). The graph is for the yearlings data set but a similar pattern holds for the other data set and also if the results are split by gender. Only 32% of members had received any comments at all, suggesting that this feature is ignored by many active members. The power law shape indicates that a cumulative advantage or rich-get-richer approach may be occurring [1]. It is possible, for example, that members who have many comments in their profile attract many more partly because of this reason. The largest number of comments on a single profile was 16,178—these seemed to be part of a long series of conversations with MySpace friends, with each conversation made up of a long series of short instant messaging style MySpace comments. This user had a

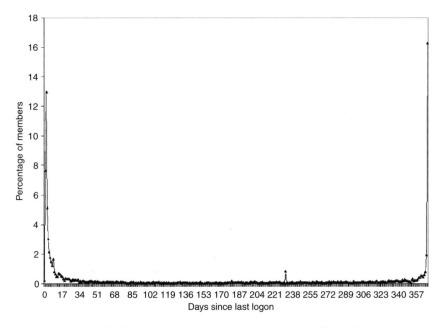

Fig. 7. The range of days since the last logon of March 10 members.

MySpace age of 16 at the time when most comments were made, and some of the comments seemed to refer to a game that was taking place.

5. Friendship

The key element in SNSs is friendship. This section focuses mainly on socializing SNSs, for which the meaning of friendship is least defined and most investigated.

5.1 Why Do We Form SNS Friendships?

The general definition of a friend is "one attached to another by affection or esteem" [74], but this does not reflect social network practices. Most importantly, online "friending" is typically seen as different from offline friendship [12]. To make an online friend in most SNSs, a member must first locate the potential new friend. This may be achieved through a name search or by searching for another attribute (e.g., musical taste), either in the site's internal search system or through a general search engine. Potential new friends are probably found most commonly by

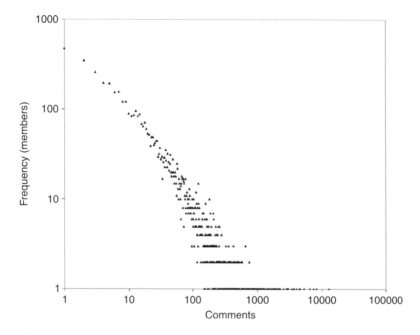

FIG. 8. The range of numbers of comments received by March 10 members (log–log scale).

noticing the person in a friend's friend list. Once the potential new friend is found, they must be invited to become a friend. Except in a few sites such as LiveJournal, friending is a reciprocal arrangement that both parties must agree to. When the other person receives the invitation, as a message next time they log in, they will see some information about the person requesting to become their friend and then can choose whether to accept or reject this offer.

The number of friends per person ranges hugely from none to over a million, with a wide spread between [12]. For people with many friends, the meaning of friendship is clearly not that given in a dictionary. One difference is that MySpace includes many sites of musicians and these can be friended in the normal way. This is easily identifiable as a fan relationship even though it is ostensibly reciprocal and equal. The musicians benefit from the relationship because it performs a marketing function. In addition, some "ordinary" members seek to collect friends as a kind of hobby with the competitive element of trying to gain the most, sometimes attracting the label "whore" from those who do not appreciate the activity [12]. For the majority of members, there are many reasons for wanting or accepting somebody as a social network friend even when they are not a real friend and danah boyd gives the following list, summarized from interviews with many Friendster and MySpace users:

1. Acquaintances, family members, colleagues
2. It would be socially inappropriate to say no because you know them
3. Having lots of Friends makes you look popular
4. It's a way of indicating that you are a fan (of that person, band, product, etc.)
5. Your list of Friends reveals who you are
6. Their Profile is cool so being Friends makes you look cool
7. Collecting Friends lets you see more people (Friendster)
8. It's the only way to see a private Profile (MySpace)
9. Being Friends lets you see someone's bulletins and their Friends-only blog posts (MySpace)
10. You want them to see your bulletins, private Profile, private blog (MySpace)
11. You can use your Friends list to find someone later
12. It's easier to say yes than no

(boyd [13])

This list contains an interesting variety of reasons, including social navigation opportunities (7, 11), access to information (8–10), identity performance (3–6), other personal relationships (1), politeness (2), and laziness (12). A survey of student users of MySpace and/or Facebook found that almost all used it to keep in touch with old friends and also to keep in contact with current friends [82].

A study of LiveJournal's nonreciprocal friending found additional practices. Since the LiveJournal focus is on the blogs produced, friending is designed primarily to represent interest in blogs. The number of people who have friended a blog author may thus be an indicator of the quality of their blog. Members sometimes seek to get people to friend them to get status for their blog in this way, or may offer to friend someone in return for a service, such as reading and commenting on their blog ([34]; see also [79]). Similar motivations have been found for YouTube [59] and Cyworld [42]. Although Cyworld is a socializing SNS, photographs, customization, and diaries seem to be important content, with the number of minihompy visitors apparently being an indicator of value or success [42]. Related to this, Twitter members could be classified as information seekers, information providers, or reciprocal friendship makers based upon their (nonreciprocal) friending patterns [51]. One final reason, which could be added to the list above, is that friending is sometimes used primarily as a communication facilitating convenience, for example, to coordinate offline activities [34].

5.2 Which Types of People Do We Friend?

The saying "birds of a feather flock together" (academic term: *homophily*) applies to offline friendship: similar people tend to become friends. Based upon predominantly US research, significant predictors of offline friendship include similarity in terms of race and ethnicity, age, religion, education, occupation, and gender [73]. This study categorized two types of homophily: baseline and inbreeding. Baseline homophily covers the degree of friendship similarity that can be explained by environmental factors; for example, children tend to have friends of their own age partly due to the organization of schooling into age groups. Inbreeding homophily is the degree of friendship similarity that is not explainable by environmental factors; for instance, if black students in a 90% white college had on average 50% black friends, then this suggests a degree of inbreeding friendship (e.g., for solidarity against a proportion of prejudiced students). As a result of this research, SNS friendship should be expected to display a degree of both types of homophily.

A quantitative study of Facebook investigated the profile factors that were most associated with friendship based on the profiles of 30,773 members of one US university network in April 2006 [58]. About half of the friendships were between members at the same institution. Undergraduates were found to have more friends than graduates and faculty and people who filled in more profile information tended to have more friends.[1] There was a small gender effect, with women having more friends than men. Also in terms of gender, it seems that both males and females choose a majority of female friends in MySpace [90], although this violates the homophily principle (see above) for males.

An investigation into ethnicity factors for Facebook friendship within 10 Texas colleges found that race homophily was a very strong factor determining friendship within institutions, with the extent of race factors varying between institutions and between racial groups [72]. To give an extreme example, two black students at Texas A&M University are 16.5 times more likely to be Facebook friends than two random students at the institution (i.e., strong ''inbreeding homophily''). Universities in Texas (and elsewhere in the US) have significantly different student racial profiles from each other, so this additional racial clustering within universities exacerbates the existing partial ethnic separation which has potential negative social consequences (see, e.g., [11]). For MySpace, online friends (especially those that interact most online) tend to also be offline friends, with MySpace perhaps often serving to allow friends to communicate or ''hang out'' outside school hours [12, 18].

Some SNSs implement features that actively encourage communication (and hence eventual friendship) between people that are not already offline friends. This can clearly impact upon the type of people who become friends. LinkedIn promotes making new professional contacts through friends of friends and between

---

[1] One implication from this study for designers was that encouraging members to fill in profile information might make them more active users.

people from the same workplace and university. This presumably harnesses occupation homophily and education homophily. Making friend connections via browsing friends' friend lists is probably the most common method in most SNSs. It seems likely that it is not the norm in role-playing SNS like Gaia Online and Club Penguin, however: typical friends may not be offline friends, because friends of friends are unlikely to be recognized as offline acquaintances or friends. In Gaia Online, friends are probably made primarily through encounters in forums and collaborative games—with friendships formed on a casual basis or perhaps through shared enjoyment in social interaction, the game or topic of discussion.

In the microblogging site Twitter, people appear to join communities based upon shared interests, so friendship seems likely to reflect this phenomenon [51]. Similarly, it is probable that SNS friendship circles broadly follow offline friendship patterns in terms of factors like age, gender, and nationality [43]. The Japanese site mixi explicitly attempts to bring people together not on the basis of shared or topic interests, but on the basis of offline geography. To support the latter, it includes features so that a user comment on an event (it gives the example of a bakery opening) may be seen by others living nearby [55].

The information requested by an SNS from a user when they register influences how easy people are to find and befriend. The lack of ethnic and international information in mixi, for example, would make it difficult for ethnic minorities and those with overseas connection to make friendships with others on the basis of ethnic and/or overseas connections because the data sample is not in the system to be queried [55]. This particularly affects questions that have a predefined set of answers built into the system. Komaki uses Nakamura's [75] concept of "menu-driven" identities to describe this situation. BlackPlanet, AsianAve, MiGente, and Glee also seem to attempt to bring together strangers via their dating features and their "Secret Admirer" game which is based upon identifying and tracking random attractive strangers. In addition to ethnic variations, a comparison of US rural and urban users has shown significant differences in friendship patterns. Rural users tended to have fewer and less geographically distributed friends [36].

5.3 MySpace Investigation

Figure 9 shows the distribution of friends for the yearlings—the graph for all members is similar. The graph is based upon the number of friends reported by MySpace on the profile page, which tends to be a small overestimate of the actual number of friends [78]. The graph shape is a power law, as is common with network data [1, 84], but it should be noted that users with zero or one friends are absent because they were excluded in the data filtering stage. The power law appears to show three different slopes: one for 9 or fewer friends, one for 10–80 friends, and a

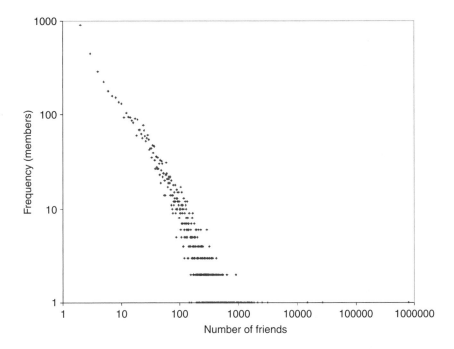

F<small>IG</small>. 9. The range of numbers of friends for 10 March 2007 members (log–log scale).

third slope for over 80 friends. This would be consistent with a few friends tending to represent offline friends, more friends also including a number of acquaintances, and a large number of friends predominantly being strangers (see also [90]). This suggests that there are different friending dynamics at work, or that different concepts of MySpace friendship are being used. A majority of members have 18 or fewer friends and the largest number in this sample was 796,365.

Figure 9 is strikingly different from a similar graph for Facebook, which has a much more hooked shape and an almost flat left-hand side [38]. It seems that Facebook users, until 2006 at least, tended to have many more friends (median 144) and it was much rarer for individuals to have few friends. This suggests that the incentives to friend in Facebook are much higher than in MySpace, or it is much easier to do. This may be because Facebook is based upon networks of organizations (particularly universities) and it is relatively easy to find members of the same organization in Facebook. Perhaps coincidentally, 150 has been claimed to be the largest effective human social group size [28].

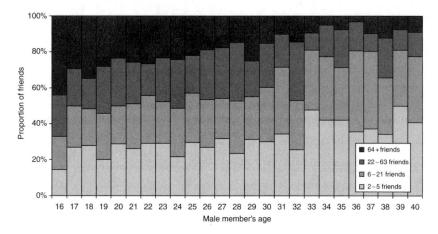

Fig. 10. An age breakdown of the number of friends for male 10 March 2007 MySpace members.

There is almost gender equality in the number of friends: males have a median of 19 friends and females have a median of 16; this difference is not statistically significant (March 10 data, Mann–Whitney U-test, $p = 0.065$). As mentioned above, males and females prefer a majority of female friends and prefer a majority of females in the top friends list [90]. There is also a significant trend for younger members to have more friends (Fig. 10). The same trend is evident for both males and females, and Fig. 10 illustrates the pattern for males (the graph for females is almost identical and is not shown). A further investigation has shown that friendship homophily is prevalent in MySpace in many dimensions, including age, ethnicity, and religion [92].

6. Friendship Issues

Social network friendship can be a big issue for users for whom social networks form an important part of their lives. This can cause two particular types of problem: the first occurs when there is a mismatch between norms of use between a person and their friends, and the second is an online variant of offline friendship issues. In addition, online friendship can have specific positive or negative impacts on members.

The *treatment of friends* becomes an issue when two online friends use different interpretations of the term. If one person views SNS friends as real friends but the other views them as casual acquaintances, then there is the potential for the latter to take actions that would be seen as a breach of trust; such actions might include defriending due to inactivity [34]. If someone thought that they had lost a real friend for such a reason, then this would be distressing. In contrast, if the first person asked a friend to do a favor that would be normal to ask of a real friend, then the second person might be offended at the liberty taken by somebody whom they did not view as a real friend [34]. Friends and their activities can impact on the perception of members in at least two ways: having more attractive friends gives positive reinforcement, as does negative comments on male members' profiles, but negative comments on a female member's profile has a negative impact [97].

The issue of *identifying close friends* has been investigated in MySpace, which gives insights into how offline friendship issues can reappear in a new way online [12]. The top 8/top 12 friends in MySpace are those friends that are displayed on the member's profile page rather than being relegated to secondary pages listing all friends. MySpace users can select which friends are shown on their profile page (not possible with Facebook) and so these are normally the most important friends—perhaps best friends and most regarded musicians. The choice of top friends can be an issue with offline friends that can cause stress and resentment because it is a highly visible public statement of importance [12]. Assuming that the first top friend is the most important one, if someone changes their best friend, then reflecting this change in such an obvious way as reordering the top friends list is a potential source of trouble.

Cyworld has a form of close friendship that is similar to kinship but may play a role like that of top friends in MySpace. The terms cyberbuddies and cyberrelatives have both been used to describe Cyworld friends [42], with the latter term reflecting the kinship analogy used within Cyworld friendships.

Online friendship can also be used to *repair offline friendships*. A study of Cyworld has found that its design takes advantage of Korean social norms to provide an environment in which types of emotional communication can occur online that would not necessarily occur offline between friends [54]. The authors emphasize that Korea has a collectivist culture supporting different kinds of interpersonal relationships and different kinds of communication styles to those in more individualist countries, such as in Europe, the US, and Canada. In particular, it is difficult to express emotions offline because these are implicit in relationships and do not often need to be spoken. Cyworld can help offline friendship issues by providing an environment in which users feel more comfortable to express emotion, for example, to mend broken relationships after an argument. Related to this, SNS friendships may also particularly help people who are unhappy or who have low self-esteem [31].

One perhaps negative impact of online friendship is that it can generate *social pressure to update* SNS profiles. It seems that Korean Cyworld members may feel this pressure particularly strongly (e.g., to update their diary, upload and decorate pictures, or change their profile customization) to attract enough visitors to validate their popularity, because friends directly ask why they have not updated their minihompy recently, or perhaps because Korean culture includes a high sensitivity to the feelings and opinions of others [42].

7. Privacy and Security

The issue of SNS privacy is different from that of offline privacy for technical reasons. Boyd [16] has identified four properties that differentiate the "networked publics" for an SNS profile from the normal offline public situation. These are persistence (most SNS actions exist for much longer than speech and some may be effectively permanent), searchability (some or all SNS information can be searched for in search engines or internal site search services), replicability (almost anything digital can be easily copied), and invisible audiences (except for BlackPlanet, Glee, AsianAve, and MiGente, most SNSs do not report who views a user's page).

Privacy is particularly important for many SNSs because of the number of children that use them. There have been media reports of pedophiles using SNSs to identify and groom children and about 7% of US teens, mostly girls, have felt uncomfortable when approached online by a stranger [86]. Profile information may also be used by criminals for identity theft purposes (e.g., [50]), by stalkers to locate the homes or telephone numbers of their targets, by parents worried about children (e.g., wondering what they are talking about with friends), or by potential employers checking applicants' backgrounds. In addition, profiles may contain information that the owners might consider embarrassing if it was widely known, such as their sexuality, relationship status, or details of personal problems. Individual members may use SNSs to communicate informally with friends, discussing topics and using language that they would not want others (e.g., parents, teachers, and employers) to read; this provides another privacy need.

Some of these concerns might be relatively minor in practice: for example, students seem to be mainly unconcerned about future employers checking their profiles, although this might be due to a focus on current rather than future privacy threats [95]. In addition to young users having special privacy needs, there are differences based upon other factors such as gender and geography. For example, in the US rural women tend to have stronger privacy needs than urban users or rural men [36].

7.1 System Affordances and Policies

Many SNSs, including MySpace and Facebook, have a basic minimum privacy setting together with additional layers of privacy that users can choose to add. In MySpace, the minimum basic level of privacy is quite low: visitors must log in to

MySpace in order to view others' pictures, videos, and blogs but most other aspects can be made world-visible, including to search engines (as of April 2008). In contrast, only minimal Facebook information is normally accessible in search engines and in full profile information is normally only be visible to friends and others within the same network. This perhaps contributes to Facebook members' greater willingness to share identifying information, although, in practice, MySpace members are not discouraged by privacy concerns from meeting new people online [30]. Within both sites, members can select a privacy level that displays minimal information. MySpace private profiles display a picture, a name, a personal message, gender, age, mood, general geographic location, and last login date. Search engines are banned from indexing private MySpace profiles (using the metatag: `<meta name = ''robots'' content = ''noindex''/>`). Facebook minimal listings are similar, containing name, picture, and some friends' pictures; members can opt to not be listed in search engines.

LinkedIn has a similar privacy policy to Facebook to support its business networking. Users can opt to hide all their information from search engines and unknown users, or select which elements of their profile to reveal to them (called the ''public profile''). Cyworld is slightly different: users can segment their content into different levels of privacy, keeping some ''secret folder'' information for themselves alone [54]. In MySpace, and probably in all other SNSs, users probably implement their own privacy policy by not including information too personal for others to see—assuming that other forms of communication can be used for this, if necessary [18]. MySpace supports this policy in a sense, by warning users under 18 about the risks of uploading a personal picture or disclosing private information [18].

Anonymity is the core privacy strategy of child-friendly sites like Club Penguin. Perhaps because of its additional security, Japanese site mixi makes a relatively large amount of information visible to all users, including blood type, favorites, hobbies, and a brief biography [55].

Exceptionally, security issues are relatively minimal in the Korean Cyworld SNS because it has a strict identity verification system, in line with common practice in South Korea [54]. Similarly, for security reasons mixi only allows new members to join that are invited by existing members, and requires them to be 18-years old [55].

7.2   Marketing and Surveillance

As the examples above illustrate, the privacy settings of SNSs can be quite extensive and seem to offer, in theory, sufficient privacy for most purposes. The exception is access to profile information by the host company. Most SNSs use profile information for their own targeted advertising [81] and although this allows them to be free, it has privacy and ethical implications. For example, Facebook has been criticized for allowing loan advertising to be targeted at young people (e.g., http://news.bbc.co.uk/1/hi/uk/7395344.stm). Access to large amounts of personal data is common to many Internet applications, including online email and search engines, and means that some Internet companies can discover extensive information about their users [100]. This can be used for marketing purposes and perhaps also in criminal and government investigations, including counterterrorism. Specific concerns have been raised about the selling of profile information to advertisers to help them set up targeted marketing campaigns (e.g., via Facebook's Beacon technology), leading Facebook to give unhappy members easier access to stop this (http://news.bbc.co.uk/1/hi/uk/7395344.stm).

7.3   User Perceptions and Strategies

Despite the extensive availability of privacy options in SNSs, they may not be used or fully understood by all members (e.g., [41, 69]). Perhaps in response to this, young users may have a policy of not mentioning very private topics in SNSs but use another online or offline mode of communication to discuss them [69]. Another important user strategy for privacy is the use of a nickname or pseudonym to retain anonymity from nonfriends. This seems to occur rarely in Facebook but to be more common in MySpace [95].

One study has systematically analyzed a random sample of the public MySpace profiles of youths under 18 to discover how much personal information was revealed [46]. The results showed that the majority of members were responsible in not disclosing personal information. For example, only 0.3% included their phone number and 8.8% reported their full name. A significant minority discussed alcohol use (18.1%), tobacco use (7.5%), or marijuana use (1.7%); however, some of which they would presumably wish to keep secret from parents, teachers, and law enforcement agencies. Another survey has shown that most online US adults were careful with posting personal information but that the majority (60%) felt comfortable with the amount of data about them that was online [70]. The majority of US teenagers with online social network profiles were aware of some privacy issues and took some steps to protect their online safety (including publishing false information) or to protect some of their content from access from others, including parents. Regardless of this, most teens believe that they could be identified from their profile by someone who was prepared to invest sufficient time [61]. Overall, however, security issues in social networks seem to have been exaggerated in terms of serious threats to online young people [99].

A study of privacy issues related to YouTube has emphasized the extent to which users consciously choose a privacy strategy to meet their needs. This strategy may be quite subtle and include recognition that their videos may be almost impossible for strangers to find even if they are publicly available to be viewed. Lange [59] identifies the "publicly private" strategy of making full information available to everyone but recognizing that only friends are likely to access it, and the "privately public" strategy of ensuring that a set of videos were widely viewed but limiting access to personal information. This distinction explains why the Facebook news feeds feature caused resentment when it was released: ostensibly it is privacy neutral because it repackages existing public information (what users have been doing) but it delivers this information prominently to friends, many of whom could perhaps be relied upon not to seek it out. As a result, some users who felt safe to conduct activities publicly were not happy to have these activities broadcast to all their Facebook friends [15].

7.4 Software Issues

Relatively little SNS software development is reported in academic papers or otherwise publicly described, but some research has tackled relevant issues. One study analyzed the extent to which anonymized social network data, as given by companies for use in research, could be mined to recover the identity of members. Both theoretical arguments and a case study of LiveJournal data were used to demonstrate that network structure information could be used to reveal apparently private information about some members from the anonymized data [5]. This is an indication that apparently private data could be extracted from social networks by those willing to expend sufficient effort. A second study took an opposite perspective, developing software that could save SNS members from spam friendship requests by identifying fake or marketing profiles [101]. It could be useful to developers to understand how communities are formed. Techniques for this have been demonstrated through a mathematical modeling approach to understanding community formation in LiveJournal which found a clear relationship between a member's tendency to join a community and the number of their friends that were already members [4].

7.5 MySpace Investigation

Table IV gives information on privacy settings as well as an overall gender breakdown. It shows that females and newer members are more likely to set their profiles to private. It also reveals that a majority of members are female, especially for more recent members.

Figure 11 gives more detailed information about the revelation of personal information, broken down by age. In terms of privacy settings, all users aged 14 and 15 must have private profiles, according to MySpace policy. In addition, 10% of

M. THELWALL

TABLE IV
PRIVACY SETTINGS FOR MYSPACE ACCOUNTS

	Yearlings		All members	
Privacy setting	Female	Male	Female	Male
Public (%)	36	45	45	59
Private (%)	64	55	55	41
Total	8976	7388	8764	8199

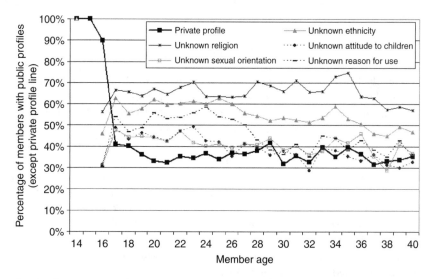

FIG. 11. The percentage of members with private profiles and the percentage of members with public profiles that have not answered a range of standard profile questions.

the 16-year olds had changed their profile from private to public since becoming 16. For the remainder of users, about 30–40% set their profiles to private, and there is little difference between ages. All users with public profiles must declare a marital status, but other personal information is optional. The remainder of the lines on Fig. 11 illustrate the proportion of users *with public profiles* that have not given definite answers to a range of standard questions. This information is part of the set of additional questions that members can choose to answer or ignore. There is a tendency for older users to answer more of these questions, as evidenced by the downward trend to most lines. Least popular overall is the declaration of a religion, and most popular are attitudes to children (e.g., ''I don't want kids,'' ''Proud parent'') and sexual orientation. It also seems that reasons for use (friendship, dating, network-ing, and serious relationships) are given significantly more frequently by those who are 28+ than by younger users.

8. Language

Relatively little research has investigated SNS language but much is known about other electronic communication styles. These styles are probably all found to some extent in a typical SNS and so are reviewed here before a discussion of SNS-specific findings. The Internet and other forms of CMC have given rise to numerous spelling and other language variations. Internet messaging and mobile phone text messaging abbreviations like m8 and l8r are well known, as are pictograms like :-) [94] and numerous international variations [3, 60, 77]. It is also known that language varies between software and between devices, depending upon the affordances of the technology and the social context in which it is used [45]. For example, abbrevia-tions initially developed for quick mobile phone text messaging using keypads might subsequently be used in email, where they are not convenient, to show group membership [24]. There are many different varieties of "Internet language" and CMC language, even for English, and the following list indicates some features that may be found in them [25, 39, 40, 83, 94]:

- Acronyms, for example, irl (in real life), lol (laugh out loud), bfn (bye for now)
- Abbreviations, for example, h8, @
- Portraying an accent, humorous spelling, or phonetic spelling, for example, luv, choon (tune), wiv for with, lata for later, clipping the final "g" of words ending in "ing"
- Letter and number homophones, for example, h8, 2, r, u, cu, k (for qu in French)
- Merged words, for example, cu, carcrash, seeya, ad hoc omitting spaces between words
- Repeated letters for emphasis, for example, helllloooo, hiiiii
- Frequent use of swear words
- Use of all lower case letters, or all upper case letters
- Omission of all punctuation or omission of apostrophes, for example, dont
- Slang, for example, scaggy, hotty
- Spelling mistakes, for example, copyed, doign, mixs
- Use of numbers for similar-looking letters, for example, c0de, 5tyll, l3t (let)
- Pictograms, for example, :-), >8-|

- Interjections, for example, boohoo, muahzz, awwww, haha
- Shortened, fragmented, or otherwise incomplete sentences, perhaps missing all verbs
- Multiple languages within a sentence

The language of SNSs probably contains all of the above with the frequency varying considerably according to context. A professional and business-oriented site like LinkedIn is likely to contain predominantly formal language, whereas a general social network like MySpace contains very informal content. Even within a SNS, the language is likely to vary. For example, MySpace profile comments (shown on members' profile pages and typically written by their friends) use all of the features listed above, with only around 3% of English comments exclusively using formal standard English [93]. An important theme in MySpace's comment language is playfulness and creativity, perhaps because messaging friends is a social activity that should not be treated too seriously. Swearing is common, but rarely in an abusive context [88]. Language switching also appears likely to be common in some non-English speaking populations [21].

In contrast to comments, which are typically two-way communication and not intended to be frequently read, most of the rest of profile page contents may potentially be viewed by all visitors or by all friends and hence may be constructed with more care. Similarly, the blog element of MySpaces may tend to adopt a diary-like style. Although there have been newspaper reports of the threat to written language standards caused by the various new forms of electronic communication, it seems that people are able to switch writing style easily between contexts. Emphasizing this point, a 2008 US survey found that teenagers did not think that sending short electronic messages was a form of writing [63].

8.1   MySpace Investigation

The data for this part are the list of comments from the profile pages of all yearlings with public profiles. These comments were parsed from the profile pages and then scanned to eliminate common spam comments using simple string matching (e.g., *CashGift*, *ringtones*). The comments were then split into words (via whitespace characters) and statistics compiled on the number of words per comment and the most common words used.

Table V lists the most common terms in the MySpace comments, after converting all letters to lower case. The items are predominantly English but some are Spanish, French, and Italian. In contrast to general English, date-related terms are particularly common and some Internet-only terms are present (e.g., *ur*, :-), *lol*, *u*) as well as abbreviated spellings like *im* for I'm, and *2* for to and too. A punctuation mark is

TABLE V
THE 100 MOST COMMON WORDS IN THE MARCH 10 MYSPACE COMMENT DATA

Rank	Word	Rank	Word	Rank	Word	Rank	Word
1	2007	26	are	51	jul	76	can
2	i	27	up	52	y	77	some
3	you	28	dec	53	know	78	miss
4	to	29	get	54	jun	79	one
5	the	30	just	55	out	80	i'm
6	a	31	but	56	sep	81	going
7	2008	32	be	57	if	82	about
8	and	33	was	58	.	83	from
9	u	34	how	59	good	84	when
10	mar	35	we	60	see	85	or
11	for	36	this	61	lol	86	its
12	me	37	at	62	what	87	well
13	feb	38	apr	63	do	88	e
14	my	39	nov	64	been	89	back
15	in	40	with	65	hope	90	am
16	is	41	de	66	que	91	en
17	it	42	all	67	ur	92	by
18	on	43	te	68	not	93	he
19	of	44	ya	69	got	94	un
20	your	45	no	70	will	95	as
21	so	46	may	71	la	96	n
22	have	47	aug	72	new	97	da
23	love	48	oct	73	2	98	o
24	jan	49	like	74	:)	99	x
25	that	50	im	75	go	100	el

included at rank 58 because it occurs frequently surrounded by whitespace, which is rare in standard English.

9. Software Issues

9.1 Programming SNS Applications

Many SNSs make additional functionality available to members via programs written in Java or Flash. There are three approaches to this in terms of openness. Gaia Online's Flash games are designed or commissioned by Gaia and there are only a few different types. In conjunction with the MochiAds games-based advertising network, Gaia Online has run an online competition to find new games to add to its small portfolio (Gaia Online/Mochi Media press release: http://www.marketwire.com/mw/release.do?id=857312).

Facebook is more open than Gaia Online, having launched Facebook Platform in May 2007, an application programming interface (API) allowing any programmer to create applications to run in Facebook. If a member sees an application that they wish to use, then they have to register with the application in order to add it to their profile. Once in their profile, the application is typically allowed to access some of their personal information and post news stories to their personal feed so that it can embed smoothly within the SNS. The applications tend to be interactive so are able to communicate with multiple members.

The Facebook *(Lil) Green Patch* application is a typical example. It allows members to send a picture of a plant to a friend, for displaying in their profile. To send or receive a plant, you must have registered with the application. Hence, the sender must first register and attempt to send a plant to a selected friend. The friend will then receive a notification that they have been sent a gift and this notification will tell them how to register for the application. If they register, then the application will be allocated space within the user's profile and can use this space to display the gift picture. The (Lil) Green Patch application can also have access to members' news feeds so that others can be notified about the exchange of gifts. Presumably, applications are successful if they are charming or interesting enough for users to want to have them in their profile. Another popular type of application is the comparative quiz: friends can answer questions about a selected topic, such as favorite films, and then forward the quiz to their friends. If their friends take the same quiz, then a score is reported about how well their tastes match. Other games are competitive, with the goal being to beat the opponent or attain the highest score.

A claim has been made that applications running in SNSs, such as those written for Facebook Platform, are potentially very powerful marketing devices that operate in a new way. Fogg [33] has coined the term mass interpersonal persuasion for this type of phenomenon, describing six key components: a persuasive experience, an automated structure, social distribution, a rapid cycle, a huge social graph, and measured impact. Most of these are self-evident and rely on the ability for SNSs to rapidly transmit ideas through a form of viral marketing. The ability to measure impact is particularly interesting. Facebook applications are able to send information back to their creators to report on how they are used, with one developer claiming to embed 200 measurement points into an application [33]. The instant feedback of these metrics allows the creators to try different methods of persuading users to adopt the application and to quickly identify successful strategies. As a result, a successful Facebook application is likely to have an invitation statement that has a proven persuasive ability and is also perhaps customized for the type of person sending the invitation. The success of many applications has been spectacular, but there has been a backlash against some of the persuasive practices, in the form of Facebook groups like "Official Facebook Petition: To ban the inviting of friends on Applications," which had over a million members in June 2008.

OpenSocial is a November 2007 (alpha status release) Google proposal for a universal SNS API. The purpose of the API was to allow developers to write application that would run on any SNS that supported the core features. The API allowed developers to create applications that used JavaScript and HTML alone, rather than Flash or Java, although it has been criticized as being too weak, not secure, and not portable enough. Google claimed that OpenSocial was being implemented by Friendster, Hi5, IMEEM, LinkedIn, MySpace, and its own Orkut (http://code.google.com/apis/opensocial/, accessed 4 May 2008). Apparently in reaction to this, Facebook announced Facebook Open Platform (http://developers.facebook.com/news.php?blog=1&story=117) and released some of the source code for Facebook Platform in June 2008 (http://developers.facebook.com/opensource.php/).

9.2   Using SNS Data

Some SNSs, including Flickr and Last.FM, have made available sections of their data for others to access, via an API. This allows programmers to construct non-SNS applications that use SNS data. Last.FM has a Web service interface (http://www.audioscrobbler.net/data/webservices/) for its AudioScrobbler database of the music tastes of individuals so that researchers and developers could access this huge database of musical tastes. The Flickr API (http://www.flickr.com/services/api/) gives access to information about the images and tags entered in Flickr: it is freely available for noncommercial purposes (e.g., [2]) and available by agreement for commercial applications. At the moment, however, these opportunities seem to be SNS byproducts rather than core to SNS functionality or future developments.

Computer scientists have already used SNS data on a large scale for published data mining applications, and this seems to be a promising general direction for future research. For example, a text analysis of 100,000 social network profiles was able to create crossdomain "taste maps" based upon word co-occurrences and using machine learning techniques [68]. This approach was then used for a detailed analysis of taste in MySpace [67]. Another visualization-based project used social network data to map friendship connections [44]. A very large-scale study of Flickr and Yahoo! 360° illustrates a more theoretical approach, attempting to understand the topology of community formation and the key types of roles in terms of friend formation [56]. Some Google research into Orkut shows the potential commercial applications of data mining in social networks: a study of how to recommend communities to Orkut users based upon existing community membership [87]. Finally, some SNSs have the potential to be mined to discover aspects of public opinion, although a study of news in Live Spaces found that there was very little evidence of nontrivial topics being discussed in a way that was easy to mine [91].

10. Conclusions

It is clear from the discussions above and research reviewed within this chapter that many different types of site have social network functionality. Perhaps, the core sites are those like MySpace, Cyworld, and Facebook that emphasize the recreational side of SNSs. These have been enormously successful in terms of growth, probably based mainly on viral spreading amongst groups of friends and acquaintances. Social networking is an international phenomenon, but the most popular sites vary by country. This is partly due to language issues but in some cases there is not an obvious reason why a country has adopted a particular SNS (e.g., Orkut in Brazil). The core members are normally assumed to be teens and although these seem to be particularly heavy users, they are in a minority, even within teen-friendly MySpace. There are some small gender and education divisions in SNS usage and membership, but these are not strong. The largest difference, at least in the US, seems to be ethnic: with successful SNSs that are targeted at one section of the community (e.g., BlackPlanet, AsianAve, and MiGente).

The evidence about how SNSs are used is fragmentary because although there are a few studies of specific sites or types of user, there is too little information to make many generalizations about how the different types of SNS are used. It seems clear that members exploit the affordances of a particular SNS in varied ways, rather than following a common pattern. For example, although Facebook is primarily about social communication between friends, game playing is also important for some members, whereas finding out about friends of friends is important for others. The evidence about the utility of overcoming geographic distance is mixed: for some users this is a key aspect but online communication seems to be most frequent between people who often meet face-to-face at school, college, or (perhaps) work.

The concept of friendship varies between sites and between individuals. Friends in LinkedIn are ''contacts'' and in LiveJournal are often people who wish to read the friend's journal. In MySpace, a member's friends could be just their close personal offline friends, could also include acquaintances, or could include a large number of strangers. The range of reasons given by MySpace members for friending or accepting a friend request includes relatively trivial ones, such as the need to avoid giving offence by refusing a request. In many sites, a person's friends may include celebrities or bands that they are a fan of, stretching the meaning of the term friend. The differing meanings of friendship are a potential cause of conflict when two users interpret the rights and responsibilities associated with it differently.

Although privacy and security are commonly discussed issues, it seems that SNS owners take personal security seriously and give users control over who can see certain information about them. Users also tend to be aware of the issues and often take steps to protect their privacy online. There is a tension, however, between the need to reveal enough information to use a site effectively and the need to protect it from unwanted others.

Linguistically, socializing SNSs are probably between blogs and chatrooms in terms of the formality of language used. In particular, comments exchanged between friends are relatively permanent, if unlikely to be viewed after they have disappeared from the main page (e.g., because 50 comments have subsequently been posted). Moreover, unless the comment facility is used to engage in a real-time conversation, for which instant messaging would be more natural, the commenter has the time to be careful with their composition, if they desire. Nevertheless, the evidence from MySpace is that comments are rarely made using correct formal English and that slang, spelling deviations/mistakes and fragmented or incomplete sentences are common. This could be explained by social rather than technological factors. Users may deliberately use informal language and comic elements to reinforce friendship ties or group membership.

Many social networking sites include embedded applications for additional connectivity or game playing. Some sites, including Orkut and Facebook, give open access to some of their functionality so that other developers can create new applications that can be added to profile pages. It seems possible that Google's OpenSocial will emerge as a standard for SNS so that applications can be created that run on multiple sites. Such applications may never be allowed on sites for which the recreational social element is less important, such as LinkedIn.

10.1   Current and Future Developments

The future will probably bring more connectivity between SNSs and mobile phones as a logical step toward ubiquity. The microblogging SNS Twitter allows mobile phones to be used easily to update sites and to receive broadcast status updates from friends (also available in Facebook)—for both information dissemination and reporting daily activities [51]. This follows Flickr and Cyworld, which have allowed users to upload photographs from their mobile phones for a long time (Cyworld since 2004), with Cyworld having a range of other mobile phone services, such as paying to be texted the number of visitors [42]. Dodgeball is an interesting mobile phone-based SNS that uses geographic information to prompt members with information such as the location of nearby interesting places and even friends of friends but it does not seem to have gained a major user base. Nevertheless, it seems to have a significant influence on the behavior of its users, particularly in terms of bringing people together for offline social activities [49].

A second important direction is to increase connectivity between competing sites so that friends can be transferred from one to another or communication between people on different sites may be supported. The social network browser Flock supports this in a sense because it makes it easy to switch between the different SNSs in order to quickly maintain multiple profiles. There is already a mechanism for open expression of friendship relationships, the XFN (XML Friends Network) microformat (http://www.gmpg.org/xfn/). If adopted by SNSs or a third-party application, this could be used to build extended multisite friendship relationships. MySpace's data availability project from May 2008 (http://news.bbc.co.uk/1/hi/technology/7391405.stm) addresses the issue in a different way by allowing members to synchronize selected profile information (including friend lists) across different SNS services. This initiative was designed to make it easier for people with multiple SNS memberships to update them all. Data security in MySpace system is handled by the open source OAuth protocol.

A third new direction is facilitating the importing of social network functionality into traditional Web sites so that developers can easily allow visitors to connect and interact via existing social networks. This has been supported to some extent for a long time via traditional hyperlinks, such as the BBC's standard ''Bookmark with: Delicious, Digg, reddit, Facebook, StumbleUpon'' links at the bottom of many of its stories. Facebook Connect, in May 2008, was introduced to allow third-party ''partner'' Web sites to incorporate some elements of Facebook interactivity (http://developers.facebook.com/news.php?blog=1&story=108). A similar initiative is Google Friend Connect (May 2008, http://news.bbc.co.uk/1/hi/technology/7397470.stm, http://www.google.com/friendconnect/) which is a service allowing Web sites to easily add SNS features (using Google's OpenSocial API, see above) for existing SNS members by logging on to their SNS of choice, as long as it supports OpenSocial. Google's initiative is more generic than that of Facebook but it remains to be seen which is most successful. Neither is completely open in the sense that users have to be approved. It is not clear whether the approval hurdle will ever be removed because this would allow SNS branding or features to appear on Web sites that might be seen as problematic to many SNS users (e.g., pornography, hate groups).

A fourth new direction is for social networking sites to add extra functionality to become more like portal sites. This occurred in May 2008 to Cyworld in Korea, which added a large search panel to the top of its home page. This was seen as a response to SNS saturation in South Korea [52] so that Cyworld had to change from being a pure SNS service into being a general portal to the Internet in order to retain its members or their activity level.

In terms of business models, there are currently three main types: advertising (e.g., Facebook), micropayments (e.g., Cyworld, partially Gaia Online), and premium membership (e.g., mixi, Flickr). It seems likely that advertising will remain the dominant overall source of revenue because the commercial logic of selling targeted advertising on the basis of users' personal data within the system seems irresistible. Perhaps, mixed-model strategies based upon advertising and micropayments or premium membership will become the norm. This is because there are advantages to micropayment—for example, supporting the social function of gift exchanging and allowing more powerful connections to mobile phones without prohibitive one-off charges. In contrast, premium membership (e.g., to add extra storage space or features) has the advantage that it allows a mature site to add expensive functionality, and hence become more attractive and guard against the power users in the system having to move elsewhere. This business model would also allow popular SNSs to keep adding additional features in order to be come larger and more powerful, perhaps adding most services found popular with the users of any other similar site.

The future will probably also see more researchers taking advantage of the friendship connection data implicit in SNSs to model patterns of friendship or the forces involved in social activities. One such study is based upon data supplied by agreement with Facebook [66], but other studies could also use publicly available data in MySpace or other SNSs. Computing research may develop data mining predictive algorithms that might help to make SNSs more user-friendly by making intelligent suggestions for future activities (e.g., [47, 85]) or may make intelligent socially relevant applications such as identifying suicide risks from the contents of their profiles [48]. Marketers will probably also exploit these sites in increasingly innovative ways to make closer connections with their customers [9].

It is difficult to speculate about the overall future of SNSs because they have emerged so rapidly that it seems possible that new variants will emerge to replace the current generation. The core idea of contacting friends online and reconnecting with former friends (e.g., classmates) is so strong that social networking in some form seems to be an inevitable part of the future of the Web. It is not clear whether the future promises a few powerful sites that dominate social networking and can be used for many types of activity, from business networking to socializing. In contrast, there may be an ever-increasing range of specialist SNS that offer functionality to support clearly defined user needs. There are two opposing factors at work here. SNSs benefit from large numbers because more people bring more chances to interact. Conversely, SNSs can benefit from being restrictive because people will probably not be able to use a site fully to chat with their friends if they know that a boss or parent is also a friend and will see what they are doing. Perhaps, future SNS functionality will include ways around this problem or people will naturally use multiple SNSs, one for each aspect of their life (e.g., work, school friends, and close friends).

ACKNOWLEDGMENT

Thank you to David Stuart for comments on an earlier draft of this chapter.

REFERENCES

[1] Adamic L. A., and Huberman B. A., 24 March 2000. Power-law distribution of the World Wide Web. *Science*, **287**: 2115a.
[2] Angus E., Thelwall M., and Stuart D., 2008. General patterns of tag usage amongst university groups in Flickr. *Online Information Review*, **32**(1): 89–101.
[3] Anis J., 2007. Netography: Unconventional spelling in French SMS text messages. In *The Multilingual Internet: Language, Culture, and Communication Online*, (B. Danet and S. C. Herring, Eds.), pp. 87–115. Oxford University Press, Oxford.
[4] Backstrom L., Huttenlocher D., Kleinberg J., and Lan X., 2006. Group formation in large social networks: Membership, growth, and evolution. In *Proceedings of 12th International Conference on Knowledge Discovery in Data Mining (KDD-2006)*, pp. 44–54. ACM Press, New York.
[5] Backstrom L., Dwork C., and Kleinberg J., 2007. Wherefore art thou r3579x? Anonymized social networks, hidden patterns, and structural steganography. In *Proceedings of the 16th International Conference on World Wide Web*, pp. 181–190.
[6] Bainbridge W. S., 2007. The scientific research potential of virtual worlds. *Science*, **317**(5837): 472–476.
[7] Baker J. R., and Moore S. M., 2008. Distress, coping, and blogging: Comparing new MySpace users by their intention to blog. *CyberPsychology & Behavior*, **11**(1): 81–85.
[8] Beer D., 2008. Social network(ing) sites . . . revisiting the story so far: A response to danah boyd & Nicole Ellison. *Journal of Computer-Mediated Communication*, **13**(2): 516–529.
[9] Bernoff J., and Li C., 2008. Harnessing the power of the oh-so-social Web. *MIT Sloan Management Review*, **49**(3): 36–42.
[10] Birch M., 20 May 2008. Talk at the Innovation Edge. London.
[11] Bonilla-Silva E., and Embrick D. G., 2007. "Every place has a ghetto. . .": The significance of whites' social and residential segregation. *Symbolic Interaction*, **30**(3): 323–345.
[12] boyd D., 2006. Friends, Friendsters, and MySpace Top 8: Writing community into being on social network sites. *First Monday*, **11**(2) (retrieved 23 June 2007 from http://www.firstmonday.org/issues/issue2011_1012/boyd/index.html).
[13] boyd D., 2006. Friendster lost steam. Is MySpace just a fad? *Apophenia Blog Essay (June 24)*, (retrieved 30 April 2008 from http://www.danah.org/papers/FriendsterMySpaceEssay.html).
[14] boyd D., 2007. Viewing American class divisions through Facebook and MySpace. *Apophenia Blog Essay (June 24)*, (retrieved 12 July 2007 from http://www.danah.org/papers/essays/ClassDivisions.html).
[15] boyd D., 2008. Facebook's privacy trainwreck: Exposure, invasion, and social convergence. *Convergence*, **14**(1): 13–20.
[16] boyd D., 2008. Why youth (heart) social network sites: The role of networked publics in teenage social life. In *Youth, Identity, and Digital Media*, (D. Buckingham, Ed.), pp. 119–142. MIT Press, Cambridge, MA.
[17] boyd D., and Ellison N., 2007. Social network sites: Definition, history, and scholarship. *Journal of Computer-Mediated Communication*, **13**(1) (retrieved 10 December 2007 from http://jcmc.indiana.edu/vol13/issue1/boyd.ellison.html).

[18] Brake D., 2008. Shaping the 'me' in MySpace: The framing of profiles on a social network site. In *Digital Storytelling, Mediatized Stories: Self-Representations in New Media*, (K. Lundby, Ed.), pp. 285–300. Peter Lang, New York.

[19] Byrne D., 2007. Public discourse, community concerns, and their relationship to civic engagement: Exploring black social networking traditions on blackplanet.com. *Journal of Computer-Mediated Communication*, **31**(1) (retrieved 18 May 2008 from http://jcmc.indiana.edu/vol13/issue1/byrne.html).

[20] Byrne D., 2008. The future of (the) 'race': Identity, discourse and the rise of computer-mediated public spheres. In *MacArthur Foundation Book Series on Digital Learning: Race and Ethnicity Volume*, (A. Everett, Ed.), pp. 15–38. MIT Press, Cambridge, MA.

[21] Carroll K. S., 2008. Puerto Rican language use on MySpace.com. *Centro Journal*, **20**(1): 96–111.

[22] Choi J. H.-J., 2006. Living in Cyworld: Contextualising Cy-Ties in South Korea. In *Use of Blogs (Digital Formations)*, (A. Bruns and J. Jacobs, Eds.), pp. 173–186. Peter Lang, New York.

[23] Corcoran K. T., March/April 2004. BlackPlanet's universe. *Stanford Magazine*, (retrieved 18 June 2008 from http://www.omarwasow.com/Stanford_Magazine_2004.pdf).

[24] Crystal D., 2006. Language and the Internet. 2nd edn. Cambridge University Press, Cambridge, UK.

[25] del-Teso-Craviotto M., 2006. Language and sexuality in Spanish and English dating chats. *Journal of Sociolinguistics*, **10**(4): 460–480.

[26] Donath J., 2007. Signals in social supernets. *Journal of Computer-Mediated Communication*, **13**(1) (retrieved 17 June 2008 from http://jcmc.indiana.edu/vol13/issue1/donath.html).

[27] Donath J., and Boyd D., 2004. Public displays of connection. *BT Technology Journal*, **22**(4): 71–82.

[28] Dunbar R., 1996. Grooming, Gossip and the Evolution of Language. Faber and Faber Limited, London.

[29] Dutton W. H., and Elsper E. J., 2007. The Internet in Britain 2007. Oxford Internet Institute, Oxford.

[30] Dwyer C., Hiltz S. R., and Passerini K., 2007. Trust and privacy concern within social networking sites: A comparison of Facebook and MySpace. In *Proceedings of AMCIS 2007*. Keystone, CO (retrieved 18 May 2008 from http://csis.pace.edu/~dwyer/research/DwyerAMCIS2007.pdf).

[31] Ellison N. B., Steinfield C., and Lampe C., 2007. The benefits of Facebook ''friends:'' Social capital and college students' use of online social network sites. *Journal of Computer-Mediated Communication*, **12**(4): 1143–1168.

[32] Escher T., 2007. The geography of (online) social networks. *Web 2.0, York University*, (retrieved 18 September 2007 from http://people.oii.ox.ac.uk/escher/wp-content/uploads/2007/2009/Escher_York_ presentation.pdf).

[33] Fogg B. J., 2008. Mass interpersonal persuasion: An early view of a new phenomenon. *Lecture Notes in Computer Science*, **5033**: 23–34.

[34] Fono D., and Raynes-Goldie K., 2007. Hyperfriendship and beyond: Friendship and social norms on LiveJournal, Association of Internet Researchers (AOIR-6), Chicago. In *Internet Research Annual Volume 4: Selected Papers from the Association of Internet Researchers Conference*, (M. Consalvo and C. Haythornthwaite, Eds.), Peter Lang, New York.

[35] Fulgoni G., 2007. Consumer trends in social networking. *ComScore*, (retrieved 8 May 2008 from http://www.comscore.com/blog/2007/2010/consumer_trends_in_social_netw.html).

[36] Gilbert E., Karahalios K., and Sandvig C., 2008. The network in the garden: An empirical analysis of social media in rural life. In *Proceedings of the SIGCHI Conference on Human Factors in*

Computing Systems. (retrieved 24 January 2008 from http://social.cs.uiuc.edu/people/gilbert/papers/chi2008-rural-gilbert.pdf).

[37] Golder S. A., and Huberman B. A., 2006. The structure of collaborative tagging systems. *Journal of Information Science*, **32**(2): 198–208.

[38] Golder S. A., Wilkinson D., and Huberman B. A., 2007. Rhythms of social interaction: Messaging within a massive online network. In *3rd International Conference on Communities and Technologies (CT2007)*, East Lansing, MI.

[39] Grinter R. E., and Eldridge M., 2003. Wan2tlk? Everyday text messaging. In *CHI 2003*, pp. 441–448.

[40] Grinter R. E., Palen L., and Eldridge M., 2006. Chatting with teenagers: Considering the place of chat technologies in teen life. *ACM Transactions on Computer–Human Interaction*, **13**(4): 423–447.

[41] Gross R., Acquisti A., and Heinz H. J., 2005. Information revelation and privacy in online social networks. In *Proceedings of the 2005 ACM Workshop on Privacy in the Electronic Society*, pp. 71–80.

[42] Haddon L., and Kim S. D., 2007. Mobile phones and Web-based social networking—Emerging practices in Korea with Cyworld. *Journal of the Communications Network*, **6**: 5–12.

[43] Hargittai E., 2007. Whose space? Differences among users and non-users of social network sites. *Journal of Computer-Mediated Communication*, **13**(1) (retrieved 10 June 2008 from http://jcmc.indiana.edu/vol13/issue1/hargittai.html).

[44] Heer J., and Boyd D., 2005. Vizster: Visualizing online social networks. In *Information Visualization 2005*, pp. 32–39. IEEE, New York.

[45] Herring S. C., 2002. Computer-mediated communication on the Internet. *Annual Review of Information Science and Technology*, **36**: 109–168.

[46] Hinduja S., and Patchin J. W., 2008. Personal information of adolescents on the Internet: A quantitative content analysis of MySpace. *Journal of Adolescence*, **31**(1): 125–146.

[47] Hsu W. H., Lancaster J., Paradesi M. S. R., and Weninger T., 2007. Structural link analysis from user profiles and friends networks: A feature construction approach. In *Proceedings of ICWSM-2007*, Boulder, CO, pp. 75–80.

[48] Huang Y.-P., Goh T., and Liew C. L., 2007. Hunting suicide notes in Web 2.0—Preliminary findings. In *Ninth IEEE International Symposium on Multimedia—Workshops, Proceedings*, pp. 517–521. IEEE, Los Alamitos, CA.

[49] Humphreys L., 2007. Mobile social networks and social practice: A case study of Dodgeball. *Journal of Computer-Mediated Communication*, **13**(1) (retrieved 5 June 2008 from http://jcmc.indiana.edu/vol2013/issue2001/humphreys.html).

[50] Jagatic T., Johnson N., Jakobsson M., and Menczer F., 2007. Social phishing. *Communications of the ACM*, **5**(10): 94–100.

[51] Java A., Song X., Finin T., and Tseng B., 2007. Why we Twitter: Understanding the microblogging effect in user intentions and communities. In *WebKDD*, San Jose, CA (retrieved 18 May 2006 from http://workshops.socialnetworkanalysis.info/websnakdd2007/papers/submission_2021.pdf).

[52] Jin-seo C., 19 May 2008. Social networking embracing search engines, games. *The Korea Times*, (retrieved 27 May 2008 from http://www.koreatimes.co.kr/www/news/nation/2008/2005/2133_24408.html).

[53] Joinson A. N., 2008. Looking at, looking up or keeping up with people? Motives and use of Facebook. In *Proceeding of the Twenty-Sixth Annual SIGCHI Conference on Human Factors in Computing Systems*, pp. 1027–1036.

[54] Kim K.-H., and Yun H., 2007. Cying for me, Cying for us: Relational dialectics in a Korean social network site. *Journal of Computer-Mediated Communication*, **13**(1) (retrieved 19 December 2008 from http://jcmc.indiana.edu/vol13/issue11/kim.yun.html).

[55] Komaki R., Preprint. Do Web interfaces have politics? A Case of mixi, a Japanese Social Network Site.

[56] Kumar R., Novak J., and Tomkins A., 2006. Structure and evolution of online social networks. In *Proceedings of 12th International Conference on Knowledge Discovery in Data Mining (KDD-2006)*, pp. 611–617. ACM Press, New York.

[57] Lampe C., Ellison N., and Steinfield C., 2006. A face(book) in the crowd: Social Searching vs. social browsing. In *Proceedings of the 2006 20th Anniversary Conference on Computer Supported Cooperative Work*, pp. 167–170.

[58] Lampe C. A. C., Ellison N., and Steinfield C., 2007. A familiar face(book): Profile elements as signals in an online social network. In *Proceedings of the SIGCHI Conference on Human Factors in Computing Systems*, pp. 435–444.

[59] Lange P. G., 2007. Publicly private and privately public: Social networking on YouTube. *Journal of Computer-Mediated Communication*, **13**(1) (retrieved 8 May 2008 from http://jcmc.indiana.edu/vol2013/issue2001/lange.html).

[60] Lee C. K. M., 2007. Text-making practices beyond the classroom context: Private instant messaging in Hong Kong. *Computers and Composition*, **24**(3): 285–301.

[61] Lenhart A., and Madden M., 18 April 2007. Teens, privacy and online social networks: How teens manage their online identities and personal information in the age of MySpace. In *Pew Internet & American Life Project*, (retrieved 2 May 2008 from http://www.pewinternet.org/PPF/r/2211/report_display.asp).

[62] Lenhart A., Madden M., Macgill A. R., and Smith A., 19 December 2007. Teens and social media: The use of social media gains a greater foothold in teen life as they embrace the conversational nature of interactive online media. In *Pew Internet & American Life Project*, (retrieved 1 May 2008 from http://www.pewinternet.org/PPF/r/2230/report_display.asp).

[63] Lenhart A., Arafeh S., Smith A., and Macgill A. R., 24 April 2008. Writing, technology and teens. In Pew Internet & American Life Project, (retrieved 1 May 2008 from http://www.pewinternet.org/PPF/r/2247/report_display.asp).

[64] Lerman K., 2006. Social networks and social information filtering on Digg. In *ArXiv.org (also a poster at International Conference on Weblogs and Social Media)*, (retrieved 23 April 2007 from http://arxiv.org/abs/cs.HC/0612046).

[65] Lewis N., 2008. To see the future of the Internet, look East. Spiked. (retrieved 27 May 2008 from http://www.spiked-online.com/index.php?/site/article/5166/).

[66] Lewis K., Kaufman J., Gonzalez M., Wimmer A., and Christakis N. A., 2008. Tastes, ties, and time: A new (cultural, multiplex, and longitudinal) social network dataset using Facebook.com. *Social Networks*, **30**(4): 330–342.

[67] Liu H., 2007. Social network profiles as taste performances. *Journal of Computer-Mediated Communication*, **13**(1) (retrieved 5 June 2008 from http://jcmc.indiana.edu/vol2013/issue2001/liu.html).

[68] Liu H., Maes P., and Davenport G., 2006. Unraveling the taste fabric of social networks. *International Journal on Semantic Web and Information Systems*, **2**(1): 42–71.

[69] Livingstone S., 2008. Taking risky opportunities in youthful content creation: Teenagers' use of social networking sites for intimacy, privacy and self-expression. *New Media & Society*, **10**(3): 393–411.

[70] Madden M., Fox S., Smith A., and Vitak J., 2007. Digital footprints: Online identity management and search in the age of transparency. In *Pew Internet & American Life Project*, (retrieved 1 May 2008 from http://www.pewinternet.org/PPF/r/2229/report_display.asp).

[71] Malinowski B., 1923. The problem of meaning in primitive languages. In *The Meaning of Meaning: Routlledge & Kegan Paul*, (C. K. Ogden and I. A. Richards, Eds.), pp. 296–346.

[72] Mayer A., and Puller S. L., 2008. The old boy (and girl) network: Social network formation on university campuses. *Journal of Public Economics*, **92**(1–2): 329–347.

[73] McPherson M., Smith-Lovin L., and Cook J. M., 2001. Birds of a feather: Homophily in social networks. *Annual Review of Sociology*, **27**: 415–444.

[74] Merriam-Webster, n.d. Friend (noun) (retrieved 30 April 2008 from http://www.merriam-webster.com/cgi-bin/dictionary?book=Dictionary&va=friend).

[75] Nakamura L., 2007. Digitizing Race: Visual Cultures of the Internet. University of Minnesota Press, Minneapolis, MN.

[76] O'Reilly T., 2006. Levels of the Game: The Hierarchy of Web 2.0 Applications. (retrieved 4 June 2007 from http://radar.oreilly.com/archives/2006/2007/levels_of_the_game.html).

[77] Palfreyman D., and Al Khalil M., 2007. "A funky language for teenzz to use": Representing Gulf Arabic in instant messaging. In *The Multilingual Internet: Language, Culture, and Communication Online*, (B. Danet and S. C. Herring, Eds.), pp. 43–63. Oxford University Press, Oxford.

[78] Parks M. R., 2008. Characterizing the Communicative Affordances of MySpace: A Place for Friends or a Friendless Place? International Communication Association, Montreal, QC.

[79] Pearson E., 2007. Digital gifts: Participation and gift exchange in LiveJournal communities. *First Monday*, **12**(5) (retrieved 5 June 2008 from http://firstmonday.org/issues/issue2012_2005/pearson/index.html).

[80] Perkel D., 2006. Copy and paste literacy: Literacy practices in the production of a MySpace profile. In *Informal Learning and Digital Media*, (retrieved 23 April 2007 from http://www.dream.dk/uploads/files/perkel%2020Dan.pdf).

[81] Preibusch S., Hoser B., Gürses S., and Berendt B., 2007. Ubiquitous social networks—Opportunities and challenges for privacy-aware user modelling. In *Proceedings of Workshop on Data Mining for User Modeling*. Corfu, Greece (retrieved 10 June 2008 from http://vasarely.wiwi.hu-berlin.de/DM.UM2007/Proceedings/2005-Preibusch.pdf).

[82] Raacke J., and Bonds-Raacke J., 2008. MySpace and Facebook: Applying the uses and gratifications theory to exploring friend-networking sites. *CyberPsychology & Behavior*, **11**(2): 169–174.

[83] Radić-Bojanić B., 2006. Fragmentation/integration and involvement/detachment in chatroom discourse. *SKASE Journal of Theoretical Linguistics*, **3**(1) (retrieved 3 March 2008 from http://www.skase.sk/Volumes/JTL2005/2004.pdf).

[84] Rousseau R., 1997. Sitations: An exploratory study. *CyberMetrics*, **1**(1)(retrieved 25 July 2006 from http://www.cindoc.csic.es/cybermetrics/articles/v2001i2001p2001.html).

[85] Schedl M., Knees P., and Pohle T., 2008. Towards an automatically generated music information system via Web content mining. *Advances in Information Retrieval*, **4956**: 585–590.

[86] Smith A., 14 October 2007. Teens and Online Stranger Contact. (retrieved 1 May 2008 from http://www.pewinternet.org/PPF/r/2223/report_display.asp).

[87] Spertus E., Sahami M., and Buyukkokten O., 2005. Evaluating similarity measures: A large-scale study in the Orkut social network. In *Proceedings of 11th International Conference on Knowledge Discovery in Data Mining (KDD-2005)*, pp. 678–684.

[88] Thelwall M., 2008. Fk yea I swear: Cursing and gender in a corpus of MySpace pages. *Corpora*, **3**(1): 83–107.

[89] Thelwall M., 2008. How are social network sites embedded in the Web? An exploratory link analysis. *Cybermetrics*, **12**(1) (retrieved 27 April 2008 from http://www.cindoc.csic.es/cybermetrics/articles/v12i1p1.html).

[90] Thelwall M., 2008. Social networks, gender and friending: An analysis of MySpace member profiles. *Journal of the American Society for Information Science and Technology*, **59**(8): 1321–1330.

[91] Thelwall M., 2008. No place for news in social network Web sites? *Online Information Review*, **21**(6) **32**(6): 726–744.

[92] Thelwall M., 2009. Homophily in MySpace. *Journal of the American Society for Information Science and Technology* **60**(2): 219–231.

[93] Thelwall M., 2009. MySpace comments. *Online Information Review* (in press).

[94] Thurlow C., 2003. Generation Txt? The sociolinguistics of young people's text-messaging. *Discourse Analysis Online*, **1**(1) (retrieved 3 January 2008 from http://extra.shu.ac.uk/daol/articles/v2001/n2001/a2003/thurlow2002003-paper.html).

[95] Tufekci Z., 2008. Can you see me now? Audience and disclosure regulation in online social network sites. *Bulletin of Science, Technology & Society*, **28**(1): 20–36.

[96] Tufekci Z., 2008. Grooming, gossip, Facebook and MySpace: What can we learn about these sites from those who won't assimilate? *Information, Communication & Society*, **11**(4): 544–564.

[97] Walther J., Van der Heide B., Kim S., Westerman D., and Tong S. T., 2008. The role of friends' appearance and behavior on evaluations of individuals on Facebook: Are we known by the company we keep? *Human Communication Research*, **34**: 28–49.

[98] Weida C. L., 2007. Technopotters and Webs of clay: Digital possibilities for teaching ceramics. *Teaching Artist Journal*, **5**(3): 183–190.

[99] Ybarra M. L., and Mitchell K. J., 2008. How risky are social networking sites? A comparison of places online where youth sexual solicitation and harassment occurs. *Pediatrics*, **121**(2): E350–E357.

[100] Zimmer M., 2008. The gaze of the perfect search engine: Google as an infrastructure of dataveillance. In *Web Search: Multidisciplinary Perspectives*, (A. Spink and M. Zimmer, Eds.), pp. 77–99. Springer-Verlag, Berlin.

[101] Zinman A., and Donath J., August 2007. Is Britney Spears spam? In *Fourth Conference on Email and Anti-Spam*, Mountain View, CA.

Highly Interactive Scalable Online Worlds

GRAHAM MORGAN

School of Computing Science, Newcastle University,
Newcastle upon Tyne NE1 7RU, United Kingdom

Abstract

The arrival, in the past decade, of commercially successful virtual worlds used for online gaming and social interaction has emphasized the need for a concerted research effort in this media. A pressing problem is that of incorporating ever more elaborate gaming scenarios into virtual worlds while ensuring player numbers can be measured in the millions. This problem reaches across a number of research areas in computing science and has already received attention from the research community in its own right. In this chapter, the major problems associated to the provisioning of expected player interaction in large-scale virtual worlds is described together with how research efforts may tackle such problems. Conclusions are drawn from observations of related work and a number of future challenges highlighted.

1. Introduction

There are a number of commercial solutions to online gaming within which players may participate in virtual worlds that are persistent in nature. Such games are commonly termed *massively multiplayer online role-playing games* (MMORPGs), which is usually shortened to MMOs. Vendors generate revenue from such gaming environments by regular financial subscriptions made by players and/or from the value of virtual world artifacts (e.g., virtual land sales, percentage taken from the interplayer trading of virtual world artifacts, sale of additional vendor-created virtual world storylines and artifacts). Fundamental to measuring the financial success of such games is the number of players actively participating: the more players there are the higher the financial rewards for a vendor. For example, World of Warcraft has boasted over 10 million subscriptions at its peak (subscriptions are typically $14 per month) [13]. An inability to attract sufficient player numbers leaves such gaming environments unprofitable and ultimately a wasted business venture. Such a waste is significant as the budget for bringing such games to market may be in excess of $10 million [16], with some placing the figure closer to $50 million [110]. In addition, once an online game is up and running, the maintenance costs may require total investment, including startup, of close to $500 million to contemplate competing as a market leader [110]. These are the figures commonly discussed as of 2008; in years to come, one may assume that vendors of such games discuss investment of in excess of $1 billion. These games are expected to become an integral part of many individuals' leisure time. Having only been around for a decade yet attaining a significant business status, the notion of carrying out research into online gaming should be taken seriously by industrialists and academics alike.

As the number of participating players is an indication of financial success, a pressing research problem is the need to provide scalable solutions for MMOs. One may assume that scalability has been achieved as no new players are ever turned away from a commercial MMO. However, scalability should be measured not only by how many players can log into a virtual world, but how many players can interact with each other at any one point in time and what level of interaction is afforded. Presenting the most attractive gaming scenarios via rich interaction provides a competitive edge in MMOs and is one element of online worlds that players will immediately identify as desirable. This is because vendors attempt to immerse players in their online worlds. Such immersion is only achievable by the ability to afford heightened realism via a highly responsive environment together with minimal hindrance to in-world player interaction.

There is no doubt that existing commercial solutions have achieved success and brought to market a series of excellent products. The purpose of this chapter is not to indicate that their efforts are not admirable, but to indicate that these are the first steps taken in this area and one may assume that significant improvements will be expected in the future. A subset of such improvements will be related to player interaction within a virtual world whilst maintaining scalability. As this is a fundamental challenge in creating MMOs, research efforts are still required in this area.

There are already a number of research efforts addressing scalability and interactivity in MMOs, with a number of academics contributing to ever more appropriate solutions for over 20 years. Early works do address the scalability/interactivity problem and do provide many of the techniques that modern commercial products base their solutions on. More recently works have continued to address scalability and interactivity in the context of MMOs, yet such works appear in a number of different areas of computing science (e.g., graphics, distributed systems, and parallel simulation). As such, the MMO researcher is faced with a wide variety of different approaches and possible solutions. Furthermore, there exists a large body of work conducted that is not achieved in the context of MMOs, but may provide MMO researchers with a valuable resource. In the future, researchers in other fields may recognize the significance their work may have for MMOs and tailor their solutions appropriately.

The aim of this chapter is to provide an introductory text which explores the problems of MMO scalability and to describe research efforts that may be of benefit.

This is achieved by first describing the type of gaming scenarios that may occur in MMOs and relating such scenarios to classic problems so far tackled in distributed systems research. Related work is then presented that is directly or indirectly related to MMOs. A series of challenges associated to MMO scalability and interactivity is then presented that are still to be tackled successfully, posing a number of questions that reinforce the difficulty of such challenges. Finally, conclusions are presented with a brief view of what future challenges may hold for the MMO researcher.

2. Gaming Scenarios

In this section, we wish to ignore, for the moment, implementation details and concentrate on the basic model for describing gaming scenarios. We assume gaming scenarios are prolonged instances of interaction between players in a virtual world. This is not an attempt to actually determine what a game is in essence, but simply a description relating to the mechanics of interaction required to provision a gaming scenario. What defines a game in relation to human interaction is a field of study best left to psychology [7]. For the purposes of this chapter, a virtual world gaming scenario is considered to be similar to gaming scenarios found in the real world.

To promote a tutorial-type style, descriptions are presented in an informal way. Formalisms that present the most accurate descriptions are not presented. Such formalisms do exist in other texts and can be gained by the reader via the references presented.

2.1 A Classic Model

A gaming scenario, in its simplest descriptive form, is a series of events witnessed and generated by artifacts of a virtual world. Artifacts may be player controlled (e.g., avatars representing the embodiment of a player) or nonplayer controlled. Nonplayer-controlled artifacts commonly refer to either an algorithm implementing some subroutine to present automated interaction or periodically generated events within a virtual world (such as the onset of sunset). For clarity, all artifacts with the ability to cause events are considered in the same manner here. Therefore, a simple model of a gaming scenario could be described as follows: An artifact, say A_1, generates a series of events, say E_1 and E_2, which may be witnessed by a different artifact, say A_2. A_2 itself may generate a series of events that may also be witnessed by A_1, say E_3 and E_4, with an additional artifact, say A_3, witnessing the events E_2 and E_3 only. In this simple example, two artifacts have generated four events between them and such artifacts have witnessed all these events with a third artifact having

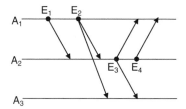

FIG. 1. Space–time diagram describing propagation of virtual world events.

only witnessed a subset of events. We show this example in the space–time diagram in Fig. 1 (arrows indicate the "witnessed" property and black dots represent events).

The act of "witnessing" an event by an artifact may be represented, in its simplest form, via message passing between artifacts: an artifact, say A_1, generates an event, say E_1, that results in a message, say M_1, been sent from A_1 to A_2 to enable A_2 to witness event E_1. This notion of message passing brings our model for gaming scenarios inline with the more general model for distributed computing.

The distributed computing model is now, briefly, described. This description may be found in much more detail penned by other authors (e.g., [11, 20, 54]). However, the description is provided here for completeness and to allow the novice reader sufficient understanding of the model to ease comprehension of this section as a whole. Although reasoning about gaming scenarios with reference to the distributed computing model may appear obvious, this has not been achieved previously with the same detail as presented here.

The distributed computing model is represented by a number of processes connected by a communications network that allows interprocess information flow (message passing) with the overall state of a system described in terms of events and their effect on local processes and channels [54]. Processes may act independently of each other (autonomously) and events may be described in terms of *local* (*internal*— occur at a single process), *send* (sending of a message), and *receive* (receiving of a message). In relation to our discussion so far, we can see that artifact and process are, for all practical purposes, describing the same notion at this level of abstraction. Therefore, to align with other literature artifacts will be described as processes from now on.

Figure 2 updates the diagram in Fig. 1 to include the send and receive events. In Fig. 2A, E_i^x should be read as i identifying the type of event (internal, send, and receive) and x identifying the original event as described in Fig. 1 (to allow comparison). In Fig. 2B, the more appropriate notation is used where i is the artifact (now identified as P for process) associated to the event and x is the number of an event at an artifact (allowing all events to be identified in a unique manner).

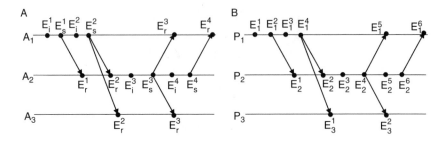

FIG. 2. Space–time diagram including internal, send, and receive events.

The state of a distributed computing model may be considered either globally, or on a per-process basis. Events dictate state change at the process where they occur and the intermediary information link on which they may pass as a message. Considering the space–time diagrams, it is clear that events are ordered in a linear manner at each process. Such a linear ordering is said to represent the *execution* of a process. The global state of a system is said to be represented by the cumulative state of all processes and information flows at a single instance in time. However, as taking such a snapshot is unlikely for many real-world systems, a *consistent global* state suffices. In such a state, the premise that all received messages must have been sent must hold, with researchers commonly using this view to describe their systems.

Different assumptions may be made regarding the distributed computing model. These assumptions, ultimately, must reflect the deployment environment of a system. Two basic assumptions that tend to divide the distributed computing community are those pertaining to the reliability of communication links and processes. Processes may fail via a crash manner (faulty processors stop) [85] or byzantine manner (faulty processors continue to produce output) [58] (one must realize there are a number of varying failure models found between these two extremes). Communication links are commonly modeled as either asynchronous (message and processing delays are bounded but unknown) or synchronous (message and processing delays are bounded and known) [92]. For example, systems deployed over the Internet within which compromised (hacked) computers may be present typically favor asynchronous/byzantine-type models, whereas real-time, failure safe, hardware-controlled colo-cated private network-type systems may be more likely represented via synchronous/crash models. Achieving synchronous/crash model environments for deployment requires an overreaching control over all aspects of implementation and is therefore difficult to achieve in many circumstances.

An assumption may be drawn that the modeling of gaming scenarios has its foundations in the theoretical research of distributed computing and, therefore, the same theoretical approach may be used: event generation and dissemination amongst a collection of processes over time can be used to reason about a gaming scenario. This provides researchers into online multiuser virtual worlds with a wealth of existing research from distributed computing on which to draw upon. Indeed, such fundamental work needs to be understood to allow for any reasoning about, and engineering of, the mechanics of gaming scenarios.

2.2   Cause and Effect

Hinted at in the previous section but not explicitly described is the notion of a *causal relationship* between events. This relationship is a key element for aiding in the reasoning about a distributed computing model and, therefore, making progress toward attaining valid gaming scenarios.

The events generated in a gaming scenario may manifest themselves in a variety of ways in a virtual world and may be described via a variety of application-dependent types. As a gaming scenario progresses, one may assume that the type of one or more events generated by a process may be based on the knowledge of previous events witnessed by such a process. This observation is obvious when considering the alternative: if all processes generated events without consideration of previous events, then one would find it inconceivable that a gaming scenario could be described at all (player choice based on current game state is not possible). In essence, when viewed globally we may deduce that an event, say E_1 may have caused an event, say E_2. This is the classic "happens before" relationship as described by Lamport [56] and indicates that E_1 "happened before" E_2 ($E_1 \rightarrow E_2$). The consideration of causal relationships throughout a distributed computation provides a partial ordering of events; partial as simultaneous events (those that do not share a causal relation) may be arbitrarily ordered with respect to each other.

To exemplify the importance of causality, consider a gaming scenario consisting of four players (P_1, P_2, P_3, and P_4). The goal of the game is for a player to shoot all other players. The virtual world is constructed from a number of different rooms and players may not shoot beyond the room they are within. For clarity, we describe the gaming scenario in plain English first: P_2 enters a room (containing P_1, P_3, and P_4) and is shot by P_1 while P_4 leaves the room and P_1 and P_3 reload their guns at some point during the gaming scenario. To allow this gaming scenario to proceed, there is a need to propagate event notification, that is, different players must be informed when certain events happen so they may react. As such, the order in which messages are received is important to ensuring causal relations between events are viewed appropriately by each player. Common practice is to uniquely identify messages in space–time diagrams to afford discussion not only for events but also to associated messages. Furthermore, the notion of a *broadcast* message (same message sent to all

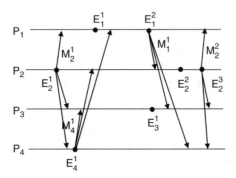

FIG. 3. Causality in gaming scenarios.

possible recipients) is introduced to describe notification of an event for more than one player. A message is described using m_i^j, where i denotes the sending process and j denotes the number of the message sent by the sending process. j is commonly termed a *logical clock*, in that the message is time stamped not with wall clock time but with a logic-based progression (usually incremental integers).

Using the diagram in Fig. 3, we now describe the scenario stating when events occur. In this model, we assume messages are not lost, processes do not fail, and message transit is FIFO. P_2 enters the room where P_1, P_3, and P_4 reside (E_2^1) at approximately the same time as P_4 leaves the room (E_4^1), which is witnessed by all players via M_2^1 and M_4^1, respectively. P_1 loads their gun (E_1^1) and shoots their gun at P_2 (E_1^2). The firing of the gun is seen by all (M_1^1). P_2 realizes they are shot (M_1^1) and dies (E_2^2), informing all other players of their mortal wound (M_2^2). During the shooting of P_2, P_3 reloads their gun (E_3^1). A number of events can be ordered arbitrarily with respect to each other (e.g., E_1^1 and E_3^1), with many events exhibiting causal relations (e.g., $E_2^1 \rightarrow E_1^1 \rightarrow E_1^2 \rightarrow E_2^2 \rightarrow E_2^3$).

By considering Fig. 3, we can identify important information about the gaming scenario and make some judgment on a game's validity. This can only be achieved by retaining the causal ordering of events. In our example, this was the case. However, by considering the impact of message latency on our model, the ability to maintain causal ordering becomes a challenging issue.

In Fig. 4, message latency plays an important factor. Consider the message associated to P_3 being notified of P_2's entrance to the room (M_2^1) delayed. As a result, P_3 is notified that P_2 is shot before P_3 realizes that P_2 is in the room. Due to the lack of preserving causality, P_1 has gained an unfair advantage over P_3 as the opportunity to shoot P_2 was only made available to P_1.

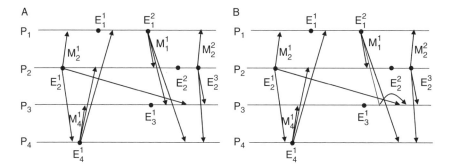

FIG. 4. Causal violation.

To preserve causality in Fig. 4A, there is a need to ensure that P_3 witnesses E_2^1 (M_2^1) before E_1^2 (M_1^1). The term *witness* is not adequate for describing this process and what actually is required is a distinction to be made between the receiving of a message by a process and the ability to act on such a message. This introduces the classic send, receive, and *deliver* approach to describing message handling in distributed computations: although P_3 received M_1^1 before M_2^1, P_3 does not actually deliver M_1^1 until it has delivered message M_2^1 (preserving causal ordering). This delayed delivery is shown in Fig. 4B.

2.3   Ordering

Although causality is an important element that should not be ignored when modeling gaming scenarios, it is by no means the only ordering constraint that should be considered. Sometimes causal ordering is not a sufficiently strong ordering guarantee for the purposes of modeling gaming scenarios. Returning to the example in Fig. 4A, the inability to afford an equal opportunity to both P_1 and P_3 in attempting to shoot P_2 is considered a problem. This problem will manifest itself in the virtual world by presenting two different views of the gaming arena to P_1 and P_3: one with P_2 present (P_1) and one without P_2 present (P_3). Even with causal relations maintained, a similar problem may occur with respect to realizing who is in the room at the beginning of the gaming scenario.

Consider Fig. 5 where message transit times are greater than zero and may vary for different links in a network. In this instance, M_2^1 is delayed and arrives at P_4 after M_4^1 has been sent (no causal relationship exists between E_2^1 and E_4^1 nor their associated messages M_2^1 and M_4^1). Played out in a virtual world, P_1 will witness P_2 enter the room (P_1, P_2, P_3, and P_4 present) then P_4 leave the room (P_1, P_2, and P_3

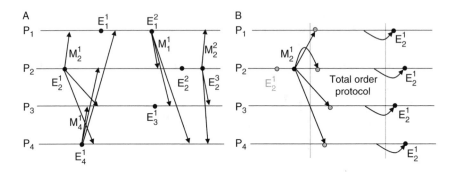

Fig. 5. Different views.

present). P_3, on the other hand, witnesses P_4 leaving the room (P_1 and P_3 present) before P_2 enters the room (P_1, P_2, and P_3 present). There is no causal relationship present between E_2^1 and E_4^1 as M_2^1 and M_4^1 arrive at their destinations after E_2^1 and E_4^1 have occurred (indicating that one event could not have caused the other). Unfortunately, the manifestation of this in the virtual world still provides inconsistencies. This indicates that although some events may not be causally related as they happen simultaneously, in a logical sense, there may still be a need to impose some form of ordering on them to preserve a gaming scenario's validity.

To ensure that P_1 and P_3 install the same consecutive views relating to when P_2 and P_4 are present in the room, an ordering guarantee stronger than causal ordering is required. *Total ordering* [12] is capable of ensuring that all participants view global events in the same order. This is not simply a case of ensuring that M_2^1 and M_4^1 are received in the same order at P_1 and P_3, but the order in which all participants (including P_2 and P_4) receive M_2^1 and M_4^1 must be the same. In fact, to ensure the total ordering of global events at all participants, the events themselves must gain their ordering from the underlying protocol governing message delivery. If this was not the case, then P_2's view would be that of leaving a room before P_4 entered, whereas P_4's view would be that of entering a room with P_2 still present.

Total ordering is achieved with the use of a broadcast to all participants, allowing all participants to ensure they are observing the same ordering of message delivery. Figure 5(B) identifies these steps with respect to P_2 leaving the room. The event equivalent to leaving the room (E_2^1) is attempted (but not carried out—i.e., a request to leave the room by a player) at the originating participant (P_2). This event is shown in a shaded manner to distinguish this from the processing of an event. Once the initial broadcast has been achieved, a number of further message passing will be required to ensure total ordering (not shown) until eventually E_2^1 is delivered to all participants, including the originator P_2.

Total ordering is primarily designed to ensure consistency of state for deterministic state machines [86], particularly useful in replication schemes used in fault tolerance (e.g., [73, 69]). The guarantee that if all replicas receive the same messages in the same order then their states will not deviate (this cannot be guaranteed for nondeterministic state machines). Therefore, state change events should always be propagated across all replicas to ensure states remain mutually consistent. If this route was followed in the example, then local events would need to be propagated to ensure all processes maintained a mutually consistent view of the state of a gaming scenario (e.g., E_1^1).

2.4 Dynamic Environments

When discussing total ordering in the previous section, a broadcast (message sent to all) was used as the basic message dissemination technique. For practical purposes, this is not appropriate as one may expect only a subset of participants to be involved in any one gaming scenario at a time. Therefore, the *multicast* is a more appropriate message dissemination technique, allowing players to join and leave gaming scenarios as they wish. Multicast introduces the concept of a "group." A group identifies the recipient of a multicast message with the membership of a group having the ability to change over time. In the example in Fig. 5, P_2 and P_4 change the membership of the group of players who are "in the room." The problem of "who is in the room," discussed in the previous two sections, highlights another problem that requires more than ordering protocols to aid in deriving an appropriate solution. This problem relates to determining exactly when messages are deliverable in the presence of dynamic group membership. We continue to use the "who is in the room" example to describe the issues that arise.

In Figs. 4 and 5, P_4 is still receiving messages after they have left the playing area (the room). Therefore, a more appropriate approach would be to restrict multicast messages to include only those inside the room. We would like participants to install the views of room occupancy as follows: P_1 and P_3 ($\{P_1, P_3, P_4\}$ followed by $\{P_1, P_2, P_3\}$), P_2 ($\{P_2\}$ followed by $\{P_1, P_2, P_3\}$), and P_4 ($\{P_1, P_3, P_4\}$ followed by $\{P_4\}$). Notice how P_2 and P_4 have views that only include themselves at some point to hinder the inappropriate multicasting of messages (we assume there is nobody else outside in neighboring rooms).

The ordering of views in a dynamic environment alone is ineffective if we do not order the event-dependent messages with respect to view changes. For example, we may be able to ensure that all participants provide the same view changes in the same, total, order. However, if the set of messages in such views varies from participant to participant, we will not solve the problem highlighted in Fig. 5. Therefore, there needs to be some guarantee to ensure the same set of messages is

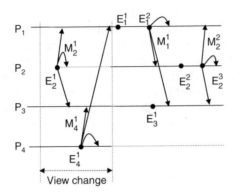

FIG. 6. View changes.

delivered to all participants in the same view, disallowing message delivery when view changes are being determined. For example, in Fig. 6 the view change event occurs at the initial steps of the gaming scenario, therefore, this view change should complete to ensure all participants' progress with the same messages delivered in the appropriate views. As with ordering, multiple messages will be required to allow all participants to realize the appropriate group membership changes.

Virtual synchrony [10] is the term used to describe the total ordering of view changes with respect to other messages (e.g., the ones responsible for propagating events). Notice that the definition of virtual synchrony does not impose total order on other messages, just the view changes with respect to all other messages. Therefore, it is quite conceivable to have a causal ordering with virtual synchronous systems.

2.5   Reaching Agreement

An underlying problem that arises frequently in distributed computing models is that of *agreement*. In essence, the previous examples are strongly related to agreement as one may assume that agreement on message ordering and group membership is a requirement that processes must satisfy. The agreement problem assumes that a process has an initial value to share with all other processes in its group (all processes must agree on this value) [58]. Alternatively, all processes may have their own, initial, value and all processes must agree on a single value [58]. The latter scenario is known as the *consensus problem* but, for the basic interpretation made here, can be viewed in the same manner as the agreement problem.

Consensus is the cornerstone of many fault-tolerant systems, as reaching consensus on who has failed is a problem that must be handled. For example, if three replica services provide failover for clients, all nonfaulty replicas must agree on who is faulty to allow failover to proceed appropriately. In addition to fault tolerance and consensus, other flavors of consensus exist: approximate agreement (where agreement is to determine values similar to each other) and probabilistic agreement (where agreement is sought with a high probability) [54].

While considering agreement, it is worth realizing that it is impossible to implement an agreement protocol in asynchronous environments when in the presence of faulty processes [39]. One simple way to visualize this impossibility result is to consider how one may tell the difference between a correct process and a failed one. Basically, when message and processing delays are unknown, it is impossible to tell if a process is slow or failed; how long will you wait for a response? For a broader discussion on the impossibility to resolve a number of problems in distributed computations in general, the reader is referred to Fich and Ruppert [38].

Circumventing the impossibility problem of reaching agreement in asynchronous environments has been tackled extensively in the literature on fault-tolerant computing. Two variations are available. One utilizes the notion of unreliable failure detectors [18, 19]; described in very brief, but clear terms: allow incorrect suspicion of failure to prevail, as long as some agreement on failed processors may be reached in a number of correct processors at some point in the future (reducing the outcome to a probabilistic chance of success). The compromise made is that correct processes may be incorrectly identified as failed during this process. Another variation, and most widely used, is via transactions: two-phase commit may be used to indicate to a group of processes the steps of preparing a value for committing, then demanding that such a value be "committed" to all participating processes' states [43, 44, 59]. The sacrifice here is that processes guarantee to commit the required state change they promised to and may not participate further until such guarantee is satisfied. Both these approaches carry substantial messaging overheads. In particular, transactions rely on persistent storage to ensure that when a process returns to correct operation any outstanding transactions may be committed. For a discussion relating these two approaches, identifying their differences and similarities, the reader should note the paper [84].

2.6   Groups

A collection of protocols that provide the message dissemination abstractions discussed so far (possibly more) are commonly termed *group communication protocols* [10]. Such systems are primarily the domain of the fault-tolerant research community and concentrate on asynchronous environments, with many design and implementation variations possible. This area of research has provided a substantial number of papers and software products. This is primarily due to the many assumptions that can be made regarding the deployment environment and the behavior of group members themselves. As the impossibility result is something that cannot be circumvented, the ability to "inch" toward ever more appropriate solutions is a quest taken up by many [54].

Software products that provide group communication services have a number of components: ordering protocols (possibly more than one), failure detectors (based on unreliable failure detectors), group membership protocols (providing dynamic groups), and reliable multicast (commonly termed *atomic multicast*—termed *atomic broadcast* in the literature as consideration of subgroups not necessarily considered in the basic problem description) [18]. In addition to these basic services, such products may also provide: overlapping groups (members may simultaneously belong to more than one group) [74], open groups (allowing processes to send messages into groups that they are not a member of—the standard alternative is the closed group approach) [69], and partitionable operation (due to incorrect suspicion of failure, or network link failure, groups may partition into multiple, distinct, subgroups) [33] (Fig. 7).

Although there are many minor variations available for the developer to choose from when designing group communication protocols, the primary design choice when considering ordering of messages is between *symmetric* and *asymmetric* approaches [36]. In the symmetric approach, all group members cumulatively assume responsibility for message delivery guarantees, requiring group members to participate in a number of message passing rounds with all other group members. In the asymmetric approach, a single group member (sequencer) assumes responsibility. Nonsequencer group members unicast their messages to the sequencer, which orders such messages and subsequently multicasts (in order) to group members. An underlying network that provides FIFO message ordering is required for the trivial implementation of asymmetric ordering. In practical situations, asymmetric ordering can provide significant performance benefits over symmetric approaches as

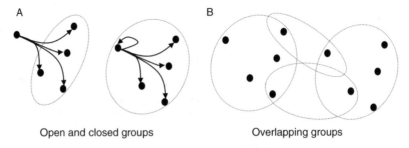

Open and closed groups   Overlapping groups

FIG. 7. Some group configurations.

fewer messages are required (unicast as opposed to multicast) and messages arrive in the appropriate order. However, when a sequencer fails, no forward progression can be made until a new sequencer is elected (usually from the remaining group members). Sequencer election (sometime called leader election) faces the impossibility result (agreement required) and is not a trivial issue and may be extremely time consuming to accomplish (possibly resulting in multiple sequencers which must be handled) [42, 97].

2.7   Timely Progression

Not mentioned so far, yet of great importance to modeling gaming scenarios appropriately, is the need for timely progression. In the previous sections, there was a logical view taken of gaming scenarios with the length of time required to execute events and send messages not considered. However, virtual worlds are expected to provide players with the illusion of real-time (or at least near real-time) interaction. Events that appear to occur "too slowly" may destroy such an illusion and render the gaming experience inappropriate: virtual synchrony, total ordering, and failure-free environments (if such an environment could be created) will not prevent excessive delays in event propagation from ruining a gaming scenario. For example, in Fig. 6 it may be possible to implement total ordering and virtual synchrony appropriately, but there is nothing in this logical view of the world preventing P_1 from viewing the leaving of P_2 and the arrival of P_4 before P_3 in (real) global time. By not considering time, we are not providing a "fair" gaming scenario for players. All observations so far have been made in "logical time."

Synchronous environments provide an opportunity to include timing when describing gaming scenarios. For example, if one realizes that message delays and process delays have a known bound, then synchronization of local clocks may be achieved with minimal effort. Once this step has been achieved, then placing timeouts on the expectation of player interaction can be worked into an implementation. Furthermore, given the known timeouts associated to a system, some design choices may be made to determine what gaming scenarios are actually possible and prevent needless explorations of gaming scenarios that are impractical.

Gaining a synchronous environment is difficult. In practice, developers attempt to focus on certain elements of a system that may be made synchronous, possibly using enhanced networking protocols and hardware devices to gain as close to a synchronous environment as practically possible (e.g., [32, 104]). However, even with such approaches, a major problem with gaining a universally synchronous environment is the presence of third-party devices that are simply beyond a developers/systems control but a necessary part of an overall system's operation. In commercial online gaming, these are many (e.g., ISP, home console, gaming interface, and variable player interaction times).

If one does not consider real time (wall clock time), then there could be anomalous behavior exhibited by a system. This is because logical time may create an ordering of events that does not reflect the same ordering when viewed in wall clock time. For example, consider two events E_1 created by P_1 at 10.15am and an event E_2 created by P_2 at 10.30am. If no causality exists between such events, then it is quite conceivable that these events may be viewed in the order E_2 followed by E_1 in a virtual world. The virtual world will be consistent, but the behavior of the virtual world may appear distinctly odd to players. Therefore, wall clock time is a concern to any that wish to model gaming scenarios appropriately and logical time alone, although important for attaining consistency, is only a partial solution.

2.8   Best Effort

Considering the difficulty, and in some cases the impossibility, of providing gaming scenarios that reflect real-world interactions in commercial virtual world solutions there is a need to make compromises. Compromises must be handled in the game play itself. In other words, the illusion of interaction is maintained while the underlying protocols governing such interaction do not always provide the required message delivery guarantees.

After acknowledging that erroneous situations will occur with respect to message delivery, a developer must decide how much effort (time/processing) the underlying system expends to progress toward appropriate modeling of a gaming scenario at the expense of real-time requirements. In the research community primarily concerned with online virtual worlds, this has been termed the *consistency/throughput tradeoff* (this term originally concerned itself with the throughput of a network as opposed to additional message passing requirements) [95]. Basically, the consistency referred to is the desire to allow all players to have a mutually consistent view of a gaming scenario. However, in commercial virtual worlds, this manifests itself not so much in nonconsistency of views but in restrictions on what is and is not possible in gaming scenarios.

In practical solutions, the consistency/throughput tradeoff manifests itself most visibly when a virtual world is required to be scalable. Scalability in virtual worlds is commonly measured as the number of participants that can be supported simultaneously. As protocols enforcing a degree of consistency tend to produce message volumes that grow rapidly when participant numbers rise and message delivery delays tend to be related to the slowest participant, scalability is difficult to achieve. To achieve scalability, there is a need to send fewer messages and not to wait too long before messages become deliverable. Three approaches exist to allow consistency to be "traded" in favor of scalability requirements. These three approaches approximate to the three elements of the distributed computing model described so far:

- *Messages*—relax delivery guarantees
- *Events*—allow players to witness "approximated" events
- *Players*—only inform players of events they may be interested in

Relaxing message delivery guarantees equate to allowing some messages to be "lost" (either at process buffer overflow or network level), and tolerating inappropriate order delivery (possibly with varying view inconsistencies with respect to group membership). Approximated events reduce the need for message passing for event propagation. An event, say E_1, occurs at one process, say P_1, but is not disseminated to other processes, say P_2 and P_3. P_2 and P_3 create the (approximated) event locally (without message passing). When creating such an event, some prediction method may be used (a technique commonly used is *dead reckoning*) [66]. The approximated event will be different, but (hopefully) within some error bound as to allow such an event to present an appropriate progression in a gaming scenario. Limiting the number of processes that are sent messages via the identification of player interaction, again, reduces the need for message passing. The basic idea is simple: only send messages to those processes that are actually interested in them and prevent the sending of messages to processes that are not interested in them [113].

Considering the optimization approaches suggested, guarantees for message delivery for online gaming are more relaxed that those found in the fault-tolerant community's approach to group communications. However, the goals both communities are attempting to achieve are not dissimilar and share a common model. For example, online gaming must approximate a group membership protocol (only sending game events to those interested in them) and at least some messages must be delivered to receiving nodes at some ordering level to afford correct, and expected, player interaction.

3. Related Work

In this section, we describe a number of related works that have contributed to the current state of the art for large-scale virtual worlds. The earliest works are considered first, followed by descriptions of commercial solutions. The more specific issues affecting scalability (synchronization and load balancing) are then described. At this point, the discussion of related work broadens to include those works that were not carried out in the context of virtual worlds, but tackle similar problems.

3.1 Early Days

The early pioneers in the creation of virtual worlds came from a variety of research backgrounds: high-performance graphics, human–computer interaction, commercial gaming, virtual reality, and military simulation. Many of the basic notions of what it takes to build scalable virtual worlds were discovered and experimented with in these early days. One of the truly admirable aspects of this early work is that real systems were built and demonstrated in both academic and commercial settings. All the techniques that attempt to gain increased scalability (see Section 2.8) were all demonstrated in these early systems for the first time. The work is substantial (it was quite a busy area in the 1980s and 1990s) and whole books have been written about these systems (e.g., [76, 95]). Only the most relevant developments that directly relate to the attempts of scalability are discussed here.

Throughout the 1980s (1983 onwards) SIMNET (simulator network) [66] was developed to provide the American military with a virtual battlefield on which to train individuals. A number of simulators (e.g., tank) could be networked together. The successor to SIMNET and DIS (distributed interactive simulation) aimed to standardize and generalize a protocol for use in more heterogeneous environments as SIMNET was not an "open" platform [48]. In these early systems, message ordering and reliability guarantees are *deliver when receive* (no further message passing to enforce any ordering or reliability). Dead reckoning was used to lower the message passing burden with participant numbers expected to be less than 1000 (designed for around 500). No central server was used, with a peer-to-peer architecture assumed. Participants could arrive and leave at arbitrary points throughout the execution of a simulation. Messages were lost, or arrived out of order. Inevitably, inconsistencies in the simulations would occur (conveniently termed "the fog of war" [95]). Inconsistencies aside, these two early systems provided functioning virtual worlds that served their training purposes well for the American military [76] with increasing standardization resulting in the *high-level architecture* (HLA) [29].

The DIS-to-HLA transition may be viewed in a similar light as the RPC-to-CORBA transition that occurred in the mid-1990s in middleware technologies; bringing a greater degree of standardization to how a distributed application may be structured. The HLA went much further than DIS in its prescriptions, indicating artifact representation in a virtual world. Immediately after the introduction of the HLA, the amount of work in online worlds appears to have decreased in the literature, possibly due to the USA's Department of Defense's instruction that all future work in this area must be HLA based, one cannot say for sure. However, since the late 1990s, the most successful online worlds have been commercial and non-HLA compliant.

In addition to the high-cost military projects, a number of PC games appeared in the 1990s that could support networking. As with SIMNET and DIS, no respect was paid to message delivery guarantees (e.g., deliver when receive, send multiple times if important [51]). Such games limited player numbers (4 or less for Doom) with players quite often expected to be colocated on the same LAN to ensure network latency would not hinder game play. Even before these games existed, players had enjoyed online virtual worlds in the form of *multiuser dungeons* (MUD) [4] and novel commercial games that afforded limited networking [72]. These early attempts were more a forerunner of *Internet relay chat* (IRC) as communications manifested themselves in the form of text messages between players with little graphical representation. In addition, these works are not well documented and only messages on a variety of newsgroups afford insight into the technical aspects of such systems. For these reasons, these works do not afford a significant insight into constructing large-scale virtual worlds.

Pioneering academic work in virtual worlds resulted in NPSNET [113] (and its descendents 2–4). The military and early commercial work was not documented in the academic literature at the time; therefore, NPSNET presented the first major advances in understanding how to build online virtual worlds in the public domain. For example, NPSNET-IV could interact with DIS and utilize IP multicast for more judicious use of bandwidth [64]. NPSNET used dead reckoning to ease the messaging burden. However, message delivery guarantees were best effort and inconsistencies would still be an issue. Further academic works extended ideas and concepts originated in NPSNET. PARADISE allowed a more intricate modeling for dead reckoning [94] and reduced message sending with the ability to retrieve state information for artifacts that send messages infrequently [49]. This protocol was termed the "log-based receiver-reliable multicast," and allowed receivers that noticed a missing message (by way of logical timestamps) to retrieve such messages from a persistent logging server. In actuality, the protocol is not reliable in the same context as atomic multicast is considered reliable and did not solve ordering issues.

From the perspective of group communications, DIVE (distributed interactive virtual environment) presents an excellent case study [15, 47]. DIVE is considered a *collaborative virtual environment* (CVE), where emphasis is primarily based on collaboration of participants as opposed to realistic simulation (e.g., shared drawing) and was built on the first fully functioning group communications toolkit (ISIS) [9] in the early 1990s. ISIS provides many of the elements described in Section 2 (e.g., total and causal ordering, virtual synchrony, and failure detection) and so provided DIVE with the strongest consistency possible of all virtual worlds (before and since). Unfortunately, choosing a fully functioning group communications service appears to have been a problem, as later versions of DIVE sacrificed their consistency in favor of scalability (dropping the use of ISIS). With ISIS, DIVE could not support more than 20–30 participants without significant deterioration of interactivity between participants in the virtual world [63]. This was the first and last time that the fault-tolerant approach to group communication services would be used to support a virtual world as ISIS clearly demonstrated the lack of scalability. Such scalability is of little issue when dealing with three or seven replicas, but it is an issue when requiring real-time virtual world access for hundreds, thousands possibly millions of participants.

In the mid- to late 1990s, a CVE was developed named MASSIVE (model, architecture, and system for spatial interaction in virtual environments) [45]. MASSIVE provided a novel model for attempting to capture the degree of interaction between participants. The *aura–nimbus* model allowed an artifact in a virtual world to "express" their interest in, and their influence over, other artifacts. This model was actually developed prior to MASSIVE (spatial model) [5] and experimented in a limited manner within the DIVE system, yet is always associated with MASSIVE. Figure 8A shows an example of the aura–nimbus model where the aura of P_3 is overlapping with the nimbus of P_1 and the nimbus of P_2, indicating that P_3 is sending messages to P_1 and P_2. This model is restricting message passing by only sending messages to those participants that are interested in them. Therefore, one may assume that this provides an opportunity for trading consistency in favor for scalability. However, the original intention of this model was to enhance interaction (on a per-artifact basis) rather than gain scalability. MASSIVE went through a number of developments, with the long running project producing a further two versions (MASSIVE-2 and MASSIVE-3) [46]. In practice, the aura and nimbus are represented as boxes in MASSIVE (possibly due to their ease of overlap identification in three dimensions and the fact this distracts little from the core requirement of determining interaction) [6].

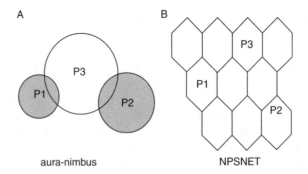

FIG. 8. Regionalization of the virtual world.

Restricting message passing in favor of achieving scalability was actually attempted in the first instance by NPSNET. In NPSNET, regions of the virtual world were divided into hexagonal areas, with artifacts in the same (or bordering) regions capable of exchanging messages (Fig. 8B). Hexagonal areas were chosen as there are at most three bordering areas (as opposed to four when using squares). This provided less area of the virtual world (and therefore choice) when disseminating messages as artifacts reach area borders. For example, when a boundary change occurred, it may be best practice to disseminate messages within multiple areas to lessen ambiguity over which artifacts should receive which messages.

When considering message dissemination techniques via the use of regions, the size of the regions becomes important for dictating the type of interaction possible within a virtual world. A region must be of sufficient size as to ensure players have the ability to engage in gaming scenarios in one region before entering another region [78]. When a player traverses a region boundary a region's membership must be updated (identify a region a player belongs to). Determining a region size that is suitable for all types of player interactions in a virtual world may not be possible. For example, if region size is decided when considering the top speed of a fighter aircraft then the presence of soldiers traveling on foot may give rise to unnecessary message exchange between foot soldiers. If region size is more suited to foot soldiers, then a fighter aircraft may traverse region boundaries with such frequency that region membership may not be resolved in a timely fashion (traverse a region in less time than it takes to realize regional membership changes resulting in an inability for fighter aircraft to engage in gaming scenarios).

Auras and regions have their advantages and disadvantages. Regions do not afford the accurate degree of interaction as auras appear to provide on a per-artifact basis, but the implementation overhead for regions is much lower than auras. This is because there is no discovery stage required when deciding upon the appropriate message recipients in the region approach. For example, an IP multicast address may be associated to each region and as long as an artifact can realize which region they are in, they can subscribe and multicast to the appropriate multicast address. On the other hand, aura overlap must be detected before message recipients may be realized in the aura approach. This will require an initial protocol step with the sole purpose of identifying appropriate message recipients. This proved an expensive step in practice and can severely limit the scalability of aura-based approaches.

Other early works continued the exploration into spatial subdivision exhibited first by NPSNET and then in a different manner by MASSIVE. For example, SPLINE introduced the notion of locales which assumed a much more independent view for each spatial subdivision [2, 3]. Each subdivision may be described within its own coordinate system, with the appropriate transformations matrices to allow transition from one locale to another. BrickNet uses a more descriptive mechanism (not necessarily based on virtual world geography) to allow related artifacts to be grouped together and become visible to each other (associated to different virtual environments) [93].

3.2   Persistent Worlds

The virtual worlds described in the previous section do not provide persistent environments. That is, they do not exist as some simulated persistent geographic location at some known, accessible, address. Persistent virtual worlds allow participants to enter a virtual world that provides a degree on continuity; artifacts may be created and persist over periods of time and the results of events on artifacts may persist. For example, a participant may purchase a virtual car; drive their car to the end of a virtual road; return some days, months, or even years later; and retrieve their car. Of course, someone else may have procured the car and driven it elsewhere in the meantime, but the continuity provided by persistence of artifacts is a factor that aids in classifying these virtual worlds.

Public access persistent virtual worlds available over the Internet present vendors with a commercial opportunity. The computer games industry has been able to use these worlds to generate revenue in a number of ways: pay-per-play (often the client program is free, or sold for a small one-off payment, with subscriptions required to allow players to participate) (e.g., [23, 34, 96, 107]), artifact sales (participants trade artifacts with commission gained on sales) (e.g., [35]), client extensions (client-side extensions are sold that allow access to additional virtual world areas/storylines) (e.g., [101, 108]), and land sales (areas of the virtual world are sold to participants) (e.g., [61]). As these gaming arenas grow, one may envisage economic structures developing not too dissimilar in variety to those that exist in the real world [17]. This area of online gaming has grown from an insignificant financial element of the games industry in the late 1990s to become a multibillion dollar industry in its own right as of 2008 [1].

Persistent virtual world implementations are server based, allowing vendors to regulate the provision of ever-evolving alternate realities to maintain player interest and, most importantly, restrict participation to subscribed players. Player consoles connect to a server that provides players with access to a virtual world. Typically, a player's console holds a subset of game state with players informing each other of their actions via the exchange of messages between consoles. Such communication is achieved via a server, allowing the regulation of player interaction and game state to be recorded and stored onto a persistent medium if required. As revenue is generated on a per-player basis, the more players that can be supported by a virtual world the more revenue may be generated. Therefore, scalability of a server, in terms of player numbers, is of great importance to ensure commercial success.

To satisfy the demand for processing resources, clusters of servers are employed to cumulatively maintain game state and manage player interactions. The additional processing resources required to support an increase in player numbers is satisfied via the addition of servers to a cluster. This approach to server cluster configuration will be familiar to any developer working with scalable service solutions found in almost all Internet applications; utilize a collection of geographically colocated nodes organized into a cluster that cumulatively support online services (e.g., search engines, e-commerce, and enterprise information portals). Such nodes are standard computers in their own right, and may operate as service providers independently of each other. Such computers are general purpose and not necessarily tailored for high-performance multiprocessor solutions, making them a cost efficient approach to server-side scalability.

Figure 9 provides an overview of a typical server cluster solution for providing scalable online worlds. Although a simplified view, this will suffice for descriptive purposes. The load balancer ensures players are directed to an appropriate server that may satisfy their service requests (e.g., updating avatar appearance or location). The application logic is where user participation is enacted and overall governance of the virtual world occurs (e.g., avatars fighting, trading artifacts between users). Artifacts, including player's avatars, which populate the virtual world, together with their current state are stored in the data store tier and retrieved as and when required by the application tier. Updates made to persistent artifacts in the application logic tier must be registered in the data store tier to ensure continuity of the virtual world.

Vendors of commercial persistent virtual worlds do not tent to describe in detail the techniques used to achieve scalability at the server side (which is to be expected for a commercial enterprise in a competitive market). However, there is an article describing EverQuest's approach in general terms [55]: a mixture of regions and

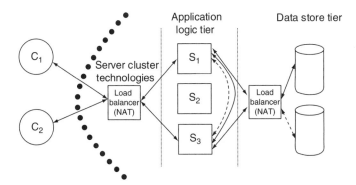

FIG. 9. Classic n-tier server-side solution.

duplicate worlds with each duplicate world supporting approximately 2000–3000 players with each world divided into regions based on the geography of the virtual world (the term used in the literature for duplicate worlds is *shards*). As regionalization is associated to virtual world geography, this approach is closely related to NPSNET's approach of subdividing the virtual world geography. A duplicate world is itself supported by a cluster of servers, with regions used to aid in allocating the processing requests originated from player actions amongst such servers as and when required. Due to the similarities in game play and the existence of duplicate worlds, one may assume that all commercial approaches to implementation of distributed player load across the application tier to be similar. There is no player interaction allowed across duplicate worlds although players may pass from one region to another.

Duplicate worlds and geographic regionalization present a three-step approach to identifying localized game play (1) players do not interact across different duplicate worlds, (2) players do not interact across different regions, and (3) players interact intricately with other players they specifically target (e.g., click on with mouse). This approach provides two distinct forms of interaction (1) a general, viewing type style, where players can see the actions of others in their region (assuming appropriate line of sight) and (2) an intricate manner where players directly interact with each other in a user directed way. The latter form of interaction requires consistency to be greater as ordering of events are usually crucial in determining the outcome of an intricate gaming scenario (the server must resolve player interaction). The consistency can be weaker in the general style of interaction as summary information could be propagated between players. For example, in a fight between two players in a virtual world attacks must be regulated (e.g., ordered, not lost in transit) between engaged players (e.g., spells, hitting, and shooting) to provide an outcome (e.g., decreased health, loss of inventory). However, for players watching a fight between other players there is only a need to view a series of fighting moves and the end result (that may or may not reflect the actual fight moves as enacted between the fight participants).

Initiating intricate play is via a handshake protocol at the start of an intricate interaction request (specifics vary slightly across commercial implementations, but there is a need for player identification made by the server to initiate such interaction). In the case of player P_1 attacking player P_2, the server will poll P_2 to ensure that intricate interaction may commence. This is to ensure P_2 is actually in a state to which it can respond appropriately and, possibly carrying out some check to ensure P_2 is not at a disadvantage due to inconsistencies between P_1 and P_2's views of the virtual world. This is especially the case if P_1's actions could have an important impact on game play if not responded to in a timely manner (e.g., P_1 attacking P_2). This protocol may be manifested as part of game play itself to ensure players are fully aware of a requested interaction (e.g., a request is provided to P_2 that may be declined or accepted—either at a player's discretion or transparently by a player's console based on local game state).

An interesting observation in implementation similarities between asymmetric ordering and intricate interaction may be made. Clearly, commercial solutions are relying on sequencer (the server) to regulate intricate interaction (ordering of events) between players. Indeed, direct communication between player consoles is to be avoided in this respect; therefore, no leader election protocol is required between player consoles if a server fails. If a server fails, one may assume that failover may be employed (but there have been instances that show this may not be the case [99]). The importance of allowing server failover specifically for persistent virtual worlds has recently been recognized as a serious problem and is an aim in Sun Microsystems' Darkstar Project [98]. This project looks to hold some promise of bringing a general purpose middleware platform to market that eases the creation of online persistent virtual worlds.

3.3 Synchronization

In Section 2, gaming scenarios are discussed with reference to the model used for describing distributed computation. This approach was shown to allow a degree of reasoning when considering the validity of gaming scenarios. As mentioned earlier, this model is primarily used in the domain of fault-tolerant computing where assurances of a system's correctness are paramount and every effort is taken to ensure message reliability and delivery requirements may satisfy such assurances. Unfortunately, probably due to the lack of timing considerations in the model and the failure of ISIS to provide an environment of any "useful" scalability, research into message ordering and reliability protocols for online gaming held little interest to the fault-tolerant community. Instead, the research community that has proceeded to make progress in this area has been the *parallel and distributed simulation* community.

Although the end goals of these two research communities are dissimilar, there are similarities between work carried out in the fault-tolerant community and the parallel and distributed simulation community. They share the same basic model of events, messages, and processes and the same concern for preserving causality. However, the parallel and distributed simulation community does not contend with the same rigorous requirements associated to reliable systems (e.g., total ordering, atomic multicast, and virtual synchrony). For this fact alone, their algorithms will undoubtedly have a lower message passing overhead and less of a delay between receiving a message and delivery of a message, providing more opportunity for scalability than that witnessed by utilizing ISIS in DIVE.

Synchronization is the term used to describe the end goal of algorithms designed within the parallel and distributed simulation community. There are two basic approaches described in the literature to achieve synchronization [102] (1) *conservative*—messages are received but delivery delayed until delivery guarantees can be satisfied and (2) *optimistic*—messages are delivered as they are received with a possibility that messages may become "undelivered" and then "redelivered" to correct violations of delivery guarantees realized at a later date (i.e., when receiving a logically stamped later message).

Work on conservative approaches can be traced back to the 1970s (e.g., [14, 21]) and appear at a similar time to Lamport's paper on logical clocks (however, Lamport's interest in this area reaches back to the 1960s). One may assume that conservative approaches share a great deal in common to the approaches carried out in the fault-tolerant community as delayed delivery is utilized. Therefore, the developers of virtual worlds find the optimistic approach more inviting than conservative approaches as messages may be delivered without delay, favoring real-time requirements (e.g., [106]). In addition, the virtual world may be capable of a degree of prediction (e.g., dead reckoning), allowing the application developer to either prejudge certain ordering irregularities or hide them in gaming scenarios when they occur.

The Time Warp [52] mechanism is a well-known optimistic approach. In simple terms, when a process receives a message with a (logical) timestamp lower than a message that has previously been delivered, delivery of such a message (or messages if there are more than one) are rolled back and redelivered together with the recently received message in the appropriate timestamp order. To limit rollback to an appropriate level, there is an identification placed on the length of history possible for rollback.

Conservative and optimistic approaches have been used to attempt synchronization in gaming scenarios with Ferretti and Roccetti providing a convenient discussion of the state of the art together with some interesting comparisons made between the techniques [81]. Optimistic approaches tend to favor scenarios that can provide a degree of determinism, and may not be suitable for intricate interaction where rollback is not feasible. For example, when two players are engaging in intricate interaction in a persistent virtual world (as described in Section 3.2) the notion that some results may be rolled back may deter from an appropriate gaming scenario. In addition, the overhead of rollback may provide a processing burden that is detrimental to the overall performance of a virtual world if it occurs sufficiently often enough. This may outweigh the alternative approach of delayed delivery found in conservative approaches. The decision on the approach used by a developer is not always straightforward.

Ferretti and Roccetti [37] have pioneered a number of optimistic synchronization techniques specifically for use in online gaming. A series of works clearly demonstrate the scalability of their optimistic approaches for use over the Internet. Their schemes are based on loose synchronization of physical clocks [25] and the ability, through negative acknowledgments, to discard events considered "obsolete" in the virtual world. As their approaches are optimistic, they deliver messages as they are received, gaining scalability by preventing the sending of some messages due to recognition of the obsolete events with which they are associated.

Including wall clock time (as opposed to logical time) when attempting to gain some ordering guarantees for message delivery has been shown to provide value. Delta-causality (Δ-causality) places a limit on the degree of causality between messages by identifying a window of time within which causal relations are maintained [109]. Attempts are not made to ensure causality for messages that arrive too late to be of use. This approach is particularly useful for streamed data (such as voice over IP—VOIP), where out-of-date message delivery only detracts from the perceived quality of the output stream. Yavatkar [109] is set in the context of streamed media and implemented as *multiflow conversation protocol* (MCP). The authors argue that wall clock time is a useful mechanism and practical synchronization is possible (measured in milliseconds) given modern clock synchronization techniques (even across the Internet) [57].

The field of distributed real-time systems has provided substantial amounts of research in an effort to maintain causality in message delivery guarantees. The two basic approaches to satisfying such guarantees are via *clock-driven* and *timer-driven* techniques. Clock driven is associated to clock synchronization (as discussed in Δ-causality), whereas timer driven relies on local timers only and requires some form of acknowledgment message. Veríssimo [103] has documented these two approaches, providing an interesting comparison. Probably, the two most popular works relating to clock-driven approaches are Δ-protocol [26] family and MARS [53]. The Δ-protocol family and Δ-causality are not to be confused, as each work appears quite distinct in the literature (Δ-causality having been attempted in the context of multimedia streams without acknowledgment of the earlier work associated to the Δ-protocol family).

Other attempts at preserving causality in message delivery have been suggested that may be directly, or indirectly, related to modeling gaming scenarios that exploit application-level knowledge. For example, Δ-protocol family has been extended for use in small-scale distributed embedded systems [112] and an attempt to use application knowledge to "ignore" causal relations between some messages has been suggested [80]. Another approach proposes the notion of, and coins the phrase, *critical causality* [111]. Critical causality identifies that the only causal relation of concern is the directly proceeding event. For example, assume P_1 receives a message m_1 from P_2 informing of event E_1. P_1 then receives a message m_2 from P_3 informing of event E_2. P_1 then generates an event E_3 and disseminates this event to P_1 and P_2 via a multicast m_3. In this scenario, E_2 and E_3 are said to be critically ordered (meaning that m_2 must be delivered before m_3 where appropriate). One must note that critical causality is not transitive and the authors assume that critical causality is appropriate for modeling gaming scenarios. The authors of this approach suggest an algorithm which does not place delay on delivery by making sure a process sends both messages that share a critical ordering (in our example, P_1 will send m_2 and m_3 together). This algorithm does not guarantee that critical causality is maintained, but is a best effort approach with experiments indicating that critical causality will be preserved 99% of the time in a realistic setting [111].

3.4   Load Balancing

Assuming the approach described in Fig. 9, the problem of scalability becomes one of load balancing of resources. Furthermore, to avoid wasting resources load balancing must be achieved in an efficient manner (i.e., not have substantial amounts of overprovision at the server side). Load-balancing schemes basing their approaches on virtual world geography for online gaming described in the literature may be classified as follows (1) duplicate, (2) distinct, and (3) partial duplicate. These approaches are shown in Fig. 10. Please note that in general purpose clustered solutions for scalable service provision, the duplicate and distinct approaches are commonly termed *homogeneous* and *heterogeneous* clustering, respectively.

In the duplicate server approach, each server holds a complete duplicate of the virtual world containing all artifacts. A server will assume responsibility for "ownership" of an artifact, and inform all other servers of updates carried out on

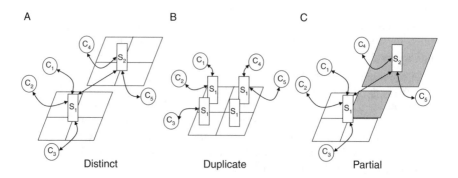

Fɪɢ. 10. Load-balancing options.

such artifacts (relating to messages originated at a player's console). This requires servers to pass messages between themselves to ensure gaming scenarios are modeled appropriately. With the volume of data present on each server there may be opportunities to make use of dead-reckoning techniques to ease the message dissemination overhead. Synchronization of servers is required and so some protocol governing message delivery guarantees will be desirable in this approach. A detailed description of an implementation of this approach has been demonstrated [75] with a number of other works (e.g., [27, 37]) advocating this approach due to a number of possible benefits: *failover*—if one server fails, other servers may assume responsibility for the failed server's clients (as all servers have some knowledge of cumulative game state); *scalability*—increased client numbers are satisfied by increased server numbers; and *responsiveness*—local servers may satisfy the demands of local clients.

In the distinct server approach, different areas of a virtual world are maintained by different servers (possibly defined in a similar manner as regions in NPSNET). There is minimum interserver communications and a single gaming scenario is executed on a single server. The main benefit of this approach is that consistency of interaction becomes an issue to be resolved between a single server and associated player consoles. There is no need for interserver communications to model interaction as synchronization between duplicate servers is not warranted to model a gaming scenario. However, a limiting factor is the problem of "full" regions: there is a processing limit dictated by server resource availability on any one particular region. For example, in Second Life this manifests itself as areas been incapable of supporting a level of activity in the virtual world defined by server resources [82] (this is actually on a per-duplicate world/shard basis and manifests itself as disjoint islands). Full regions exhibit themselves in the virtual world as "crowding." Unfortunately, crowding is not an uncommon occurrence as players tend to gravitate toward popular events in virtual worlds. In addition, there is a requirement to handle process resource handover between servers when players move from one region to another. This problem in itself has warranted a number of research papers (e.g., [31, 82]).

The partial duplication approach is similar to the duplicate server approach apart from the fact that not all the servers are aware of all virtual world interactions. Localized game play is used to identify where synchronization requirements need to be satisfied across servers. In essence, this approach lies between duplicate server and distinct server approaches. In this approach, regions may be allocated to servers dynamically at runtime to alleviate the "full region" problem found in the distinct server approach. Alternatively, load balancing may be achieved by players being assigned to servers and full synchronization between servers is required to model interaction appropriately, possibly using auras as a basis of determining interaction.

This approach has been demonstrated successfully in the context of auras identifying areas of interest to aid in dictating which servers should enact interserver communications to satisfy gaming scenarios [62, 71].

In Section 3.1 the aura and region approaches were described, and in Section 3.2 EverQuest's approach to identifying localized game play was described. The reader should by now recognize that EverQuest (and similar commercial products) use regions as a form of load balancing. The identification of localized game play is conveniently used to identify load distribution across the application tier and implement the distinct server approach. Unfortunately, commercial solutions, like EverQuest, do exhibit the crowding phenomenon resulting in exhaustion of server resources and full regions. Left unchecked, the effects of crowding may result in a slowdown in game play or, in worst case scenarios, a complete inability to enact player interaction. This may be considered the same problem of consistency management that the distinct server approach is attempting to alleviate: without regionalization, the virtual world itself (single region) may become populated by a sufficiently large number of players as to make the consistency problem unmanageable. In commercial solutions, the number of players allowed into a duplicate world is rarely above 2500 to offset the problem of resource exhaustion; better to prevent failure in player interaction than allow it. In essence, players load balance themselves by choosing duplicate worlds to enter and are barred from entering those duplicate worlds that are "full" or not available due to maintenance issues.

In the presence of server clustering, there is an opportunity to alleviate the crowding problem by dynamically associating processing requirements generated by player actions during runtime. This takes the form of load-balancing player activities across servers with respect to regions and assumes the partial duplicate server approach. The literature provides a number of solutions to load balancing across server clusters suitable for MMORPGs. Regions may be reduced in size by subdividing them further (allocating servers to these additional subdivisions) [105]. Other methods distribute responsibility for region execution to a particular server at runtime based on the volume of players in a region [30], while other methods dynamically resize regions during runtime [50]. Such approaches may be fine tuned further to ensure that the cost of moving responsibility for execution to another server is minimized [22].

EverQuest also describes runtime allocation of resources from within small clusters of servers responsible for a duplicate virtual world. Although no great technical detail is provided on how this is achieved [55], the premise of this approach appears to be player driven: when player enacts a particular action (e.g., opening a door, entering into battle) processing resources are allocated to satisfy the increased processing requirements.

Commercial approaches aside, there are a number of other works in the area of scalable server-side solutions that may be appropriate. A notable contribution is work carried out by IBM. IBM has produced region-based services that make use of standards such as Web/Grid services [90]. Regions are again used in this work, providing a platform that would allow a similar approach to implementation than would be expected in the commercial approach already discussed. Other works (e.g., RING [41]) do employ multiple servers, allocating regions of virtual worlds to different servers, providing a similar approach to scalability (regions to servers) as advocated in the common commercial approach. Recently, The Darkstar Project from Sun Microsystems is tackling the scalability issue without dependency on duplicate worlds and instead advocates the scalability problem be solved by distributing tasks over a collection of servers (irrelevant of geographic location of the world). Experimental results are not yet available demonstrating scalability, but this is a project that should be monitored for results in the future [98].

4. Core Problems

There has been a large spectrum of work that is directly or indirectly related to scalable online gaming. In recent years the volume of research related to this area has increased rapidly; many papers on scalability have appeared in the annual ACM SIGCOMM workshop on *network and system support for games* (*NetGames*), an excellent resource for the latest developments in the area. Many other works have appeared sporadically in a variety of other conferences, ranging from graphics to networking. Correlating such work is a nontrivial task as useful knowledge related to online gaming research may be found in a number of different genres not necessarily produced by researchers primarily concerned with online gaming (e.g., distributed simulation, fault tolerance, real-time systems, streamed multimedia, human–computer interaction). The different genres within online gaming themselves produce their own focused works (e.g., nonpersistent first-person shooter [28, 65] and streamed content for game artifacts [82]).

Considering the wide spectrum of research activity associated to online gaming, one must not lose fact of the basic requirements that need to be satisfied when constructing large-scale online gaming worlds. We can structure these requirements into three logical steps that must be achieved to make large-scale online games a reality. In their simplest abstraction, these basic steps are described as follows:

1. Determine, based on virtual world state, which artifacts are and are not interacting
2. Enable required message dissemination between nodes in a network (e.g., servers, player consoles) while prohibiting needless message dissemination between nodes

3. Manage message delivery to attain appropriate synchronization to afford intended gaming scenarios

Each of these steps is now considered in turn, concentrating on a number of open questions that each requirement highlights.

4.1   Where Am I?

Primarily, virtual world geography is used to determine which artifacts should be interacting. This is not as simple as defining a virtual world distance within which interaction between two artifacts becomes possible. For example, when a virtual world is divided into static regions an artifact close to a region boundary may actually be closer to artifacts in neighboring regions than artifacts in their own region. The aura/nimbus approach appears more appealing as this issue does not arise. Furthermore, the aura/nimbus model allows areas of interest to be specified on a per-artifact basis (allowing for varying types of artifacts to express varying degrees of influence and interest). Unfortunately, this requires additional processing requirements to determine what interaction is occurring at any one point in time. The only option at this point is to employ a real-time collision detection algorithm to identify such interaction; a substantial processing overhead if in excess of a million artifacts exist at any one time in a virtual world [70]. Furthermore, this is a distributed computation in itself to be carried out across multiple nodes. How does one achieve such a service in a timely manner [78]?

In commercial solutions, the problem is tackled by using regions and simply constructing the virtual world to hide the hindrance of interaction found in the static region approach. For example, constructing a large wall preventing players from seeing what is within other regions is a simple, if not elegant, solution. Even with regions and an appropriately constructed virtual world, the process of moving from one region to another still requires processing time to allow a server cluster to allocate processing resources effectively. Basically, a player must be slowed down in some way when process resource allocation is changed at the server side due to region changes. Maybe the player can ride on a train between regions, or maybe a door between regions takes time to open. Either way, some game play element must be seamlessly incorporated into a virtual world in a less as intrusive way as possible. When in excess of a few million players are changing regions frequently how can timely requirements be satisfied?

A major drawback with static regions is the possibility that they may become full, hindering player participation. Research has been associated to this problem, with regions been able to spread their processing resources across multiple server nodes if required. However, this may be more process intensive and, therefore, time consuming to achieve than simply allowing interserver message passing in the first place and distributing load on a per-player basis between servers [62]. If this is the case, what tradeoff must be made between the provision of a free-roaming virtual world that players enjoy and the strictly regulated transition of region boundaries?

4.2   Who to Tell?

Assuming the nontrivial problem of determining where all players are in a virtual world is solved, identifying which events should be propagated to which players needs to be addressed. Once a single oracle-type service that identifies interaction in a timely manner exists, this information then has to be implemented using some (approximated) group membership protocol to ensure messages may then be disseminated appropriately across nodes in a network to allow interaction. The less accurate the group membership protocol is the more needless messages will be sent. However, the more accurate the protocol is the more time, and message passing, will be required to achieve identification of message recipients. During runtime, how can such a tradeoff be monitored and tailored to guarantee that player expectations associated to gaming scenarios are to be achieved?

The simple solution would be to send all messages to all artifacts within a particular region or to send messages to all artifacts that a player may influence. Unfortunately, this solution is not ideal, especially if a large number of players are present and player consoles receive messages that they are simply not interested in. Witnessing players move around a virtual world is required to aid immersion, but just because a player can view other players does not necessarily indicate that such a player is interested in all events generated by visible players. Therefore, one may envisage that all messages are not to be treated the same. For example, assume a player, say P_1, generates two events, say E_1 and E_2, and another player, say P_2, is only interested in E_2 but not E_1. A group-based system modeling this approach will require two distinct groups (message dissemination of E_1 and E_2 is handled separately). Add another player, say P_3, who is interested in E_1 and E_2 and not only do we have another group, but there exists a causal relationship that may be maintained for P_3's view of P_1's actions. This may be modeled via overlapping groups, but the more groups we add the more the processing burden increases and the more time is used up determining message recipients. At what point does group management become so burdensome as to hinder interactivity?

4.3   How to Inform?

Consider a virtual world within which the mechanism of realizing player locations has been achieved and the identification of suitable message recipients accomplished both in a timely manner. All that is left is to enact message delivery in a manner that satisfies the ordering and reliability guarantees that satisfy the desired player interaction requirements. Such ordering and reliability guarantees will be based on the relevance of messages, and their associated events, to players. For example, intricate interaction between two players will require sufficient ordering and reliability guarantees to ensure game play scenarios progress appropriately. A third player may still be interested in viewing this progression in game play, but may be indifferent to the actual details, possibly requiring summary-type information using aggregated messages (e.g., which player won a particular battle). If this is the case, then how are aggregated messages related to the ordering and delivery guarantees of the messages they represent? What type of protocol could manage such relationships between messages when different recipients have differing ordering and reliability requirements for the same set of messages?

Treating all messages with the strongest deliverable and reliability guarantees possible has been shown to be problematic when attempting to achieve scalability (ISIS in DIVE); yet modern commercial persistent virtual worlds require something similar for modeling intricate game play. The existence of a server can ease the ordering burden (utilizing asymmetric approaches), but such a server must provide some form of failover to ensure a robust environment. An added complication occurs when attempting to avoid resource exhaustion, requiring multiple servers to satisfy message ordering and reliability guarantees to model a single gaming scenario. How does one balance load efficiently yet minimize time-consuming message delays that are the result of spreading load over multiple servers? How can failover be achieved while ensuring real-time requirements are satisfied?

5. Conclusions and Further Work

Engineering a scalable virtual world is a nontrivial task that requires a broad range of skills from different areas of computing science. Although commercial virtual worlds exist and have been successful (accounting for over $1 billion in revenue in the USA and Europe by 2006, not including Asia [87]); these worlds can become ultimately more successful. This statement is made as the research accomplished so far, although admirable, needs to expand and become inclusive of a number of fields of computing science.

In the first part of this chapter, gaming scenarios are described using the common model for identifying progression in a distributed computation. This provides a convenient and readily understandable description of possible gaming scenarios. A number of errors in gaming scenarios were highlighted that could occur if progression of a distributed computation is not regulated in some way. An attempt is made to relate the problems in gaming scenarios to the more general problems found in distributed computation. This allows a reasoned discussion on what is and what is not possible when developing online games and the possible research direction for addressing the problem of ensuring appropriate gaming scenarios are achieved. This highlights the advances made in the distributed systems community as worthy of serious scrutiny from the online games developer when attempting to create appropriate gaming scenarios for large-scale virtual worlds.

In related work, a number of academic, military, and commercial efforts are listed that have made progress toward the current state of the art for scalable online gaming. Works are described that may provide the essence of a number of solutions for advancing the state of the art of scalable online games. This is an important issue to address, as there are a number of research efforts that can make significant contributions to the development of large-scale, highly interactive, virtual worlds yet are rarely considered in the gaming literature.

After considering related work, a section is provided that attempts to highlight a number of significant issues to be addressed if advancement in large-scale, highly interactive, virtual worlds is to be made. This is represented in a simplified, three-stepped approach that appears obvious at first glance, but conceals nontrivial problems that provide a focus for the online gaming researcher. A series of questions are posed without answers to bring to the fore a number of research issues. However, these questions are not exhaustive and may find their solutions by combining solutions highlighted in the related work section of this chapter.

This chapter is now concluded with a number of research problems that go beyond the basic problem of scalability while maintaining highly involving gaming scenarios.

5.1 Advanced Interest Management

Identifying which artifacts are interacting is a nontrivial problem; however, one can envisage ever more elaborate schemes for actually defining and describing the influence and interest associated to such interaction. Interaction in the real world may consist of a highly complex series of events and creates complex relationships between artifacts which may last sometime (e.g., parcel in plane makes plane heavier). Describing the manner of interaction between participants requires a language capable of expressing a variety of techniques. Although some languages have been proposed (e.g., [79]), they tend to be limited in their expressiveness [95]. Existing solutions use fixed interaction patterns (server based or direct communications between user consoles). Varying this choice at runtime has never been considered. Judiciously, exercising a choice regarding such patterns may be the key to achieving interactivity and scalability.

To accommodate a wide variety of interaction requirements, an interest management scheme must combine location and discovery services with interaction techniques from a variety of gaming genres:

- *Discovery*. Given the scale of a virtual world, there is a need to provide users with the ability to find scenarios they wish to participate in.
- *Abstract*. Allow users to exert far-reaching degrees of influence on a virtual world, say moving an army of 20,000 soldiers, via minimal effort (e.g., a few mouse clicks).
- *Realistic*. To heighten the sense of realism, users interact with the each other in a manner similar to that of the real world.

Envisage combining the expressions of interest exhibited in discovery, abstract, and realistic interaction into a single interest management solution. For example, a discovery service may utilize knowledge of realistic and abstract interaction services to allow a player to locate an appropriate gaming scenario (e.g., finding communities of players collaborating on a task). Developing a single interest management solution for abstract and realistic services will provide a highly interactive virtual world for participants and raises interesting questions. For example, how does a single player's management of a whole city (abstract services) influence the realistic services supporting interacting players inhabiting such a city?

The area of research concerned with scalable *message-oriented middleware* (MOM) may offer some insight into this challenging problem. In MOM systems, messages may be propagated between sender and receiver based on the subject matter of a message, rather than the identity of the sender. To aid in this MOM systems can provide scripting languages that allow receivers to express their interest in particular message types. This approach has already been experimented with [8, 71] with some success. However, apart from these works, the tailoring of MOM systems for use in highly interactive large-scale virtual worlds is rarely considered.

Work by Minson and Theodoropoulos [67] has tackled the problem of interest management in a novel way and provide further insights into gaining advanced interest management systems of the future. Their work centers on the investigation of event dissemination via push and pull methods of internode communications. They show by considering interest management from the "bottom-up," intricacies are present that affect performance that are often hidden when solely concentrating on interest management as purely an in-world problem. They demonstrate their approaches quite successfully via first-person shooter architectures using cell division to attain scalability [68].

5.2   Standardization and Interorganizational Issues

With the commercialization of virtual worlds, a practical engineering solution to scalability must consider two additional issues:

1. *Interorganizational.* Delivering a commercial solution to end users requires the cooperation of a number of different organizations (e.g., content providers, hosting provision, and Internet service providers).
2. *Middleware.* To ensure development costs remain acceptable, a commercial solution must be constructed using readily available middleware tools and services (e.g., security, reliability, persistence, and scalability).

An example of interorganizational complexities is highlighted by the diagram in Fig. 11, taken from IBM [91]: A games software house produces a game that is made available by some hosting entity supported by a number of service providers that cooperate to deliver a gaming experience to players via some, possibly propriety, gaming device. This interorganizational approach results in service provision that crosses organizational boundaries, requiring the emulation of electronic equivalents of contract-based business management practices. *Service-level agreements* (SLAs) provide an opportunity to define such contracts in a way that interorganizational information sharing may be defined, monitored, and enforced.

The cost of developing distributed applications is reduced if existing middleware may be exploited efficiently by a developer. For example, by using an implementation of the J2EE component architecture, say JBoss [40], a developer may engineer a scalable server-side application. Services such as transactions, persistence, security, and load balancing may be incorporated into an application by a JBoss application server with configuration guidance from an application programmer.

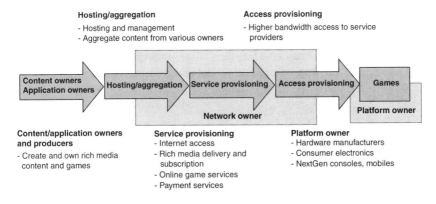

FIG. 11. Business value chain for online gaming.

Interorganizational and component middleware research has focused on e-commerce client/server style interactions (e.g., stock purchase): there are no J2EE component-type architectures for online game developers. Work carried out by IBM to demonstrate Grid technologies does provide introductory work in this area [83, 89, 90] and Sun's Darkstar Project may well provide such a platform in the future [98]. However, the use of SLAs and standard middleware may not be sufficient for modeling advanced virtual worlds.

At the moment, virtual worlds are quite disjoint environments. For example, the commercial model dictates that whatever is achieved in World of Warcraft is nontransferable to other vendor's sites (vendors do not wish to encourage departures from their own worlds). However, with the advent of standardization and SLA-governed interaction, the future may provide a more unified vision of a virtual world allowing artifacts to be seamlessly transferred between vendors. Ultimately, this may result in a single virtual place where vendors primarily become content providers as opposed to world developers. Artifacts currently have value in commercial virtual worlds, and are regularly traded for real money. However, once the virtual world becomes as accessible and standardized as the modern-day Internet, then it will be content that will be the most valuable asset.

The ease of access and standardization of virtual worlds together with associated game engine technologies may yield exciting possibilities. For example, a player may purchase the latest car from one vendor and pay another vendor to race this car around a purpose built arena in a virtual world. Another player may purchase an aircraft and fly over the race track and witness the other player driving their car. Should we let the players interact? Would they want to? Could gaming scenarios grow from disjoint gaming scenarios? Would they make sense? Could they be regulated? Any number of questions may be raised. Linden Labs [61] do allow user-derived content development in their Second Life product; however, this is a different proposition to allowing Activision to create the next Gotham Racing in the same virtual world as Rockstar's Grand Theft Auto. Even in the arena of Second Life, where products usually cost less than $1000 there has been legal issues raised [88]. Consider what legal issues may be raised if a company invested over $30 million (typical cost of top selling game title) in such a world and that investment came to be worth in excess of $400 million (sales value of Grand Theft Auto 4 in first week of release [100]).

5.3 Content Management

To ensure financial success in commercial virtual worlds, player interest must be maintained over prolonged periods of time (measured in years). Therefore, a virtual world must continue to provide new and challenging scenarios to encourage user participation. This can be achieved by periodically introducing new content (e.g., artifacts, rules, stories, and areas) and ensuring all content exhibits a degree of persistence to provide a heightened sense of continuing community. In the previous section, the discussion centered on the content ownership and management of gaming scenarios created by multiple vendors. However, a more difficult problem may be the actual maintenance and continual improvements to virtual world content. Even now, many commercial virtual worlds are struggling to maintain in excess of 10–20 million separate items of content. The prospect of evolving such artifacts and gaming scenarios into ever more elaborate environments seems an insurmountable problem.

Faced with the problem of content management, companies are restricted to manual updates by their own developers or by players. Companies may have good reasons to manage content: coherent storylines and directing the overall look and feel of a gaming scenario. However, this is a burdensome task when millions of artifacts exist. Therefore, an alternative approach has arisen where players are encouraged to create such content, albeit at the expense of a company's ability to direct gaming scenarios [61].

When companies manage content, the use of client-side updates coupled with additions at the server side is common (e.g., [101, 108]). Updates to client's software are an additional revenue stream for a company. Such updates are achieved by the company releasing "expansion packs" (software updates) which the user must purchase to participate in new gaming scenarios. To ensure existing users may continue to participate without "expansion packs," the company isolates new scenarios from existing content. This is achieved by adding a new area to a virtual world. In reality, existing content is not evolved, but increased in the form of additional areas.

Second Life [61], by Linden Labs, allows player content creation with a financial revenue model based on real estate and trading: the main type of revenue for Linden Labs relates to the purchase of land and paying of ground rent. An innovative aspect of Second Life is the ability players have for creating content. Such content may then be traded between users. No client-side updates are required to access new content (beyond the original downloading of the client game software itself). A scripting language allows artifacts to be instilled with behavior, allowing players to provide their own virtual world scenarios. This approach provides Second Life players with the most powerful content creation tool available today for online virtual worlds with players providing a wealth of content. Content creation via players has been achieved before Second Life in Active Worlds [114], but it is Second Life's scripting language that provides the dynamic content required to create gaming scenarios. However, even Second Life's approach has its limitations. The following example is used to highlight such limitations.

In a virtual world that already allows players to navigate ships between ports, there is a desire to evolve an economic market by introducing "trade" and "cargo." Once introduced, players will be able to trade between ports via ships carrying cargo. There is a requirement to modify the artifact ship to enable the carrying of cargo. The new concept of trade will require modification to the rules governing the virtual world itself. Ports will assume the role of trade hubs and must be enhanced to recognize their role in trading.

In this example, it is not sufficient to just add content, but existing content (ships, ports) must also be altered to enhance them with the ability to participate in trade. This requires updates in the data store tier (e.g., amount of cargo that a ship can carry) and updates in the application logic tier to enhance functionality (e.g., unload/ load cargo) (see Fig. 9). Furthermore, other artifacts not mentioned in the example must be designated as cargo. This in itself will require updates to other artifacts in the data store tier (e.g., weight, size, and owner) and additions in the application logic tier (e.g., in transit, set owner, and change value). Finally, the concept of trade itself is quite fundamental and not easily captured within one single artifact, requiring recognition in the rules governing a virtual world (e.g., supply, wealth, and exchange).

The core research problem is the need to ease creation and amendment of existing program code together with changes in persistent data representations to allow far-reaching evolutionary change in virtual worlds. This has to be achieved by limiting manual intervention (automating change) without disruption to the virtual world (runtime safe content management).

Existing approaches to company and player-derived content evolution cannot realize the trading example as existing content cannot be changed appropriately to accommodate new content. In Second Life, propagation of change from one artifact to another is limited and inhibited between artifacts belonging to different owners. Even using such an inhibitive approach Second Life has been plagued by problems (failure of simulation due to erroneous scripts [60]). The more controlled approach used in company-driven content change has faired better in terms of virtual world correctness (but failures still happen [24]). This safety has come at the expense of limiting existing content updates to simple bug fixes and only allowing new content distinct from existing content. Fundamentally, all existing approaches severely limit content evolution in favor of safety and the programming burden is immense.

A new code fragment representing an artifact may be manually created. However, the adaptation of the system to accommodate the new artifact should be sufficiently automated to lessen the development burden and ensure safety. One avenue of exploration that may be useful for engineering evolutionary change in virtual worlds is *reflection*. One use of reflection is to allow the self-reorganization of a system. In essence, reflection could be employed to enable self-reorganization of code fragments and associated attributes to allow far-reaching evolutionary change in a safe manner. Work at Lancaster University in the UK identified the role that reflection may play in online game construction for satisfying scalability, persistence, and responsiveness requirements [77]. Reflective middleware platforms may play a significant role in the future of server-side virtual world development.

In the end, a virtual world that dates and is unable to keep pace with player expectations will eventually become financially unsustainable. When this occurs, the vendor has no option but to turn the virtual world off.

ACKNOWLEDGMENTS

The author gratefully acknowledges members of his team here at Newcastle who have contributed to research related to MMOs over the past few years: Fengyun Lu, Kier Story, Simon Parkin, and Dan Martin. Their research was funded by a number of sources, but primarily by the *Engineering and Physical Sciences Research Council* (EPSRC) of the UK.

REFERENCES

[1] Anecdotal Evidence from Computer and Video Game Survey.com, 2008. (http://www.video-games-survey.com/online_gamers.htm).

[2] Barrus J. W., Waters R. C., and Anderson D. B., 1996. Locales and beacons: Efficient and precise support for large multi-user virtual environments. In *Proceedings of the 1996 Virtual Reality Annual International Symposium (VRAIS'96)*, 30 March–3 April 1996, p. 204. IEEE Computer Society, Washington, DC.

[3] Barrus J. W., Waters R. C., and Anderson D. B., November 1997. Locales: Supporting large multiuser virtual environments. *IEEE Computer Graphics and Applications*, **16**(6): 50–57.

[4] Bartle R., 1990. Early MUD history (http://www.mud.co.uk/richard/mudhist.htm).

[5] Benford S., and Fahlén L., 1993. A spatial model of interaction in large virtual environments. In *Proceedings of the Third Conference on European Conference on Computer-Supported Cooperative Work (ECSCW)*, (G. de Michelis, C. Simone, and K. Schmidt, Eds.), 13–17 September 1993, Milan, Italy, pp. 109–124. Kluwer Academic Publishers, Norwell, MA.

[6] Benford S., Greenhalgh C., Rodden T., and Pycock J., July 2001. Collaborative virtual environments. *Communications of the ACM*, **44**(7): 79–85.

[7] Berne E., 1979. The Games People Play. Ballantine Books, New York, NY.

[8] Bharambe A. R., Rao S., and Seshan S., 2002. Mercury: A scalable publish-subscribe system for Internet games. In *Proceedings of the Workshop on Network and System Support for Games (NetGames'02)*, 16–17 April 2002, Braunschweig, Germany, pp. 3–9. ACM Press, New York, NY.

[9] Birman K. P., 1986. Isis: A system for fault-tolerant distributed computing. Technical Report, UMI Order Number: TR86-744, Cornell University.

[10] Birman K. P., 1993. The process group approach to reliable distributed computing. *Communications of the ACM*, **36**(12): 37–53.

[11] Birman K., 2005. Reliable Distributed Systems: Technologies, Web Services, and Applications. Springer-Verlag, Berlin.

[12] Birman K., and Joseph T., 1987. Reliable communication in the presence of failure. *ACM Transactions on Computer Systems*, **5**(1): 47–46.

[13] Blizzard Entertainment press release, 22 January 2008. World of Warcraft® Reaches New Milestone: 10 Million Subscribers, Paris, France (http://eu.blizzard.com/en/press/080122.html).

[14] Bryant R. E., 1997. Simulation of packet communication architecture computer systems. Technical Report, UMI Order Number: TR-188, Massachusetts Institute of Technology.

[15] Carlsson C., and Hagsand O., 1993. DIVE—A platform for multiuser virtual environments. *Computers & Graphics*, **17**(6): 663–669.

[16] Carpenter A., 11 June 2003. Applying Risk Analysis to Play-Balance RPGs. Gamasutra (http://www.gamasutra.com/features/20030611/carpenter_01.shtml).

[17] Castronova E., 2007. Synthetic Worlds: The Business and Culture of Online Games. University of Chicago Press, Chicago, IL.

[18] Chandra T. D., and Toueg S., 1996. Unreliable failure detectors for reliable distributed systems. *Journal of the ACM*, **43**(2): 225–267.

[19] Chandra T. D., Hadzilacos V., and Toueg S., 1992. The weakest failure detector for solving consensus. In *Proceedings of the Eleventh Annual ACM Symposium on Principles of Distributed Computing (PODC'92)*, Vancouver, BC, Canada, pp. 147–158. ACM Press, New York, NY.

[20] Chandy K. M., and Lamport L., 1985. Distributed snapshots: Determining global states of distributed systems. *ACM Transactions on Computer Systems*, **3**(1): 63–75.

[21] Chandy K. M., and Misra J., 1979. Distributed simulation: A case study in design and verification of distributed programs. *IEEE Transactions on Software Engineering*, **SE-5**(5): 440–452.

[22] Chim J., Lau R., Leong H. V., and Si A., December 2003. CyberWalk: A Web-based distributed virtual walkthrough environment. *IEEE Transactions on Multimedia*, **5**(4): 503–515.

[23] City of Heroes Site. (http://www.cityofheroes.com/).

[24] CNet. 'World of Warcraft' battles server problems (http://news.com.com/World+of+Warcraft+battles+server+problems/2100-1043_3-6063990.html).

[25] Cristian F., 1989. Probabilistic clock synchronization. In *Distributed Computing*, vol. 3, pp. 146–158. Springer-Verlag, Berlin.

[26] Cristian F., Aghili H., and Strong R., 1985. Atomic broadcast from simple message diffusion to Byzantine agreement. In *International Symposium on Fault-Tolerant Computing (FTCS-15)*, June 1985, Ann Arbor, MI, pp. 200–206.

[27] Cronin E., Kurc A. R., Filstrup B., and Jamin S., May 2004. An efficient synchronization mechanism for mirrored game architectures. In *Multimedia Tools and Applications*, vol. 23(1), pp. 7–30. Springer-Verlag, Netherlands.

[28] Cronin E., Kurc A. R., Filstrup B., and Jamin S., May 2004. An efficient synchronization mechanism for mirrored game architectures. *Kluwer Multimedia Tools and Applications*, **23**(1): 7–30.

[29] Dahmann J. S., Fujimoto R. M., and Weatherly R. M., December 1997. The Department of Defense High Level Architecture. In *Proceedings of the 29th Conference on Winter Simulation*, (S. Andradóttir, K. J. Healy, D. H. Withers, and B. L. Nelson, Eds.). *Winter Simulation Conference*, Atlanta, GA, pp. 142–149. IEEE Computer Society, Washington, DC.

[30] Das T. K., Singh G., Mitchell A., Kumar P. S., and McGee K., 1997. NetEffect: A network architecture for large-scale multi-user virtual worlds. In *Proceedings of the ACM Symposium on Virtual Reality Software and Technology* (Lausanne, Switzerland). *VRST '97*. ACM Press, New York, NY, pp. 157–163.

[31] De Vleeschauwer B., Van Den Bossche B., Verdickt T., De Turck F., Dhoedt B., and Demeester P., 2005. Dynamic microcell assignment for massively multiplayer online gaming. In *Proceedings of the 4th ACM SIGCOMM Workshop on Network and System Support for Games (NetGames'05)*, October 2005, Hawthorne, NY, pp. 1–7. ACM Press, New York, NY.

[32] Delporte-Gallet C., and Fauconnier H., 2001. An example of real-time group communication system. In *Proceedings of the 21st International Conference on Distributed Computing Systems Workshops (ICDCSW'01)*.

[33] Dolev D., Malki D., and Strong R., 1996. A framework for partitionable membership service. In *Proceedings of the Fifteenth Annual ACM Symposium on Principles of Distributed Computing (PODC'96)*, p. 343. ACM Press, New York, NY.

[34] Eve Online Site (http://www.eve-online.com/).

[35] EverQuest Site (http://everquest.station.sony.com/).

[36] Ezhilchelvan P. D., Macedo R., and Shrivastava S. K., 1994. Newtop: A fault-tolerant group communication protocol. Technical Report, UMI Order Number: BROADCAST#TR94-48, University of Bologna.

[37] Ferretti S., and Roccetti M., 2005. Fast delivery of game events with an optimistic synchronization mechanism in massive multiplayer online games. In *Proceedings of the 2005 ACM SIGCHI International Conference on Advances in Computer Entertainment Technology (ACE'05)*, 15–17 June 2005, Valencia, Spain, vol. 265, pp. 405–412. ACM Press, New York, NY.

[38] Fich F., and Ruppert E., 2003. Hundreds of impossibility results for distributed computing. *Distributed Computing*, **16**(2–3): 121–163.

[39] Fischer M. J., Lynch N. A., and Paterson M. S., 1985. Impossibility of distributed consensus with one faulty process. *Journal of the ACM*, **32**(2): 374–382.

[40] Fleury M., and Reverbel F., 2003. The JBoss extensible server. In *Proceedings of the ACM/IFIP/ USENIX International Middleware Conference (Middleware 2003)*, LNCS, pp. 344–373. Springer-Verlag, Berlin.

[41] Funkhouser T. A., 1995. RING: A client–server system for multi-user virtual environments. In *Computer Graphics, 1995 SIGGRAPH Symposium on Interactive 3D Graphics*, Monterey, CA, pp. 85–92.

[42] Garcia-Molina H., 1982. Elections in a distributed computing system. *IEEE Transactions on Computers*, **31**(1): 47–59.

[43] Gray J., 1979. Notes on Database Operating Systems: An Advanced Course. Springer-Verlag, Berlin.

[44] Gray J., 1980. A transaction model. In *Lecture Notes in Computer Science*, vol. 85, pp. 282–298. Springer-Verlag, Berlin.

[45] Greenhalgh C., and Benford S., 1995. Virtual reality tele-conferencing: Implementation and experience. In *Proceedings of the Fourth Conference on European Conference on Computer-Supported Cooperative Work (ECSCW)*, 10–14 September 1995, Stockholm, Sweden, (H. Marmolin, Y. Sundblad, and K. Schmidt, Eds.), pp. 165–180. Kluwer Academic Publishers, Norwell, MA.

[46] Greenhalgh C., Purbrick J., and Snowdon D., 2000. Inside MASSIVE-3: Flexible support for data consistency and world structuring. In *Proceedings of the Third International Conference on Collaborative Virtual Environments (CVE'00)*, San Francisco, CA, (E. Churchill and M. Reddy, Eds.), pp. 119–127. ACM Press, New York, NY.

[47] Hagsand O., January 1996. Interactive multiuser VEs in the DIVE system. *IEEE MultiMedia*, **3**(1): 30–39.

[48] Hofer R. C., and Loper M. L., 1995. DIS today [distributed interactive simulation]. In *Proceedings of the IEEE*, vol. 83(8), pp. 1124–1137.

[49] Holbrook H. W., Singhal S. K., and Cheriton D. R., October 1995. Log-based receiver-reliable multicast for distributed interactive simulation. *SIGCOMM Computer Communication Review*, **25**(4): 328–341.

[50] Hori M., Iseri T., Fujikawa K., Shimojo S., and Miyahara H., 2001. Scalability issues of dynamic space management for multiple-server networked virtual environments. In *Proceedings of the IEEE Pacific Rim Conference on Communications, Computers and Signal Processing (PACRIM)*, August 2001, vol. 1, pp. 200–203.

[51] Id Software's Original README.TXT File for Shareware Doom v1.8 can be viewed at http://www. classicdoom.com/doominfo.htm.

[52] Jefferson D. R., 1985. Virtual time. *ACM Transactions on Programming Languages and Systems*, **7**(3): 404–425.

[53] Kopetz H., Damm A., Koza C., Mulazzani M., Schwabl W., Senft C., and Zainlinger R., January 1989. Distributed fault-tolerant real-time systems: The mars approach. *IEEE Micro*, **9**(1): 25–40.

[54] Kshemkalyani A. D., and Singhal M., 2008. Distributed Computing: Principles, Algorithms, and Systems. Cambridge University Press, Cambridge.

[55] Kushner D., April 2005. Engineering EverQuest. *IEEE Spectrum*, **42**(7): 34–39.

[56] Lamport L., 1978. Time, clocks and the ordering of events in a distributed system. *Communications of the ACM*, **21**, 558–564.

[57] Lamport L., 1984. Using time instead of timeout for fault-tolerant distributed systems. *ACM Transactions on Programming Languages and Systems*, **6**(2): 254–280.

[58] Lamport L., Shostak R., and Pease M., July 1982. The Byzantine generals problem. *ACM Transactions on Programming Languages and Systems*, **4**(3): 382–401.

[59] Lampson B., and Sturgis H., 1976. Crash recovery in distributed storage systems. Technical Report, Computer Science Laboratory, Xerox Parc, Palo Alto.

[60] Linden Lab 2007. Security and second life, http://blog.secondlife.com/2006/10/09/security-and-second-life/, viewed August 2007.

[61] Linden Lab, Second Life Site (http://secondlife.com/).

[62] Lu F., Parkin S., and Morgan G., 2006. Load balancing for massively multiplayer online games. In *Proceedings of the 5th ACM SIGCOMM Workshop on Network and System Support for Games (NetGames'06)*, October 2006, Singapore, ACM Press, New York, NY.

[63] Macedonia M. R., and Zyda M. J., January 1997. A taxonomy for networked virtual environments. *IEEE MultiMedia*, **4**(1): 48–56.

[64] Macedonia M. R., Brutzman D. P., Zyda M. J., Pratt D. R., Barham P. T., Falby J., and Locke J., 1995. NPSNET: A multi-player 3D virtual environment over the Internet. In *Proceedings of the 1995 Symposium on Interactive 3D Graphics (SI3D'95)*, 9–12 April 1995, Monterey, CA, ACM Press, New York, NY.

[65] Martin D., van Moorsel A., and Morgan G., 2008. Efficient resource management for game server hosting. In *Proceedings of the 2008 11th IEEE Symposium on Object-Oriented Real-Time Distributed Computing (ISORC)*, May 2008, IEEE Computer Society, Washington, DC.

[66] Miller D. C., and Thorpe J. A., 1995. SIMNET: The advent of simulator networking. In *Proceedings of the IEEE* **83**(8): pp. 1114–1123.

[67] Minson R., and Theodoropoulos G., 2005. An adaptive interest management scheme for distributed virtual environments. In *Proceedings of the 19th Workshop on Principles of Advanced and Distributed Simulation. Workshop on Parallel and Distributed Simulation*, 1–3 June 2005, pp. 273–281. IEEE Computer Society, Washington, DC.

[68] Minson R., and Theodoropoulos G., 2008. Push–pull interest management for virtual worlds. In *Proceedings of the 2008 11th IEEE Symposium on Object-Oriented Real-Time Distributed Computing (ISORC)*, May 2008, pp. 189–194. IEEE Computer Society, Washington, DC.

[69] Morgan G., and Shrivastava S. K., 2000. Implementing flexible object group invocation in networked systems. In *Proceedings on Dependable Systems and Networks (DSN 2000)*, pp. 439–448.

[70] Morgan G., and Storey K., 2005. Scalable collision detection for massively multiplayer online games. In *Proceedings of the IEEE 19th International Conference on Advanced Information Networking and Applications (AINA'05)*, Taiwan, vol. 1, pp. 873–878. IEEE Computer Society, Washington, DC.

[71] Morgan G., Lu F., and Storey K., 2005. Interest management middleware for networked games. In *Proceedings of the 2005 Symposium on Interactive 3D Graphics and Games (I3D'05)*, April 2005, Washington, DC, pp. 57–64. ACM Press, New York, NY.

[72] Morningstar C., and Farmer F. R., 1991. The lessons of Lucasfilm's habitat. In *Cyberspace: First Steps*, pp. 273–302. MIT Press, Cambridge, MA.

[73] Moser L. E., Melliar-Smith P. M., and Narasimhan P., 2000. Consistent object replication in the Eternal system. *Theory and Practice of Object Systems*, **4**(2): 81–92.

[74] Mostefaoui A., and Raynal M., 1993. Causal multicasts in overlapping groups: Towards a low cost approach. Technical Report. UMI Order Number: BROADCAST#TR93-09, University of Bologna.

[75] Müller J., and Gorlatch S., July 2006. Rokkatan: Scaling an RTS game design to the massively multiplayer realm. *Computer Entertainment*, **4**(3): 11.

[76] Neyland D. L., 1997. Virtual Combat: A Guide to Distributed Interactive Simulation. Stackpole Books, Mechanicsburg, PA.

[77] Okanda P., and Blair G., 2003. The role of structural reflection in distributed virtual reality. In *Proceedings of the ACM Symposium on Virtual Reality Software and Technology (VRST'03)*, 1–3 October 2003, Osaka, Japan, pp. 140–149. ACM Press, New York, NY.

[78] Parkin S. E., Andras P., and Morgan G., 2006. Managing missed interactions in distributed virtual environments. In *Proceedings of the Virtual Environments 2006: 12th Eurographics Symposium on Virtual Environments*, 8–10 May 2006, Portugal, pp. 101–108. Eurographics Association, Aire-la-Ville, Switzerland.

[79] Powel E. T., Mellon L., Watson J. F., and Tarbox G. H., 1996. Joint precision strike demonstration (JPSD) simulations architecture. In *Proceedings of the 14th Workshop on Standards for the Interoperability of Distributed Simulations*, Orlando, FL, pp. 807–810.

[80] Roberts D. J., Strassner J., Worthington B. G., and Sharkey P., 1999. Influence of the supporting protocol on the latencies induced by concurrency control within a large scale multi user distributed virtual reality system. In *International Conference on Virtual Worlds and Simulation (VWSIM), SCS Western Multi-conference'99*, vol. 31, pp. 70–75.

[81] Roccetti M., Ferretti S., and Palazzi C. E., May 2008. The brave new world of multiplayer online games: Synchronization issues with smart solutions. In *Proceedings of the 2008 11th IEEE Symposium on Object-Oriented Real-Time Distributed Computing (ISORC)*, pp. 587–592. IEEE Computer Society, Washington, DC.

[82] Rosedale P., and Ondrejka C., September 2003. Enabling player-created online worlds with grid computing and streaming. Gamasutra.

[83] Saha D., Sahu S., and Shaikh A., 2003. A service platform for on-line distributed games. In *Proceedings of the Workshop on Network and Systems Support for Games (NetGames)*, May 2003.

[84] Schiper A., and Raynal M., April 1996. From group communication to transactions in distributed systems. *Communications of the ACM*, **39**(4): 84–87.

[85] Schlichting R. D., and Schneider F. B., 1983. Fail-stop processors: An approach to designing fault-tolerant computing systems. *ACM Transactions on Computer Systems*, **1**(3): 222–238.

[86] Schneider F. B., 1990. Implementing fault-tolerant services using the state machine approach: A tutorial. *ACM Computing Surveys*, **22**(4): 299–319.

[87] Screen Digest report by Piers Harding-Rolls, 2006. Western world massively multiplayer online games market: 2006 review and forecasts to 2011 (http://www.screendigest.com).

[88] Second Life News Center, Reuters 31 May 2007. Judge rules against 'one-sided' TOS in Bragg lawsuit.

[89] Shaikh A., Sahu S., Rosu M., Shea M., and Saha D., 2004. Implementation of a service platform for on-line games. In *Proceedings of the Workshop on Network and Systems Support for Games (NetGames)*.

[90] Shaikh A., Sahu S., Rosu M.-C., Shea M., and Saha D., 2006. On demand platform for online games. *IBM Systems Journal*, **45**(1): 7–19.

[91] Sharp C., IBM, 2004. Middleware to enable new business models in the online games industry, http://www-106.ibm.com/developerworks/webservices/library/ws-intgame, as viewed May 2004.

[92] Shatz S. M., 1984. Communication Mechanism for Programming Distributed Systems, pp. 21–28. IEEE Computer Society Press, Los Alamitos, CA.

[93] Singh G., Serra L., Png W., Wong A., and Ng H., 1995. BrickNet: Sharing object behaviors on the Net. In *Proceedings of the Virtual Reality Annual International Symposium (VRAIS'95)*, 11–15 March 1995, p. 19. IEEE Computer Society, Washington, DC.

[94] Singhal S. K., and Cheriton D. R., 1995. Exploiting position history for efficient remote rendering in networked virtual reality. *Presence*, **4**(2): 169–193.

[95] Singhal S., and Zyda M., 1999. Networked Virtual Environments: Design and Implementation. Addison-Wesley, Reading, MA.

[96] Star Wars Galaxies Site (http://starwarsgalaxies.station.sony.com/).

[97] Stoller S. D., 2000. Leader election in asynchronous distributed systems. *IEEE Transactions on Computers*, **49**(3): 283–284.

[98] Sun Microsystems, Project Darkstar (http://www.projectdarkstar.com/).

[99] Terdiman D., April 2006. 'World of Warcraft' battles server problems. CNET News.com (http://news.cnet.com/World-of-Warcraft-battles-server-problems/2100-1043_3-6063990.html).

[100] The BBC, 29 April 2008. GTA game 'to break sales records' (http://news.bbc.co.uk/1/hi/technology/7372736.stm).

[101] Trials of Obi-Wan Site (http://starwarsgalaxies.station.sony.com/trialsofobiwan/).

[102] Tyrer H. W., 1994. Advances in distributed and parallel processing: System paradigms and methods. Ablex Publishing, Norwood, NJ.

[103] Veríssimo P., 1996. Causal delivery protocols in real-time systems: A generic model. *Real-Time Systems*, **10**(1): 45–73.

[104] Veríssimo P., and Casimiro A., 2002. The timely computing base model and architecture. *IEEE Transactions on Computers*, **51**(8): 916–930.

[105] Vleeschauwer B., et al., 2005. Network and system support for games. In *Proceedings of the 4th ACM SIGCOMM Workshop on Network and System Support for Games (vNetGames'05)*, Hawthorne, NY, pp. 1–7.

[106] Wang X., Turner S. J., Low M. Y., and Gan B. P., 2005. Optimistic synchronization in HLA-based distributed simulation. *Simulation*, **81**(4): 279–291.

[107] World of Warcraft Site (http://www.worldofwarcraft.com).

[108] Wrath of the Lich King Site (http://www.worldofwarcraft.com/wrath/).

[109] Yavatkar R., 1992. MCP: A protocol for coordination and temporal synchronization in multimedia collaborative applications. In *Proceedings of the IEEE International Conference on Distributed Computing Systems (ICDCS)*, vol. 12, pp. 606–613.

[110] Zenke M., June/July 2008. Land of Fire: The Rise of the Tiny MMO. Game Developer Magazine, United Business Media.

[111] Zhou S., Cai W., Turner S. J., Lee B., and Wei J., August 2007. Critical causal order of events in distributed virtual environments. *ACM Transactions on Multimedia Computing, Communications, and Applications*, **3**(3): 15.

[112] Zuberi K. M., and Shin K. G., 1996. A causal message ordering scheme for distributed embedded real-time systems. In *Proceedings of the 15th Symposium on Reliable Distributed Systems (SRDS'96)*, October 1996, p. 210. IEEE Computer Society, Washington, DC.

[113] Zyda M., and Pratt D., 1991. NPSNET: A 3D visual simulator for virtual world exploration and experimentation. SID In *International Symposium Digest of Technical Papers*, vol. XXII, pp. 361–364.

[114] Active Worlds Site (http://www.activeworlds.com/).

The Future of Social Web Sites: Sharing Data and Trusted Applications with Semantics

SHEILA KINSELLA

Digital Enterprise Research Institute, National University of Ireland, Galway, Ireland

ALEXANDRE PASSANT

Digital Enterprise Research Institute, National University of Ireland, Galway, Ireland

JOHN G. BRESLIN

Digital Enterprise Research Institute, National University of Ireland, Galway, Ireland

Department of Electronic Engineering, National University of Ireland, Galway, Ireland

STEFAN DECKER

Digital Enterprise Research Institute, National University of Ireland, Galway, Ireland

AJIT JAOKAR

University College London, United Kingdom

Abstract

In recent years, there has been an explosion in the number of Social Web sites which allow the creation of knowledge through simplified user contributions via blogs, wikis, and the deployment of online social networks. As more Social Web sites form around the connections between people and their objects of interest, and as these "object-centered networks" grow bigger and more diverse, more intuitive methods are needed for representing and navigating the objects in these sites: both within and across Social Web sites. Also, to better enable user access to multiple sites, interoperability among Social Web sites is required in terms of both the expressed data (content objects, person-to-person networks, etc.) and the social applications in use (e.g., widgets) on each site. This requires representation mechanisms for data and applications on the Social Web in an interoperable and extensible way. The Semantic Web provides such representation mechanisms: it can be used to link people and objects by representing the heterogeneous ties that bind us all to each other (either directly or indirectly). In this chapter, we will describe methods that build on agreed-upon Semantic Web formats to describe people, content objects, the connections that bind them together explicitly or implicitly, and embeddable application widgets on Social Web sites, thereby enabling these sites to interoperate by appealing to some common semantics. We will also focus on how a social aspect can be added to data such as software project and widgets descriptions, so that one can combine social networking, trust, and relationship aspects with those representation models. We will also look at how developers can use the Semantic Web to augment the ways in which they create, reuse, and link content on social networking sites and Social Web sites. In particular, we will see how both data and applications can be shared on the Web, thanks to these semantics.

1. Introduction

Since it was founded, the Web has been used to facilitate communication not only between computers but also between people. Usenet mailing lists and Web forums allowed people to connect with each other and enabled communities to form, often around topics of interest. The social networks formed via these technologies were not explicitly stated, but were implicitly defined by the interactions of the people involved. Later, technologies such as IRC (Internet Relay Chat), instant messaging and blogging continued the trend of using the Internet to build communities.

Social networking sites (SNSs) such as Friendster (an early SNS previously popular in the US, now widely used in Asia), Orkut (Google's SNS), LinkedIn (an SNS for professional relationships), and MySpace (a music- and youth-oriented service)—where explicitly stated networks of friendship form a core part of the Web site—have become part of the daily lives of millions of users, and generated huge amounts of investment since they began to appear around 2002. Since then, the popularity of these sites has grown hugely and continues to do so. Boyd and Ellison [10] recently described the history of SNSs, and suggested that in the early days of SNSs, when only the SixDegrees service existed, there simply were not enough users: "While people were already flocking to the Internet, most did not have extended networks of friends who were online." A graph from Internet World Stats[1] shows the growth in the number of Internet users over time. Between 2000 (when SixDegrees shut down) and 2003 (when Friendster became the first successful SNS), the number of Internet users had doubled.

Content-sharing sites with social networking functionality such as YouTube (a video-sharing site), Flickr (for sharing images), and last.fm (a radio and music community site) have enjoyed similar popularity. The basic features of an SNS are profiles, friend's listings and commenting, often along with other features such as private messaging, discussion forums, blogging, and media uploading and sharing. Many content-sharing sites such as Flickr and YouTube also include some social networking functionality. In addition to SNSs, other forms of Social Web sites include wikis, forums, and blogs. Some of these publish content in structured formats enabling them to be aggregated together. The Social Web or "Web 2.0" has enabled community-based knowledge acquisition with efforts like the Wikipedia demonstrating the "wisdom of the crowds" in creating the world's largest online encyclopedia. Although it is difficult to define the exact boundaries of what structures or abstractions belong to the Social Web, a common property of such sites is that they facilitate collaboration and sharing between users with low technical barriers, although usually on single sites.

A limitation of current Social Web sites is that they are isolated from one another like islands in a sea. For example, different online discussions may contain complementary knowledge and topics, segmented parts of an answer that a person may be looking for, but people participating in one discussion do not have ready access to information about related discussions elsewhere. As more and more Social Web sites, communities, and services come online, the lack of interoperation among them becomes obvious: a set of single data silos or "stovepipes" has been created, that is, there are many sites, communities, and services that cannot interoperate with each other, where synergies are expensive to exploit, and where reuse and interlinking of data is difficult and cumbersome. The main reason for this lack of interoperation is that for the most part in the Social Web, there are still no common standards for knowledge and information exchange and interoperation available. RSS (Really Simple Syndication), a format for publishing recently updated Web content such as blog entries, could be a first solution for interoperability among Social Web sites, but it has various limitations that make it difficult to be used efficiently in such a context, as we will see later.

However, the Semantic Web effort aims to provide the tools that are necessary to define extensible and flexible standards for information exchange and interoperability. The Scientific American article from Berners-Lee et al. [4] defined the Semantic

---

[1] http://www.internetworldstats.com/emarketing.htm.

Web as "an extension of the current Web in which information is given well-defined meaning, better enabling computers and people to work in cooperation." The last couple of years have seen large efforts going into the definition of the foundational standards supporting data interchange and interoperation, and currently a well-defined Semantic Web technology stack exists, enabling the creation of defining metadata and associated vocabularies. The Semantic Web effort is in an ideal position to make Social Web sites interoperable. The application of the Semantic Web to the Social Web can lead to a "Social Semantic Web" (Fig. 1), creating a network of interlinked and semantically rich knowledge. This vision of the Web will consist of interlinked documents, data, and even applications created by the end users themselves as the result of various social interactions, and it is modeled using machine-readable formats, so that it can be used for purposes that the current state of the Social Web cannot achieve without difficulty.

A semantic data "food chain" (see Fig. 2), that is, producers, collectors, and consumers of semantic data from social networks and Social Web sites, can lead to something greater than the sum of its parts: a social Semantic Web where the islands of the Social Web can be interconnected with semantic technologies, and Semantic Web applications are enhanced with the wealth of knowledge inherent in user-generated content.

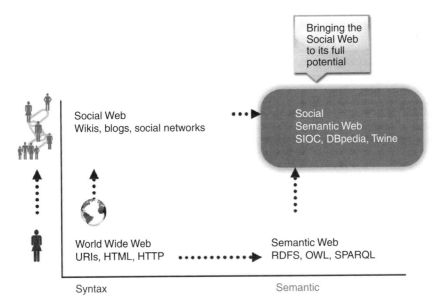

Fig. 1. The Social Semantic Web.

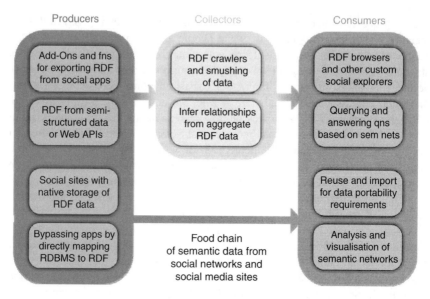

Fig. 2. A food chain for semantic data on the Social Web.

Applying semantic technologies to Social Web sites can greatly enhance the value and functionality of these sites. The information within these sites is forming vast and diverse networks which can benefit from Semantic Web technologies for representation and navigation. Additionally, to easily enable navigation and data portability across sites, mechanisms are required to represent data in an interoperable and extensible way. These are termed semantic data producers.

An intermediary step which may or may not be required is for the collection of semantic data. In very large sites, this may not be an issue as the information in the site may be sufficiently linked internally to warrant direct consumption after production, but in general, may users make small contributions across a range of services which can benefit from an aggregate view through some collection service. Collection services can include aggregation and consolidation systems, semantic search engines, or data lookup indexes.

The final step involves consumers of semantic data. Social networking technologies enable people to articulate their social network via friend connections. A social network can be viewed as a graph where the nodes represent individuals and the edges represent relations. Methods from graph theory can be used to study these networks, and we will describe how social network analysis (SNA) can consume semantic data from the food chain.

Also, representing social data in RDF (Resource Description Framework), a language for describing Web resources in a structured way, enables us to perform queries on a network to locate information relating to a person or people. Interlinking social data from multiple sources may give an enhanced view of information in distributed communities, and we will describe applications to consume this interlinked data.

In this chapter, we will begin by describing various social networking sites and Social Web sites, along with some of their limitations and initial approaches to leverage semantics in social networks, blogs, wikis, tagging, and software descriptions. We will discuss the representation methods that can be used by semantic producers to represent data (user profiles, feeds, content) and applications (widgets) for porting and sharing amongst users and sites. We will then describe the collection stage in a "semantic data food chain," giving examples of queries that can be used to consolidate aggregates of data from Social Web sites. We will also discuss how trust mechanisms in consuming applications can be leveraged via the distributed social graph, so that users can decide who to accept any new data or applications from. Finally, we will give our conclusions and ideas for future work.

2. Social Web Sites and Approaches to Add Semantics

2.1 Social Networks

The "friend-of-a-friend effect" often occurs when someone tells someone something and they then tell you—linked to the theory that anybody is connected to everybody else (on average) by no more than six degrees of separation. This number of six degrees came from a sociologist called Stanley Milgram who conducted an experiment in the late 1960s. Random people from Nebraska and Kansas were told to send a letter (via intermediaries) to a stock broker in Boston. However, they could only give the letter to someone that they knew on a first-name basis. Amongst the letters that found their target (around 20%), the average number of links was around 5.5 (rounded up to 6). While this experiment does not prove the theory of six degrees of separation, it does demonstrate that most individuals are not separated by many links. Some other related ideas include the Erdös number (the number of links required to connect scholars to mathematician Paul Erdös, a prolific writer who coauthored over 1500 papers with more than 500 authors), and the Kevin Bacon game (the goal is to connect any actor to Kevin Bacon, by linking actors who have acted in the same movie).

It is often found that even though one route is followed to get in contact with a particular person, after talking to them there is another obvious connection that was not previously known about. This is part of the small-world network theory [45], which says that most nodes in a network exhibiting small-world characteristics (such as a social network) can be reached from every other node by a small number of hops or steps.

There has been a proliferation of SNSs which Boyd and Ellison [10] define as a category of Web sites consisting of user profiles, which other users can comment on, and a traversable social network originating from publicly articulated lists of friends. The idea behind such services is to make people's real-world relationships explicitly defined online—whether they be close friends, business colleagues, or just people with common interests. Most SNSs allow one to surf from a list of friends to find friends-of-friends, or friends-of-friends-of-friends for various purposes. While the majority of these sites are for purely social reasons, others have additional purposes such as LinkedIn which is targeted toward professionals.

Before 2002, most people networked using online services such as OneList (a mailing list service), ICQ (an instant messaging program), or eVite (a site for sending invitations). The first big SNS in 2002 was Friendster; in 2003, LinkedIn and MySpace appeared; then in 2004, Orkut and Facebook (by a college student for college students) were founded; these were followed by Bebo (targeting both high school and college students) in 2005. Social networking services usually offer the same basic functionalities: network of friends listings (showing a person's "inner circle"), person surfing, private messaging, discussion forums or communities, events management, blogging, commenting (sometimes as endorsements on people's profiles), and media uploading. In general, these sites do not usually work together and therefore require you to re-enter your profile and redefine your connections when you register for each new site.

Some motivations for SNS usage include building friendships and relationships, arranging offline meetings, curiosity about others, arranging business opportunities, or job hunting. People may want to meet with local professionals, create a network for parents, network for social (dating) purposes, get in touch with a venture capitalist, or find out if they can link to any famous people via their friends.

In addition to relationship management, social networks are sometimes used for viral marketing [34], although recent results indicate that this might be less effective than often assumed. For example, Knorr-Cetina [31] reports that "the additional purchases that resulted from recommendations are just a drop in the bucket of sales" and that "marketers should take heed that even if viral marketing works initially, providing excessive incentives for customers to recommend products could backfire by weakening the credibility of the very same links they are trying to take advantage of."

A key feature of these sites is community-contributed content that may be tagged and can be commented on by others. That content can be virtually anything: blog entries, board posts, videos, audio, images, wiki pages, user profiles, bookmarks, events, etc. Already, sites are being proposed where live multiplayer video games will appear in browser-embedded windows just as YouTube does for videos, with running commentaries going on about the games in parallel. Tagging is common to many social networking Web sites—a tag is a keyword that acts like a subject or category for the associated content. Folksonomies (a portmanteau of the words "folks" and "taxonomies," meaning collaboratively generated, open-ended labeling systems) emerge from the use of tagging on a given platform and enable users of these sites to categorize content using the tags system, and to thereby visualize popular tag usages via "tag clouds" (visual depictions of the tags used on a particular Web site, similar to a weighted list in visual design, that provides an overview of the different categories and topics used within a community).

Even in a small-sized SNS, there can be a lot of links available for analysis, and these data are usually meaningless when viewed as a whole, so one usually needs to apply some SNA techniques.[2] Apart from comprehensive textbooks in this area [44], there are many academic tools for examining social networks and performing common SNA routines. For example, the tool Pajek[3][3] can be used to drill down into various social networks. A common method is to reduce the amount of relevant social network data by clustering. One can choose to cluster people by common friends, by shared interests, by geographic location, by tags, etc.

In SNA, people are modeled as nodes or "actors." Relationships (such as acquaintanceship, coauthorship, friendship, etc.) between actors are represented by lines or edges. This model allows analysis using existing tools from mathematical graph theory and mapping, with target domains such as movie actors, scientists and mathematicians (as already mentioned), sexual interaction, phone call patterns, or terrorist activity. There are some useful tools for visualizing these models, such as Vizster[4] by Heer and Boyd [26], based on the Prefuse[5] open-source toolkit.

2.2 Leveraging Semantics in "Object-Centered" Social Networks

Social networks exist all around us—at workplaces as well as within families and social groups. They are designed to help us work together over common activities or interests, but anecdotal evidence suggests that many SNSs lack such common

---

[2] http://lrs.ed.uiuc.edu/tse-portal/analysis/social-network-analysis/.
[3] http://vlado.fmf.uni-lj.si/pub/networks/pajek/.
[4] http://jheer.org/vizster/.
[5] http://prefuse.org/.

objectives [27]. Instead, users often connect to others for no other reason than to boost the number of friends they have in their profiles.[6] Many more browse other users' profiles simply for curiosity's sake. These explicitly established connections become increasingly meaningless because they are not backed up by common objects or activities.

The act of connecting sometimes becomes a site's primary (only) activity. In fact, some sites act simply as enhanced address books: although potentially useful for locating or contacting someone, they provide little attraction for repeat visits. This is a flaw with the current theory. As Jyri Engeström, cofounder of the Jaiku.com microblogging site (microblogging is a lightweight form of blogging that consists of short message updates), put it, "social network theory is good at representing links between people, but it doesn't explain what connects those particular people and not others." Indeed, many are finding that SNSs are becoming increasingly boring and meaningless.

Another problem is that the various SNSs do not usually work together. You thus have to re-enter your profile and redefine your connections from scratch when you register for each new site. Some of the most popular SNSs probably would not exist without this sort of "walled garden" approach, but some flexibility would be useful. Users often have many identities on different social networks. Reusable profiles would let them import existing identities and connections (from their own home page or another site they are registered on), thereby forming a single global identity with different views (using systems such as OpenID,[7] e.g., an open standard that enables users to log in to many Web sites using a single sign-on).

Engeström has theorized[8] that the longevity of Social Web sites is proportional to the "object-centered sociality" occurring in these networks, that is, the degree to which people are connecting via items of interest related to their jobs, workplaces, favorite hobbies, etc. Similarly, Jordan and colleagues [28] advocate *augmented social networks*, in which citizens form relationships and self-organize into communities around shared interests.

On the Web, social connections are formed through the actions of people—via the content they create together, comment on, link to, or for which they use similar annotations. Adding annotations to items in social networks (using topic tags, geographical pinpointing, etc.) is particularly useful for browsing and locating interesting items and people with similar interests. Content items such as blog entries, videos, and bookmarks serve as the lodestones for social networks, drawing

---

[6] http://www.russellbeattie.com/notebook/1008411.html.

[7] http://www.openid.net/.

[8] http://www.zengestrom.com/blog/2005/04/why_some_social.html.

people back to check for new items and for updates from others in their network. For many of the Social Web sites, success has come from enabling communities formed around common interests, where the users are active participants who as well as consuming information also provide content and metadata. In this way, it is probable that people's SNS methods will continue to move closer toward simulating their real-life social interaction, so that people will meet others via something they have in common, not by randomly approaching each other—eventually leading toward more realistic interaction methods with friends.

Virtual worlds such as Second Life have already begun to provide a user experience which is more faithful to reality. Users interact via avatars in a three-dimensional environment where they can move between different areas and social-ize with other residents. An important aspect of Second Life is that the world is largely user-created. Residents can buy land, construct houses, and create objects. It is also possible to trade with other users, as well as buy or sell using the world's internal currency, the Linden Dollar. Second Life's world encourages residents to meet and stay in touch with other users with similar interests via themed areas and events—a prime example of object-centered sociality.

Figure 3 illustrates an object-centered social network for three people. Bob and Carol are connected through bookmarked Web sites that both have annotated, as well as through events they are both attending. Alice and Bob have matching tags on media items, and they subscribe to the same blogs.

Although object-centered social networks can fix one problem (that of sites becoming boring), the remaining challenge is how to achieve interoperability among SNSs and, ultimately, content-creation facilities on the Web. As more social networks form around connections between people and their objects of interest, and as these object-centered social networks grow bigger and more diverse, more intuitive methods are needed for representing and navigating the information in these networks—within and across SNSs. Also, to better enable navigation across sites, interoperability among SNSs is required in terms of both the content objects and the person-to-person networks expressed on each site. That requires representa-tion mechanisms to interconnect people and objects on the Web in an interoperable, extensible way [11].

Semantic Web representation mechanisms are ideally suited to describing people and the objects that link them together in such object-centered networks, by record-ing and representing the heterogeneous ties that bind each to the other. By using agreed-upon Semantic Web formats to describe people, content objects, and the connections that bind them together, social networks can also interoperate by appeal-ing to common semantics. Developers are already using Semantic Web technologies to augment the ways in which they create, reuse, and link content on social networking and Social Web sites [15]. These efforts include the Friend-of-a-Friend

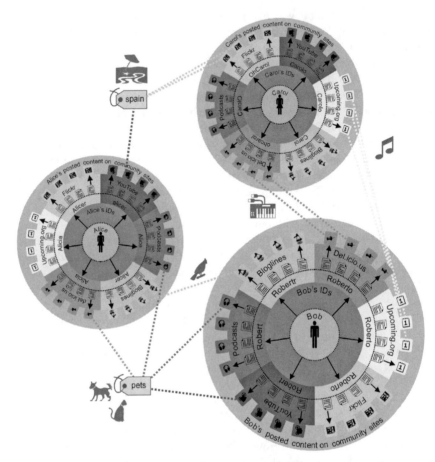

Fig. 3. Users form object-centered social networks (using their possibly multiple online accounts) around the content items they act on via social Web sites.

(FOAF) project[9] for describing people and relationships, the Nepomuk social semantic desktop[10] which is a framework for extending the desktop to a collaborative environment for information management and sharing, and the Semantically Interlinked Online Communities (SIOC) initiative[11] for representing online

---

[9] http://www.foaf-project.org/.
[10] http://nepomuk.semanticdesktop.org/.
[11] http://sioc-project.org/.

discussions. Some SNSs, such as Facebook, are also starting to provide query interfaces to their data, which others can reuse and link to via the Semantic Web.[12]

The Semantic Web is a useful platform for linking and for performing operations on diverse person—and object-related data gathered from heterogeneous SNSs. In the other direction, object-centered networks can serve as rich data sources for Semantic Web applications. This linked data can provide an enhanced view of individual or community activity in localized or distributed object-centered social networks. In fact, since all these data are semantically interlinked using well-given semantics (e.g., using the FOAF and SIOC ontologies), in theory it makes no difference whether the content is distributed or localized. All of these data can be considered as a unique interlinked machine-understandable graph layer (with nodes as users and related data and arcs as relationships) over the existing Web of documents and hyperlinks, that is, a Giant Global Graph as Tim Berners-Lee recently coined.[13] Moreover, such interlinked data allow advanced querying capabilities, for example, "show me all the content that Alice has acted on in the past three months."

As Tim Berners-Lee said in a 2005 podcast,[14] Semantic Web technologies can support online communities even as "online communities. . .support Semantic Web data by being the sources of people voluntarily connecting things together." For example, SNS users are already creating extensive vocabularies and annotations through folksonomies [38]. Because a consensus of community users is defining the meaning, these terms are serving as the objects around which those users form more tightly connected social networks.

2.3 Blogs

A blog, or Weblog, is a user-created Web site consisting of journal style entries displayed in reverse chronological order. Entries may contain text, links to other Web sites, and images or other media. Often, there is a facility for readers to leave comments on individual entries, which make blogs an interactive medium. Blogs may be written by individuals, or by groups of contributors. A blog may function as a personal journal, or it may provide news or opinions on a particular subject.

The growth and take-up of blogs over the past 5 years has been impressive, with a doubling in the size of the "blogosphere" every 6 or so months (according to statistics from Technorati[15]). Over 100,000 blogs are created everyday, working out at about

---

[12] http://www.openlinksw.com/blog/~kidehen/?id=1237.
[13] http://dig.csail.mit.edu/breadcrumbs/node/215.
[14] http://esw.w3.org/topic/IswcPodcast.
[15] http://technorati.com/weblog/2007/04/328.html.

one a second. Nearly, 1.5 million blog posts are being made each day, with over half of bloggers still contributing to their sites 3 months after the blog's creation.

RSS feeds are also a useful way of accessing information from your favorite blogs, but they are usually limited to the last 15 or 20 entries, and do not provide much information on exactly who wrote or commented on a particular post, or what the post is talking about. Some approaches like SIOC (more later) aim to enhance the semantic metadata provided about blogs, forums, and posts, but there is also a need for more information about what exactly a person is writing about. Blog entries often refer to resources on the Web and these resources will usually have a context in which they are being used could be described. For example, a post which critiques a particular resource could incorporate a rating, or a post announcing an event could include start and end times.

When searching for particular information in or across blogs, it is often not that easy to get it because of "splogs" (spam blogs) and also because of the fact that the virtue of blogs so far has been their simplicity—apart from the subject field, everything and anything is stored in one big text field for content. Keyword searches may give some relevant results, but useful questions such as "find me all the Chinese restaurants that bloggers reviewed in Dublin with a rating of at least 5 out of 10" cannot be posed, and you cannot easily drag-and-drop events or people or anything (apart from Uniform Resource Locators—URLs) mentioned in blog posts into your own applications.

2.4   Adding Semantics to Blogs

There have been some approaches to tackle the issue of adding more information to blog posts, so that queries can be made and the things that people talk about can be reused in other posts or applications (because not everyone is being served well by the lowest common denominator that we currently have in blogs). One approach is called "structured blogging,"[16] and the other is "semantic blogging": both approaches can also be combined together.

Structured blogging is an open-source community effort that has created tools to provide microcontent from popular blogging platforms such as WordPress and Movable Type. The term microcontent indicates a unit of data and associated metadata communicating one main idea and accessible at a URI. Sources of micro-content include microformats,[17] which enable semantic markup to be embedded directly within XHTML. Microformats therefore provide a simple method of

---

[16] http://structuredblogging.org/.
[17] http://microformats.org/.

expressing content in a machine-readable way, facilitating reuse and aggregation. An example of a microformat is hReview, which allows for the structured description of reviews within Web pages. Another approach to annotating XHTML documents is RDFa (Resource Description Framework in attributes)[18] which makes it possible to embed semantics in XHTML attributes in such a way that enables the data to be mapped to RDF.

Although the original effort has tapered off, structured blogging is continuing through services like LouderVoice,[19] a review site which integrates reviews written on blogs and other Web sites. In structured blogging, packages of structured data are becoming post components. Sometimes (not all of the time) a person will have a need for more structure in their posts—if they know a subject deeply, or if their observations or analyses recur in a similar manner throughout their blog—then they may best be served by filling in a form (which has its own metadata and model) during the post creation process. For example, someone may be writing a review of a film they went to see, or reporting on a sports game they attended, or creating a guide to tourist attractions they saw on their travels. Not only do people get to express themselves more clearly, but blogs can start to interoperate with enterprise applications through the microcontent that is being created in the background.

Take the scenario where someone (or a group of people) is reviewing some soccer games that they watched. Their after-game soccer reports will typically include information on which teams played, where the game was held and when, who were the officials, what were the significant game events (who scored, when and how, or who received penalties and why, etc.)—it would be easier for these blog posters if they could use a tool that would understand this structure, presenting an editing form with the relevant fields, and automatically create both HTML and RSS with this structure embedded in it. Then, others reading these posts could choose to reuse this structure in their own posts, and their blog reading/writing application could make this structure available when the blogger is ready to write. As well as this, reader applications could begin to answer questions based on the form fields available—"show me all the matches from South Africa with more than two goals scored," etc.

At the moment, structured blogging tools provide a fixed set of forms that bloggers can fill in for things like reviews, events, audio, video, and people—but there is no reason that people could not create custom structures, and news aggregators or readers could autodiscover an unknown structure, notify a user that a new structure is available, and learn the structure for reuse in the user's future posts.

---

[18] http://www.w3.org/TR/xhtml-rdfa-primer/.
[19] http://www.loudervoice.com/.

Semantic Web technologies can also be used to enhance any available post structures in a machine-readable way for more linkage and reuse. Blog posts are usually only tagged on the blog itself by the post creator, using free-text keywords such as "scotland," "movies," etc. (or can be tagged by others using social book-marking services like del.icio.us or personal aggregators like Gregarius). Technorati, the blog search engine, aims to use these keywords to build a "tagged Web." Both tags and hierarchical categorizations of blog posts can be further enriched using the SKOS (Simple Knowledge Organization Systems) framework for repre-senting vocabularies. However, there is often much more to say about a blog post than simply what category it belongs in.

This is where semantic blogging comes in. Traditional blogging is aimed at what can be called the "eyeball Web"—that is, text, images, or video content that is targeted mainly at people. Semantic blogging aims to enrich traditional blogging with metadata about the structure (what relates to what and how) and the content (what is this post about—a person, event, book, etc.). Already RSS and Atom (a format for syndicating Web content) are used to describe blog entries in a machine-readable way and enable them to be aggregated together. However by augmenting these data with additional structural and content-related metadata, new ways of querying and navigating blog data become possible.

In structured blogging, microcontent such as microformats or RDFa is positioned inline in the (X)HTML (and subsequent syndication feeds) and can be rendered via CSS. Structured blogging and semantic blogging do not compete, but rather offer metadata in slightly different ways (using microcontent and RDF, respectively). There are already mechanisms such as GRDDL (Gleaning Resource Descriptions from Dialects of Languages)[20] which can be used to move from one to the other and allows one to provide RDF data from embedded RDFa or microformats. Extracted RDF data can then be reused as would any native RDF data, and so it may be processed using common Semantic Web tools and services.

The question remains as to why one would choose to enhance their blogs and posts with semantics. Current blogging offers poor query possibilities (except for searching by keyword or seeing all posts labeled with a particular tag). There is little or no reuse of data offered (apart from copying URLs or text from posts). Some linking of posts is possible via direct HTML links or trackbacks, but again, nothing can be said about the nature of those links (are you agreeing with someone, linking to an interesting post, or are you quoting someone whose blog post is directly in contradiction with your own opinions?). Semantic blogging aims to tackle some of these issues, by facilitating better (i.e., more precise) querying when compared with

---

[20] http://www.w3.org/TR/grddl/.

keyword matching, by providing more reuse possibilities, and by creating "richer" links between blog posts.

It is not simply a matter of adding semantics for the sake of creating extra metadata, but rather a case of being able to reuse what data a person already has in their desktop or Web space and making the resulting metadata available to others. People are already (sometimes unknowingly) collecting and creating large amounts of structured data on their computers, but these data are often tied into specific applications and locked within a user's desktop (e.g., contacts in a person's address book, events in a calendaring application, author and title information in documents, audio metadata in MP3 files). Semantic blogging can be used to "lift" or release these data onto the Web, as in the semiBlog[21] application (now called Shift) which allows users to reuse metadata from Apple Mac desktops in blog posts. For example, Aidan can write a blog post which he annotates using metadata about events and people from his desktop calendaring and address book applications. He publishes this post onto the Web, and John, reading this post, can reuse the embedded metadata in his own desktop applications. As well as semiBlog, other semantic blogging systems have been developed by HP,[22] the National Institute of Informatics, Japan[23] and MIT.[24]

Also, conversations often span multiple blog sites in blog posts and their comments, and bloggers may respond to the entries of other users in their own blogs. The use of semantic technologies can also enable the tracking of these distributed conversations. Links between units of conversation could even be enhanced to include sentiment information, for example, who agrees or disagrees with the initial opinion.

2.5 Wikis

A wiki is a Web site which allows users to edit content through the same interface they use to browse it, usually a Web browser, while some desktop-based wikis also exist. This facilitates collaborative authoring in a community, especially since editing a wiki does not require advanced technical skills. A wiki consists of a set of Web pages which can be connected together by links. Users can create new pages, and change existing ones, even those created by other members. One of the most well-known wikis is the Wikipedia free online encyclopedia. Wikis are also being used for free dictionaries, book repositories, event organization, and software

---

[21] http://semiblog.semanticweb.org/.
[22] http://www.hpl.hp.com/personal/Steve_Cayzer/semblog.htm.
[23] http://www.semblog.org/.
[24] http://theory.csail.mit.edu/~dquan/iswc2004-blog.ppt.

development. They have become increasingly used in enterprise environments for collaborative purposes: research projects, papers and proposals, coordinating meetings, etc. SocialText[25] produced the first commercial open-source wiki solution, and many companies now use wikis as one of their main intranet collaboration tools. However, wikis may break some existing hierarchical barriers in organizations (due to a lack of workflow mechanisms, open editing by anyone with access, etc.) which means that new approaches toward information sharing must be taken into account when implementing wiki solutions. This is why some argue that Enterprise 2.0 [36], that is, the use of social software in or within companies, raises more philosophical issues than technical ones.

There are hundreds of wiki software systems now available, ranging from MediaWiki, the software used on the Wikimedia family of sites, and PurpleWiki, where fine-grained elements on a wiki page are referenced by purple numbers, to Odd-Muse, a single Perl script wiki install, and WikidPad, a desktop-based wiki for managing personal information. Many are open source, free, and will often run on multiple operating systems. The differences between wikis are usually quite small but can include the development language used (Java, PHP, Python, Perl, Ruby, etc.), the database required (MySQL, flat files, etc.), whether attachment file uploading is allowed or not, spam prevention mechanisms, page access controls, RSS feeds, etc.

The Wikipedia project consists of over 250 different wikis, corresponding to a variety of languages. The English-language one is currently the biggest, with over 2 million pages, but there are wikis in languages ranging from Gaelic to Chinese. A typical wiki page will have two buttons of interest: "Edit" and "History." Normally, anyone can edit an existing wiki article, and if the article does not exist on a particular topic, anyone can create it. If someone messes up an article (either deliberately or erroneously), there is a revision history so that the contents can be reverted or fixed by the community. Thus, while there is no predefined hierarchy in most wikis, content is autoregulated, thanks to an emergent consensus within the community, ideally in a democratic way (for instance, most wikis include discussions pages where people can discuss sensible topics). There is a certain amount of ego-related motivation in contributing to a wiki—people like to show that they know things, to fix mistakes, and fill in gaps in underdeveloped articles (stubs), and to have a permanent record of what they have contributed via their registered account. By providing a template structure to input facts about certain things (towns, people, etc.), wikis also facilitate this user drive to populate wikis with information.

---

[25] http://www.socialtext.com/.

2.6   Adding Semantics to Wikis

Typical wikis usually enable the description of resources in natural language. By additionally allowing the expression of knowledge in a structured way, wikis can provide advantages in querying, managing, and reusing information. Wikis such as the Wikipedia have contained structured metadata in the form of templates for some time now (to provide a consistent look to the content placed within article texts), but there is still a growing need for more structure in wikis. Templates can also be used to provide a structure for entering data, so that it is easy to extract metadata about the topic of an article (e.g., from a template field called "population" in an article about London). Semantic wikis bring this to the next level by allowing users to create semantic annotations anywhere within a wiki article text for the purposes of structured access and finer-grained searches, inline querying, and external information reuse. Generally, those annotations are designed to create instances and properties of domain ontologies (either explicit ontologies or ontologies that will emerge from the usage of the wiki itself), whereas other wikis use semantic annotations to provide advanced metadata regarding wiki pages. There are already about 20 semantic wikis in existence, and one of the largest ones is Semantic MediaWiki, based on the popular MediaWiki system. Semantic MediaWiki allows for the expression of semantic data describing the connection from one page to another, and attributes or data relating to a particular page.

Let us take an example of providing structured access to information in wikis. There is a Wikipedia page about JK Rowling that has a link to "Harry Potter and the Deathly Hallows" (and to other books that she has written), to Edinburgh because she lives there, and to Scholastic Press, her publisher. In a traditional wiki, you cannot perform fine-grained searches on the Wikipedia data set such as "show me all the books written by JK Rowling," or "show me all authors that live in the UK," or "what authors are signed to Scholastic," because the type of links (i.e., the relationship type) between wiki pages are not defined. In Semantic MediaWiki, you can do this by linking with [[author of::Harry Potter and the Deathly Hallows]] rather than just the name of the novel. There may also be some attribute such as [[birthdate:=1965-07-31]] which is defined in the JK Rowling article. Such attributes could be used for answering questions like "show me authors over the age of 40" or for sorting articles, since this wiki syntax is translated into RDF annotations when saving the wiki page. Moreover, page categories are used to model the related class for the created instance. Indeed, in this tool, as in most semantic wikis that aim to model ontology instances, not only do the annotations make the link types between pages explicit, but they also make explicit the relationships between the concepts referred to in these wiki pages, thus bridging the gap from documents plus hyperlinks to concepts plus relationships. For instance, in the previous example, the annotation will not model that "the page about JK Rowling is author of the page about Harry Potter and the Deathly Hallows" but rather that "the person JK Rowling is author of the novel Harry Potter and the Deathly Hallows."

Since Semantic MediaWiki is completely open in terms of the wiki syntax for annotating content, extracted data may be subject to heterogeneity problems. For instance, some users will use [[author of:xxx]] while others will prefer [[has written: xxx]], leading to problems when querying data. Other wikis such as OntoWiki, IkeWiki, or UfoWiki assist the user when modeling semantic annotations, to avoid those heterogeneity issues and provide data that are based on predefined ontologies.

Some semantic wikis also provide what is called inline querying. A question such as "?page dc:creator EyalOren" (or find me all pages where the creator is Eyal Oren) is processed as a query when the page is viewed and the results are shown in the wiki page itself. Also, when defining some relationships and attributes for a particular article (e.g., "foaf:gender Male"), other articles with matching properties can be displayed along with the article. Moreover, some wikis feature reasoning capabilities, for example, retrieving all instances of foaf:Person when querying for a list of all foaf:Agent(s) since the first class subsumes the second one in the FOAF ontology.

Finally, just as in the semantic blogging scenario, wikis can enable the Web to be used as a clipboard, by allowing readers to drag structured information from wiki pages into other applications (e.g., geographic data about locations on a wiki page could be used to annotate information on an event or a person in your calendar application or address book software, respectively).

2.7   Tags, Tagging, and Folksonomies

Apart from providing a means to define and manage social networks, one of the most important features of Social Web sites is the ability to upload and share content with others, either with anyone subscribed to (or just browsing) the Web site or else within a restricted community. Various media files can be shared, such as pictures, videos, bookmarks, slides, etc. To make this content more easily discoverable, users can add free-text keywords, or tags, to any content that they upload. For example, this chapter could be tagged with "Semantic Web," "social networks," and "SIOC" on a scientific bibliography management system such as bibsonomy.org. While the same content can be tagged by various users on the same system, anyone can use their own tags. Yet, most services suggest existing tags for a given item when someone begins tagging it.

The main advantage of tagging for end users is that one does not have to learn a predefined vocabulary scheme (such as a hierarchy or taxonomy) and one can use the keywords that fit exactly with his or her needs. Web sites that support tagging benefit from the "wisdom of the crowds" effect. Tags evolve quickly according to the needs of the users, and these tags, combined with the tagging actions and the frequency with which they are used, lead to the emergence of a folksonomy, that is, a user-driven, open and evolving classification scheme. Moreover, tags can be used for various purposes, and Golder and Huberman [24] have identified seven different functions that tags can play for end users, from topic definition to opinion forming and even self-reference.

In spite of its advantages when annotating content, tagging leads to various issues in information retrieval. Since a single tag can refer to various concepts, it can lead to ambiguity. For instance, "paris" can refer to a city in France, a city in the USA or even a person. Moreover, various tags can be used to define the same idea, so that a user must run various queries to get the content related to a given concept. Such heterogeneity is mainly caused by the multilingual nature of tags (e.g., "Semantic Web" and "Web semantique") but also due to the fact people will use acronyms or shortened versions ("sw" and "semweb"), as well as linguistic and morphosyntactic variations (synonyms, plurals, case, etc.). Finally, since a folksonomy is essentially a flat organization of tags, the lack of relationships between tags makes it difficult to suggest related content, especially when there is a gap of expertise between people tagging content and the ones looking for it. Someone searching for the tag "Semantic Web" will not easily be able to find content tagged with "RDFa," even though there is a clear relationship between both.

2.8   Adding Semantics to Tags and Related Objects

Numerous works related to the links between tags, the tagging process, folksonomies, and the Semantic Web have been published during the last couple of years. We can divide these into two general approaches: the ones aiming to define, mine, or automatically link to ontologies from existing folksonomies, and works based on defining Semantic Web models for tags and related objects (e.g., tagging, tag clouds, etc.). Again, the border between both is not very precise and some approaches combine both.

The first set of approaches is based on the idea that emergent semantics naturally appears through the use of tags, relying on various methods to achieve this goal. For example, Specia and Motta [43] combine automatic tag filtering, clustering, and mapping with ontologies already available on the Web to extract ontologies from existing folksonomies in a completely automated approach. Another approach involving a social aspect is the one defined by Mika [38], which uses SNA to extract ontologies from the Flickr folksonomy, based on the way that the community shares and uses tags.

Regarding the second approach, various models have been proposed to define Semantic Web vocabularies for tagging. Representing tags using Semantic Web technologies offer various advantages: providing a uniform, machine-readable and extendable way to represent tags as well as other concepts such as tagging actions, tag clouds, the relationships between tags and the meanings that they carry. While tag-based search is the only way to retrieve tagged content at the moment (and leads to the aforementioned problems), these new models allow advanced querying capabilities such as "retrieve all the content tagged with something relevant to the Semantic Web field" or "give me all the tags used by Bob on Flickr and Alice on del.icio.us." Moreover, having tags and tagged content published in RDF allows one to easily link to it from other Semantic Web data, and to reuse it across applications.

The Tag Ontology[26] provides an initial model to represent tags and tagging actions in RDF, based on the ideas of Gruber [25] and on a common mathematical model of tagging that defines it as a tripartite relationship involving a "Tag," a "User," and a tagged "Resource." This ontology defines the Tag class by subclassing skos:Concept, which means that each tag has a given URI (Uniform Resource Identifier). This offers the ability to interlink tags together with semantic relationships, as this model permits. SCOT (Social Semantic Cloud of Tags) [29] aims to represent tag clouds, and so defines a model to represent the use and co-occurrence of tags on a given social platform, allowing one to move his or her tags from oneservice to another and to share tags with others. Finally, MOAT (Meaning of a Tag) [40] aims to represent the meaning of tags using URIs of existing domain ontology instances from existing public knowledge bases (such as Geonames, a geographical database, or DBpedia, a data set of structured information extracted from Wikipedia), thus creating a bridge between folksonomies and existing ontologies or knowledge bases. It also provides a framework using this model, the goal of which is to let people easily bridge the gap between simple free-text tagging and semantic indexing.

Some tools already used some of these models to provide advanced and more precise querying tag-based capabilities to their users, including gnizr (a tag-sharing application), SweetWiki (a wiki engine), int.ere.st (a tag-sharing service based on SCOT), and LODr[27] (a tag aggregation and interlinking application based on MOAT).

2.9   Software Project Descriptions

Software descriptions are also required for the embeddable applications or "widgets" that are now proliferating many of the big social networking Web sites. Third-party developers are now creating their own applications that can be added

---

[26] http://www.holygoat.co.uk/projects/tags/.
[27] http://lodr.info.

by users to their own social networking profiles. For example, a user may choose to add a widget to their profile showing a map of places they have visited in the world, or enabling some other functionality which may not be natively offered by the Social Web site. Soon after Facebook added a developer's interface to their site, 4000 third-party applications had been made available and 70,000 developers had signed up to the developer community. Facebook's active user count also jumped 70% in the 4 months after this contributable application layer was added. In parallel, Google has initiated the OpenSocial project,[28] which allows developers to create application widgets that can be deployed across a range of OpenSocial-enabled social networking sites. However, there is an important question in relation to these widgets: how does one trust the source of an application? For example, does a user have to browse the complete source code (as a developer would), or can they just rely on some social networking aspect, that is, trusting applications from people they know?

Before widgets, many applications were already produced on the Web, mainly from open-source developer communities. In these communities, the social aspects of software project hosting and directory services are present but may not be immediately obvious. Web sites like SourceForge,[29] Savannah,[30] or BerliOS Developer[31] offer tools for developers to manage their projects (source code repositories, versioning, FTP space, etc.); Freshmeat[32] or Ohloh[33] allow them to reference and give visibility to their projects; and Slashdot[34] provides the latest "hot" news from the developer community and information on some projects. Yet, as with many Social Web sites, one problem is that developers must subscribe to each hosting Web site independently, filling in their personal details on each one, and entering their project description again and again on each directory-like Web site.

Beyond project hosting, these Web sites generally offer various social interaction tools for project tracking (such as blogs, wikis, and mailing lists) which can provide a social aspect to a software project. Thus, while the software development itself does not necessary involve a social aspect (for instance, source code write access might be delegated to only a restricted of users), users can be part of the process, for instance by reporting bugs and participating on the mailing list, answering blog posts, or editing a project wiki page to suggest new functionalities. Software development can thus benefit from the participation of online communities in the

---

[28] http://opensocial.org/.
[29] http://sourceforge.net/.
[30] http://savannah.gnu.org/.
[31] http://developer.berlios.de/.
[32] http://freshmeat.net/.
[33] http://ohloh.net/.
[34] http://slashdot.net/.

development process, even if users are not directly "in touch" with the source code itself. Moreover, if those tools are not provided by the project hosting service itself, developers can easily set them up using freely available tools on the Web.

2.10   Adding Semantics to Software Project Descriptions

As for blogs and wikis, a project description that describes a software application usually depends on the Web site it has been created on. There is thus a need for a common metadata modeling scheme for describing applications, in order to provide a unified way to represent it wherever it comes from.

DOAP[35] (Description of a Project) is an RDF vocabulary that aims to achieve this goal. It defines a "Project" class with various properties, such as its maintainers, its license, subversion access, etc. Moreover, since it is RDF-based, DOAP can be reused with existing vocabularies. In particular, from a social networking point of view, DOAP can be linked to FOAF to specify the developers of a project (with their associated identifying URIs) rather than just having a plain-text name, which can often raise ambiguity or heterogeneity problems.

If a user decides to install a widget or application on their social networking service, they usually have to trust some third-party service that may provide them with a certificate which they can decide whether to trust or not. An alternate approach is to leverage the social graphs of publishers and consumers of application widgets. Let us suppose someone writes a Facebook or OpenSocial widget and they want to distribute it, using this new approach. A user may choose to trust applications written by people connected to them in their (distributed) social graph by no more than two degrees of separation.

It is possible to use semantics to represent the various parts required in this scenario: FOAF can be used to describe people and their (distributed) social graph; while DOAP can be used to describe software projects, with the widget or application as a component of this software projects. We then connect the application project and the person together using FOAF–DOAP relationships.

By using such representations, the social graph (that is used here to determine whether to install a widget or not) does not have to be locked into one site, but rather can be distributed across any site that can be part of the larger interconnected social graph. As long as a publisher is part of the FOAF network, they do not even have to be on the particular social networking service where you install the application. This

---

[35] http://doap-project.org/.

means that one can trust an OpenSocial widget on one social networking site if its author is someone he or she knows on another Social Web site, where both sites have representations on the Semantic Web.

3. Producers of Social Semantic Data

Applying Semantic Web technologies to online social spaces allows for the expression of different types of relationships between people, objects and concepts. By using common, machine-readable ways of expressing individuals, profiles, social connections, and content, they provide a way to interconnect people and objects on the Web in an interoperable, extensible way.

On the conventional Web, navigation of social data across sites can be a major challenge. Communities are often dispersed across numerous different sites and platforms. For example, a group of people interested in a particular topic may share photos on Flickr, bookmarks on del.icio.us, and hold conversations on a discussion forum. Additionally, a single person may hold several separate online accounts, and may have a different network of friends on each. The information existing in these spaces is generally disconnected, lacking in semantics, and centrally controlled by single organizations. Individuals generally lack control or ownership of their own data.

Social spaces on the Web are becoming bigger and more distributed. This presents new challenges for navigating such data. Machine-readable descriptions of people and objects, and the use of common identifiers, would allow for linking diverse information from heterogeneous SNSs. This would create a starting point for easy navigation across the information in these networks.

The use of common formats allows interoperability across sites, enabling users to reuse and link to content across different platforms. This also provides a basis for data portability, where users could have ownership and control over their own data and could move profile and content information between services as they wish. Recently, there has been a push within the Web community to make data portability a reality.

Additionally, the Social Web and social networking sites can contribute to the Semantic Web effort. Users of these sites often provide metadata in the form of annotations and tags on photos, links, blogs posts, etc., social networks and semantics can complement each other. Already within online communities, common vocabularies or folksonomies for tagging are emerging through of a consensus of community members.

There are also a number of semantically enabled social applications appearing that have been enhanced with extra features due to the rich content being created in social software tools by users. The Twine application from Radar Networks is a recent example of a system that leverages both the explicit (tags and metadata) and implicit semantics (autotagging of text) associated with content items. Twine is a "knowledge networking" application that allows users to share, organize, and find information with people they trust. People create and join "twines" (community containers) around certain topics of interest, and items (documents, bookmarks, media files, etc., that can be commented on) are posted to these containers through a variety of methods. The underlying semantic data can be exposed as RDF by appending "?rdf" to any Twine URL. The DBpedia represents structured content from the collaboratively edited Wikipedia in semantic form, leveraging the semantics from many social content contributions by multiple users. DBpedia allows you to perform semantic queries on these data, and enables the linking of this socially created data to other data sets on the Web by exposing it via RDF. Revyu.com combines Web 2.0 interfaces and principles such as tagging with Semantic Web modeling principles to provide a reviews Web site that is integrated with linked data principles—a set of best practice guidelines for publishing and interlinking pieces of data on the Semantic Web. Anyone can review objects defined on other services (such as a movie from DBpedia), and the whole content of the Web site is available in RDF, therefore it is available for reuse by other applications.

3.1   FOAF

Semantic Web technologies allow for a more expressive description of a social network, enabling the use of heterogeneous nodes and link denoting different types of objects and different types of relationships. This enables us to express a model of an object-centered network where content and other items of interest can be described along with people.

The FOAF project was started in 2000 and defines a widely used vocabulary for describing people and the relationships between them, as well as the things that they create and do. Anyone can create their own FOAF file describing themselves and their social network, and the information from multiple FOAF files can easily be combined to obtain a higher-level view of the network across various sources, as shown in Fig. 4. This means that a group of people can articulate their social network without the need for a single centralized database, following the distributed principles used in the architecture of the Web.

FOAF can be integrated with any other Semantic Web vocabularies, such as SIOC, SKOS, etc. Some prominent social networking services that expose data using FOAF include Hi5 (a social networking site), LiveJournal (a social networking and blogging community site), Vox (a social networking and blogging service), Pownce (a social networking and microblogging site), and MyBlogLog

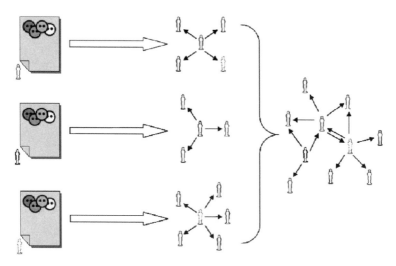

F<small>IG</small>. 4. Integrating social networks by using FOAF as a common representation format and having unique URIs for people.

(an application which adds community features to blogs). People can also create their own FOAF document and link to it from their homepage, and exporters are available for some major Social Web sites as Flickr, Twitter (a microblogging service), and Facebook. Such FOAF documents usually contain personal information, links to friends, and other related resources. The structure of the social network formed by relations expressed in FOAF documents on the Web has been studied in Ding et al. [16], particularly the small-world characteristics of the graph.

The knowledge representation of a person and their friends would be achieved through a FOAF fragment similar to that below.

```
<foaf:Person rdf:about="#JB">
    <foaf:name>John Breslin</foaf:name>
    <foaf:mbox rdf:resource="mailto:john.breslin@deri.org"/>
    <foaf:homepage rdf:resource="http://www.johnbreslin.com/"/>
    <foaf:nick>Cloud</foaf:nick>
    <foaf:depiction rdf:resource="http://www.johnbreslin.com/
      images/foaf_photo.jpg"/>
    <foaf:interest>
        <rdf:Description rdf:about="http://dbpedia.org/
        resource/SIOC" rdfs:label="SIOC"/>
    </foaf:interest>
```

```
<foaf:knows>
      <foaf:Person>
        <foaf:name>Sheila Kinsella</foaf:name>
        <foaf:mbox rdf:resource="mailto:sheila.kinsella
        @deri.org"/>
      </foaf:Person>
</foaf:knows>
<foaf:knows>
      <foaf:Person>
        <foaf:name>Stefan Decker</foaf:name>
        <foaf:mbox rdf:resource="mailto:stefan.decker
        @deri.org"/>
      </foaf:Person>
</foaf:knows>
</foaf:Person>
```

There have been a lot of complaints in recent years about the walled gardens that are social network sites. Some of the most popular SNSs would not exist without the walled garden approach, but some flexibility would be useful. Users may have many identities on different social networks, where each identity was created from scratch. A reusable profile would allow a user to import their existing identity and connections (from their own homepage or from another site they are registered on), thereby forming a single global identity with different views.

"Social network portability" is a related term that has been used to describe the ability to reuse one's own profile across various social networking sites and applications. The founder of the LiveJournal blogging community, Brad Fitzpatrick, wrote an article[36] in August 2007 from a developer's point of view about forming a "decentralized social graph," which discusses some ideas for social network portability and aggregating one's friends across sites. "The Bill of Rights for Users of the Social Web" was authored in September 2007 for Social Web sites who wish to guarantee ownership and control over one's own personal information.[37] Dan Brickley, the cocreator of the FOAF vocabulary, wrote an article entitled "The World is Now Closed" which talked about how SNSs should not define one's relationships in absolute terms and that even an aggregate social graph cannot be so clearly defined.[38]

The evolving need for distributed social networks and reusable profiles has been highlighted by several recent notable efforts. DataPortability[39] is a group whose aim

---

[36] http://bradfitz.com/social-graph-problem/.
[37] http://opensocialweb.org/2007/09/05/bill-of-rights/.
[38] http://danbri.org/words/2007/09/13/194.
[39] http://www.dataportability.org/.

is to advance standards enabling data sharing between services. DiSo (Distributed Social Networking applications) is a project from Google which aims to implement distributed social networks. Google's Social Graph API indexes publicly articulated social connections and allows users to view their social network across multiple services. These initiatives make use of existing and open standards like FOAF, microformats, and OpenID.

3.2 SIOC

The SIOC initiative is aimed at interlinking related online community content from platforms such as blogs, message boards, and other Social Web sites. In combination with the FOAF vocabulary for describing people and their friends, and the SKOS model for organizing knowledge, SIOC lets developers link discussion posts and content items to other related discussions and items, people (via their associated user accounts), and topics (using specific "tags" or hierarchical categories). As discussions begin to move beyond simple text-based conversations to include audio and video content, SIOC is evolving to describe not only conventional discussion platforms but also new Web-based communication and content-sharing mechanisms.

Since disconnected Social Web sites require ontologies for interoperation, and due to the fact that there is a lot of social data with inherent semantics contained in these sites, there is potential for high impact through the successful deployment of SIOC. Many online communities still use mailing lists and message boards as their main communication mechanisms, and the SIOC initiative has created a number of data producers for such systems to lift these communities to the Semantic Web. As well as having applications to Social Web sites, there is a parallel lack of integration between social software and other systems in enterprise intranets. So far, SIOC has been adopted in a framework of 50 applications or modules[40] deployed on over 400 sites.

A sample fragment of SIOC RDF is shown below, representing a blog post, its metadata and associated follow-up comments.

```
<sioc:Post rdf:about="http://johnbreslin.com/blog/2006/09/
    07/creating-connections-between-discussion-clouds-with-
    sioc/">
    <dc:title>Creating connections between discussion clouds
        with SIOC</dc:title>
```

---

[40] http://rdfs.org/sioc/applications.

```
<dcterms:created>2006-09-07T09:33:30Z</dcterms:created>
<sioc:has_container  rdf:resource="http://johnbreslin.
  com/blog/index.php?sioc_type=site#weblog"/>
<sioc:has_creator>
    <sioc:User  rdf:about="http://johnbreslin.com/blog/
    author/cloud/" rdfs:label="Cloud">
        <rdfs:seeAlso rdf:resource="http://johnbreslin.
        com/blog/index.php?sioc_type=user&sioc_id=1"/>
    </sioc:User>
</sioc:has_creator>
<sioc:content>SIOC provides a unified vocabulary for
  content and interaction description: a semantic layer
  that can coexist with existing discussion platforms.
    </sioc:content>
<sioc:topic rdfs:label="SemanticWeb" rdf:resource="http://
  johnbreslin.com/blog/category/semantic-web/"/>
<sioc:topic rdfs:label="Blogs" rdf:resource="http://
  johnbreslin.com/blog/category/blogs/"/>
<sioc:has_reply>
    <sioc:Post  rdf:about="http://johnbreslin.com/blog/
    2006/09/07/creating-connections-between-discussion-
    clouds-with-sioc/#comment-123928">
        <rdfs:seeAlso rdf:resource="http://johnbreslin.com/
        blog/index.php?sioc_type=comment&sioc_id=123928"/>
    </sioc:Post>
</sioc:has_reply>
</sioc:Post>
```

So far, work on SIOC has focused on producing social semantic data, but the augmentation of these data with rules to aid with reasoning is the next step (e.g., as discussed in Aleman-Meza et al. [2] by members of the ExpertFinder initiative,[41] a project to improve publication of metadata on Web pages to help automated identification of experts on particular topics). By combining information from one's explicitly defined social network and from implicit connections that may be derived through common activities (e.g., commenting on each other's content, participating in the same community areas), the suggestion of experts can be enhanced. An interesting aspect of SIOC is that it goes beyond pure Web 2.0

---

[41] http://expertfinder.info/.

services and can be used in other use cases involving the need to model social interaction within communities, either in corporate environments,[42] or for argumentative discussions [33] and scientific discourse representation, as illustrated by recent efforts[43] to align SIOC and SWAN[44] (Semantic Web applications in neuromedicine).

3.3   DOAP

As introduced in the previous section, the DOAP project provides an RDFS (RDF Schema) vocabulary for defining metadata related to software projects. As with FOAF and SIOC, this is a lightweight vocabulary, and this makes it easy for software developers who want to provide open and common descriptions of their projects using Semantic Web technologies. For instance, the next snippet of code identifies metadata about the SIOC PHP API, defined as an instance of a doap: Project, and assigned a specific URI.

```
<doap:Project rdf:about="http://sw.deri.org/svn/sw/2005/08/
  sioc/phpapi/doap.rdf#sio cexportapi">
  <doap:name>SIOC PHP Export API</doap:name>
  <doap:shortname>sioc-export-api</doap:shortname>
  <doap:shortdesc xml:lang="en">PHP API to create SIOC
    exporters</doap:shortdesc>
  <doap:description xml:lang="en">SIOC PHP Export API pro-
    vides an easy to write SIOC exporters for any PHP
    application.</doap:description>
  <doap:homepage rdf:resource="http://esw.w3.org/topic/SIOC/
    PHPExportAPI"/>
  <doap:download-page rdf:resource="http://esw.w3.org/topic/
    SIOC/PHPExportAPI"/>
  <doap:programming-language>PHP</doap:programming-
    language>
  <doap:license rdf:resource="http://usefulinc.com/doap/
    licenses/gpl"/>
  <doap:maintainer rdf:resource="http://apassant.net/alex"/>
```

---

[42] http://www.w3.org/2001/sw/sweo/public/UseCases/EDF/.
[43] http://esw.w3.org/topic/HCLSIG/SWANSIOC.
[44] http://swan.mindinformatics.org/.

```
<doap:maintainer rdf:resource="http://captsolo.net/semweb/
    foaf-captsolo.rdf#Uldis_Bojars"/>
<doap:developer rdf:resource="http://apassant.net/alex"/>
<doap:developer rdf:resource="http://captsolo.net/semweb/
    foaf-captsolo.rdf#Uldis_Bojars"/>
<doap:repository>
    <doap:SVNRepository>
        <doap:location  rdf:resource="http://sw.deri.org/
        svn/sw/2005/08/sioc/phpapi/"/>
    </doap:SVNRepository>
</doap:repository>
</doap:Project>
```

While DOAP descriptions can be created by hand, various DOAP exporters for major free software development Web sites have been written by developers (see also the RDF exporter for Ohloh[45]). These exporters allow software metadata to be available on the Web, described in a uniform way using the DOAP vocabulary (rather than just being embedded in Web pages which makes it difficult for automatic reuse by software agents).

As one can see in the above example, there are various ties between FOAF and DOAP. Since any project can have various developers or maintainers, DOAP offers the ability to use not only a name to define an author, but their URI, that is, his or her identifier on the Semantic Web, generally associated with a FOAF profile. Thanks to URI identification, and in spite of the fact that these profiles are distributed on the network, the software graph (DOAP), the identity graph (FOAF), and even the content graph (SIOC) can be connected together, providing a complete overview of the online activity and identity of people working on a given project. For instance, Fig. 5 shows how different graphs, related mainly to FOAF, SIOC, and DOAP can interact together to provide a complete Semantic Web description of a network, a widget description and a related blog post by various people, in a distributed but interlinked way.

Moreover, projects can have various topics. Here, once again, instead of relying on text strings, people can use URIs and properties from Dublin Core, a vocabulary for information resource description, to define project topics in a machine-understandable way. A good practice would be to use URIs of topics as defined on DBpedia, or other data sets from the Linked Open Data movement to make open data sets available in RDF format. The link between the project and a topic URI can

---

[45] http://rdfohloh.wikier.org/.

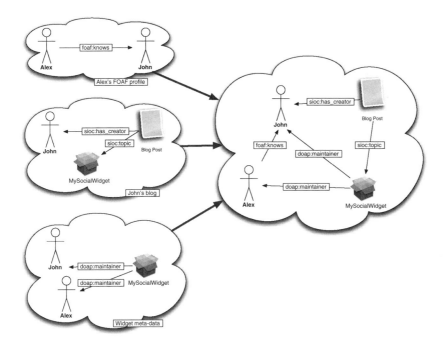

FIG. 5. Linking people, content, and social widgets across Web sites.

be defined directly by the project's author, may be extracted from the project's textual description using an NLP (natural language processing) algorithm, or can by added by the author via free-text keyword tagging using MOAT as explained earlier. For instance, since our example project is related to Semantic Web technologies, and particularly to the SIOC vocabulary, the following code mentions the links between the project and those topics, uniquely identified with their DBpedia URIs.

```
<doap:Project rdf:about="http://sw.deri.org/svn/sw/2005/08/
   sioc/phpapi/doap.rdf#sioc exportapi">
      <dc:subject rdf:resource="http://dbpedia.org/resource/
         Semantic_Web"/>
      <dc:subject rdf:resource="http://dbpedia.org/resource/
         SIOC"/>
</doap:Project>
```

Once again, and with reference to the earlier tagging section, expressing these URIs offers new capabilities regarding information exchange and modeling (we will also exemplify this later).

4. Collectors of Social Semantic Data

The semantic social data available on the Web are distributed across numerous sources and are stored in many different formats. In some cases, these data may be published in such a way that it can be consumed directly by applications, for example, in an RDF store with a SPARQL (Simple Protocol and RDF Query Language) endpoint. Alternatively, it may be necessary to first gather and process the data, for example, when it is stored in documents which need to be crawled and indexed. In the following, we describe issues with interpreting social data from mined the Web, inferring relations from semantic data, and technical aspects of collecting data.

4.1   The Web as a Source of Social Network Data

Common traditional methods of collecting social network information include administering questionnaires, conducting interviews or performing observational studies, and studying archival records. There are some fundamental differences between the networks acquirable by these methods and the networks retrievable from the Internet. Extracting data from the Web present a different set of challenges but also offer some advantages over traditional methods.

A major advantage of mining online social networks for analysis is the much lower cost of acquiring data due to the reduced time and effort involved. Also, the scale of the social information available online is unprecedented. In the past, acquisition of social network data of the order of millions of nodes would have been impossible; with the social data now freely available on the Internet, it is easy. In addition, networks collected from the Web are evidence-based and objective. Unlike interviews or questionnaires, results are not dependent on the accurate recall of the subjects, who may interpret questions differently, or may be unwilling to cooperate. Furthermore, while it is unlikely you will get a 100% participation rate in a survey, especially on a large network, if you have access to a full Web data set you can analyze a whole network. Finally, electronic data collection easily enables longitudinal studies, allowing the dynamics of networks to be investigated, as opposed to surveying, where repeated data collection would be time-consuming and maybe impossible if the subjects are unwilling or unable to repeat the survey.

However, the accuracy of social network data mined from the Internet can be highly questionable. People can easily misrepresent themselves or others. Depending on Internet usage habits, some people will have far more information available about them online than others. This means that the social networks extracted from the Web may not give a balanced representation of real-life social networks. There is also the question of how exactly to interpret information from the Internet, for example, the strength of the relationship implied. The people on an individual's contact list on an

SNS may encompass a spectrum from close friends to distant acquaintances or even strangers. Another problem is that there are likely to be errors in Web data, for example, resulting from typos, inconsistent spelling of names, and variations on names.

Semantic Web technologies can greatly assist the process of harvesting social networks. The use of common, structured formats means that social network data can easily be aggregated from multiple, heterogeneous sources. References to the same person or resource can be identified across multiple sources and consolidated. Much of the effort needed to construct a model of a social network is removed and the need for human effort is lessened. It is possible to do reasoning on the data and infer relations from certain properties. Additionally, it is possible to extract a network of typed nodes and links.

Harvesting and analyzing social data from the Web raises important ethical issues. It involves using data for purposes which were not intended by the users who uploaded for their use and that of their friends. Trust and provenance of information are important aspects that should be taken into consideration. At a technical level, the ability to confirm the origin of data is important, and at a more social level, a means to express trust in sources is also required [14, 23]. We believe that advanced policies are also needed to let users define who can access which part of their social data, and to which extent it can be reused.

4.2   Collecting and Aggregating Data

Data on the Semantic Web are published in different ways, so different methods may be required to collect them. Additional processing may also be required to merge data from multiple sources.

Crawling. Due to the linked nature of social networks, given URIs to seed members of the network, we can follow links from these nodes to their friends, and then their friends-of-friends and so on. This can be done by simply following rdf:seeAlso links. Additional knowledge about the structure of the data can be used to improve the task. For example, the SIOC Crawler [5] uses knowledge of the ontology's structure to incrementally retrieve new SIOC data in threads. For widgets and project descriptions, crawling is also important since there is a need to easily find a software project without having to manually browse the complete Semantic Web. We will later detail an architecture that can be used to achieve this goal. To ease the crawling of published data, site suppliers can provide a semantic sitemap[46] on their Web site, so that crawling agents know where to find related RDF data.

Exporters. For some platforms, exporters are available which generate a structured RDF representation of the data. These allow information in a relational database or

---

[46] http://sw.deri.org/2007/07/sitemapextension/.

other structured stores to be automatically transformed into RDF. Exporters make it easy for users to maintain semantic representations of their data. For example, there are SIOC exporters available for platforms including mailing lists [17], Web forums and blogs [12], and existing Web 2.0 services such as Flickr.

Object consolidation. An important task in extracting social data from the Web is merging identifiers of equivalent instances occurring across different sources. This involves identifying instances representing the same object, and unifying them into one entity. Object consolidation (or "smushing") can be performed for instances which share the same value for inverse functional properties or IFPs [37], for example, using foaf:mbox.[47] Another option is to provide explicit identification using instances of the OWL (Web Ontology Language) sameAs property between various resources that identify the same person or data, in spite of different URIs. This best practice allows one to unify all of their identities from various exporters (e.g., Flickr, Twitter, Facebook, etc.) and to then query their complete social network with a single entry point, as Fig. 6 shows. Finally, it can also be achieved

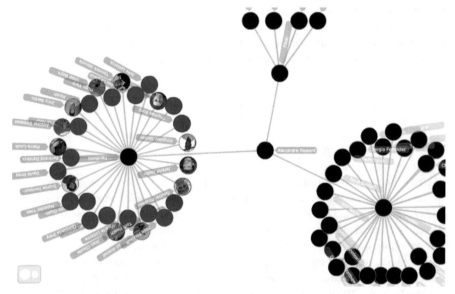

FIG. 6. Identity consolidation and social network browsing using data exported from various social Web sites.[48] (Partial view of the social network.)

---

[47] Defining a property as inverse functional (owl:InverseFunctionalProperty) implies that if two resources share the same value for that property, they are the same even if they have different URIs. FOAF defines various IFPs (foaf:mbox, foaf:opened).

[48] http://apassant.net/home/2008/01/foafgear.

by considering various alternative criteria and if a certain threshold is reached in similarity between two instances, they can be considered equal [1]. Yet, while one can define such rules within his or her own restricted social graph, it may lead to unexpected results on the complete Web (for instance, since different people will sometimes have the same name) and identity management on the Semantic Web is a vast research topic.

4.3 Crawling and Browsing Software Descriptions

As with FOAF profiles or any RDF data, DOAP files may be distributed over the network, which can make it difficult for end users or developers to discover them. To solve this problem, an architecture was proposed by Bojārs et al. [6] involving various components acting together (1) a Firefox plug-in, called Semantic Radar, whose goal is to discover RDF documents from HTML pages (either using auto-discovery links or thanks to embedded RDFa); (2) a ping service for Semantic Web documents, called PingTheSemanticWeb[49] (PTSW), which stores a fresh listing of RDF files it has received pings about; and (3) a collaborative and open directory of DOAP projects, called doap:store.[50] In fact, while all of these components were developed separately, they all act with each other to provide a complete Semantic Web food chain.

When people browse the Web using Semantic Radar, the plug-in sends a ping to PTSW each time an RDF file is found. PTSW then stores a link to this RDF file in its database, and provides a list of pinged documents to developers (which may then be organized by type). In this system, discovering documents and storing pings is not only dedicated to DOAP, but can be useful for people who are looking for FOAF or SIOC files. Finally, in this architecture, doap:store fetches the list of new DOAP files on a regular basis to provide a directory of DOAP projects that can then be queried and browsed. doap:store was one of the first tools to use this architecture, but anyone can benefit from it, by focusing on creating the application rather than finding and crawling the data. An interesting point in this workflow is the social process it involves. Since anyone can contribute just by browsing the Web, this means that any user can be a part of the Semantic Web document discovery process, weaving the "architecture of participation" principle from Web 2.0 into the Semantic Web.

---

[49] http://pingthesemanticweb.com.
[50] http://doapstore.org.

4.4 Inferring Relationships from Aggregated Data

The simplest way of extracting a social network from the Web is to look at explicitly stated connections. Social networking sites and other types of social software allow users to express lists of friends. Blogging platforms may allow users to add a blogroll which is a list of favorite blogs. Depending on the platform, these connections may indicate a directed or undirected link between users. For example, blogroll links are frequently unreciprocated, and are therefore directed, but many SNSs require both users to consent to the link, creating undirected ties. A sample query for extracting the social network formed by explicit foaf:knows relationships follows using the SPARQL query language.

```
PREFIX rdf:<http://www.w3.org/1999/02/22-rdf-syntax-ns#>
PREFIX foaf:<http://xmlns.com/foaf/0.1/>

SELECT ?s ?o
WHERE {
    ?s rdf:type foaf:Person.
    ?o rdf:type foaf:Person.
    ?s foaf:knows ?o.
}
```

In addition to explicitly stated person-to-person links, there are many implicit social connections present on the Web. Links between people may be inferred due to links to some common objects, for example, appearing in the same pictures, tagging the same documents, and replying to each other's blog posts. These connections indicate relationships of varying strengths—for example, email communication may be interpreted as stronger evidence of a real tie than the case of one person replying to another's blog post. Co-occurrence of names in documents would be an even weaker sign of a relation. A sample query for extracting the implicit social network formed by replies to posts follows.

```
PREFIX rdf:<http://www.w3.org/1999/02/22-rdf-syntax-ns#>
PREFIX sioc:<http://rdfs.org/sioc/ns#>
PREFIX foaf:<http://xmlns.com/foaf/0.1/>

SELECT ?author1 ?author2
WHERE {
    ?post1 rdf:type sioc:Post.
    ?post1 foaf:maker ?author1.
    ?post1 sioc:has_reply ?post2.
    ?post2 rdf:type sioc:Post.
    ?post2 foaf:maker ?author2.
}
```

Instead of running queries to retrieve those implicit relationships, we can define rules to make them explicit and to state the acquaintance of users on a Weblog. For instance, we can consider that there is a formal agreement relationship between two users (modeled with an arg:agreedWith relationship) as soon as one replies to a post from the other one using "I agree" in his or her answer.[51] To model this rule, we rely here on the SPARQL CONSTRUCT pattern, which can be used to produce new statements from existing ones. Thus, we can apply the following query on our triple store, and then put the created RDF graph in the store itself, so that the relationship will become explicit. The produced statements may then be used to extract a more precise social network within a blogging community when querying data.

```
PREFIX rdf:<http://www.w3.org/1999/02/22-rdf-syntax-ns#>
PREFIX sioc:<http://rdfs.org/sioc/ns#>
PREFIX foaf:<http://xmlns.com/foaf/0.1/>
CONSTRUCT {
    ?author2 arg:agreedWith ?author1.
} WHERE {
    ?post1 rdf:type sioc:Post.
    ?post1 foaf:maker ?author1.
    ?post1 sioc:has_reply ?post2.
    ?post2 rdf:type sioc:Post.
    ?post2 foaf:maker ?author2.
    FILTER REGEX(?post2, "I agree", "i").
}
```

While the above examples result in simple networks of people and untyped ties, more complex social networks consisting of multiple node and link types can also be studied. These examples are only possible through linking people and content in and across sites. Traditional, nonsemantic queries like in SQL would be limited to one site and would require some kind of join on a user/content table. However, the use of shared semantically rich vocabularies makes it possible to perform operations like these on data originating from many different sources.

5. Consumers of Social Semantic Data

Once data have been collected and aggregated, or made directly accessible through a SPARQL endpoint, it can be studied or used in applications. As the information is in a structured format, it can easily be converted into the formats required by popular

---

[51] Ideally, more advanced pattern matching and NLP methods should be used to define agreement between two users on a Weblog.

social network analysis and visualization tools. RDF data can also be queried directly to return some set of items that fit certain criteria that a user is interested in. In the following, we describe these two ways of using semantic social data.

5.1 Social Network Analysis

SNA uses methods from graph theory to study networks of individuals and the relationships between them. The individuals are often referred to as nodes or actors, and they may represent people, groups, countries, organizations, or any other type of social unit. The relations between them can be called edges or ties, and can indicate any type of link, for example, acquaintance, friendship, coauthorship, and information exchange. Ties may be undirected, in which case the relationship is symmetric, or directed, in which case the relationship has a specific direction and may not be reciprocated.

The nodes in a social network can be seen as analogous to entities in an RDF graph, where a <subject, predicate, object> triple indicates a directed tie from the subject node to an object node, and the predicate indicates the type of the relationship. While SNA methods are generally applied to social networks, they can be used to analyze any kind of networked data.

We can apply mathematical measures from SNA to get interesting information about a social network. The more complex methods of network analysis cannot be performed directly on a graph in RDF format, but must be converted to a representation more suited to network analysis. An RDF graph can be loaded into a network analysis program such as Pajek or UCINET [9] which can perform various measures and visualizations. Alternatively, a library like JUNG [39], which provides analysis and visualization methods, can be used to develop custom analytic or visual tools.

Locating important individuals. Centrality measures can be used to locate key players in a network [44]. Degree centrality is based on the number of connections a person has. This measure locates individuals who are connected to a large number of others. In a directed graph, indegree is the number of incoming connections and outdegree is the number of outgoing connections. Closeness centrality is calculated based on the total shortest distance to all other nodes in the network. This measure can be an indicator of people who can most quickly communicate information to the whole network. Betweenness centrality is based on the number of shortest paths on which a node lies. A node which scores highly according to this metric may occupy a strategic position and function as a bridge between different parts of the network. Flink [37] applies these measures to a social network of Semantic Web researchers in order to investigate whether the network position of a scientist is related to their performance.

Extracting communities. We may be interested in finding subgraphs or small communities within a larger graph. This enables the restriction of network to a manageable size for performing further analysis. Algorithms exist for partitioning a network into different groups, for example, that of Girvan and Newman [21]. Alternatively, if there is a particular individual of interest we can extract their ego network, the area of the graph focused around them. For example, spreading activation algorithms can activate an input node or nodes, and propagate the activation from these to locate those individuals which are most strongly connected and therefore receive the most activation [30].

Characterizing a social network. There are some interesting whole network properties that can be investigated to gain an understanding of the overall structure of the network [44]. Centralization measures the degree to which the network has a leader. Cohesiveness measures the well-connectedness of the network. These measures can also be used to make comparisons between different networks.

Visualizing a social network. By creating a pictorial image of a social network, it may be possible to get an improved insight into the structure of the graph. A visual representation can help analysts to understand the network better themselves, and also aid in explaining features of the network to others [19]. Flink provides visualizations of the ego networks of individual researchers and allows users to browse members of the Semantic Web research community.

5.2 Querying an RDF Graph

By representing social data in RDF and putting it in a store with a SPARQL endpoint (i.e., an access point where remote SPARQL queries can be run via HTTP), we can perform queries to extract interesting information about users, communities, and content. In the following, we discuss some example scenarios and illustrate them with sample queries.

Finding a person's ego network. Identifying an ego-centric network centered around a focus person involves finding all people to whom they are connected to online. This means searching over all their accounts, and across all SNSs of which they are a member. Below is a simple example query over FOAF data to get all friends of persons with a particular email address sha1sum. We use the hash of an email address as an identifier (since the foaf:mbox_sha1sum is defined as an owl: InverseFunctionalProperty in FOAF), as the focus person is likely to have different URIs on different sites.

```
PREFIX foaf:<http://xmlns.com/foaf/0.1/>
SELECT DISTINCT ?o
WHERE {
```

```
?s foaf:mbox_sha1sum "9a348bd34fe67b15f388c95c2cb9b4bfc
    9073797".
?s foaf:knows ?o.
}
```

Finding a person's implicit social links. While locating a person's explicitly stated connections goes some way to locating their social network, they may have more acquaintances with whom they are implicitly linked. It is possible to identify additional potential acquaintances of a person via objects to which they are both connected. The example below shows a query to find all people with the same workplace, school, or project as the focus person. We could also consider people who are coauthors of some documents, or who have replied to each other's SIOC-enabled posts.

```
PREFIX foaf:<http://xmlns.com/foaf/0.1/>
SELECT DISTINCT ?s
WHERE { {
    <http://sw.deri.org/~sheila/foaf.rdf#me>foaf:workplace-
        Homepage ?o.
    ?s foaf:workplaceHomepage ?o.
} UNION {
    <http://sw.deri.org/~sheila/foaf.rdf#me>foaf:schoolHo-
        mepage ?o.
    ?s foaf:schoolHomepage ?o.
} UNION {
    <http://sw.deri.org/~sheila/foaf.rdf#me>foaf:project?o.
    ?s foaf:project ?o.
}}
```

We can carry out simple reasoning by expressing a set of rules to describe when such implicit links create a social connection between people and when they may not. For example, we may decide that two people are socially connected if one posts a comment on someone else's blog post; alternatively, we may conclude that a weak link exists if two people posted on the same lengthy discussion thread and that no social connection exists.

Aggregating a person's Web contributions. This means retrieving content that a person has contributed to various sources on the Web; for example, all blog posts and comments on other blogs, chat logs, mailing list, and forum posts. This is a difficult problem to perform with a normal search engine as people may share their name with other people, or may use different account names on different sites. A sample query over SIOC data is shown below, to get all posts created by a particular user.

```
PREFIX rdf:<http://www.w3.org/1999/02/22-rdf-syntax-ns#>
PREFIX foaf:<http://xmlns.com/foaf/0.1/>
PREFIX sioc:<http://rdfs.org/sioc/ns#>
SELECT DISTINCT ?post
WHERE {
     ?post rdf:type sioc:Post.
     ?post sioc:has_creator <http://www.mindswap.org/blog/
        author/hendler/#foaf>.
}
```

Yet, since this query is based on a precise URI, it will not retrieve content created by the same user while using another URI (for instance, http://example.org/hendler). One option to retrieve this content is to define owl:sameAs statements between this URIs and other URIs of the same user, such as:

```
<http://example.org/hendler>owl:sameAs<http://www.mind-
   swap.org/blog/author/hendler/#foaf>.
```

Then, by adding these statements in the triple store that holds the data, and assuming it supports reasoning based on owl:sameAs, the query will also retrieve posts that have http://example.org/hendler as a sioc:has_creator.

A second way to do retrieve the person's contributions is to run the query not based on the URI, but based on an IFP, such as the foaf:mbox or foaf:openid. Since OpenID aims to become a standard for authentication on the Web, this can be a useful way to retrieve all the contributions of a given user no matter which Social Web site it comes from—providing the person signs in using the same OpenID URL—and this method is shown in the following query:

```
PREFIX rdf:<http://www.w3.org/1999/02/22-rdf-syntax-ns#>
PREFIX foaf:<http://xmlns.com/foaf/0.1/>
PREFIX sioc:<http://rdfs.org/sioc/ns#>
SELECT DISTINCT ?post
WHERE {
     ?post rdf:type sioc:Post.
     ?post sioc:has_creator ?user.
     ?user foaf:openid<http://example.org/hendleropenid>.
}
```

Locating a community around a topic. We may be interested in extracting a community centered around a certain topic, using tags, keywords, and other metadata to find people who are talking about a certain thing. The query below locates posts with the topic "Semantic Web" and returns the URIs of the authors of these posts.

```
PREFIX rdf:<http://www.w3.org/1999/02/22-rdf-syntax-ns#>
PREFIX rdfs:<http://www.w3.org/2000/01/rdf-schema#>
PREFIX sioc:<http://rdfs.org/sioc/ns#>
PREFIX foaf:<http://xmlns.com/foaf/0.1/>
SELECT DISTINCT ?author
WHERE {
    ?post rdf:type sioc:Post.
    ?post foaf:maker ?author.
    ?post sioc:topic ?post_topic.
    ?post_topic rdfs:label "semantic web".
}
```

Yet, this query will not retrieve posts written in French, for example, using a "Web semantique" string instead of the "Semantic Web" phrase. However, if people were encouraged to use a precise URI instead of the simple tag, such as http://dbpedia.org/resource/Category:Semantic_Web, we would then be able to retrieve all related posts. Moreover, using those URIs, we can run even more advanced queries, as in the example of retrieving all posts related to the Semantic Web, we could also show those for which the topic is directly related to this URI (e.g., RDFa, SKOS, etc.), as the following query does, emphasizing the benefits of combining data from various data sets, interlinked together in the whole Semantic Web graph.

```
PREFIX rdf:<http://www.w3.org/1999/02/22-rdf-syntax-ns#>
PREFIX rdfs:<http://www.w3.org/2000/01/rdf-schema#>
PREFIX sioc:<http://rdfs.org/sioc/ns#>
PREFIX foaf:<http://xmlns.com/foaf/0.1/>
SELECT DISTINCT ?author
WHERE {
    ?post rdf:type sioc:Post.
    ?post foaf:maker ?author.
    ?post sioc:topic ?topic.
    ?topic ?rel <http://dbpedia.org/resource/Category:
       Semantic_Web>.
}
```

As with the example queries in Section 4, the queries above can be performed on data originating from various diverse sources.

Locating software projects from people you trust. If we consider that a user will only trust software applications written by people that they have added as personal connections (represented on the Semantic Web using FOAF), the following query will retrieve projects in which one of the maintainers of a project is in their network, where the original user is identified with $uri:

```
PREFIX rdf:<http://www.w3.org/1999/02/22-rdf-syntax-ns#>
PREFIX rdfs:<http://www.w3.org/2000/01/rdf-schema#>
PREFIX sioc:<http://rdfs.org/sioc/ns#>
PREFIX foaf:<http://xmlns.com/foaf/0.1/>
PREFIX doap:<http://usefulinc.com/doap/ns/doap#>
SELECT DISTINCT ?project ?friend
WHERE {
    ?project rdf:type doap:Project.
    ?project doap:maintainer ?friend.
    <$uri>foaf:knows ?friend.
}
```

Moreover, as explained earlier, instead of giving a URI, one can use an IFP to identify themselves, such as an email address or an OpenID URL.

A similar query can be used if one decides to trust not only their direct friends, but also their friends-of-friends as shown below, retrieving the project, its maintainer, and the person that acted as an intermediary connection:

```
PREFIX rdf:<http://www.w3.org/1999/02/22-rdf-syntax-ns#>
PREFIX rdfs:<http://www.w3.org/2000/01/rdf-schema#>
PREFIX sioc:<http://rdfs.org/sioc/ns#>
PREFIX foaf:<http://xmlns.com/foaf/0.1/>
PREFIX doap:<http://usefulinc.com/doap/ns/doap#>
SELECT DISTINCT ?project ?friend ?friendofafriend
WHERE {
    <$uri>foaf:knows ?friend.
    ?friend foaf:knows ?friendofafriend.
    ?project rdf:type doap:Project.
    ?project doap:maintainer ?friendofafriend.
}
```

Moreover, the query could be extended to express various degrees of connectivity. The current SPARQL specification only allows node–arc–node queries, which means that for each desired path length, the query must be adapted. However, a SPARQL "path" extension like SPARQLer [32] can be used with appropriate SPARQL engines, allowing us to write queries like "find all projects from people I'm connected to via a path of between 1 and 3 (inclusive) foaf:knows relationships."

Locating a software project related to a particular topic. Similar to the earlier example of blog posts and associated topics, where projects are related to some topics using URIs rather than keywords, projects around a particular topic can easily be found. Once again, we show how various data sets interlinked with URIs in this "Giant Global Graph" can enable us to perform advanced queries. Moreover, this can be combined with a social networking aspect. The following query will retrieve all projects with a topic related to the Semantic Web created by people known to a user with the identifier $uri:

```
PREFIX rdf:<http://www.w3.org/1999/02/22-rdf-syntax-ns#>
PREFIX rdfs:<http://www.w3.org/2000/01/rdf-schema#>
PREFIX sioc:<http://rdfs.org/sioc/ns#>
PREFIX foaf:<http://xmlns.com/foaf/0.1/>
PREFIX doap:<http://usefulinc.com/doap/ns/doap#>

SELECT DISTINCT ?project ?friend
WHERE {
        ?project rdf:type doap:Project.
        ?project doap:maintainer ?friend.
        ?project foaf:topic ?topic.
        ?topic ?rel <http://dbpedia.org/resource/Category:
           Semantic_Web>.
        <$uri>foaf:knows ?friend.
}
```

6. Future Work

6.1   Leveraging Semantics in Multimedia-Enabled Social Web Sites

A key feature of the new Social Web is the change in the role of user from just a consumer of content, to an active participant in the creation of content. For example, Wikipedia articles are written and edited by volunteers; Amazon.com uses information about what users view and purchase to recommend products to other users; Slashdot moderation is performed by the readers. One area of future work in relation to social networks on the Semantic Web is the application of semantic techniques to take even more advantage of community input to provide useful functionality. As an example, we will look at the area of multimedia management.

There is an ever increasing amount of multimedia of various formats becoming available on the Internet. Current techniques to retrieve, integrate, and present these media to users are deficient and would benefit from improvement. Semantic technologies make it possible to give rich descriptions to media, facilitating the process of locating and combining diverse media from various sources. Making use of online communities can give additional benefits. Two main areas in which social networks and semantic technologies can assist multimedia management are annotation and recommendation. Some efforts such as DBTune[52] already provide musical content exported to the Semantic Web, and recent work has been done in order to use that interlinked musical content for music-based recommendations [41].

Social bookmarking systems like del.icio.us allow users to assign shared free-form tags to resources, thus generating annotations for objects with a minimum amount of effort. The informal nature of tagging means that semantic information cannot be directly inferred from an annotation, as any user can tag any resource with whatever strings they wish. However, studying the collective tagging behavior of a large number of users allows emergent semantics to be derived [46]. Through a combination of such mass collaborative "structural" semantics (via tags, geotemporal information, ratings, etc.) and extracted multimedia "content" semantics (which can be used for clustering purposes, e.g., image similarities or musical patterns), relevant annotations can be suggested to users when they contribute multimedia content to a community site by comparing new items with related semantic items in one's implicit/explicit network.

Another way in which the wisdom of crowds can be harnessed in semantic multimedia management is in providing personalized social network-based recommender systems. Liu et al. [35] present an approach for semantic mining of personal tastes and a model for taste-based recommendation. Ghita et al. [20] explore how a group of people with similar interests can share documents/metadata and can provide each other with semantically rich recommendations. The same principles can be applied to multimedia recommendation, and these recommendations can be augmented with the semantics derived from the multimedia content itself (e.g., the information on those people depicted or carrying out actions in multimedia objects[53]).

6.2   Privacy and Deliberate Fragmentation

Some challenges must also be overcome regarding the online identity aspect and authentication/privacy for users of Social Web sites. An interesting aspect of social networking and media-sharing Web sites is that most people use various Web sites

---

[52] http://dbtune.org.
[53] http://acronym.deri.org/.

because they *want* to fragment their online identity: uploading pictures of friends on MySpace, forming business contacts on LinkedIn, etc. Under each persona, a user may reveal completely different facets of their personality. People may wish to share many of their identities with certain contacts, but retain more privacy when dealing with others. For example, many people are careful to keep their personal life distinct from their professional life. However just as people may wish to keep separate identities for some purposes, it can also be beneficial to be able to connect these personas, when desired. Members of online communities often expend a lot of effort into forming relationships and building their reputation. Since reputation determines how much trust other people will place in an individual, it can be of very real value and therefore the ability to maintain a reputation across different identities could be very beneficial.

While the Semantic Web and in particular reasoning principles (such as leveraging IFPs) allow us to merge these data and provide vocabularies, methods, and tools for data portability among Social Web sites [7, 8], this identity fragmentation must be taken into account. It implies a need for new ways to authenticate queries or carry out inferencing, by delivering data in different manners depending on, for instance, which social subgraph the person requesting the data belongs to (family, coworker, etc.). Here, Web 2.0 efforts like oAuth[54] are of interest. oAuth is an open protocol which enables users to allow applications access their protected data stored in accounts they hold with other services. Also relevant is the recent proposal for RDFAuth.[55] Moreover, advanced social aspects of contextualizing information delivery may be added later. The nature of each relationship (e.g., work, family, romantic, friendship) could be taken into account, as well as the current status, location, or mood of a user. In some cases, external influences such as the political climate in a country may be considered in determining what kind of information to share about an individual. Additionally, as relationships evolve over time, the processing of requests could be updated accordingly.

6.3 Using Wikipedia as a Reputation System with Embedded Semantics

As a global, independent and neutral framework to which we can all contribute content, Wikipedia could serve as the basis for a de-facto global and open reputation system. At the moment, Wikipedia does not provide much information on people's reputations, that is, those who make changes to articles are not very visible on

---

[54] http://oauth.org/.
[55] http://blogs.sun.com/bblfish/entry/rdfauth_sketch_of_a_buzzword.

Wikipedia and are not treated as experts as such. On the Wikipedia Web site, it is often the case that the contributor who may know the most about an article is not clearly identified in the Wikipedia article as being the foremost expert.

There have been various attempts to establish reputation sites on the Web, for example, Naymz, which may help a person to improve their visibility in search engines. However, there is a problem with these sites in that a person's reputation can only be truly reflected online if they regularly contribute to the site and maintain an up-to-date version of their profile with all of their achievements. Another issue is that people who already have a good reputation will most probably not join these sites, perhaps due to time constraints, or if reputation is related to the number of connections or endorsements one has (which may be by invitation).

Wikipedia can be improved by the addition of a global reputation system with embedded semantics. This could be achieved by placing larger emphasis on the discussion pages in the Wikipedia, and by introducing threaded structures in these pages from which expertise would emerge. For example, experts could emerge from their actions in discussion pages when their suggested changes have been accepted, highlighting those who made the best changes on the article page itself.

If we include microcontent such as microformats or RDFa in these pages, we solve two problems at one stroke (1) Wikipedia benefits from a richer reputation framework where people can be motivated to add contextual semantic information to make their content better searchable (directly benefiting their own reputations) and (2) this can also move forward the Semantic Web, by solving the issue of who will be motivated to add the semantics to the Semantic Web and why. This information can also be used to power services like QDOS that aim to measure people's digital status online.

6.4 A Common Social Networking Stack

So far, SNSs use explicit representations of social networks primarily for visualization and browsing purposes. Yet, some research prototypes show that social networks are actually useful for more than just ego surfing to discover unexpected links in networks of friends. For example, some efforts are under way to examine email filtering and ranking based on social networks [18, 22] Explicitly represented social networking information can also provide a means for assessing a piece of information's importance and relevance for many other kinds of information filtering (e.g., in semantic attention management [42]) and routing, in general.

Rather than building a separate social networking layer into tools (with all the created maintenance problems), information space and application architects need to fold it into the technology stacks (see Fig. 7). Nepomuk does this for the desktop, but given the evolution toward ubiquitous computing and the so-called "Internet of

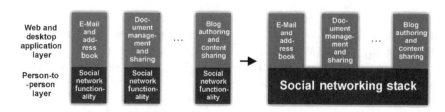

Fɪɢ. 7. Making social networking a shared component across various desktop and Web applications.

things," which will deliver much more information, the Internet infrastructure itself might need to be augmented to include social networking infrastructure to keep users from drowning in an ocean of unconnected and meaningless information. Just as the social semantic desktop Nepomuk[56] provides an operating system layer for representing and exchanging information on the desktop, information creation on the Web and the Internet should take existing connections between content objects and people into account to provide meaning for this information. For example, SNSs might include mechanisms to automate the creation of connections among information items or to route information based on existing relationships between people and content items.

A social networking stack needs to take into account a person's relevant objects of interest and provide some limited data portability (at the very least, for their most highly used or rated items). Through this, the actions and interactions of a person with other users and objects (exhibiting relevant properties) in existing systems can be used to create new user or group connections when a person registers for a new social networking site or application. Also, instead of having a fragmented view of one's network in each application, the social networking stack would let a user use all of their person-to-person connections in any application. To enable the sharing of existing contacts and to aid with the creation of new ones, the cross-application social networking stack will require a number of layers:

1. **Personal authentication and authorization layer.** This layer would use OpenID, Sxip,[57] or some other single sign-on mechanism to authenticate that an individual is who they claim to be, and would in turn ensure that they are authorized to make use of their social network connections (layer 2) and/or leverage previously created content items (layer 3).

---

[56] http://nepomuk.semanticdesktop.org/.
[57] http://sxip.com/.

2. **Social network access layer.** This layer would utilize the social networking contacts created by an individual across various platforms, for example, by collecting FOAF "knows" relationships from multiple sites. However, access control is required as social connections may not always be bidirectional: that is, there has to be some consent from both sides for certain transactions. For example, Alice may create a connection to Bob in order to view Bob's public content, but Bob may have to approve the connection in the reverse direction if Alice ever wants to send him a direct message. This layer would not only ensure that the required directional links exist for various interactions, but would also verify that the source of this social network information is valid.

3. **Content object access layer.** This layer would collect a person's relevant content objects, and verify that they are allowed to reuse data/metadata from these objects in the current application. This could be achieved using SIOC as a representation format, aggregating a person's created items (through their user accounts) from various site containers. For reputation purposes, this layer would also verify that these items were in fact created by the authenticated individual on whatever sites they reference. This may require provenance of information as well as signing of RDF graphs [13] and possibly advanced policies for dealing with identity theft.

For the implementation of a social networking stack, various architectural alternatives exist: the existing Domain Name System (DNS) system is an example of a possible architecture, but creates a central point of control. A peer-to-peer approach is another possibility which would be worthwhile to explore, especially since it preserves the distributed aspect.

The availability of a social networking stack would also have an effect on existing networking layers: social routing algorithms are able to deliver information directly to people for whom the information is relevant—email filtering and routing with social networks being just a simple example.

7. Conclusions

In this chapter, we have described the significance of community-oriented and content-sharing sites on the Web, the shortcomings of many of these sites as they are now, and the benefits that semantic technologies can bring to social networks and Social Web sites. Online social spaces encouraging content creation and sharing have resulted in the formation of massive and intricate networks of people and associated content. However, the lack of integration between sites means that these networks are disjoint and users are unable to reuse data across sites. As well as content, many third parties are producing application widgets that can be added by users to their Social Web site profiles, but mechanisms for trusting the source of these widgets can be improved or augmented with information derived from social network connections. There is a need for Semantic Web technologies that can solve some of these issues and improve the value and functionality of online social spaces. The process of creating and using semantic data in the Social Web can be viewed as a sort of food chain of producers, collectors, and consumers. Semantic data producers publish information in structured, common formats, such that it can easily be integrated with data from other diverse sources. Collectors, if necessary, aggregate and consolidate heterogeneous data from other diverse sources. Consumers may use these data for analysis or in end-user applications.

In this way, it becomes possible to integrate diverse information from heterogeneous sites, enabling improved navigation and the ability to query over data. There are also advantages for those interested in studying social networks, as the Semantic Web makes freely available large-scale, multirelational data sets for analysis. In this chapter, we described some methods by which consolidated facts and content can be extracted from people and content networks aggregated from multiple social networks and Social Web sites. We also presented some of our ideas for future work, including the need for more semantics as the focus of Social Web sites moves toward the provision of multimedia content; requirements for privacy and occasional fragmentation of a user's aggregated semantic content; and how a reputation system with embedded semantics could be deployed in a large-scale community site. Finally, based on observations that form and deployment are evolving toward object-centered networks and driven by the need to exploit information assessment methods, we described the direct integration of a social networking layer into the technology stack of clients (the desktop) and the Internet itself.

ACKNOWLEDGMENT

This work was supported by Science Foundation Ireland under Grant No. SFI/02/CE1/I131.

REFERENCES

[1] Aleman-Meza B., Nagarajan M., Ramakrishnan C., Ding L., Kolari P., Sheth A. P., Arpinar I. B., Joshi A., and Finin T., 2006. Semantic analytics on social networks: Experiences in addressing the problem of conflict of interest detection. In *Proceedings of the 15th International Conference on the World Wide Web*, Edinburgh, Scotland.
[2] Aleman-Meza B., Bojars U., Boley H., Breslin J. G., Mochol M., Nixon L. J. B., Polleres A., and Zhdanova A. V., 2007. Combining RDF vocabularies for expert finding. In *Proceedings of the 4th European Semantic Web Conference (ESWC'07)*, June 2007, Innsbruck, Austria.

[3] Batagelj V., and Mrvar A., 1998. Pajek—Program for large network analysis. *Connections*, **21**(2): 47–57.

[4] Berners-Lee T., Hendler J. A., and Lassila O., May 2001. The semantic Web. *Scientific American*, **284**(5): 34–43.

[5] Bojārs U., Heitmann B., and Oren E., 2007. A prototype to explore content and context on social community sites. *The SABRE Conference on Social Semantic Web (CSSW 2007)*, September 2007, Leipzig, Germany.

[6] Bojārs U., Passant A., Giasson F., and Breslin J. G., 2007. An architecture to discover and query decentralised RDF data. In *The 3rd Workshop on Scripting for the Semantic Web at the 4th European semantic Web Conference (ESWC'07)*, June 2007, Innsbruck, Austria.

[7] Bojārs U., Breslin J. G., Finn A., and Decker S., 2008. Using the semantic Web for linking and reusing data across Web 2.0 communities. In *Special Issue on the Semantic Web and Web 2.0. The Journal of Web Semantics*, **6**, 21–28.

[8] Bojārs U., Passant A., Breslin J. G., and Decker S., 2008. Social network and data portability using semantic Web technologies. In *Proceedings of the BIS 2008 Workshop on Social Aspects of the Web*, May 2008, Innsbruck, Austria.

[9] Borgatti S. P., Everett M. G., and Freeman L. C., 2002. UCINET for Windows: Software for Social Network Analysis. Analytic Technologies, Harvard, MA.

[10] Boyd D. M., and Ellison N. B., 2007. Social network sites: Definition, history, and scholarship. *Journal of Computer-Mediated Communication*, **13**(1).

[11] Breslin J. G., and Decker S., November/December 2007. The future of social networks on the Internet: The need for semantics. *IEEE Internet Computing*, **11**, 86–90.

[12] Breslin J. G., Harth A., Bojārs U., and Decker S., 2005. Towards Semantically-Interlinked Online Communities. In *Proceedings of the 2nd European Semantic Web Conference (ESWC'05)*, May 2005, Heraklion, Greece, LNCS, vol. 3532, pp. 500–514.

[13] Carroll J. J., Bizer C., Hayes P., and Stickler P., 2005. Named graphs, provenance and trust. In *Proceedings of the 14th International Conference on the World Wide Web (WWW2005)*, pp. 613–622. ACM Press, Chiba, Japan.

[14] Choi H. C., Kruk S. R., Grzonkowski S., Stankiewicz K., Davis B., and Breslin J. G., 2006. Trust models for community aware identity management. In *Proceedings of the Identity, Reference and Web Workshop at the 15th International World Wide Web Conference (IRW2006, WWW2006)*, May 2006, Edinburgh, Scotland.

[15] Decker S., and Frank M., 2004. The social semantic desktop. Technical Report 2004-05-02, Digital Enterprise Research Institute, National University of Ireland, Galway, May 2004. (http://www.deri.ie/fileadmin/documents/DERI-TR-2004-05-02.pdf).

[16] Ding L., Zhou L., Finin T., and Joshi A., 2005. How the semantic Web is being used: An analysis of FOAF documents. In *Proceedings of the 38th Hawaii International Conference on System Sciences (HICSS'05)*.

[17] Fernandez S., Berrueta D., and Labra J. E., 2007. Mailing lists meet the semantic Web. In *Proceedings of the BIS 2007 Workshop on Social Aspects of the Web*, April 2007, Poznan, Poland.

[18] Fisher D., Hogan B., Brush A. J., Smith M. A., and Jacobs A., 2006. Using social sorting to enhance email management. In *Proceedings of the Human–Computer Interaction Consortium (HCIC'06)*, ACM Press, New York, NY. (http://research.microsoft.com/research/pubs/view.aspx?type=Publication&id=1600).

[19] Freeman L. C., 2000. Visualizing social networks. *Journal of Social Structure*, **1**(1).

[20] Ghita S., Nejdl W., and Paiu W. R., 2005. Semantically rich recommendations in social networks for sharing, exchanging and ranking semantic context. In *Proceedings of the 4th International Semantic Web Conference*, November 2005, Galway, Ireland.

[21] Girvan M., and Newman M. E. J., 2002. Community structure in social and biological networks. In *Proceedings of the National Academy of Sciences of the United States of America*, **99**(12): 7821–7826.

[22] Golbeck J., and Hendler J., 2004. Reputation network analysis for email filtering. In *Proceedings of the 1st Conference on Email and Anti-Spam, Microsoft Research*. (http://www.ceas.cc/papers-2004/ 177.pdf).

[23] Golbeck J., Parsia B., and Hendler J., 2003. Trust networks on the semantic Web. In *Proceedings of Cooperative Intelligent Agents*, August 2003, Helsinki, Finland.

[24] Golder S., and Huberman B. A., April 2006. The structure of collaborative tagging systems. *Journal of Information Sciences*, **32**(2): 198–208.

[25] Gruber T., 2007. Ontology of folksonomy: A mash-up of apples and oranges. *International Journal on Semantic Web and Information Systems*, **3**(2).

[26] Heer J., and Boyd D., 2005. Vizster: Visualizing online social networks. In *IEEE Symposium on Information Visualization (InfoVis 2005)*, October 2005, Minneapolis, MN.

[27] Irvine M., 9 October 2006. Breaking up with social-networking sites. *The Seattle Times*. (http:// seattletimes.nwsource.com/html/living/2003292646_onlinebacklash09.html).

[28] Jordan K., Hauser J., and Foster S., 2003. The augmented social network: Building identity and trust into the next-generation Internet. *First Monday*, **8**(8). (http://www.firstmonday.org/issues/issue8_8/ jordan/index).

[29] Kim H. L., Yang S. K., Breslin J. G., and Kim H. G., 2007. Simple algorithms for representing tag frequencies in the SCOT exporter. In *The IEEE/WIC/ACM International Conference on Intelligent Agent Technology*, pp. 536–539. IEEE Computer Society, Washington, DC.

[30] Kinsella S., Harth A., Troussov A., Sogrin M., Judge J., Hayes C., and Breslin J. G., 2007. Navigating and annotating semantically-enabled networks of people and associated objects. In *Accepted for the 4th Conference on Applications of Social Network Analysis (ASNA 2007)*, September 2007, University of Zurich, Switzerland.

[31] Knorr-Cetina K., 1997. Sociality with objects: Social relations in postsocial knowledge societies. *Theory, Culture & Society*, **14**(4): 1–30.

[32] Kochut K., and Janik M., 2007. SPARQLeR: Extended SPARQL for semantic association discovery. In *Proceedings of the 4th European Semantic Web Conference (ESWC'07)*, Lecture Notes in Computer Science, vol. 4519, pp. 145–159. Springer-Verlag, Berlin.

[33] Lange C., Bojārs U., Groza T., Breslin J. G., and Handschuh S., 2008. Expressing Argumentative Discussions in Social Media Sites. In *Proceedings of the 1st International Workshop on Social Data on the Web (SDOW 2008) at the 7th International Semantic Web Conference (ISWC 2008)*, October 2008, Karlsruhe, Germany (ISSN 1613-0073).

[34] Leskovec J., Adamic L. A., and Huberman B. A., 2006. The dynamics of viral marketing. In *Proceedings of the ACM Conference on Electronic Commerce*, pp. 228–237. ACM Press, New York, NY.

[35] Liu H., Maes P., and Davenport G., 2006. Unraveling the taste fabric of social networks. *International Journal on Semantic Web and Information Systems*, **2**, 42–71.

[36] McAfee A., 2006. Enterprise 2.0: The dawn of emergent collaboration. *MIT Sloan Management Review*, **47**(3): 21–28.

[37] Mika P., 2005. Flink: Semantic Web technology for the extraction and analysis of social networks. *Web Semantics: Science, Services and Agents on the World Wide Web*, **3**(2–3): 211–223.

[38] Mika P., 2005. Ontologies are us: A unified model of social networks and semantics. In *International Semantic Web Conference*, Lecture Notes in Computer Science, pp. 522–536. Springer-Verlag, Berlin.

[39] O'Madadhain J., Fisher D., White S., and Boey Y., 2003. The JUNG (Java Universal Network/Graph) Framework. University of California, Irvine, CA.

[40] Passant A., and Laublet P., 2008. Meaning of a tag: A collaborative approach to bridge the gap between tagging and linked data. In *Proceedings of the WWW2008 Linked Data on the Web Workshop (LDOW2008)*, April 2008, Beijing, China.

[41] Passant A., and Raimond Y., 2008. Combining social music and semantic Web for music-related recommender systems. In *Proceedings of the 1st International Workshop on Social Data on the Web (SDOW 2008) at the 7th International Semantic Web Conference (ISWC 2008)*, October 2008, Karlsruhe, Germany (ISSN 1613-0073).

[42] Petrie C., 2006. Semantic attention management. *IEEE Internet Computing*, **10**(5): 93–96.

[43] Specia L., and Motta E., 2007. Integrating folksonomies with the semantic Web. In *Proceedings of the 4th European Semantic Web Conference (ESWC'07), semantic Web: Research and Applications*, May 2007, Innsbruck, Austria, LNCS, vol. 4519, pp. 624–639.

[44] Wasserman S., and Faust K., 1994. Social Network Analysis: Methods and Applications. Cambridge University Press, Cambridge.

[45] Watts D. J., and Strogatz S. H., 1998. Collective dynamics of 'small-world' networks. *Nature*, **393**(6684): 409–410.

[46] Wu X., Zhang L., and Yu Y., 2006. Exploring social annotations for the semantic Web. In *Proceedings of the 15th International Conference on World Wide Web*, May 2006, Edinburgh, Scotland.

Semantic Web Services Architecture with Lightweight Descriptions of Services

TOMAS VITVAR

Semantic Technology Institute,
University of Innsbruck, Austria

JACEK KOPECKY

Semantic Technology Institute,
University of Innsbruck, Austria

JANA VISKOVA

Department of Information Networks,
University of Zilina, Slovakia

ADRIAN MOCAN

Semantic Technology Institute,
University of Innsbruck, Austria

MICK KERRIGAN

Semantic Technology Institute,
University of Innsbruck, Austria

DIETER FENSEL

Semantic Technology Institute,
University of Innsbruck, Austria

Abstract

The goal of semantic Web services research and development is to introduce semantics for service descriptions and to enable an automation for various tasks of a service integration process. Recent developments in semantic Web services aim to introduce bottom-up approach to service modeling allowing to build incremental layers on top of existing service descriptions while at the same time enhance existing SOA technologies. An important step in this direction has been made in the W3C by the SAWSDL WG proposing a framework for annotating WSDL services with arbitrary semantic descriptions. In this chapter, we show how lightweight semantic service model called WSMO-Lite can build on top of SAWSDL and how such service model can be used for various tasks within the service integration process in a semantic Web services architecture and its service technology. Ultimately, our goal is to allow incremental steps on top of existing service descriptions, enhancing existing SOA capabilities with intelligent and automated integration.

1. Introduction

Web services and particularly technologies that enable them, such as WSDL (Web Service Description Language)[1] and SOAP[2] are widely acknowledged for their potential to revolutionize computing. Web service technologies enable so-called Service-Oriented Architectures (SOAs), a software architecture where functionality is abstracted as services with well-defined interfaces, independent of operating systems, programming languages, or any other technologies which underline the applications. The major driver behind adoption of SOA architectures in enterprises is to address requirements for flexibility and dynamism. However, existing SOA will prove difficult to scale without a proper degree of automation. SOAs success depends on resolving fundamental challenges that existing SOA technologies do not sufficiently address, namely search, integration, and mediation. In large-scale, open and service-centric environments, thousands of services will have to be discovered, adapted, and orchestrated based on user needs. Depending on XML only descriptions, this technology only offers manual support for integration which usually operates on rigid configuration of workflows or services. Although flexible and extensible, XML only defines the structure and syntax of data. The extension of SOA with semantics offers a scalable solution that is more adaptive to changes in business requirements. The goal is to design a semantic Web service (SWS) architecture and a technology promoting personalization and adaptability of business requirements on-the-fly. SWS architecture defines a service model where semantics is used for rich description of both services offered and capabilities required by potential users and on the top defines essential functionalities for the dynamic integration of services. The SWS architecture aims to solve users goals by means of logical reasoning over semantic descriptions while users, not aware of the processing logic, only care about the result and its quality.

2. SWS Architecture

The SWS architecture enables an open and service-centric environment where service orientation, intelligence and seamless integration are the key to providing services to their users. Following principles drive SWS architecture research, design, and implementation:

---

[1] http://www.w3.org/TR/wsdl.
[2] http://www.w3.org/TR/2000/NOTE-SOAP-20000508/.

- *Service-oriented principle* represents a distinct approach for analysis, design, and implementation which further introduces particular principles of service reusability, loose coupling, abstraction, composability, autonomy, and discoverability.
- *Semantic principle* allows a rich and formal description of information and behavioral models enabling automation of certain tasks by means of logical reasoning. Combined with the service-oriented principle semantics allows to define scalable, semantically rich and formal service models and ontologies allowing to promote total or partial automation of tasks such as service discovery, contracting, negotiation, mediation, composition, invocation, etc.
- *Problem-solving principle* follows problem-solving methods (PSM) as one of the fundamental concepts of the artificial intelligence. It underpins the ultimate goal of the architecture which lies in so-called goal-based discovery and invocation of services. Users (service requesters) describe requests as goals semantically and independently from services while the architecture solves those goals by means of logical reasoning over goal and service descriptions. Ultimately, users do not need to be aware of processing logic but only care about the result and its desired quality.

With respect to the service-oriented principle, SWS distinguishes two types of services, namely middleware services and business services. Middleware services are the main facilitators for search, integration, and mediation of business services. On the other hand, business services are exposed by back-end systems of service providers which are subject of integration within the architecture. Through the functionality of the both types of services, the SWS architecture aims to support business users who consume the functionality of business services through some domain applications, and engineers (i.e., enterprise architects, application programmers, and domain experts) who perform the development and administrative tasks related to configuration of business services within the SOA lifecycle, that is, modeling, deployment, assembling, management, and maintenance of business services. As Fig. 1 depicts, the SWS architecture introduces the three main layers: business services layer, middleware services layer, and problem-solving layer. We further detail a semantic services model for business services, and define a scope of required functionality for the middleware services.

2.1   Middleware Services Layer

In the SWS architecture, middleware services reside in the Semantic Execution Environment (SEE) middleware. They mainly operate on the semantic service model of business services with aim to facilitate the seamless integration of business

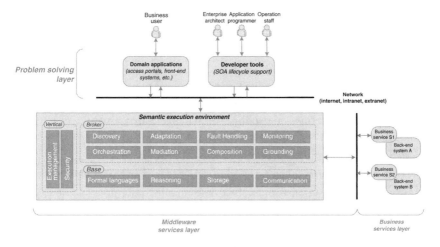

FIG. 1. Semantic Web services architecture.

services. The functionality of the middleware services is being specified within the OASIS SEE Technical Committee[3] with reference implementations of WSMX [16] and IRS-III [7]. In this section, we describe various general functionalities for middleware services in vertical, base, and broker sublayers.

The vertical sublayer defines a framework that is used across the broker and base layers but which remains invisible to them:

- Execution Management defines a control for distributed execution of middleware services.
- Security defines a secure communication, that is, authentication, authorization, confidentiality, data encryption, traceability, or nonrepudiation support applied within execution scenarios in the architecture.

The broker sublayer defines the functionality for various *service use tasks*:

- Discovery defines tasks for identifying and locating business services which can achieve a goal.
- Adaptation defines an adaptation within particular integration process according to users' requirements (e.g., service contracting, selection, ranking, validation).

---

[3] http://www.oasis-open.org/committees/semantic-ex/.

- Orchestration defines the execution of a composite process (business process) together with a conversation between a service requester and a service provider within that process.
- Monitoring defines a monitoring for the execution of business services. It gathers information on invoked services, for example, QoS related or for identifying faults during execution.
- Fault handling defines a handling of faults occurring within execution of business services.
- Mediation defines interoperability at the data and process levels.
- Composition defines a composition of services into an executable workflow.
- Grounding defines transformations from semantic descriptions to nonsemantic descriptions of business services.

The base sublayer defines functionality that is not directly required for a service use tasks; however, it is required by the broker layer for successful operation:

- Formal languages define semantic languages used for semantic description of services, goals, and ontologies.
- Reasoning defines reasoning functionality over semantic descriptions.
- Storage and communication defines persistence mechanism for various elements (e.g., repositories for services, ontologies) as well as inbound and outbound communication of the middleware.

2.2   Business Services Layer

The SWS architecture adopts the specification of the Semantic Service Stack for describing business services. In the core, a lightweight Web service modeling ontology (WSMO-Lite) provides a conceptual model for various aspects of business services described using various W3C-compliant semantic languages. WSMO-Lite together with semantic languages provides grounds for the semantic technology which is well suited for the SWS architecture underlying principles. In Section 3, we describe the model for business services in more detail.

2.3   Problem-Solving Layer

Through this layer, users can formulate or identify goals, submit goals, interact with the architecture during processing, and get desired results. End users can perform these activities through some domain applications; engineers can perform them through some management tools—that is, an integrated development environment. The reference implementations of the IDE framework developed for our SWS architecture are the Web Service Modeling Toolkit (WSMT) [20, 21] and WSMO studio.[4] In Section 5, we describe the WSMT in more details.

3. Model for Business Services

The major driver behind development of the Semantic Service Stack is to augment existing service descriptions already available on the Web or within enterprise environments. Service specifications allow one to describe service offerings so that an up-front decision on whether and how to consume services functionality can be made. Most of the specifications used today are expressed in WSDL. Their uptake will further enable environments where thousands of services will have to be searched, integrated, and mediated, and where automation will be the key enabler of service provisioning to end users.

In 2007, the W3C finished its work on semantic annotations for WSDL and XML schema (SAWSDL). SAWSDL defines simple extensions for WSDL and XML schema used to link WSDL components with arbitrary semantic descriptions. It thus provides the grounds for a bottom-up approach to semantic service modeling: it supports the idea of adding small increments (and complexity) on top of WSDL, allowing results from various existing approaches to be adopted. As the basis for bottom-up modeling, SAWSDL is independent of any particular semantic technology, that is, it does not define any types, forms, or languages for semantic descriptions. On top of SAWSDL, WSMO-Lite defines concrete semantic service descriptions and thus embodying the semantic layer of the Semantic Service Stack. With the ultimate goal to support real-world challenges in intelligent service integration, WSMO-Lite addresses the following requirements:

- Identify the types and a simple vocabulary for semantic descriptions of services (a service ontology) as well as languages used to define these descriptions.
- Define an annotation mechanism for WSDL using this service ontology.
- Provide the bridge between WSDL, SAWSDL, and (existing) domain-specific ontologies such as classification schemas, domain ontology models, etc.

Even though we adopt the base Web service model from WSDL and SAWSDL, WSMO-Lite is inspired in the WSMO framework [12]. However, in WSMO-Lite we only tackle semantic description of Web services, notably leaving user goals and mediators out of scope; and we value ease of use over semantic expressiveness.

---

[4] http://www.wsmostudio.org.

3.1 Semantic Service Stack

As Fig. 2 depicts, there are two levels in the Semantic Service Stack, namely semantic and nonsemantic level. When a service engineer describes a business service using the model in Fig. 2, the SWS architecture processing the business service description can apply various service automation tasks to automate the service integration process. As we have mentioned earlier, the model allows to reuse existing service descriptions already available in WSDL and enhance those description with appropriate semantic descriptions for purposes of service automation. Section 3.2 (Listing 1) shows the WSMO-Lite service ontology encoded in RDFS, Listing 2 shows an example of a concrete service ontology as an extension of the WSMO-Lite service ontology from the telecommunications domain, and finally Section 3.4 describes example annotations for a corresponding WSDL service using the telecommunications ontology.

The service tasks that SWS architecture automates include service discovery, adaptation, mediation, composition, invocation, etc. (see the broker sublayer of the middleware services layer in Section 2.1). From the business service perspective, we further denote such SWS architecture functionality a *client*. Through these tasks, the client or service engineer (depending on the level of automation) decides whether to bind with the service or not. To facilitate such decisions, services should describe their offers using so-called service contracts. The Semantic Service Stack adopts the following general types of service contracts:

- *Information model* defines the data model for input, output, and fault messages.
- *Functional descriptions* define service functionality, that is, what a service can offer to its clients when it is invoked.
- *Nonfunctional descriptions* define any incidental details specific to the implementation or running environment of a service.

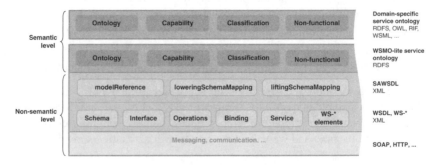

Fig. 2. Semantic Service Stack.

- *Behavioral descriptions* define external (public choreography) and internal (private workflow) behavior.
- *Technical descriptions* define messaging details, such as message serializations, communication protocols, and physical service access points.

In the following sections, we show how the Semantic Service Stack represents the above general description types for service contracts at the two different levels.

3.1.1   Nonsemantic Level

In regard to SOA technology developments today, the Semantic Service Stack represents service contracts at the nonsemantic level using the existing de-facto and de-jure standards: WSDL, SAWSDL, and related WS-* specifications. They all use XML as a common flexible data exchange format. Service contracts are represented as follows:

- *Information model* is represented using XML schema.
- *Functional description* is represented using a WSDL interface and its operations.
- *Nonfunctional description* is represented using various WS-* specifications, such as WS-policy, WS-reliability, WS-security, etc.
- *Behavioral description* is represented using the WS-* specifications of WS-BPEL (for the workflow) and WS-CDL (for the choreography).
- *Technical description* is represented using WSDL binding for message serializations and underlying communication protocols, such as SOAP, HTTP; and using WSDL service for physical endpoint information.

WSDL uses XML as a common flexible data exchange format and applies XML schema for data typing. WSDL aims to describe the Web service on a syntactic level: it specifies what messages look like rather than what they mean. It describes a Web service on three levels:

- ○ Reusable abstract interface defines a set of operations, each representing a simple exchange of messages described with XML schema element declarations.
- ○ Binding describes on-the-wire message serialization; it follows the structure for SOAP or HTTP.
- ○ Service represents a single physical Web service that implements a single interface; the Web service can be accessed at multiple network endpoints.

While SAWSDL does not fall into any of the service contract descriptions, it is an essential part of the nonsemantic level of the stack, providing the ground for the semantic layer. SAWSDL is a set of extensions for WSDL, which provides a standard description format for Web services allowing for a simple extension layer on top of WSDL. SAWSDL defines extension attributes that we apply to elements both in WSDL and in XML schema to annotate WSDL interfaces, operations, and their input and output messages. The SAWSDL extensions take two forms: model references that point to semantic concepts and schema mappings that specify data transformations between messages XML data structure and the associated semantic model. Table I summarizes the complete syntax introduced by SAWSDL.

Model references. A model reference is an extension attribute, sawsdl:model Reference, that we can apply to any WSDL or XML schema element to point to one or more semantic concepts. The value is a set of URIs, each one identifying some piece of semantics. Model references generically refer to semantic concepts, thus serve as hooks for attaching semantics. As well illustrate later, we can use model references to describe the meaning of data or to specify the function of a Web service operation.

Schema mappings. SAWSDL provides two attributes for attaching schema mappings, namely sawsdl:liftingSchemaMapping and sawsdl:loweringSchemaMapping. Lifting mappings transform XML data from a Web service message into a semantic model (for instance, into RDF data that follows some specific ontology), whereas lowering mappings transform data from a semantic model into an XML message. Lifting and lowering transformations are useful for communicating with a Web service within the SWS architecture, for example, the client software will lower some of its semantic data into a request message and send it to the Web service; when the client software receives the response message, it can lift the data contained in the message for semantic processing (see Fig. 3 and Section 4.2 for more details).

WSDL 1.1 support. Although SAWSDL is built primarily for WSDL 2.0, it also supports the older and more prevalent version, WSDL 1.1. Essentially, both model references and schema mappings apply in the same places in both WSDL versions. However, the XML schema for WSDL 1.1 allows only element extensions on

TABLE I
SAWSDL ATTRIBUTE EXTENSIONS

Name	Description
modelReference	A list of references to concepts in some semantic models (XML attribute)
liftingSchemaMapping	A list of pointers to alternative data-lifting transformations (XML attribute)
loweringSchemaMapping	A list of pointers to alternative data-lowering transformations (XML attribute)
attrExtensions	Attaches attribute extensions where only element extensibility is allows (XML element)

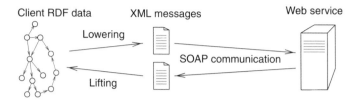

Fig. 3. Lifting and lowering in Web service communication.

operations, so a WSDL 1.1 document with the SAWSDL modelReference attribute on an operation would not be valid. To overcome this obstacle, SAWSDL defines the element attrExtensions to carry extension attributes in places where only element extensibility is allowed. Instead of putting the model reference directly on the operation element, SAWSDL can put it on the attrExtensions element, then insert that into the operation element.

3.1.2 Semantic Level

The Semantic Service Stack represents service contracts at the semantic level using the WSMO-Lite service ontology as follows (see Section 3.2 for a detailed description of WSMO-Lite):

- *Information model* is represented using a domain ontology that the service uses for description of functional, nonfunctional, or behavioral descriptions.
- *Functional descriptions* are represented as capabilities and/or functionality classifications. A capability defines conditions which must hold in a state before a client can invoke the service, and effects which hold in a state after the service invocation. Classifications define the service functionality using some classification ontology (i.e., a hierarchy of categories).
- *Nonfunctional descriptions* are represented using an ontology, semantically representing some policy or other nonfunctional properties.
- *Behavioral descriptions* are not represented explicitly in WSMO-Lite. Section 3.5 shows how the public part of the behavioral description of a Web service may be derived from the functional descriptions of its operations.
- *Technical descriptions* are not represented semantically in the service ontology, as they are sufficiently covered by the nonsemantic description in WSDL.

To create or reuse domain-specific service ontologies on top of the Semantic Service Stack, a service engineer can use any W3C-compliant language with an

RDF syntax.[5] This preserves the choice of language expressivity according to domain-specific requirements. Such languages may include RDF Schema (RDFS), Web Ontology Language (OWL) [17], Rule Interchange Format (RIF),[6] or Web Service Modeling Language (WSML) [12].

RDF. The W3C has produced several language recommendations for representation and exchange of knowledge on the Semantic Web. At the core, the Resource Description Framework (RDF) represents information in graph-based models with so-called triples, that is, statements in the form "subject, predicate, object." The subjects and objects link the triples into a graph. Thus, RDF can be used to represent the syntax of data using graph models while it does not define any semantics for any of the subjects, predicates, and objects. RDF provides various serializations including RDF/XML[7] and Notation 3 (N3).[8]

RDFS. On top of RDF, RDFS defines constructs that allow the expression of some semantics for the RDF model: RDFS allows the definition of classes describing the terminology of the domain of discourse, properties of those classes, as well as class and property hierarchies (i.e., subClassOf and subPropertyOf). Thus, RDFS provides the minimal set of constructs that allow the specification of lightweight ontologies.

On top of RDFS: OWL, WSML, and RIF. Where the expressivity of the RDFS is not sufficient for modeling of the required knowledge, various specializations of RDFS can be used. Such specializations are being developed both inside and outside of W3C along the lines of knowledge representation paradigms of Description Logic (DL) and Logic Programming (LP). OWL provides further vocabulary along with a formalism based on Description Logics. On the other hand, WSML defines several variants allowing for both paradigms of Description Logics (WSML-DL) and Logic Programming (WSML-Flight, WSML-Rule). All WSML variants can be represented using RDF syntax and they are layered on top of RDFS. While WSML-DL has a direct mapping to OWL, WSML-Rule is the basis of the Web Rule Language (WRL) specification which serves as an input for the W3C Rule Interchange Format Working Group (RIF WG). RIF WG aims to produce a core rule language for the Semantic Web together with extensions that allow rules to be translated between different rule languages. The detailed description of WSML its compliance with standards can be found in de Bruijn et al. [9].

---

[5] http://www.w3.org/RDF/.
[6] http://www.w3.org/2005/rules/.
[7] http://www.w3.org/TR/rdf-syntax-grammar/.
[8] http://www.w3.org/DesignIssues/Notation3.html.

3.2   WSMO-Lite Service Ontology

Listing 1 shows the WSMO-Lite service ontology in RDFS, serialized in Notation 3. Below, we explain the semantics of the WSMO-Lite elements:

```
 1 @prefix rdfs: <http://www.w3.org/2000/01/rdf−schema#> .
 2 @prefix rdf: <http://www.w3.org/1999/02/22−rdf−syntax−ns#> .
 3 @prefix owl: <http://www.w3.org/2002/07/owl#> .
 4 @prefix wl: <http://www.wsmo.org/ns/wsmo−lite#> .
 5
 6 wl:Ontology rdf:type rdfs:Class;
 7    rdfs:subClassOf owl:Ontology.
 8 wl:FunctionalClassificationRoot rdfs:subClassOf rdfs:Class.
 9 wl:NonFunctionalParameter rdf:type rdfs:Class.
10 wl:Condition rdf:type rdfs:Class.
11 wl:Effect rdf:type rdfs:Class.
```

LISTING 1. WSMO-Lite service ontology.

- *wl:Ontology* (lines 6–7) defines a container for a collection of assertions about the information model of a service. Same as *owl:Ontology*, *wl:Ontology* allows for metadata such as comments, version control, and inclusion of other ontologies. *wl:Ontology* is a subclass of *owl:Ontology* since as we already mentioned, it has a special meaning of the ontology used as the service information model.

- *wl:FunctionalClassificationRoot* (line 8) marks a class that is a root of a classification which also includes all the RDFS subclasses of the root class. A classification (taxonomy) of service functionalities can be used for functional description of a service.

- *wl:NonFunctionalParameter* (line 9) specifies a placeholder for a concrete domain-specific nonfunctional property.

- *wl:Condition* and *wl:Effect* (lines 10–12) together form a *capability* in functional service description.

Below, we describe the resolutions of major points that came up while WSMO-Lite was under development in the Conceptual Models for Services Working Group.[9]

Relation of WSMO-Lite to WSMO. WSMO-Lite has been created due to a need for lightweight service ontology which would directly build on the newest W3C

---

[9] http://cms-wg.sti2.org.

standards and allow bottom-up modeling of services. On the other hand, WSMO is an established framework for SWSs representing a top-down model identifying semantics useful in a semantics-first environment. WSMO-Lite adopts the WSMO model and makes its semantics lighter in the following major aspects:

- WSMO defines formal user goals and mediators, while WSMO-Lite treats mediators as infrastructure elements, and specifications for user goals as dependent on the particular discovery mechanism used. They both can be adopted in the running environment in combination with WSMO-Lite.
- WSMO-Lite only defines semantics for the information model, functional and nonfunctional descriptions (as WSMO Service does) and only implicit behavior semantics (see below). If needed, an application can extend WSMO-Lite with its own explicit behavioral descriptions, or it can adopt other existing technologies.
- While WSMO uses the WSML language for describing domain-specific semantic models, WSMO-Lite allows the use of any ontology language with an RDF syntax (see Section 3.1 for more details).

WSMO-Lite defines behavioral descriptions through functional annotations of operations. While WSMO-Lite does not have a special construct for behavioral descriptions, they are described declaratively with functional (capability) annotations of service operations. Such annotations can be transformed into a WSMO choreography [30], using the algorithm described in Section 3.5. WSMO-Lite does not deal with annotations of existing WS-BPEL processes, which may also describe Web service behavior. Semantic annotation of processes is an independent research effort led by the business process community and its use in combination with WSMO-Lite services is an open research question.

Dependency of WSMO-Lite on SAWSDL. As we already mentioned, WSMO-Lite has been created to address the need for a concrete service ontology as the next evolutionary step after SAWSDL. For this reason, it might seem that WSMO-Lite is also SAWSDL-dependent. However, WSMO-Lite uses SAWSDL only as an annotation mechanism for WSDL while the WSMO-Lite service ontology can be used with any machine-readable service descriptions in combination with an appropriate annotation mechanism.

Concrete semantics for conditions and effects. To work with conditions and effects, it is necessary to define the environment in which these axioms are evaluated. Such an environment depends on the particular logical language in which the axioms are expressed. WSMO-Lite does not prescribe any concrete language for functional service semantics, and therefore it cannot define semantics for conditions and effects as they are language-dependent.

3.3   Background Definitions

In this section, we provide some background definitions for semantic as well as nonsemantic descriptions of the Semantic Service Stack, namely ontology (used to describe information model, functionality classification ontology, and ontology for nonfunctional descriptions), capability, WSDL descriptions, and SAWSDL annotations. We use these definitions in subsequent sections of this chapter. In addition, we illustrate the types of service descriptions on the example ontology shown in Listing 2. The example ontology describes a telecommunication service (lines 9–24); the capability for a concrete Video-on-Demand (VoD) subscription service (lines 26–39) (the condition and the effect); a nonfunctional property describing the pricing (lines 44–48); and a simple functionality classification (lines 50–53). We also define the *wsml:AxiomLiteral* data type (line 42) for WSML-Rule axioms so that a client can correctly process them according to the WSML specification.

Ontology. The ontology is a fundamental building block for all types of semantic descriptions offered by WSMO-Lite, that is, WSMO-Lite represents the services information model, functional as well as nonfunctional descriptions as an ontology. In our work, we use a general definition of the ontology

$$\Omega = (C, R, E, I), \tag{1}$$

where the sets C, R, E, and I in turn denote classes (unary predicates), relations (binary and higher-arity predicates[10]), explicit instances (extensional definition), and axioms (intensional definition) which describe how new instances are inferred. A particular axiom common in I is the *subclass* relationship: if c_1 is subclass of c_2 (written as $c_1 \sqsubset c_2$), every instance of c_1 is also an instance of c_2. We call this axiom out because it is necessary for Definition 2 below.

We distinguish several subtypes of ontologies: we denote an *information model* ontology as $O_I \equiv \Omega$; a *functionality classification ontology* with root $r \in C$ as $O_F(r) = \Omega$; and an ontology for *nonfunctional descriptions* as $O_N \equiv \Omega$.

The ontology can be expressed in various languages as outlined in Section 3.1. As RDF and RDFS are the base languages, we illustrate the representation of RDF and RDFS ontology in Table II. However, other languages such as OWL or WSML can also be used, especially when expressing logical conditions (e.g., capability). Note that in Table II symbols such as c, r_1, etc., on the left-hand side are translated into URIs c and r_1, etc., on the right-hand side using a bijective naming function N: *symbol* $\rightarrow$ *uri*. For instance, instead of r_1 we could write $N(r_1)$, but we chose the

---

[10] Note that a minimal definition would combine the sets of classes and relations as a set of predicates, but we choose to split them, due to familiarity and also reuse in further definitions.

TABLE II

ONTOLOGY IN RDFS

Information semantics construct	RDFs triples
$c \in C$	c rdf:type rdfs:Class
$c \in C \wedge c(e) \in E$	e rdf:type c
$r \in R$, r is a binary predicate	r rdf:type rdf:Property
$r \in R \wedge r(a,b) \in E$	$a\ r\ b$
$r \in R$	r rdf:type rdfs:Class
r is an n-ary predicate with parameters $r_1,\ldots,r_n$	r_1 rdf:type rdf:Property
	$\vdots$
	r_n rdf:type rdf:Property
$r \in R \wedge r(a_1,\ldots,a_n) \in E$	$\_{:}x$ rdf:type r
	$\_{:}x\ r_1\ a_1$
	$\vdots$
	$\_{:}x\ r_n\ a_n$
$(\forall a, \forall b : r(a,b) \Rightarrow c(a)) \in I$	r rdfs:domain c
$(\forall a, \forall b : r(a,b) \Rightarrow c(b)) \in I$	r rdfs:range c
$(\forall a : c_1(a) \Rightarrow c_2(a)) \in I$	c_1 rdfs:subClassOf c_2
$(\forall a, \forall b : r_1(a,b) \Rightarrow r_2(a,b)) \in I$	r_1 rdfs:subPropertyOf r_2
Other axioms are expressed in some rule language	

former for readability. Equation 1 allows predicates with arity higher than two; however, RDFS only defines classes (unary predicates) and properties (binary predicates). For the higher-arity predicates, it is a common style to represent an n-ary predicate as a class, with attributes (properties with preset domain) representing the n-parameters.

In general, to model ontologies you can use classes of objects, attributes/relations and axioms. Classes of objects define the terminology of the domain of discourse. For example, in Listing 2 (lines 12–24) a simple ontology of a telecommunication service is shown in RDFS language. Here, the Service (line 16) stands for the class of all services that can be put in a subsumption relation by means of the subClassOf construct (line 24). Attributes define relations between classes, and point to data types. For example, in Listing 2, the Customer class has the relations hasService (line 13) and hasConnection (line 17). These relations point to classes for the parts of the Customer class. Please note that relations subClassOf, hasService, hasConnection, etc., are ontology relations, that is, intentional definitions of the ontology. Apart from relations, intentional definitions also include arbitrary complex logical expressions (axioms) over other definitions of the ontology. We show examples of logical expressions for some descriptions of services later encoded in the WSML language.

```
 1  /* namespaces and prefixes */
 2  @prefix rdfs: <http://www.w3.org/2000/01/rdf−schema#> .
 3  @prefix rdf: <http://www.w3.org/1999/02/22−rdf−syntax−ns#> .
 4  @prefix wl: <http://www.wsmo.org/ns/wsmo−lite#> .
 5  @prefix ex: <http://example.org/onto#> .
 6  @prefix xs: <http://www.w3.org/2001/XMLSchema#> .
 7  @prefix wsml: <http://www.wsmo.org/wsml/wsml−syntax#> .
 8
 9  /* ontology example */
10  <> rdf:type wl:Ontology.
11
12  ex:Customer rdf:type rdfs:Class .
13  ex:hasService rdf:type rdf:Property ;
14      rdfs:domain ex:Customer ;
15      rdfs:range ex:Service .
16  ex:Service rdf:type rdfs:Class .
17  ex:hasConnection rdf:type rdf:Property ;
18      rdfs:domain ex:Customer ;
19      rdfs:range ex:NetworkConnection .
20  ex:NetworkConnection rdf:type rdfs:Class .
21  ex:providesBandwidth rdf:type rdf:Property ;
22      rdfs:domain ex:NetworkConnection ;
23      rdfs:range xs:integer .
24  ex:VideoOnDemandService rdfs:subClassOf ex:Service .
25
26  /* capability description example */
27  ex:VideoOnDemandSubscriptionPrecondition rdf:type wl:Condition ;
28      rdf:value """
29          ?customer[hasConnection hasValue ?connection]
30              memberOf Customer and
31          ?connection[providesBandwidth hasValue ?y]
32              memberOf NetworkConnection and
33          ?y > 1000
34      """^^wsml:ExpressionLiteral .
35
36  ex:VideoOnDemandSubscriptionEffect rdf:type wl:Effect ;
37      rdf:value """
38          ?customer[hasService hasValue ?service]
39      """^^wsml:ExpressionLiteral .
40
41  /* non−functional property example */
42  ex:PriceSpecification rdfs:subClassOf wl:NonFunctionalParameter .
43  ex:VideoOnDemandPrice rdf:type ex:PriceSpecification ;
44      ex:pricePerChange "30"^^ex:euroAmount ;
45      ex:installationPrice "49"^^ex:euroAmount .
46
47  /* classification example */
48  ex:SubscriptionService rdf:type wl:FunctionalClassificationRoot .
49  ex:VideoSubscriptionService rdfs:subClassOf ex:SubscriptionService .
50  ex:NewsSubscriptionService rdfs:subClassOf ex:SubscriptionService .
```

LISTING 2. Example of domain-specific service ontology.

Capability. Functional description of a service as a capability is defined here as

$$K = \left(\Sigma, \phi^{\text{pre}}, \phi^{\text{eff}}\right), \tag{2}$$

where $\Sigma \subseteq (\{x\} \cup C \cup R \cup E)$ is the signature of symbols, that is, identifiers of elements from C, R, E of some ontology O_I complemented with variable names $\{x\}$; ϕ^{pre} is a condition which must hold in a state before the service can be invoked, and ϕ^{eff} is the effect, a condition which must hold in a state after the successful invocation. Conditions and effects are defined as statements in logic $L(\Sigma)$. In the example ontology in Listing 2, the condition (lines 27–34) specifies that the customer must have a connection with minimal bandwidth required by the service, and the effect (lines 36–39) specifies that the customer is subscribed to the VoD service as a result of the service invocation.

In addition, we define a capability and a category restriction. In Definition 1 below, we specify a *restriction* relationship (partial ordering) between capabilities, and in Definition 2 we define an analogous relationship between categories in a functionality classification. Practically, if a capability/category K_1 is a restriction of another capability/category K_2, any discovery algorithm that discovers K_1 as a suitable capability/category for some goal would also discover K_2 as such.

Definition 1 (capability restriction) A capability $K_1 = \left(\Sigma, \phi_1^{\text{pre}}, \phi_1^{\text{eff}}\right)$ is a restriction of $K_2 = \left(\Sigma, \phi_2^{\text{pre}}, \phi_2^{\text{eff}}\right)$ (written as $K_1 \leq K_2$) if the condition ϕ_1^{pre} only holds in states (denoted as s) where also ϕ_2^{pre} holds, and if the same is true for the effects:

$$K_1 \leq K_2 \Leftrightarrow \forall s : (\text{holds}(\phi_1^{\text{pre}}, s) \Rightarrow \text{holds}(\phi_2^{\text{pre}}, s)) \wedge$$
$$\left(\text{holds}(\phi_1^{\text{eff}}, s) \Rightarrow \text{holds}(\phi_2^{\text{eff}}, s)\right). \tag{3}$$

Definition 2 (category restriction) For two functionality categories K_1 and K_2 from classification $O_F(r)$, K_1 is a restriction of K_2 (written as $K_1 \leq K_2$) if $K_1 \subset K_2$:

$$K_1 \leq K_2 \Leftrightarrow K_1 \subset K_2. \tag{4}$$

WSDL. We denote an XML schema in WSDL as S, a WSDL interface as I, and a service as W. Further, we denote $\{x\}_S$ as the set of all element declarations and type definitions of S, and $\{\text{op}\}_I$ as the set of all operations of I. Each operation $\text{op} \in \{\text{op}\}_I$ may have one input message element $m \in \{x\}_S$ and one output message element $n \in \{x\}_S$ and a corresponding MEP[11] denoted here as *op.mep*.

Annotations. According to SAWSDL, we distinguish two types of annotations, namely *reference annotations* and *transformation annotations*. A reference annotation points from a WSDL component to a semantic concept. This is denoted as the

---

[11] Message Exchange Pattern, http://www.w3.org/TR/wsdl20-adjuncts/#meps.

binary relation $ref(x, s)$, where $x \in (\{x\}_S \cup \{I\} \cup \{op\}_I)$—any WSDL or Schema component; $s \in (C \cup R \cup E \cup \{K\})$—an ontology element or a capability. SAWSDL represents ref using $modelReference$ extension attribute on the WSDL or XML schema component.

A transformation annotation specifies a data transformation called $lifting$ from a component of schema S to an element of ontology O_I; and a reverse transformation (from ontology to XML) called $lowering$. We denote these annotations as the binary relations $lower(m, f(c_1))$ and $lift(n, g(n))$, where $m, n \in \{x\}_S$. The function $f(c_1) = m$, where $c_1 \in (C \cup R)$, is a lowering function transforming data described semantically by c_1 to the XML message described by schema m (SAWSDL represents this annotation using $loweringSchemaMapping$ extension attribute on m). Analogously, function $g(n) = c_2$, where $c_2 \in (C \cup R)$, is a lifting function transforming XML data from the message n to semantic data described by c_2 (SAWSDL represents this annotation using $liftingSchemaMapping$ extension attribute on n).

3.4 Annotations and Rules

Figure 4 illustrates a set of annotations (marked $A1 \ldots A5$) and their associated rules (marked $Rule\ 1 \ldots Rule\ 5$). The rules have been refined from Vitvar et al. [32] to conform to the latest WSMO-Lite service ontology specification. The purpose of the rules is to ensure that the annotations are:

- *Complete*, that is, no gaps are left in the semantic annotations, so that the client can see all the parts of the service description; for instance, all the operations should be semantically annotated so that they are reachable to automatic discovery.

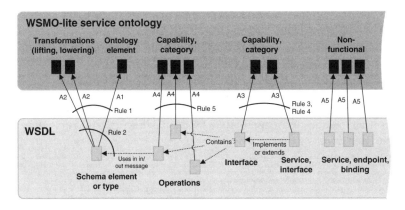

FIG. 4. Illustration of annotations and rules.

- *Consistent*, that is, no related annotations are contradictory; for instance, the schema annotations by model reference need to point to concepts that are the outputs of the lifting schema mapping transformation, or inputs of the lowering one.

A1: Annotations of XML schema (ontology). The schema used in WSDL to describe messages, that is, the element declarations and type definitions, can carry reference annotations linking to classes from the service information model ontology.

A2: Annotations of XML schema (transformations). To be able to communicate with a service, the client needs to transform data between its semantic model and the service-specific XML message structures. The schema may contain transformation annotations which specify the appropriate mappings.

```
1 <xs:element name="NetworkConnection" type="NetworkConnectionType"
2    sawsdl:modelReference="http://example.org/onto#NetworkConnection"
3    sawsdl:loweringSchemaMapping="http://example.org/NetCn.xslt"/>
```

LISTING 3. Example of annotations *A1* and *A2*.

Listing 3 shows an example of annotations *A1* and *A2* (the lowering transformation is omitted for brevity). Below, Rule 1 defines consistency of *A1* and *A2* annotations on schema components; Rule 2 defines completeness of these annotations on element declarations used as operation input and output messages.

Rule 1 (consistency) Let S be a schema and O_I be an ontology. If for any $m \in \{x\}_S$ there exist the annotations $ref(m, c_1)$ (*A1*) and $lower(m, f(c_1))$ (*A2*), then it must hold that $f(c_1) = m$. Analogously, if for any $n \in \{x\}_S$ there exist the annotations $ref(n, c_2)$ (*A1*) and $lift(n, g(n))$ (*A2*), then it must hold that $g(n) = c_2$.

Rule 2 (completeness) Let S be a schema and I be an interface. For each $m \in \{x\}_S$ where m is the input message element of any operation in $\{op\}_I$, the element must have consistent annotations $ref(m, c_1)$ (*A1*) and $lower(m, f(c_1))$ (*A2*). Analogously, for each $n \in \{x\}_S$ where n is the output message element of any operation in $\{op\}_I$, the element must have consistent annotations $ref(n, c_2)$ (*A1*) and $lift(n, g(n))$ (*A2*).

A3: Annotations of WSDL interface and service (functional). Functional descriptions (both capabilities and categories) apply both to concrete Web services and to the reusable and abstract interfaces. A reference annotation points from a service or an interface to its appropriate functional description. Listing 4 shows an example of multiple *A3* annotations:

```
1 <wsdl:interface name="NetworkSubscription"
2    sawsdl:modelReference="http://example.org/onto#VideoSubscriptionService
3        http://example.org/onto#VideoOnDemandSubscriptionPrecondition
4        http://example.org/onto#VideoOnDemandSubscriptionEffect" >
```

LISTING 4. Example of annotation *A3*.

Please note that a WSDL interface may be shared by multiple services; therefore, the functional description of the interface should be general. A concrete functional description attached to the service then refines the functional description of the interface. Additionally, aggregate interfaces or services (i.e., those that combine multiple potentially independent functionalities) may be annotated with multiple functional descriptions. Rule 3 defines consistency for *A3* annotations: each functionality of a service must be a restriction of some functionality of the service's interface (see Definitions 1 and 2). This allows discovery to first find appropriate interfaces and then only check services that implement these interfaces. Rule 4 is analogous to Rule 3 with the difference that it applies to interface extension,[12] ensuring that functionality cannot be lost through WSDL interface extension.

Rule 3 (consistency) Let W be a service and I be an interface such that W implements I. Then, for each annotation $ref(W, F)$ (*A3*), there must exist an annotation $ref(I, G)$ (*A3*) such that $F \leq G$.

Rule 4 (consistency) Let I and J be some interfaces such that I extends J. Then, for each annotation $ref(I, F)$ (*A3*), there must exist an annotation $ref(J, G)$ (*A3*) such that $G \leq F$.

A4: Annotations of WSDL interface operations (functional). Functional descriptions (both capabilities and categories) apply also to interface operations, to indicate their particular functionalities. A reference annotation points from an operation to its appropriate functional description.

Functional annotation of interface operations can be used for services whose interfaces are simply collections of standalone operations. For example, a network subscription service may offer independent operations for subscription to a bundle, cancellation of a subscription, or price inquiry. A client will generally only want to use one or two of these operations, not all three. This shows that service discovery can, in such cases, become operation discovery. Also, operation annotations can be used for defining the order in which the operations should be invoked (see Section 3.5).

Rule 5 defines completeness for *A4* annotations: all operations within an interface must be annotated with a functional description. This rule ensures that no operation is left invisible to the automated clients.

Rule 5 (completeness) For all $o \in \{op\}_I$, there must exist some functional description F (capability or category) such that $ref(o, F)$ is defined.

Please note that annotations *A3* and *A4* apply to both types of functional descriptions, that is, a capability or a category from some functional classification. It is even possible to combine them for a service, interface, and its operations.

---

[12] Interface extension is a feature of WSDL 2.0.

A5: Annotations of WSDL service, endpoints, and binding (nonfunctional).
Nonfunctional descriptions apply to a concrete instance of a Web service, that is, a
service, its endpoints, or its binding. A reference annotation can point from any of
these components to a nonfunctional property. Listing 5 shows an example of
annotation *A5*:

```
1 <wsdl:service name="ExampleCommLtd"
2     interface="NetworkSubscription"
3     sawsdl:modelReference="http://example.org/onto#VideoOnDemandPrice">
4   <wsdl:endpoint ...
5 </wsdl:service>
```

LISTING 5. Example of annotation *A5*.

Please note that nonfunctional descriptions are always specific to a concrete
service, therefore, annotating interfaces or interface operations with nonfunctional
properties is not defined. In case nonfunctional properties need to be specified on the
operations (e.g., different operations may have different invocation micropayment
prices), a WSDL binding operation components (which mirror the operations of
some interface) may be used to capture these properties. Due to the domain-specific
nature of nonfunctional properties, WSMO-Lite cannot formulate any consistency
or completeness rules for nonfunctional descriptions.

3.5   On Top of WSMO-Lite Annotations

WSMO-Lite annotations for Web services allow additional tasks on top: in
particular, we show implicit representation of a service choreography and illustrate
the overall use of WSMO-Lite annotations for various SWS tasks essential for the
SWS architecture's automated decisions about services.

3.5.1   Implicit Choreography

In this section, we show how WSMO-Lite interface operation annotations implicitly
represent a choreography, understood according to Roman and Scicluna [29] as a
protocol from a single service's point of view,[13] and formalized as an abstract state
machine (ASM, [6]) as

$$X = (\Sigma, L), \tag{5}$$

---

[13] WS-CDL defines a different type of a choreography, that is, as a common behavior of collaborating
parties. The relationship of WSMO-Lite to WS-CDL is an open research question.

where $\Sigma \subseteq (\{x\} \cup C \cup R \cup E)$ is the signature of symbols, that is, variable names $\{x\}$ or identifiers of elements from C, R, E of some ontology O_I; and L is a set of rules. Further, we denote by Σ_I and Σ_O the input and output symbols of the choreography (subsets of $C \cup R \cup E$), corresponding to the input data sent to the service and the returned output data. Each rule $r \in L$ defines a state transition $r : r^{\text{cond}} \rightarrow r^{\text{eff}}$, where r^{cond} is an expression in logic $L(\Sigma)$ which must hold in a state before the transition is executed; r^{eff} is an expression in logic $L(\Sigma)$ describing a condition which holds in a state after the execution. And finally, we use ontology elements as conditions (as in $c_1 \in O_I : c_1 \wedge \phi^{\text{pre}}$ within the algorithm), by which we mean that there exists an entity in the knowledge base which fits the description of the ontology element; for example, if the ontology element c_1 is a class, the knowledge base contains an instance of this class.

We construct the choreography from capability annotations of interface operations, according to the following algorithm.

Input:
- An interface I with operations $\{\text{op}\}_I$, ontology O_I, and a set of capabilities $\{K\}$
- *A4* annotations using capabilities from $\{K\}$ for operations $\{\text{op}\}_I$
- Consistent and complete *A1* and *A2* annotations using O_I for all input and output messages of operations $\{\text{op}\}_I$

Output:
- Choreography X with Σ_I, Σ_O, and L.

Algorithm:
1: **for all** *ref*(op, K), op $\in \{\text{op}\}_I$, $K = (\phi^{\text{pre}}, \phi^{\text{eff}}) \in \{K\}$ **do**
2:     get *ref*(m, c_1) where m is the input message of op, $c_1 \in O_I$; add c_1 to Σ_I.
3:     get *ref*(n, c_2) where n is the output message of op, $c_2 \in O_I$; add c_2 to Σ_O.
4:     **if** *op.mep* in $\{$*in–out, in-only, out-only*$\}$ **then**
5:         create the rule $r : r^{\text{cond}} = c_1 \wedge \phi^{\text{pre}}, r^{\text{eff}} = c_2 \wedge \phi^{\text{eff}}$; add r to L.
6:     **else if** *op.mep* in $\{$*out–in*$\}$ **then**
7:         create the rule $r_1 : r_1^{\text{cond}} = \phi^{\text{pre}}, r_1^{\text{eff}} = c_2$; add r_1 to L.
8:         create the rule $r_2 : r_2^{\text{cond}} = c_1 \wedge c_2, r_2^{\text{eff}} = \phi^{\text{eff}}$; add r_2 to L.
9:     **end if**
10: **end for**

The algorithm creates the sets of choreography input and output symbols from the semantic representations of the input and output messages of all the operations (lines 2–3). In addition, it creates choreography rules where the conditions contain assertions about the input messages and the effects contain assertions about output messages of operations. The algorithm creates one rule for operations with the *in–out*, *in-only*, or *out-only* MEPs (lines 4–5). Since the ASM rules always represent an *in–out* interaction, two rules need to be created for operations with the *out–in* MEP: one representing the output and one the following input interaction. To further illustrate the results of the algorithm, Table III shows the resulting rules for the four MEPs (please note that we do not currently cover fault messages). Here, a transition rule $r^{cond} \rightarrow r^{eff}$ is represented as if r^{cond} then r^{eff}; the symbols msg1...msg6 refer to schema elements used for input/output messages of operations; the symbols $c_1...c_6$ refer to identifiers of semantic descriptions of these messages; $ref(m, c)$ denotes the *A1* annotation, w is a shortening for the URI http://www.w3.org/ns/wsdl/, and *ex* is a shortening for some application URI http://example.org/onto#. With a choreography constructed according to this algorithm, the client is able to automatically invoke a service, that is, its operations in the correct and expected order (see Section 4.2 for more details).

3.5.2   Service Use Tasks

Not all annotations described in Section 3.4 are always needed, only those required by the tasks at hand in a particular domain-specific setting. Table IV provides a summary, with *A1...A5* denoting the annotations and *R1...R5* denoting

TABLE III
MEPs, Rules, and WSDL Operations

MEP and rule	WSDL operation
in–out: if $c_1 \wedge$; cnd1 then $c_2 \wedge$; eff1 $c_1 \in \Sigma_I$, ref(msg1, c_1) $c_2 \in \Sigma_O$, ref(msg2, c_2)	<operation name="op1" pattern="w: in-out" sawsdl:modelReference="ex:cnd1 ex:eff1"> <input element="msg1"/> <output element="msg2"/> </operation>
in-only: if $c_3 \wedge$; cnd2 then eff2 $c_3 \in \Sigma_I$, ref(msg3, c_3)	<operation name="op2" pattern="w: in-only"> sawsdl:modelReference="ex:cnd2 ex:eff2"> <input element="msg3"/> </operation>
out-only: if cnd3 then $c_4 \wedge$; eff3 $c_4 \in \Sigma_O$, ref(msg4, c_4)	<operation name="op3" pattern="w: out-only"> sawsdl:modelReference="ex:cnd3 ex:eff3"> <output element="msg4"/> </operation>
out–in: if cnd4 then c_5 if $c_5 \wedge c_6$ then eff4 $c_5 \in \Sigma_O$, ref(msg5, c_5) $c_6 \in \Sigma_I$, ref(msg6, c_6)	<operation name="op4" pattern="w: out-in"> sawsdl:modelReference="ex:cnd4 ex:eff4"> <output element="msg5"/> <input element="msg6"/> </operation>

TABLE IV
SERVICE TASKS, ANNOTATIONS, AND RULES

Service task	A1	A2	A3	A4	A5	R1	R2	R3	R4	R5
Service discovery			•					○	○	
Operation discovery				•						○
Composition			•							
Ranking and selection					•					
Operation invocation	•	•				•	•			
Service invocation	•	•		•		•	•			○
Data mediation	•	•				•				
Process mediation	•	•		•		•	•			○

the rules. The symbol • marks the annotations and rules required to automate a given task, and the symbol ○ marks rules that are helpful but not absolutely required:

- *Service discovery*, operating on functional descriptions (capabilities or categories), requires annotations *A3*. Rules 3 and 4 help improve the scalability of the discovery through narrowing down a set of interfaces and services to be searched. If the discovery mechanism determines that an interface is not suitable, all the services implementing it and all the interfaces extended by it can immediately be discarded from further consideration.

- *Operation discovery*, operating on functional descriptions of individual operations, requires annotations *A4*. Operation discovery might be useful with interfaces that are collections of standalone, independent operations. Rule 5 ensures that no operation is left invisible to this discovery process.

- *Composition* uses capability descriptions, that is, annotations *A3* restricted to capabilities, to put together multiple services to achieve a complex goal.

- *Ranking and selection* processes nonfunctional descriptions, that is, annotations *A5*, to select the service that most suits some particular requirements.

- *Operation invocation* is the invocation of a single operation, requiring data transformations between the semantic model on the client and the service's XML message structure. This requires *A1* and *A2* annotation, kept consistent by Rule 1. Rule 2 ensures that all operation messages have these annotations.

- *Service invocation* requires the operations of the service to be invoked in a proper order. This task therefore uses the implicit interface choreography (Section 3.5) and requires annotations *A4*. Rule 5 ensures that no operation is omitted from the choreography.

- *Data mediation* uses data annotations (*A1* and *A2*)—assuming two different schemas correspond to a single shared ontology, the *A1* annotations make it possible to discover such a correspondence, and the *A2* annotations then enable data mapping transformations: lifting from one schema and lowering to the other.

- *Process mediation* combines data mediation and choreography processing and thus requires the combined annotations *A1*, *A2*, and *A4*. As described in Haselwanter et al. [16], process mediation is applied during conversation between two services mediating their choreographies and messages.

This provides certain modularity to WSMO-Lite, enabling different environments using this service ontology to mix and match the annotations as necessary for the required tasks. On top of already being lightweight, WSMO-Lite provides value even if only parts of it are used.

4. Service Execution Model

SWS architecture defines two phases in the service integration process, namely *late-binding phase* and *execution phase* [33]. In the late-binding phase, the architecture binds a user request with a set of services "on-the-fly" through semiautomation of the *service lifecycle* by applying various tasks of service discovery, adaptation, mediation, composition, invocation, etc. In the execution phase, the architecture invokes previously bound services and manages the conversation between them. While services may have heterogeneous descriptions in terms of data and protocols, it is important to achieve their interoperability within the both phases. In this section, we describe a model for the SWS architecture execution phase and show how interoperability can be achieved between two services through combined data and process mediation. In Section 5.3, we demonstrate the execution model on a B2B scenario.

4.1 Background Definitions

Data mediation. Data mediation resolves interoperability conflicts between two services that use two different ontologies. In general, the data mediation has two stages (1) creation of alignments between *source* and *target* ontologies during *design-time* and (2) applying the alignments to resolve interoperability conflicts during *run-time*. Since the interoperability problems can greatly vary in their nature and severity, fully automatic solution for the creation of alignments are not feasible in real-world case scenarios due to the lower than 100% precision and recall of existing methods.[14] From this reason, the design-time data mediation stage is still dependent on manual support of a service engineer.

An alignment consists of a set of mappings (rules) expressing the semantic relationships that exist between the two ontologies. In particular, a mapping can specify that classes from two ontologies are equivalent while corresponding rules use logical expressions to unambiguously define how the data encapsulated in an instance of one class can be encapsulated in instances of the second class. Formally, we define an alignment A between source and target ontologies $O_s = (C_s, R_s, E_s, I_s)$ and $O_t = (C_t, R_t, E_t, I_t)$ as

$$A_{s,t} = (O_s, O_t, \Phi_{s,t}),\qquad(6)$$

where $\Phi_{s,t}$ is the set of mappings m in the form

$$m = \langle \varepsilon_s, \varepsilon_t, \gamma_{\varepsilon_s}, \gamma_{\varepsilon_t} \rangle,\qquad(7)$$

where ε_s and ε_t represent the mapped entities from the two ontologies while γ_{ε_s} and γ_{ε_t} represent restrictions (i.e., conditions) on these entities such as $\varepsilon_s \in C_s \cup R_s$, $\varepsilon_t \in C_t \cup R_t$ while γ_{ε_s} and γ_{ε_t} are expressions in logic$L(C_s \cup R_s \cup E_s)$ and $L(C_t \cup R_t \cup E_t)$, respectively.

To execute the mappings during the execution phase, these mappings must be *grounded* to rules expressed in some logical language for which a reasoning support is available (in Section 5.3, we show examples of rules in the WSML language). We obtain the set of rules $\rho_{s,t} = \Phi_{s,t}^G$ by applying the grounding G to the set of mappings Φ. Every mapping rule $\mathrm{mr} \in \rho_{s,t}$ has the following form:

$$\mathrm{mr}: \bigwedge_{i=1\ldots n}^{\{x\}} \mathrm{mr}_i^{\mathrm{head}} \rightarrow \bigwedge_{i=1\ldots n}^{\{x\}} \mathrm{mr}_i^{\mathrm{body}}\qquad(8)$$

where

$$\mathrm{mr}^{\mathrm{head}} \in \{x'\mathbf{instanceOf}\varepsilon | \varepsilon \in C_t \wedge x' \in \{x\}\}$$
$$\cup \{\varepsilon(x', x'') | \varepsilon \in R_t \wedge \varepsilon(x', x'') \in E_t \wedge x', x'' \in \{x\}\},$$
$$\mathrm{mr}^{\mathrm{body}} \in \{x'\mathbf{instanceOf}\varepsilon | \varepsilon \in C_s \wedge x' \in \{x\}\}$$
$$\cup \{\varepsilon(x', x'') | \varepsilon \in R_s \wedge \varepsilon(x', x'') \in E_s \wedge x', x'' \in \{x\}\}$$
$$\cup \{\gamma_s | \gamma_s \in L(C_s \cup R_s \cup E_s \cup \{x\})\}$$
$$\cup \{\gamma_t | \gamma_t \in L(C_t \cup R_t \cup E_t \cup \{x\})\}.$$

---

[14] The "Ontology Alignment Evaluation Initiative 2006" [10] shows that the best five systems' scores vary between 61% and 81% for precision and between 65% and 71% for recall.

A mapping rule is formed of a head and a body. The head is a conjunction of logical expressions over the target elements and describes the result of the mediation in terms of instances of the target ontology. The body is formed of a set of logical expressions over the source entities which represent the data to be mediated, plus a set of logical expressions representing conditions over both the source and the target data. In the above definitions, $\{x\}$ stands for the set of variables used by the mapping rule and x' and x'' are two particular variables.

There are situations when there is no corresponding data in the source ontology as required by the target ontology such as when mapping prices with different currency units. These issues are, however, dependant on implementation of the data mediation and the reasoning engine. In our implementation, it is possible to specify an URI for a transformation function and its parameters as placeholders for the missing target values. It is the role of the reasoning engine to fill the parameters placeholders with data from the source ontology. The data mediation engine then executes the function and gets the data for the target ontology.

Process mediation. Process mediation handles interoperability issues which occur in descriptions of choreographies of the two services. In [8], Cimpian defines five process mediation patterns:

1. *Stopping an unexpected message*: when one service sends a message which is not expected by the other service.
2. *Inversing the order of messages*: when one service sends messages in a different order than the other service expects them to receive.
3. *Splitting a message*: when a service sends a message which the other service expects to receive in multiple different messages.
4. *Combining messages*: when a service expects to receive a message which is sent by the other service in multiple different messages.
5. *Generating a message*: when one service expects to receive a message which is not supplied by the other service.

4.2   Execution Phase

Figure 5 depicts the main states of the execution phase. In this section, we define the algorithm for the execution phase and in Section 4.3, we further discuss some relevant aspects for the data and process mediation applied within the phase.

Input:
- Service W_1 and service W_2. Each such a service W contains the interface I with operations $\{op\}_I$, ontology O_I (Eq. 1), and a set of capabilities $\{K\}$ (Eq. 2).
- *A4* annotations using capabilities from K for operations $\{op\}_I$ and consistent and complete annotations *A1* and *A2* using O_I for all input and output messages

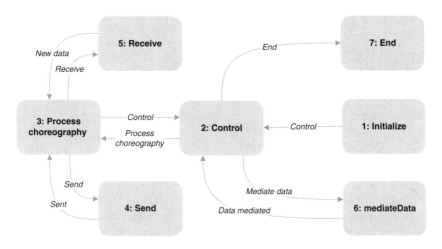

FIG. 5. Control state diagram for the execution phase.

of operations $\{op\}_I$. Using the algorithm described in Section 3.5, we construct a choreography WX (Eq. 5) with set of rules WXL.

- Mappings Φ_{12} of W_1O_I to W_2O_I and mappings Φ_{21} of W_2O_I to W_1O_I.

Uses:

- Symbols M_1 and M_2 corresponding to the processing memory of the choreography W_1X and W_2X, respectively (a memory M is a populated ontology WO_I with instance data). The content of each memory M determines at some point in time a state in which a choreography WX is. In addition, each memory has a method $M.add$ allowing to add the data to M and a flag $M.modified$ indicating whether the memory was modified. The flag $M.modified$ is set to *true* whenever the method $M.add$ is used.

- Symbols D_1 and D_2 corresponding to the set of data to be added to the memory M_1 and M_2 after one or more rules of a choreography are processed. Each D has a method $D.add$ for adding new data to the set.

- A symbol 0 corresponding to a WSDL operation of a service and symbols m, n corresponding to some XML data of the message (input or output) of the operation 0.

States 1, 2, 7: Initialize, Control, End

1: $M_1 \leftarrow \emptyset$; $M_2 \leftarrow \emptyset$
2: **repeat**
3:     $M_1.modified \leftarrow false$; $M_2.modified \leftarrow false$

4:    $D_1 \leftarrow processChoreography(W_1, M_1)$
5:    $D_2 \leftarrow processChoreography(W_2, M_2)$
6:    **if** $D_1 \neq \emptyset$ **then**
7:        $D_m \leftarrow mediateData(D_1, W_1O, W_2O, \Phi_{12})$
8:        $M_1.add(D_1); M_2.add(D_m)$
9:    **end if**
10:   **if** $D_2 \neq \emptyset$ **then**
11:       $D_m \leftarrow mediateData(D_2, W_2O, W_1O, \Phi_{21})$
12:       $M_1.add(D_m); M_2.add(D_2)$
13:   **end if**
14: **until not** $M_1.modified$ **and not** $M_2.modified$

After the initialization of the processing memory M_1 and M_2 (line 1), the execution gets to the control state when the algorithm can process choreographies (State 3), mediate the data (State 6), or end the execution (State 7). The execution ends when no modifications of the processing memories M_1 or M_2 has occurred.

State 3: $D = processChoreography(W, M)$

1: $D \leftarrow \emptyset$
2: **for all** r in WXL: $holds(r^{cond}, M)$ **do**
3:      **if** c in r^{cond}: $c \in WX\Sigma_I$ **then**
4:          $send(c, W)$
5: **end if**
6: **if** c in r^{eff}: $c \in WX\Sigma_O$ **then**
7:          $c \leftarrow receive(W)$
8:          **if** $c \neq \emptyset$ **then**
9:              $D.add(c)$
10:         **end if**
11:     **end if**
12: **end for**
13: **return** D

The algorithm executes each rule of the choreography which condition holds in the memory by processing its condition and effect in the two major steps as follows:

- For input symbol of the rule's condition (line 3), the algorithm sends the data to the service W (line 4, see State 4).

- For output symbol of the rule's effect (line 6), the algorithm receives the data from the service (line 7) and adds the data to the collection of received data D (line 9).

The result of the algorithm is the set D which contains all new data to be added to the memory M. The actual modification of the memory M with the new data is done in State 2. For correct processing of the algorithm, it is important that annotations *A1* and *A2* are consistent and complete (see Sections 3.4 and 3.5) as well as no failures occur in services. In case the annotations would not be consistent and complete, the algorithm would either ignore the received message which could in turn affect the correct processing of the choreography or wait infinitely. In addition, as we do not currently handle fault messages, the algorithm will not function properly when a failure occurs in a service.

State 4: *send(c, op)*

1: $m \leftarrow lower(c)$
2: **for all** o of which m is the input message **do**
3:    send m to W
4: **end for**

To send the data c, the algorithm first creates a corresponding message according to the *A2* annotation by transforming c to the message m using the lowering transformation function (line 1). Then, through each operation of which the message m is the input message, the algorithm sends the message m to the service W.

State 5: $c = receive(W)$

1: **if** receive m from W **then**
2:    $c \leftarrow lift(m)$
3:    **return** c
4: **else**
5:    **return** *null*
6: **end if**

When there is new data from the service W, the algorithm lifts the data (message m in XML) to the semantic representation using lifting transformation function from annotation *A2* (line 2).

State 6: $D_m = mediateData(D, O_s, O_t, \Phi)$

1: $\rho \leftarrow \emptyset; \xi_m \leftarrow \emptyset$
2: **for all** $c \in D$ **do**
3:    $\varepsilon \leftarrow getTypeOf(c);$
4:    $\varepsilon_m \leftarrow null$
5:    **for all** $m = \langle \varepsilon_s, \varepsilon_t, \gamma_{\varepsilon_s}, \gamma_{\varepsilon_t} \rangle \in \Phi$ **do**
6:       **if** $\varepsilon = \varepsilon_s$ **then**
7:          **if** $isBetterFit(\varepsilon_t, \varepsilon_m)$ **then**
8:             $\varepsilon_m \leftarrow \varepsilon_t$
9:          **end if**

10:     $m_G \leftarrow ground(m);\ \rho \leftarrow \rho \cup \{m_G\}$
11: **end if**
12: **end for**
13: $\xi_m \leftarrow \xi_m \cup \varepsilon_m$
14: **end for**
15: **if** $\xi_m = null$ **then**
16:     **return** *null*
17: **end if**
18: $D_m \leftarrow getDataForType(\xi_m, \rho)$
19: **return** D_m

The algorithm performs two steps during data mediation. Firstly, the algorithm processes mappings in order to determine the most suitable target concepts to mediate the source data to, and secondly, the algorithm transforms the mappings into an executable form and executes the mappings. Since current reasoning engines does not scale well in terms of processing time, keeping these steps separate enable high performance in processing of alignments independent of the logical language and reasoning engine used. In other words, this approach minimizes the use of the reasoning during the data mediation.

- **Step 1.** The algorithm first determines a concept for an instance data to be mediated (line 3). After that, the algorithm traverses through a set of mappings to determine the type of the target data (mediated data) (lines 5–12). Since there could be more mappings from a given source entity to the several other target entities, the algorithm determines the most suitable concept (lines 7–9). In particular, if a concept ε_s is mapped to two target concepts ε_t^1 and ε_t^2, then ε_t^1 is more suitable if ε_t^1 is a subconcept of ε_t^2 (the most specific) or if ε_t^2 can be reached via binary relationships (i.e., attributes) starting from ε_t^1 (maximal coverage).

- **Step 2.** While traversing the set of mappings, the algorithm grounds each mapping to a logical language by transforming them to a set of logical mapping rules (line 10). Finally, by using a reasoner engine, the algorithm queries and retrieves all the data of the selected target type according to the source data and the set of mapping rules (line 18).

4.3   Discussion

The data mediation ensures that all new data coming from one service are translated to the other's service ontology. Thus, no matter from where the data originate the data is always ready to use for the both services. From the process mediation point view, the data mediation also handles the splitting of messages (pattern (c)) and combining messages (pattern (d)). Since the mediated data are always added to the both memories (see State 2, lines 8, 12, and the next paragraph for additional discussion) the patterns (a) and (b) are handled automatically through processing of the choreography rules. In particular, the fact that a message will be stopped (pattern (a)) means that the message will never be used by the choreography because no rule will use it. In addition, the order of messages will be inverted (pattern (b)) as defined by the choreography rules and the order of ASM states in which conditions of rules hold. This means that the algorithm automatically handles the process mediation with help of data mediation through rich description of choreographies when no central workflow is necessary for that purpose. To fulfill the pattern (e), the algorithm might need a third-party data for which an integration workflow might be necessary. Although some of the third-party data can be gathered through transformation functions of the data mediation which can in turn facilitate some cases of pattern (e), we do not provide a general solution for this pattern. A special case of pattern (e) could be "generating an acknowledgment message" for which the algorithm should distinguish types of interactions. For example, if the algorithm is able to understand control interactions (such as acknowledgments) among all the interactions between services, it could generate an acknowledgment message (evaluation of successful reception of the message by the other service is, however, another issue).

In our algorithm, we always add all the data to the both choreographies and not only the data which could be of *potential use*, that is, the data could be used when evaluating a subsequent rule. The reason is that we use the language which allows for the intentional definitions (axioms) which are present in the information semantics and the memory, the new data might affect the evaluation of rules indirectly through such axioms. An assessment whether new data are usable would thus require a logical reasoning and would influence the scalability and the processing time. On the other hand, we do not expect a significant overhead when storing such additional data; however, we leave the evaluation for the future work.

5. Implementation

There exist several implementation efforts which aim is to build a technology for our SWS architecture. The major ones are the WSMT [20, 21], the implementation of the architecture's problem-solving layer which supports a developer through the full Software Development Cycle related to services, their implementation, semantic descriptions modeling, and deployment; and the Web Service Execution Environment (WSMX) [16], the implementation of the middleware layer of the architecture which provides various functionality for service tasks as well as core functionality to manage and coordinate middleware services. To show how our SWS technology can be used in real-world case scenarios, we work on various solutions defined by the SWS Challenge initiative.[15]

5.1 WSMX

WSMX is one of the two reference implementations of the SWS architecture's middleware layer called Semantic Execution Environment (the other implementation is called IRS-III [7]). WSMX hosts a number of components as implementations of middleware services including service discovery, adaptation, mediation, composition, invocation, etc. The core to the WSMX is the *Execution Management* and *Communication and Coordination* of components.

Execution Management. Figure 6 depicts an overview of the WSMX Execution Management. It implements the middleware kernel (microkernel) utilizing Java Management Extensions (JMX) as described in Haselwanter [15]. In the core of the management lies a management agent which offers several dedicated services. The most important one is the *bootstrap service* responsible for loading and configuring components. The Execution Management also implements *self-management* techniques through scheduled operations, and allows *administration* through a representation independent management and monitoring interface. Through this interface, a number of management consoles can be interconnected, each serving different management purposes. In particular, we have implemented terminal, Web browser and eclipse management consoles. Similarly as in other middleware systems, the Execution Management hosts a number of subsystems that provide services to components and enable intercomponent communication. For example, it provides *pool management* which takes care of handling component instances, logging, transport, and lifecycle services. The Execution Management also exploits the underlying (virtual) machine's instrumentation to monitor performance and system health metrics. The Execution Management also acts as a facade to distributed components. However, the preferred way to distribution is to organize the system as *federations of agents*. Each agent has its own Execution Management and a particular subset of functional components. To hide the complexity of the federation for the management application, WSMX provides a single *agent view*, that is, single point of access to the management and administration interfaces. This is achieved by propagating requests within the federation via proxies, broadcasts, or directories. A federation thus consists of a number of Execution Management

---

[15] http://www.sws-challenge.org.

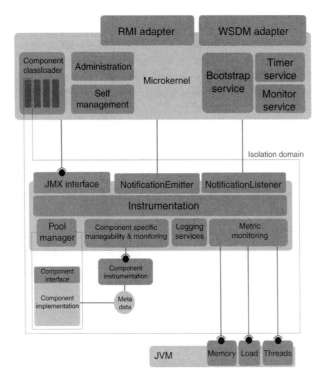

Fig. 6. Execution Management in WSMX.

services, each of them operating a kernel per one machine and hosting a number of functional components.

Communication and Coordination. The middleware avoids hard-wired bindings between components using events for the intercomponent communication. If some functionality is required, an event representing the request is created and published. A component subscribed to this event type can fetch and process the event. As depicted in Fig. 7, the exchange of events is performed via Tuple Space which provides a persistent shared space enabling interaction between components without direct exchange of events between them. This interaction is performed using a publish–subscribe mechanism. The Tuple Space enables communication between distributed components running on both local and remote machines while at the same time distribution is transparent to components. For this purpose, an additional layer provides components with a mechanism of communication with other components which shields the actual mechanism of local or remote communication.

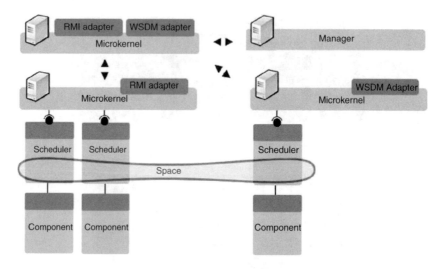

Fig. 7. Communication and Coordination in the middleware.

The Tuple Space technology used in the middleware is based on Linda [13] which provides a shared distributed space.

5.2   WSMT

WSMT is an integrated development environment for SWSs. The WSMT is implemented as a collection of plug-ins for the Eclipse[16] framework such that it can be integrated with other toolkits like the Java Development Toolkit (JDT) or the Web Tools Platform (WTP)[17] so that a developer can develop his java code, Web services, and semantic Web services side by side in the one application. The main aim of the WSMT is to support the developer through the full Software Development Cycle of his SWS from requirements, through design, implementation, testing, and deployment such that the process of developing SWSs can become cheaper to perform and remove many of the tedious activities that the developer must currently perform.

The WSMT, which has been under active development since early 2005, is made up of three main areas of functionality:

----

[16] http://www.eclipse.org.
[17] http://www.eclipse.org/webtools/.

1. **Creation and management of SWS artifacts.** The ability to quickly and cheaply create and test ontologies, Web services, mediators, etc., through a semantic language is key to the successful creation of SWSs. The WSMT provides the *WSML perspective* with multiple editors [19] for creating and testing SWS descriptions, conversion tools to and from RDF and OWL, embedded reasoners for testing the behavior of ontologies in their target environment.

2. **Creation and management of mediation mappings.** One of the key challenges in semantics is the interoperability of ontologies. In the SWS field, this becomes even more important when the service requester and service provider use different ontologies to describe the same domain. The WSMT provides the *Mapping Perspective* [25] within which mediation mappings between two or more ontologies can be created at design-time, such that they can later be executed at run-time. The tools in this perspective guide the developer through the process of creating mappings using visual cues, suggestion algorithms, and embedded testing functionality.

3. **Interfacing with Semantic Execution Environments.** Crucially once all the artifacts related to a SWS have been created, these artifacts need to be deployed to the execution environment within which they will be used. The *SEE Perspective* provides functionality for interfacing with the WSMX and IRS-III implementations of the SEEs. Artifacts can be stored to and retrieved from these environments, or can be used to invoke the functionality of the SEEs.

5.3   B2B Scenario

We use our SWS architecture technology to implement a number of scenarios described by the SWS Challenge initiative. The SWS Challenge defines a set of increasingly difficult problems on which various SOA and SWS solutions can be demonstrated. In this section, we describe a solution based on our SWS technology and the lightweight semantic service model for a SWS Challenge mediation scenario.

5.3.1   Solution Architecture

Figure 8 depicts a solution architecture for the mediation scenario. The scenario describes a trading company, called Moon, which uses a Customer Relationship Management system (CRM) and an Order Management System (OMS) to manage its order processing. The SWS Challenge organizers provide all back-end services described in WSDL as well as access to services' endpoints. Moon has signed

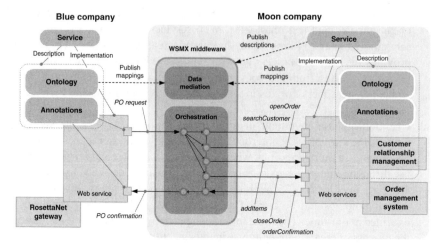

FIG. 8. Mediation scenario solution architecture.

agreements to exchange Purchase Order (PO) messages with a company called Blue using the RosettaNet standard PIP3A4.[18] There are two interoperability problems in the scenario. At the *data level*, the Blue uses PIP3A4 to define the PO request and confirmation messages while Moon uses a proprietary XML schema for its OMS and CRM systems. At the *process level*, the Blue follows PIP3A4 Partner Interface Protocol (PIP), that is, it sends out a PIP3A4 PO message, including all items to be ordered, and expects to receive a PIP3A4 PO confirmation message. On the other side, various interactions with the CRM and OMS systems must be performed in Moon to process the order, that is, get the internal ID for the customer from the CRM system, create the order in the OMS system, add line items into the order, close the order, and send back the PO confirmation.

The core of the architecture is the WSMX middleware located between Blue and Moon systems. WSMX functionality can be customized to conform to particular integration needs through choosing appropriate components and their configuration. In the scenario, we use the *orchestration* which executes the conversation and the *data mediation* which resolves the heterogeneity issues, both implemented according to the execution model from Section 4. In addition, WSMX contains the base components such as *reasoning* which performs logical reasoning over semantic descriptions as well as *communication* and *storage*. For brevity, we do not show them in the figure.

---

[18] http://www.rosettanet.org.

5.3.2 Modeling

To implement the scenario using our SWS technology, we need to model ontologies and define annotations for both Blue and Moon WSDL services. In addition, we need to define mapping rules between the two ontologies in order to facilitate data mediation. Firstly, we create ontologies in WSML language as semantic representations of the PIP3A4, CMR, and OMS XML schema. Secondly, we define *A1*, *A2*, and *A4* annotations (cf. Section 3.4), that is, annotations of XML schema messages with semantic concepts from the ontologies, lifting and lowering schema mappings, and annotations of WSDL interface operations with functional capability descriptions. Finally, we define mappings between the both ontologies.

```
1 axiom aaMappingRule23
2     definedBy
3        mediated(?X21, SearchCustomerReq)[searchString hasValue ?Y22] memberOf o1#SearchCustomerReq
4  :− ?X21[businessName hasValue ?Y22] memberOf o2#BusinessDescription.
```

LISTING 6. Mapping rules in WSML.

Listing 6 shows a sample mapping rule between the *SearchCustomerReq* concept of the CMR ontology (denoted using *o1* prefix) and *BusinessDescription* concept of the PIP3A4 ontology (denoted using *o2* prefix). The construct *mediated(X, C)* represents the identifier of the newly created target instance, where *X* is the source instance that is transformed, and *C* is the target concept we map to.

Listing 7 shows extracts of the Moon ontology (lines 1–18) and corresponding WSDL descriptions (lines 20–41). With help of *A1*, *A2* annotations (lines 23–25) and *A4* annotations (line 38) and using the algorithm described in Section 3.5 we construct a choreography with two rules (please note that the rules are defined on semantic representations of messages; the semantic messages are transformed to their XML representations using *A2* annotations during execution; for more details please refer to Section 4.2):

- The first rule defines that the message *SearchCustomerReqWsml* will be sent to the service and on result the message *SearchCustomerRespWsml* will be expected as the output message. For this purpose the message *SearchCustomerReqWsml* must be available in the memory (in our case, the data for the message are provided by the Blue after the data mediation).

- The second rule defines that the *SearchCustomerRespWsml* must be available in the memory while its *customerId* will be used for the *customerId* of the message *CreateNewOrderReqWsml* (this is defined using the *CreateOrderPrecondition* in lines 11–15). The *CreateNewOrderRespWsml* will be expected to

```
1    /* Moon's ontology */
2    /* namespaces and prefixes */
3    @prefix rdfs: <http://www.w3.org/2000/01/rdf-schema#> .
4    @prefix rdf: <http://www.w3.org/1999/02/22-rdf-syntax-ns#> .
5    @prefix wl: <http://www.wsmo.org/ns/wsmo-lite#> .
6    @prefix swsc: <http://example.org/swsc#> .
7    @prefix wsml: <http://www.wsmo.org/wsml/wsml-syntax#> .
8    @prefix xs: <http://www.w3.org/2001/XMLSchema#>
9
10   /* create order precondition (functional capability) */
11   swsc:CreateOrderPrecondition rdf:type wl:Condition ;
12        rdf:value "
13          ?customerResp[customerId hasValue ?id] memberOf SearchCustomerRespWsml and
14          ?orderReq[customerId hasValue ?id] memberOf CreateNewOrderReqWsml
15        "^^wsml:AxiomLiteral .
16
17   /* other ontology definitions suppressed due to brevity */
18   ...
19
20   /* WSDL */
21   /* XML Schema elements */
22   <xs:element name="searchCustomerReqXml" type="searchCustomerReqXmlType"
23        sawsdl:modelReference="http://example.org/swsch#searchCustomerReqWsml"
24        sawsdl:loweringSchemaMapping="http://example.org/lowerCustomerReq"
25        sawsdl:liftingSchemaMapping="http://example.org/liftCustomerReq"
26   />
27
28   /* other XML schema elements suppressed due to brevity */
29   ...
30
31   /* WSDL interface operations of the Moon's back-end systems */
32   <operation name="searchCustomer" pattern="http://www.w3.org/ns/wsdl/in-out">
33      <input element="searchCustomerReqXml"/>
34      <output element="searchCustomerRespXml"/>
35   </operation>
36
37   <operation name="createNewOrder" pattern="http://www.w3.org/ns/wsdl/in-out"
38        sawsdl:modelReference="http://example.org/swsch#CreateOrderPrecondition" >
38      <input element="createNewOrderReqXml"/>
40      <output element="createNewOrderRespXml"/>
41   </operation>
```

LISTING 7. Moon CRM/OMS ontology and WSDL extracts.

be received back. The data for the *CreateNewOrderReqWsml* will be again supplied by the Blue after the data mediation.

6. Related Work

In this section, we describe a related work in the two sections. *Semantic service models* provide background on state of the art for modeling of semantic Web services conceptual models or ontologies, and *service architectures and technologies* provide overview of existing architectures based on the use of the semantic service models.

6.1   Semantic Service Models

Web service modeling ontology (WSMO) [12] is a top-down conceptual model for semantic description of Web services which is realized in Web Service Modeling Language [12]. It has four top-level components: ontologies capture information semantics, goals describe what the user (or the system) wants to achieve, Web services model the properties of the available services, and mediators resolve any heterogeneities that might arise in a distributed system. The WSMO describes a Web service along with the similar service semantics as we define in Section 3.2; however, these semantics are specified in the Metaobject Facility (MOF).[19] In addition, the WSMO adopts the top-down approach to modeling of Web services when service semantics is not meant to be used separately but as a whole.

OWL-S [23] is divided into three subontologies—ServiceProfile, ServiceModel, and Grounding. The ServiceProfile describes what a Web Service does and provides the means by which the service can be advertised. In contrast to WSMO Goal and Web service concepts, there is no distinction in the conceptual model of OWL-S between the viewpoints of service requesters and providers. The ServiceProfile is aimed equally at advertising services offered by providers as well as those sought by requesters. Similarly to WSMO, OWL-S defines the capability a service offers as a state transition in terms of pre- and postconditions. The WSMO model explicitly considers the data and process heterogeneity problems in an open Web environment. WSMO defines the concept of mediator to tackle this. OWL-S does not model this problem explicitly, tending to treat it as more of an architectural issue. The ServiceModel is used to define the behavioral aspect of the Web Service. The ServiceModel allows for the description of different types of services: atomic, abstract, and composite. Atomic processes correspond to a single interaction with the service, for example, a single operation in a WSDL document. Composite processes have multiple steps, each of which is an atomic process, connected by control and data flow. Simple processes are abstractions to allow multiple views on the same process. These can be used for the purposes of planning or reasoning. Simple processes are not invocable but are described as being conceived as representing single step interactions. A Simple process can be realized by an atomic process or expanded to a composite process. WSMO goes further than OWL-S by modeling orchestrations describing what other Web services have to be used, or Goals to be fulfilled, to

---

[19] http://www.omg.org/technology/documents/formal/mof.htm.

perform a specific task. Additionally, WSMO allows the definition of multiple interfaces, and corresponding choreographies, for a Web service while OWL-S allows only a single service model. The final part of the conceptual model is the ServiceGrounding, providing a link between the ServiceModel and the description of the concrete realization for a Web Service provided by WSDL. Atomic processes are mapped to WSDL operations, where the process inputs and outputs, described using OWL, are mapped to the operations inputs and outputs, described using XML-Schema. The use of OWL-DL as the ontology language for OWL-S had some unwanted side effects noted in detail in Balzer et al. [2]. Included amongst these was that OWL-S does not comply with the OWL-DL specification, which places constraints on how OWL-S ontologies can be reasoned over. A second problem is that variables are not supported within OWL but are necessary when combining data from multiple cooperating processes. Additionally, a significant problem is that OWL-DL is not well suited to describing processes—an important aspect for SWS descriptions. The lack of clear separation between language layers in OWL-S and the open interpretation of OWL-S semantics if expressions in SWRL [18] or KIF [14] are combined, was a strong motivation for the MOF-style consistent layering of the WSML family of languages.

   Semantic Web services framework (SWSF) and semantic Web services ontology (SWSO) [3] were devised to provide a full conceptual model and language expressive enough to describe the process model of Web Services, and to address the shortcomings of OWL-S in this regard. The first-order logic axiomatization of SWSO is called FLOWS (first-order logic ontology for Web services) and is based on the Process Specification Language (PSL) [24], an ISO international standard process ontology. FLOWS is expressed in a language called SWSL-FOL (semantic Web services language for first-order logic). To enable logic-programming-based implementations and reasoning for SWSO, a second ontology available called ROWS (rules ontology for Web services), expressed in SWSL-Rules. ROWS is derived from FLOWS by a partial translation. The intent of the axiomatization of ROWS is the same as that of FLOWS but in some cases is weakened because of the lover expressivity of the SWSL-Rules language. Service is the primary concept in SWSO with three top level elements, derived from the three parts of the OWL-S ontology. These are Service Descriptors, Process Model, and Grounding. *Service Descriptors* provide a set of nonfunctional properties that a service may have. The FLOWS specification includes examples of simple properties such as the name, author, and textual description. The set is freely extensible. Metadata specifications for online documents including Dublin Core are also easily incorporated. Each property is modeled as a relation linking the property to the service. The *Process Model* extends the PSL generic ontology for processes with two fundamental elements, especially to cater for Web Services (1) the structured notion of atomic processes as found in OWL-S and (2) infrastructure for allowing various forms of data flow. The Process Model of FLOWS is organized as layered extension of the PSL-OuterCore ontology. The SWSO approach to *grounding* follows very closely that of OWL-S v1.1 to WSDL. Like SWSL Rules, WSMO's rule language WSML-Rule is largely based on F-Logic. The major difference between the SWSO and WSMO efforts is the focus of the former on providing a highly expressive first-order logic ontology for describing process models. WSMO uses guarded transition rules, considered as abstract state machines, to define its process model but does not have the detailed semantics of SWSO. On the other hand, SWSO adopts the OWL-S model for describing other aspects of Web services and so does not explicitly model the notion of goals or of mediators.

WSDL-S [1] is a lightweight approach for augmenting WSDL descriptions of Web Services with semantic annotations. It is a refinement of the work carried on by the METEOR-S group at the LSDIS Lab, Athens, GA to enable semantic descriptions of inputs, outputs, preconditions, and effects of Web Service operations, by taking advantage of the extension mechanism of WSDL. WSDL-S is agnostic to the ontology language and model used for the annotations of WSDL and does not introduce a detailed conceptual model for Web service. The WSDL-S specification was one of the major inputs for the SAWSDL as part of a W3C standards activity.

6.2 Service Architectures and Technologies

W3C Web service architecture [4] describes the main concepts, relationships, and models behind a Web service-based architecture. It identifies four architectural models: the message-oriented model (focuses on messages, message structure, message transport, etc.), the service-oriented model (focuses on aspects of service, action, etc.), the resource-oriented model (focuses on resources that exist and have owners), and the policy model (focuses on constraints on the behavior of agents and services). Based on this conceptual model the stakeholder's perspective is described showing how the architecture meets the goals and the requirements. The stakeholder's perspective description includes the main architectural properties and design principles of SOAs, an overview of the Web Services Technologies stack and the role of the Web Service Semantics. Our work can be seen as complementary, since it respects the same design principles, uses the same underlying technologies and above all recognizes the outmost importance of the explicitly describing the Web Service Semantics. That is, our SWS architecture's Semantic Service Stack adds semantics on top of existing technologies stack (e.g., SOAP, WSDL, etc.) and show how process such as Discovery, Composition, Choreography, etc., can be enhanced by semantics. While Booth et al. [4] define the generic principles behind Web Services Architecture, our approach realizes such an architecture (in the lines of the principles) and furthermore adds a semantic layer on top of existing standards and technologies to enable dynamic and (semi)automated discovery, composition, mediation, and invocation of semantically described Web services.

OWL-S virtual machine (OWL-S VM) [27] provides a general-purpose Web service client for the invocation of a Web service based on the process model of its OWL-S description. The architecture consists of components for executing the OWL-S process model, the grounding, and for making the Web service invocation. The OWL-S VM provides a first implementation, and therefore proof of value, of the OWL-S process model but only addresses a subset of the functionality offered by the SWS architecture described in this chapter. Our SWS architecture focuses on providing an environment where multiple semantically described services can interact. Data and process mediators are first class citizens, based on the assumption that independent services will exhibit, not only data, but also behavioral independence. Both types of mediation in our SWS architecture are based at the conceptual level on mappings between ontologies. In the OWL-S VM, data heterogeneity is handled syntactically, based on the use of XSLT. Our SWS architecture prototype, WSMX, is an open-source project where the formal execution semantics and component-based architecture descriptions are public. A detailed architecture and run-time execution semantics for OWL-S VM are not publicly available.

IRS-III [26] is an execution environment for SWSs that also uses WSMO as the underlying conceptual model. To facilitate its implementation of capability-based service invocation, IRS-III extends the definition of the WSMO Goal slightly to introduce input and output roles as well as soap bindings for these roles. Conceptually, both WSMX and IRS-III have common roots in the UPML framework of Fensel et al. [11] Although there are implementation differences, both WSMX and IRS-III implement a common system-level API to facilitate interoperability.

METEOR-S [28, 31] project of the LSDIS Lab proposes the application of semantics to existing Web service technologies. In particular the project endeavors to define and support the complete lifecycle of SWS processes. Their work includes extending WSDL to support the development of SWSs using semantic annotation from additional type systems such as WSMO and OWL ontologies. A similar approach to data mediation is taken by both WSMX and METEOR-S, based on using a common data representation format. METEOR-S proposes an enhancement of UDDI to facilitate semantic discovery as well as a framework for SWS composition. METEOR-S allows for (1) the creation of WSDL-S descriptions from annotated source code, (2) the automatic publishing of WSDL-S descriptions in enhanced UDDI registries, and (3) the generation of OWL-S descriptions, from WSDL-S, for grounding. The publication and discovery (MWSDI) module provides support for semantic publication and discovery of Web services across a federation of registries as well as a semantic publication and discovery layer over UDDI. The composition module consists of two main submodules—the constraint analysis and optimization submodule and the execution environment. The constraint analysis and optimization submodules deal with correctness and optimization of the process on the basis of quality of service constraints. The execution environment provides proxy-based dynamic binding support to an execution engine for BPEL4WS.

SWS Challenge. There have been several contributions to the SWS Challenge series of workshops which are related to our work. In particular, the entry from DEI and CEFRIEL, Milano [5], was evaluated to be the most complete at the workshop in Budva, June 2006. The DEI/CEFRIEL approach was to use the WebML language to specify their solution to the mediation problem presented by the Challenge. WebML uses entity-relations diagrams extended with Object Query Language constraints to create the data model. The authors then use an extension of WebML that permits interactions with Web services and a further extension that allows process models, specified using the Business Process Modeling Notation, to be translated into executable WebML. Process mediation is catered for at design-time through the use of GUI-based BPMN modeling tools. Data mediation is carried out by XSLT transformation between SOAP message and the internal WebML data model. The system was shown to solve the problems presented by the challenge and changes to the problem specification were able to be addressed relatively easily.

7. Conclusion

The SWS architecture presented in this chapter follows a new approach to integration and interoperation of services by means of various semantic languages and the lightweight semantic service model called WSMO-Lite. Building on the established grounds of the Web service modeling ontology and taking into account governing principles of service orientation, semantic modeling, and problem-solving methods, the architecture provides a means to total or partial automation of tasks including discovery, mediation, selection, and execution of SWSs. With respect to underlying principles, we define the architecture from several perspectives, presenting its middleware, problem-solving and business services layers. We elaborate in detail on the business service layer presenting the Semantic Service Stack, its WSMO-Lite service ontology, as well as annotation mechanism for WSDL. WSMO-Lite fills in SAWSDL annotations, and thus enables the Semantic Service Stack, open for various customizations according to domain-specific requirements, languages of required expressivity, and domain-specific ontologies. WSMO-Lite supports the idea of incremental enhancements of SAWSDL as Amit Sheth points out in [22]:

> Rather than look for a clear winner among various SWS approaches, I believe that in the post-SAWSDL context, significant contributions by each of the major approaches

will likely inuence how we incrementally enhance SAWSDL. Incrementally adding features (and hence complexity) when it makes sense, by borrowing from approaches offered by various researchers, will raise the chance that SAWSDL can present itself as the primary option for using semantics for real-world and industry-strength challenges involving Web services.

Building on the WSMO-Lite service ontology and its annotation mechanism, we also describe the execution model for services and show how data and process mediation can be applied within the execution. In addition, we describe the two major implementation efforts around our SWS architecture, namely Web Service Modeling Toolkit implementing the architecture's problem-solving layer and the Web Service Execution Environment implementing the architecture's middleware services layer. On the use case scenario from the SWS Challenge, we describe how real-world business services can be annotated using our WSMO-Lite service ontology.

One of the major aspects of the architecture is to facilitate the flexible integration of services which is more adaptive to changes in business requirements. While our SWS architecture facilitates a novel style of integration of services by means of semantic service descriptions and AI methods, some people say that such an approach is not realistic today. They argue that the complexity of semantic languages and integration techniques that depend on logical reasoning is a burden for service processing and high performance. However, the logical reasoning can efficiently help resolve inconsistencies in service descriptions as well as maintain interoperability when these descriptions change. The more complex the services' descriptions are, the more difficult it is for a human to manually maintain the integration. The semantics that promote the automation is the key to such integration's flexibility and reliability. To demonstrate the value of semantics for service descriptions as well as automation in service integration, we are working on the SWSs challenge. The SWS Challenge aims to establish a common understanding, evaluation scheme, and testbed to compare and classify various approaches to services integration in terms of their abilities as well as their shortcomings in real-world settings. Although a world full of services does not exist yet, one-click integration will be desirable. The SESA and its related activities enable such a world as well as such integration.

REFERENCES

[1] Akkiraju R., Farrell J., Miller J., Nagarajan M., Schmidt M., Sheth A., and Verma K., 2005. Web service semantics—WSDL-S. Technical report. Available at http://lsdis.cs.uga.edu/projects/meteors/wsdl-s/.

[2] Balzer S., Liebig T., and Wagner M., 2004. Pitfalls of OWL-S: A practical semantic Web use case. In *2nd International Conference on Service Oriented Computing*, pp. 289–298. ACM Press, New York.

[3] Battle S., et al., 2005. Semantic Web services framework (SWSF) overview, W3C submission. Technical report. Available at http://www.w3.org/submission/swsf/.

[4] Booth D., Haas H., McCabe F., Newcomer E., Champion M., Ferris C., and Orchard D., 2004. Web services architecture. W3C Working Group Note.

[5] Brambilla M., Celino I., Ceri S., Cerizza D., Valle E. D., and Facca F. M., 2006. A software engineering approach to design and development of semantic Web service applications. In *International Semantic Web Conference*, pp. 172–186.

[6] Brger E., and Strk R., 2003. Abstract State Machines: A Method for High-Level System Design and Analysis. Springer-Verlag, Berlin.

[7] Cabral L., Domingue J., Galizia S., Gugliotta A., Norton B., Tanasescu V., and Pedrinaci C., 2006. IRS-III: A broker for semantic Web services based applications. In *Proceedings of the 5th International Semantic Web Conference (ISWC2006)*, Athens, GA.

[8] Cimpian E., and Mocan A., 2005. WSMX process mediation based on choreographies. In *Business Process Management Workshops*, pp. 130–143.

[9] de Bruijn J., Fensel D., and Lausen H., 2007. D34v0.1: The Web compliance of WSML. Technical report, DERI. Available from http://www.wsmo.org/TR/d34/v0.1/.

[10] Euzenat J., Mochol M., Shvaiko P., Stuckenschmidt H., Šváb O., Svátek V., van Hage W. R., and Yatskevich M., 2006. Results of the ontology alignment evaluation initiative 2006. In *Proceeding of the International Workshop on Ontology Matching (OM-2006), CEUR Workshop Proceedings*, Athens, GA, vol. 225, pp. 73–95.

[11] Fensel D., Benjamins V., Motta E., and Wielinga B., 1999. UPML: A framework for knowledge system reuse. In *Proceedings of the International Joint Conference on AI (IJCAI-99)*, Stockholm, Sweden.

[12] Fensel D., Lausen H., Polleres A., de Bruijn J., Stollberg M., Roman D., and Domingue J., 2006. Enabling Semantic Web Services—The Web Service Modeling Ontology. Springer-Verlag, Berlin.

[13] Gelernter D., Carriero N., and Chang S., 1985. Parallel programming in Linda. In *Proceedings of the International Conference on Parallel Processing*.

[14] Genesereth M., and Filkes R., 1992. Knowledge Interchange Format (KIF), Stanford University Logic Group, Logic-92-1. Technical report.

[15] Haselwanter T., 2005. WSMX core—A JMX microkernel. Ph.D. Thesis, University of Innsbruck.

[16] Haselwanter T., Kotinurmi P., Moran M., Vitvar T., and Zaremba M., 2006. WSMX: A semantic service oriented middleware for B2B integration. In *Proceedings of the 4th International Conference on Service Oriented Computing*, pp. 477–483.

[17] Horrocks I., 2005. Owl: A description logic based ontology language. In *Proceedings of the International Conference on Principles and Practice of Constraint Programming*, pp. 5–8.

[18] Horrocks I., Patel-Schneider P., Boley H., Tabet S., Grosof B., and Dean M., 2004. SWRL: A semantic Web rule language combining OWL and RuleML. Technical report. Available from http://www.w3.org/Submission/2004/SUBMSWRL-20040521/.

[19] Kerrigan M., 2006. WSMOViz: An ontology visualization approach for WSMO. In *Proceedings of the 10th International Conference on Information Visualization (IV06)*, London, England.

[20] Kerrigan M., Mocan A., Tanler M., and Bliem W., 2007. Creating semantic Web services with the Web service modeling toolkit (WSMT). In *Proceedings of the Workshop on Making Semantics Work for Business (MSWFB2007) at the 1st European Semantic Technology Conference (ESTC2007)*, Vienna, Austria.

[21] Kerrigan M., Mocan A., Tanler M., and Fensel D., 2007. The Web service modeling toolkit— An integrated development environment for semantic Web services (system description). In *Proceedings of the 4th European Semantic Web Conference (ESWC2007)*, Innsbruck, Austria.

[22] Martin D., and Domingue J., 2007. Semantic Web services: Past, present and possible futures (systems trends and controversies). *IEEE Intelligent Systems*, **22**(6).

[23] Martin D., Burstein M., Hobbs J., Lassila O., McDermott D., McIlraith S., Narayanan S., Paolucci M., Parsia B., Payne T., Sirin E., Srinivasan N., et al., 2004. OWL-S: Semantic markup for Web services, W3C member submission. Technical report, W3C.

[24] Michel J., and Cutting-Decelle A., 2004. The Process Specification Language, International Standards Organization ISO TC184/SC5 Meeting. Technical report.

[25] Mocan A., and Cimpian E., 2007. An ontology-based data mediation framework for semantic environments. *International Journal on Semantic Web and Information Systems (IJSWIS)*, **3**(2): 66–95.

[26] Motta E., Domingue J., Cabral L., and Gaspari M., 2003. IRS-II: A framework and infrastructure for semantic Web services. In *The Semantic Web ISWC 2003*, Lecture Notes in Computer Science 2870 pp. 306–318. Springer-Verlag, Heidelberg.

[27] Paolucci M., Ankolekar A., Srinivasan N., and Sycara K., 2003. The DAML-S virtual machine. In *The Semantic Web—ISWC 2003* LNCS 2870, pp. 290–305. Springer-Verlag, Heidelberg.

[28] Patil A., Oundhakar S., Sheth A., and Verma K., 2004. Semantic Web services: Meteor-S Web service annotation framework. In *13th International Conference on World Wide Web,* pp. 553–562.

[29] Roman D., and Scicluna J., 2006. Ontology-based choreography of WSMO services. WSMO final draft v0.3, DERI. Available at http://www.wsmo.org/TR/d14/v0.3/.

[30] Roman D., Keller U., Lausen H., de Bruijn J., Lara R., Stollberg M., Polleres A., Feier C., Bussler C., and Fensel D., 2005. Web service modeling ontology. *Applied Ontologies*, **1**(1): 77–106.

[31] Verma K., Gomadam K., Sheth A. P., Miller J. A., and Wu Z., 2005. The Meteor-S approach for configuring and executing dynamic Web processes. Technical report. Available at http://lsdis.cs.uga.edu/projects/meteor-s/techrep6-24-05.pdf.

[32] Vitvar T., Kopecky J., and Fensel D., 2007. WSMO-Lite: Lightweight semantic descriptions for services on the Web. ECOWS.

[33] Vitvar T., Mocan A., Kerrigan M., Zaremba M., Zaremba M., Moran M., Cimpian E., Haselwanter T., and Fensel D., 2007. Semantically-enabled service oriented architecture: Concepts, technology and application. *Service Oriented Computing and Applications*, **2**(2): 129–154.

Issues and Approaches for Web 2.0 Client Access to Enterprise Data

AVRAHAM LEFF

IBM T.J. Watson Research Center,
Yorktown Heights, New York 10598

JAMES T. RAYFIELD

IBM T.J. Watson Research Center,
Yorktown Heights, New York 10598

Abstract

A new generation of Web technologies and programming styles, known collectively as "Web 2.0," is increasingly used in non-enterprise applications. Many businesses, however, continue to use "Web 1.0" applications to give users access to enterprise data. This chapter outlines the main issues that confront enterprises as they consider allowing Web 2.0 access to enterprise data. These include data security, programming style, performance tradeoffs, and deployment infrastructure. We motivate these issues and their solutions in the context of several examples.

ADVANCES IN COMPUTERS, VOL. 76
ISSN: 0065-2458/DOI: 10.1016/S0065-2458(09)01006-7

225

1. Introduction

This chapter examines how enterprises can best use the new generation of Web technologies, known collectively as "Web 2.0," to build Web applications that access, display, and update enterprise data. In this introductory section, we first define what we mean by Web 2.0 technologies and applications. We compare Web 2.0 to Web 1.0, and show where they fit into the broader context of client/ server computing.

With this background in place, in Section 2 we analyze the issues—both technical and organizational—that naive use of Web 2.0 technologies pose for enterprise data access. We present two relevant spectra: one of application types, the other of Web data-access models. We explain how, depending on the application type, Web 2.0 access to enterprise data can be provided in a way that addresses enterprise-specific concerns. Finally, we summarize our conclusions about enterprise use of Web 2.0 applications in Section 4.

1.1   Defining Web 2.0

For such a popular term (51,800,000 Google search results in mid-2008), a certain amount of confusion exists about what "Web 2.0" really means. This is because people conflate the concepts of Web 2.0 *applications* and *technology*.

Sometimes, Web 2.0 refers to a type of application. For example [30]:

> Web 2.0 is the network as platform, spanning all connected devices; Web 2.0 applications are those that make the most of the intrinsic advantages of that platform: delivering software as a continually updated service that gets better the more people use it, consuming and remixing data from multiple sources, including individual users, while providing their own data and services in a form that allows remixing by others, creating network effects through an "architecture of participation," and going beyond the page metaphor of Web 1.0 to deliver rich user experiences.

In this fairly prolix definition (elaborated elsewhere [31]), Web 2.0 applications are those that use the Internet as a collaboration platform. Web 2.0 applications improve the more they are used, and in turn, are easily incorporated into other Web 2.0 applications.

In other cases, Web 2.0 refers to the technology—software stacks, programming languages, and techniques—used by developers to build Web 2.0 applications. Some of these technologies are themselves "applications": for example, wikis [25], and "tag clouds" or social-bookmarking sites (such as [8]). In this chapter, we refer to Web 2.0 in its "technology" sense, focusing specifically on a lower-level set of Web 2.0 technologies known as Ajax [14, 15].

1.1.1 Ajax

By using Ajax (Asynchronous JavaScript and XML) technologies, developers can make Web applications behave like desktop applications in contrast to standard (Web 1.0) applications. This is done by enhancing the ability of the Web browser platform to load all, or part, of a Web page *independently* of a Web server. Thus, Ajax applications use:

- CSS (Cascading Style Sheets) [27] to reduce the amount of HTML that the server must transmit to format a Web page. The browser can cache the style sheet, using it to format content that is subsequently transmitted by the server.

- JavaScript [12], a Web client programming language, to program large portions of an application's business logic. In contrast to other approaches for executing business logic in the browser (e.g., Java applets [28]), JavaScript executes natively in a Web browser without the need to install plugins. Because the client can itself execute non-trivial portions of the application, fewer interactions between the Web browser and the server are required for the application to execute.

- The DOM (Document Object Model) [9], a platform and language-independent standard object model for representing HTML, XML, and related formats. JavaScript can use the DOM to dynamically inspect or modify arbitrary portions of a Web page, reducing the dependence on the server to generate the Web page.

- XML [34] or JSON [21] as standardized formats for client/server data transfers: JavaScript code executing in the browser can efficiently (de)serialize these data structures.

- (Most important of all), the *XmlHttpRequest* [43] object which is used to exchange data *asynchronously* with the Web server. By using *XmlHttpRequest*, a Web application can continue to interact with users while processing data requests in the background. This has two advantages. First, the application does not "freeze up," since the Web browser is not blocked while waiting for the server to process the data transfer. Second, the application can cache the data locally, and (potentially) use that data to fulfill subsequent data requests, reducing the number of client/server interactions.

Code sample 1 is a "bare-bones" illustration of how the *XmlHttpRequest* object can be used to fetch information about the first 100 employees in the company directory; load the information and display it a grid widget; and do so while continuing to construct the rest of the Web page. In practice, many developers use the libraries provided by JavaScript frameworks such as Dojo [10] and the Yahoo Interface Library [38] rather than code to the raw *XmlHttpRequest* interface. Such libraries provide a higher-level interface to the *XmlHttpRequest* function, implement exception handling, and simplify crossbrowser usage. Our code sample ignores these issues since we just want to convey how Web 2.0 applications can use Ajax to move data processing, business logic, and view construction from the server to the client. Gmail [17] and Flickr [13] are well-known applications that use Ajax technologies to dramatically improve a user's application experience.

CODE SAMPLE I   BASIC USE OF THE *XMLHTTPREQUEST* OBJECT

```
var page = beginConstructingWebPage();
var xhr = new XMLHttpRequest();
//Register an event handler to process the server's
//asynchronous response
xhr.onreadystatechange = function() {
  if(xhr.readyState == 4) {//finished
    if(request.status == 200) {//and success
      //use eval(xhr.responseText) for JSON data
      loadEmployeesIntoTable(xhr.responseXML, page);
    }
  }
}
//"open" stores its arguments for later use: specify
//an "asynchronous" request by passing "true"
xhr.open("GET","http://mycompany.com/directory?
  start=1&count=100", true);
//Pass "null" since the request is a GET and not a POST
xhr.send(null);//NOTE: The send does not block
continueConstructingWebPage();
```

1.2   Web 1.0, Web 2.0, and Client/Server Computing

This chapter focuses on the issues that must be addressed in order for enterprises to grant Web 2.0 applications access to enterprise data. In most cases, even modern enterprise Web applications resemble the Web 1.0 architecture depicted in Fig. 1. The Web browser is restricted to rendering and presenting the application's "view"; the function of any client-side "controller" logic is to select a specific view or to determine the details of the selected view. (We selected "Perl/CGI" only as examples of languages for Web 1.0 server-side business logic: historically, other languages were also used.) The bulk of the application's "controller" code—especially its business logic—executes on the server, as does the code that accesses and updates the application's data model. (Here, we refer to the well-known model/view/controller terminology introduced by Krasner and Pope [22].)

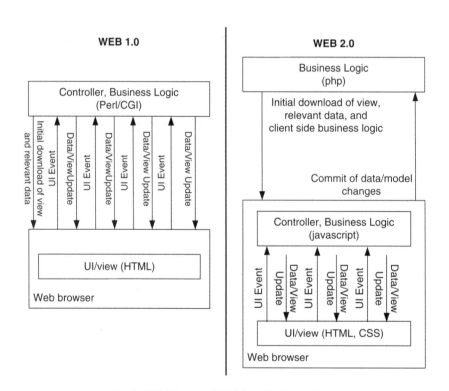

Fig. 1. Web 1.0 versus Web 2.0 application architecture.

Web 1.0 application architecture, in other words, corresponds to the "thin-client" portion in the spectrum of client/server computing. From an enterprise's perspective, Web 1.0 applications have several advantages. They enable:

- Simple distribution to, and installation of, enterprise applications on client devices. An application is deployed once on the Web server, and pulled on to Web browsers as they are needed simply by loading a URL. All of the required client software stack is already present, and users do not have to install additional plugins.
- Ubiquitous deployment since Web browsers are virtual machines that execute applications on almost all major operating systems.
- Straightforward partitioning of function between client and server. The differences between the programming model and languages (HTML, CSS, and JavaScript) for the Web client versus the Web server (Java Servlets, PHP) are well known and well defined.

The enthusiasm for Web 2.0 stems from the fact that it addresses some of the disadvantages of Web 1.0 applications:

- Web 1.0 application response time is poor because the client must do HTTP interactions with the server whenever business logic must be executed. This is because Web browsers did not initially support programming artifacts such as *XmlHttpRequest*, and thus convoluted client application architectures [4] were required to provide similar function.
- Web 1.0 clients must completely reload the Web page every time they interact with the server. This provides a poor visual impression, especially when few changes are being made to the page. This is because most of the DOM was not architected or supported on early browsers.

In short, early browsers did not provide the APIs needed for effective development of client-side applications. Thus, Web 1.0 applications focused on server-side development, where the needed APIs and tools were available.

In contrast to Web 1.0, and as shown in Fig. 1, Web 2.0 application architecture corresponds to the "fat-client" portion in the spectrum of client/server computing. The Ajax technologies discussed in Section 1.1.1 enable developers to shift a greater portion of an application's business logic and data model to the Web browser client. As a result, Web 2.0 applications can address the Web 1.0 disadvantages listed above. Importantly, Web 2.0 applications share two advantages with Web 1.0 applications: a simple distribution/installation model and a ubiquitous client platform. Thus, although Web 2.0 is a fat-client architecture in the sense that more application function is moved to the client, it avoids some of the problems that have historically bedeviled fat-client applications.

1.3 Chapter Theme

This chapter contends that enterprises will deploy Web 2.0 applications only when the interplay between the spectrum of application types and the spectrum of Web data-access models—delineated in Section 2—is clearly understood. Depending on the application type, naive use of Web 2.0 technologies will be forbidden in an enterprise context. More sophisticated use of Web 2.0 *is* compatible with enterprise concerns, and we expect that Web 2.0 will be used more broadly in the enterprise when these issues and solutions are clearly understood.

2. Enterprises and Web 2.0 Data Access

As we explained in Section 1, Web 2.0 technologies give Web developers the capability to move large portions of an application's business logic and the data it manipulates from the server to the client. Because the primary motivation for Web 2.0 is to improve application response time, Web developers prefer that the data *actually reside* on the client. In the case of applications utilizing shared data, the master copy of the data does not actually reside on the client. Instead, Web developers must use APIs that permit the client to access and update server-side data. To the greatest extent possible, a Web 2.0 developer wants to manipulate a *cached* version of the server-side data, since this can further reduce the number of client/server interactions. Perhaps more importantly, Web 2.0 developers prefer a client-centric programming model in which the client maintains strong control of the application's data. This programming model, however, can be difficult to map to the set of server-side data-access APIs that are commonly provided by enterprises.

2.1 Server-Side Data-Access APIs

A number of different data-access approaches are possible for Web 2.0 application construction. Here, we categorize these in terms of the API semantics provided by the server, because the server API semantics determine which client architectures are practical. We designate the two major variants as ODBC-CRUD and ODBC-SP. Here, "ODBC" refers to the well-known approach [16] used by enterprises to provide client access to server-side relational data. Although the ODBC approach was originally written for non-Web programming languages and environments, its design extends naturally to the Web and Ajax applications.

2.1.1 ODBC-CRUD and REST

In the ODBC-CRUD style of server API, the server allows the client to directly read and write individual data items in the database. For example, with a relational database, the client may use INSERT, SELECT, UPDATE, and DELETE SQL statements to manipulate data on the server. (Hence CRUD, for CREATE, RETRIEVE, UPDATE, and DELETE.)

To pick a simple example, assume that a Web application is used to display "all employees in a given department." In the ODBC-CRUD approach, Web developers use the following steps to access and update the required server-side relational data:

1. The developer specifies the required data in terms of the corresponding SQL statement, for example, SELECT * FROM DEPARTMENT.
2. The SQL statement is passed to a client-side API, typically written in JavaScript, to be executed by the database server.
3. A client-side JavaScript library converts the API call into an XML or JSON message that is transmitted to the server in an *XmlHttpRequest* invocation.
4. This message is interpreted on the server and a server-side API is invoked to execute the SELECT * FROM DEPARTMENT against the server-side database (after authenticating the client's credentials).
5. The server-side API packages the result of the SQL statement in XML or JSON format and sends it to the client.
6. The client-side library passes the result to the application that initiated the request.
7. Either the client-side library or the application can cache the employee data so that subsequent requests—for example, to sort the data in different ways—can be accommodated without another round-trip to the server.
8. Using an editable text field, the application allows the user to modify an employee's phone number. The change is propagated to the server by transmitting an SQL statement such as UPDATE DEPARTMENT SET PHO-NENUM = "914-555-1222" WHERE ID = "103", which is executed against the server-side database.

Using the ODBC-CRUD approach, it is straightforward to implement a cache in the client Web browser by querying the server for a set of tuples, storing the result set on the client, and subsequently allowing the client side to access and modify the result set as necessary. Other advantages of the ODBC-CRUD approach (e.g., [6, 32, 33]) are its flexibility, since it allows clients to have direct read and write access to the database using techniques that are familiar to server-side programmers in a wide variety of languages (e.g., ODBC for C, JDBC for Java, and PDO for PHP).

The REST [35, 42] programming style is a variant of ODBC-CRUD, updated for a Web environment, and not directly targeted at relational data. It shares the key characteristic of ODBC-CRUD of directly exposing collections, and individual items, of enterprise data to client-side developers. The semantics of the REST verbs (or HTTP methods [20]) directly correspond to ODBC-CRUD verbs: PUT with CREATE, GET with RETRIEVE, POST with UPDATE, and DELETE with DELETE. The use of REST verbs allows the server to abstract details of the database implementation (e.g., a particular SQL dialect) with a higher-level interface.

Although this programming style is attractive to the client-side developer, enterprises, in general, consider it to have serious flaws for developing enterprise applications. We discuss these flaws in Section 2.1.3, after contrasting the ODBC-CRUD style with the ODBC-SP programming style.

2.1.2   ODBC-SP and SOA

In the ODBC-SP style of server API, the server only allows the client to call *stored procedures* [18] on the server. Stored procedures are essentially black boxes of business logic which are defined by the server administrator and executed on the server. The ODBC-SP style is very similar to what are known as service-oriented architectures (SOA [11]).

Consider the previous example, in which a Web application is used to display "all employees in a given department." In the ODBC-SP approach, Web developers use the following steps to access and update the required server-side relational data:

1. The enterprise specifies the API for two procedures: ReadEmployees() and UpdatePhoneNumber(employeeId, phoneNumber). That is, the parameters and return values of server-side remote procedure calls are defined using an interface definition language such as WSDL [5].
2. The client-side developer invokes the ReadEmployees() procedure, using a client-side library to convert the invocation into an XML or JSON message that is transmitted to the server in an *XmlHttpRequest* invocation.
3. This message is interpreted on the server and the server-side API is invoked to execute the ReadEmployees() procedure against the server-side database (after authenticating the client's credentials). Note that the server-side implementation of this procedure may well be the SQL used in the ODBC-CRUD approach: for example, SELECT * FROM DEPARTMENT.
4. The server-side API packages the result of the procedure—a set of database tuples—in XML or JSON format and sends it to the client.
5. The client-side library passes the result to the application that initiated the request.

6. Either the client-side library or the application can cache the employee data, so that subsequent requests—for example, to sort the data in different ways—can be accommodated without another round-trip to the server.
7. Using an editable text field, the application allows the user to modify an employee's phone number. The change is propagated to the server by invoking the UpdatePhoneNumber() procedure. Using the transmitted arguments, the server updates the database, perhaps by invoking the UPDATE DEPART-MENT SET PHONENUM = "914-555-1222" WHERE ID = "103" SQL which is executed against the server-side database.

2.1.3 Comparison

In this section, we compare ODBC-CRUD and ODBC-SP to show why, from an enterprise's viewpoint, using ODBC-CRUD for server-side data-access suffers from a number of disadvantages. Enterprises tend to prefer ODBC-SP and SOA, because SOA explicitly addresses these issues architecturally, and ODBC-SP addresses them from an implementation perspective. In our previous example, the steps used by Web developers in an ODBC-CRUD approach (Section 2.1.1) are much less attractive to an enterprise than the SOA-based steps taken in an ODBC-SP (Section 2.1.2) approach.

One disadvantage of the ODBC-CRUD approach is that it forces an enterprise to expose much detail about the employee data. For example, the Web developer has to know the name of the database, the name of the employee table, and the schema used in the employee table (e.g., column names and types). Conversely, because the ODBC-SP approach is similar to a procedure call, the server is not forced to disclose information about the database schema and organization, which improves security by disclosing as little information as possible to a potential attacker. However, what we call the ODBC-CRUDV variant of the ODBC-CRUD style addresses this enterprise concern. It does this by only providing client's access to updateable database *views* [7] of the server's data, and then allowing CRUD access to these views. This makes it possible to restrict users to viewing and updating subsets of the entire database. For example, a user could be allowed to read and write only their own data. The ODBC-CRUDV approach further addresses enterprise security concerns since views allow renaming of the tables and columns in the underlying server database: additional security is thus provided by hiding the underlying schema.

Application-level security is another disadvantage of the ODBC-CRUD approach. At first glance, it is hard to understand why the authentication scheme used by ODBC for desktop application access to a database server (often just a *userid* and *password*) should not also suffice—at least in an Intranet environment—for Web client access to the same database server. Even in an Internet environment, where insecure communication is definitely an issue, technologies such as SSL can be used to encrypt client–server communication as necessary.

A closer look shows that the key difference between desktop and Web applications is the security issue of "trusted code." Authentication schemes prove only that a trusted person is *executing* the code. They do not prove that a trusted person *wrote* the code. Compared to a server-based application, it is much easier to inject malicious code into a Web 2.0 client application, and enterprises are therefore very wary about letting client-side business logic execute directly against their databases. In addition, database servers do not usually have fine-grained access control mechanisms. Typically the database does not have a userid defined for each end user of the system, but only a userid for each role that might access the database. Also, access to tables is typically granted on a per-table basis, and not on a per-row or per-column basis. In practice, the application code is typically heavily involved in verifying that only authorized users have access to only the data they are authorized to see (in addition to the access control provided by the database manager). Thus, enterprises prefer ODBC-SP over ODBC-CRUD and ODBC-CRUDV because stored-procedure code is vetted by the administrator, and so it much less likely to be malicious than code running on a client machine. Although the REST style is somewhat higher level than the ODBC-CRUD style, its verbs are by design intended to express CRUD semantics. As a result, it is problematic to use a REST API to interface to server-side business logic functions (e.g., stored procedures) other than CRUD.

2.2   Application Types

Given this background of server-side data-access APIs, an enterprise's decision regarding whether, or how, to enable Web 2.0 access to enterprise data will often depend on where a specific application lies on a spectrum of application types.

2.2.1   Situational Applications

Situational applications have been defined as software that is "designed in and for a particular social situation or context" [36]. Developers of situational applications place a great premium on flexibility (typically operating outside the usual I/T bureaucracy), and favor a client-centric programming model (perhaps, because of the lower entry barrier or because of the proportionally greater focus on an application's view). Situational applications are therefore a good candidate for a Web 2.0 programming model, specifically one in which enterprise data are accessed using a client-side cache built on top of an ODBC-CRUD server-side API. From the developer perspective, the GUI widgets can directly access and update the database as they interact with the user, without worrying much about adapting to a non-CRUD API on the server. When displaying data, for example, a grid widget can load data directly from the database table; when the user "types over" one of the grid's cells, the application can immediately perform an update on the corresponding database item.

The security issues raised in Section 2.1.3 with respect to the ODBC-CRUD approach are less of a concern in a situational application environment. Such an environment is not overly concerned with security, because security is somewhat enforced by social norms. As noted in Shirky [36]:

> Instead, in both projects the students decided that since all the users were part of the ITP community, they would simply make it easy to track the deadbeats, with the threat of public broadcast of their names. The possibility of being shamed in front of the community became part of the application design, even though the community and the putative shame were outside the framework of the application itself.

Thus, five people sharing a phone directory application do not worry much about users in the group deliberately corrupting the database, because the "honest" users will kick the dishonest users out of the group. Also, the damage that can be done by a single malicious user is limited. Note that a personal (nonshared) database is the limiting case of situational software; you will not corrupt your own database and hope to escape detection. In situational environments, the system really only needs to verify that the user is a member of the group that is allowed to access the database. Differentiating between read access and write access to server-side data is less important than for other application types.

2.2.2   View-Constrainable Applications

In contrast to situational applications, other application types cannot rely on social pressures to enforce security and integrity constraints. However, the security and integrity constraints *can* be enforced using views provided by the database server. We call such applications *view constrainable*.

By using the ODBC-CRUDV (ODBC enhanced with "views") server-side data-access API, enterprises may be willing to provide view-constrainable applications with a Web 2.0 client-centric programming style. For example, consider a phone-book application which is shared by a large number of users. All users are allowed to read the entire database, but users should only be allowed to update their own record. This can be accomplished by defining two views: a read-only view of the entire database, and an updateable view containing only the records belonging to the user.

2.2.3 Enterprise Applications

At the far end of the spectrum, *enterprise applications* are those which require tight security constraints that are incompatible with the ODBC-CRUD or ODBC-CRUDV data-access models. Although database views can reduce some risk to the enterprise, enterprises are often wary about exposing *any* schema information about the database, because any information that is exposed provides clues for a potential attack. Schema information is needed to employ *SQL Injection* techniques [37], where clients provide fragments of SQL as parameter values in the hope that the server will mistakenly execute these fragments.

Direct execution of a client's SQL may be viewed as intrinsically dangerous because SQL is a very open-ended API, and thus provides the greatest opportunity for malicious users to attempt to bypass system security. Also, database view technology is typically not sufficiently fine grained to provide security for certain applications. For example, in an HR application, managers will be allowed to see employee salaries, but may not be allowed to see an employee's personal information. In general, using only views for security is not flexible enough to enable such restrictions.

More fundamentally, enterprise applications are characterized by the fact that the business logic itself is responsible for enforcing system security and integrity. Therefore, those portions of the business logic must be validated by the enterprise before they are allowed to read and write application data. As discussed in Section 2.1.3, enterprises will not allow untrusted code to update their databases, because they cannot be sure that the code will maintain the consistency, integrity, and security constraints which are required by the business. For example, consider the funds transfer application shown in Fig. 2. It is a stylized version of the business and funds transfer logic detailed in the TPC-A transaction profile [39].

In this application, a user interacts with a funds transfer form in the browser, allowing a customer to transfer funds from one account to another. Internally, the Web 2.0 application manipulates a set of account information for the customer using the application. Although extracted from a server-side database, the Web 2.0 developer stores and manipulates the account information as an array of JavaScript objects. By caching this information on the client, a developer can achieve the Web 2.0 goal of improving response time when listing the customer's accounts. The Web 2.0 application will typically exploit the cache to allow responsive client-side information sorting or to facilitate a drag-and-drop funds transfer. As shown in the figure, to provide security and integrity guarantees, the enterprise must enforce access constraints such as "users can only read and modify their own accounts." This type of constraint *can* be handled by views in an ODBC-CRUDV style. However, the enterprise must *also* enforce additional business rules: for example,

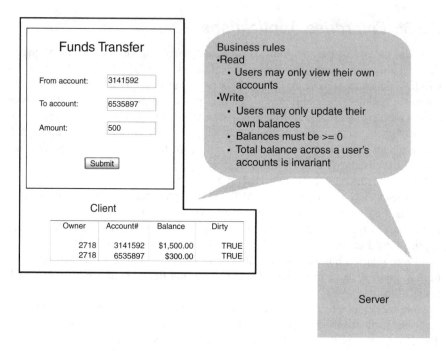

FIG. 2. Elements of a Web 2.0 funds transfer application.

the total balance in the user's accounts before and after the transfer must be the same so that a user can only transfer funds but not create or destroy funds. Such constraints cannot be specified using database views.

One way to view such constraints is as a set of invariants and postconditions on the database. The invariant is that the sum of all the funds in the user's accounts must be the same at the end of a complete database operation (e.g., transaction) as at the beginning of a transaction. Also, no account can have a balance of less than zero, because this would allow the user steal money by transferring a large sum from an empty account into a second account, and then withdrawing the money from the second account.

In theory, the database server could allow ODBC-CRUDV access to the database server, and the server could execute some server-side code before and after the transaction to verify that the client code has maintained integrity constraints. However, most enterprises choose to enforce such constraints using business logic encoded in trusted *server-side* code. Clients can propagate database updates only through the ODBC-SP data-access API. As shown in Fig. 2, Web 2.0 applications are certainly capable—from a technology perspective—of enforcing these constraints on the client. However, enterprises will simply not trust the client-side code to enforce the constraints, because enterprises feel more confident about the accuracy and reliability of server-side code. Code-signing approaches do not provide a benefit for enterprise applications. Code signing is typically used to allow a client to verify that is it executing code that was written by a known (and trusted) source. In this case, it is the server that needs to be reassured as to the provenance of the code running on the client. There is no way for the client to convince the server that it is running code from a known source.

Our use of the "funds transfer application" to characterize enterprise applications as applications that require trusted business logic in order to update enterprise data actually understates the case. Rather than consisting simply of a single "chunk" of business logic (Fig. 2), many enterprise applications include multiple such "chunks" using a *workflow* component to link multiple application steps. For example, consider an HR application that accesses an employee salary. A given employee may be authorized to see their own salary—a view-constrainable function (Section 2.2.2). However, only the employee's manager can update the salary data by initiating a workflow chain through in which two levels of management approve of the salary change. Such an application's business logic is more diffuse than in a fund's transfer scenario, as well as comprising a greater proportion of the application's overall footprint. In such cases, enterprises will be even more reluctant to trust client-resident code, and to require that server-side data be updated from server-resident code.

Note that this spectrum of application types is orthogonal to an application's semantics or function. An application may be initially coded as a situational application, and as it becomes more useful to an enterprise, become an enterprise application. In that case, its initial implementation is now unsuitable for the enterprise because it has become more critical to an enterprise's success.

2.3   Client-Side Enterprise Data Access

We now consider the implications of the interaction between the various server-side data-access models and the spectrum of application types with respect to Web 2.0 client-side access to enterprise data. We consider both the APIs and implementation for Web 2.0 client-side data access.

As we discussed previously, the preferred Web 2.0 client-side API allows the client application to directly read and write the application data. The programming model, in other words, is that the client-side data are an explicit cache of the enterprise data. The Web browser becomes another data tier of the extended enterprise, and client-side middleware must provide the typical cache functions on the new tier. For example, the client-side middleware should transparently handle cache misses on behalf of the application developer, querying the server for the required data. If the client-side API allows data to be modified, a suitable cache *write policy* must be devised. The API implementers must also examine tradeoffs between using a *write-through* write policy (every write to the cache causes a synchronous write to be made to the corresponding server-side data) and using a *write-back* policy (writes are propagated to the server only as needed, e.g., when the data are removed from the cache to make room for new data) [29]. The client-side cache middleware must also determine how modified data are merged with the enterprise's master version of the data. Transactional commit of the modified data is ideal, but difficult to do without a more complex programming model than may be suitable for Web-based frameworks [3].

Another issue that designers of the client-side cache API must address is whether the client-side data have a *single-level* or *two-level* store relationship to the corresponding server-side data. In the two-level store approach, an explicit distinction is made between the client-side version of the data (the first level) and the server-side version of the data (the second level) which is copied to the Web browser. Explicit "load" methods move the state from the server to the client, and explicit "store" methods move modified state from the client back to the server. No mechanism exists through which a client can persistently keep a "handle" to a specific component. In contrast, when a single-level store approach is used, a lifetime association exists between the client-side version of the data and the master version resident on the server. A client-side developer can reasonably speak of client-side data persisting across serial instantiations of the application. This is accomplished by referencing the data through a construct that maps between the client and server versions of the data. Tradeoffs have been identified in non-Web environments between the single-level and two-level store concepts [24]. Web 2.0 frameworks that present a client-side cache to developers must deal with this, and other, traditional cache issues.

A typical example of a direct-access API is dojo.data [40], and a similar approach is taken by ADO.NET Data Services [1]. The dojo.data API provides query-based read access to data, and direct write access to data (a more detailed description is provided in Section 3.1). The easiest server-side API for this approach is an ODBC-CRUD API. This allows the client to build a client-side cache, to populate the cache with server data on a cache miss, and to implement a write-through or write-back cache for modified data. This approach works well for situational applications, where security is limited to discriminating between allowed and disallowed clients. This approach also works well for view-constrainable applications.

However, implementation of dojo.data-style APIs is more problematic for enterprise applications. As discussed above, enterprise applications have stringent requirements for security, integrity, and consistency, which typically cannot be met by ODBC-CRUD or ODBC-CRUDV-access APIs to the server. In practice, for most applications of interest, enterprises will use SOA and ODBC-SP (stored procedure) APIs to implement updates to the server database. This presents a problem for the maintenance of client-side caches. For example, to use the funds transfer stored procedure (Fig. 2) to implement write-through or write-back caching algorithms, the client developer would have to reverse engineer the updates that were made to the client cache, and try to make the same changes to the server by using one or more funds transfer calls to the server. Sometimes, it is possible to provide stored procedures whose APIs are close enough to CRUD to build a writeable client-cache implementation, especially if the stored procedures are deliberately designed in this fashion. However, some applications do not map well to a CRUD API. Looking at the funds transfer example, it would seem necessary to define a (virtual) table, where inserting a record into this table caused a funds transfer to occur. This is significantly different from what is desired for a Web 2.0 application developer.

The "cognitive dissonance" between the need for write-back or write-through of Web 2.0 caches and the availability of only an ODBC-SP server-side API for enterprise data access recalls the problem faced by compiler developers for CISC architectures. For example, the IBM 370 [19] series mainframe and successors provided an "edit and mark" (EDMK) instruction, which could be used to do fairly complicated conversions from integer to string type. However, it was very difficult to take high-level language programs and recognize code sequences that could be implemented by EDMK. Experiences such as this led many hardware designers to conclude that it was a waste of effort to include complicated instructions such as EDMK; eventually, this observation lead to the development of RISC [26] architectures.

For enterprise applications, it is therefore impractical for client-side developers to use dojo.data-type write APIs on the client; ultimately, the developer will be forced to map updates applied to the client-side cache into invocations of server-side stored procedures. A more practical Web 2.0 approach for enterprise applications is a partition between function that only reads data and function that updates the data. Thus, in the funds transfer example, a view could be defined that shows only the accounts for the authenticated user, and the client could use dojo.read to cache data from this view. This would make a Web 2.0 approach for responsive data display feasible while satisfying enterprise concerns. However, the application must then also be enhanced to appropriately invalidate the relevant cached data when funds transfer updates are sent to the server.

An alternative type of client-side API is based on the *XmlHttpRequest* [43] API. This API is found in most modern browsers, and enables a client to make synchronous and asynchronous HTTP calls to the server. *XmlHttpRequest* is essentially a messaging API, which sends a block of bytes to the server, and receives a block of bytes in

response. This can be used as a building block for various application-specific protocols which can be used, in turn, as middleware to support applications. For example,
such a protocol was implemented by the DBC-JS [6] project. DBC-JS enables a client
to send any SQL request to the server, and to cache the results sent back to the client.
Interestingly, DBC-JS is a mix of ODBC-CRUD and ODBC-SP server APIs, because
the client can send both CRUD-type and stored-procedure-type requests to the server.
The only restrictions on what a client may execute are the database permissions set by
the server. Thus, DBC-JS can be used to implement both situational applications (using
CRUD SQL) and enterprise applications (using SQL to call stored procedures).

3.   A Closer Look at Web 2.0 Client and Server Data-Access APIs

Section 2 delineated the application types best suited for enterprise deployment of
a "preferred" Web 2.0 client-side API. Such an API is preferred by client-side
developers because it allows the client portion of the application to directly read
and write application data. Examples of this style API include dojo.data [40] and
ADO.NET Data Services [1]. In this section, we take a closer look at dojo.data, and
then examine implementations of this API that are targeted at two REST APIs for
server-side data access.

3.1   dojo.data

The dojo.data API provides a Web 2.0 framework for reading, writing, and
integrating data into other Dojo [10] libraries in general, and Dojo widgets in
particular. Interestingly, "dojo.data is a uniform data access layer that removes the
concepts of database drivers and unique data formats. All data is represented as an
item or as an attribute of an item. With such a representation, data can be accessed
in a standard fashion." [40]. Thus, dojo.data is agnostic about both the *source*
(client vs server) and the *type* of the data manipulated by the API. It includes
implementations for data stores such as XML, JSON, and ATOM. Although the
following discussion of the dojo.data API is not exhaustive, it should convey a sense
of how it presents developers with the ability to directly access and update data
regardless of the master version of the data reside.

Table I lists some of the key functions of the dojo.read API. It enables developers
to fetch and access data in a Web 2.0 style using asynchronous callback functions.
The data returned consist of a set of JavaScript objects ("items"), each having a set
of properties ("attributes"). getValue() and getAttributes() thus provide a
synchronous API to access the property values and property names of a given item.

TABLE I
DOJO.READ API: KEY FUNCTIONS

dojo.read Functions	Description	Arguments
getValue	Returns the attribute's value for the given item	Item, attribute, defaultValue
getAttributes	Returns an array containing the names of the item's attributes	Item
Fetch	Executes a query and makes the resulting set of data asynchronously available to a set of callback functions	Query object with standard properties

In contrast, the fetch() method is an event-driven, asynchronous, function that returns a desired set of items. In addition to the query itself, a developer may specify one or more of the following optional parameters:

- An onBegin function, invoked immediately before processing the query's items
- An onItem function, invoked individually on each item
- An onComplete function, invoked after all the items have been processed
- An onError function, invoked if an error occurs

Importantly, aside from these callbacks, the API does not allow developers direct access to the set of items.

In addition, optional *start*, *count*, and *sort* parameters may also be specified.

Table II lists some of the key functions of the dojo.write API. As one would expect, it includes (synchronous) CUD-like functions (R (RETRIEVE) is provided by the dojo.read API):

- newItem() corresponds to CREATE
- setValue() and unsetAttribute() correspond to UPDATE
- deleteItem() corresponds to DELETE

Other functions of the dojo.write API are needed because of the approach taken in the design of the client-side cache. In Section 2.3, we noted that cache designers must address:

- Whether to use a write-back or a write-through policy.

With the dojo.write API, the (typically) relatively large latency between client and server implies that the *asynchronous* write-back policy is superior to the write-through policy, allowing the application to continue while data are written back to the server. The processing model for the save function is therefore based on asynchronous execution of developer-supplied "onComplete" and "onError"

TABLE II
DOJO.WRITE API: KEY FUNCTIONS

dojo.write Functions	Description	Arguments
newItem	Creates a new item, setting its attributes from keyword Args	Object with item's initial state
deleteItem	Deletes the specified item	Item
setValue	Sets the specified item's attribute to the supplied value	Item, attribute, value
unsetAttribute	Deletes the value(s) associated with the specified item's attribute	Item, attribute
save	Asynchronously saves the current state of the item to the server, running the supplied callback functions when the operation completes	Object with callback function
revert	Discards state changes made by the client to its set of cached items	None
isDirty	Determines if the item has been modified since the last save operation	Item

TABLE III
DOJO.IDENTITY API: KEY FUNCTIONS

dojo.identity Functions	Description	Arguments
getIdentity	Returns an identifier for the item	Item
fetchItemByIdentity	Asynchronously fetches the item associated with the supplied identity, running the callback function when the item is loaded	Object with callback functions

callback functions. The save function operates on all (modified) items in the data store; the revert function is used to clear modifications made by the developer since the last save invocation. Developers can use the isDirty function to determine whether a given item has been modified since the last save invocation.

- Whether to use a single-level or two-level store design.

As the fetch and save functions make clear, the dojo.data API uses a *two-level store* design in which the client must explicitly move a datum's state between the server and the client. Although the getIdentity and fetchItemByIdentity functions of the dojo.identity API (see Table III) enable a client-side developer to get a "handle" to a given datum, that handle is *temporary* rather than persistent. The temporary handle is intended for the purpose of populating a given Web page; the API does not guarantee that a developer can use the handle when constructing a different Web page—let alone in a subsequent instantiation of the application.

3.2   Implementing dojo.data for the Enterprise

Having discussed dojo.data as a representative Web 2.0 client-side data-access API in Section 3.1, we now examine implementations of this API in an enterprise context. Specifically, we discuss IBM's WebSphere sMash [41] and Zazen, a research proto- type effort [23]. Microsoft's ADO.NET Data Services [2] provides analogous server- side services for its client-side Web 2.0 data API [1]. In terms of the framework presented in Section 2, sMash and Zazen provide an ODBC-CRUD server-side data- access API—specifically, a REST API. Client-side libraries implement dojo.data by mapping the API's calls to the corresponding server-side REST calls. Our discussion focuses on the sMash product, with occasional references to Zazen.

Conforming to our analysis of Section 2, sMash describes its application focus as being on 'Leveraging Web 2.0 to meet the "situational" needs of business'.

Figure 3 shows the GUI of a situational employee phonebook Web-based application. It enables members of a department to create, modify, and delete information about a given employee. sMash's *Zero Resource Model* (ZRM) defines the employee schema on the server, exposing the associated data to Web clients with a REST API. For example, the application initially populates the GUI with the entire set of department employees via this REST call:

GET http://localhost:8080/resources/employees?start=0

Fig. 3. GUI for a situational employee phonebook application.

The sMash server responds with the JSON data structure shown in Example 1; the client-side code builds the Web page shown in Fig. 3.

sMash allows developers to construct REST URLs that filter a server-side collection (such as the department's employees), returning a subset collection whose members meet the specified conditions. Filter conditions can be chained together, and the sMash run-time optimizes the composed query so that the filtering is done in the database rather than in the ZRM layer. Filter conditions are specified using a convention of

---

```
[
  {
  "firstname": "John",
  "lastname": "Doe",
  "location": "Hursley",
  "phonenumber": "914-555-1212",
  "id": 101,
  "updated": "2008-05-21 13:23:53"
  },
  {
  "firstname": "William",
  "lastname": "Smith",
  "location": "RTP",
  "phonenumber": "203-555-1212",
  "id": 102,
  "updated": "2008-05-21 13:24:08"
  },
  {
  "firstname": "Susan",
  "lastname": "Johnson",
  "location": "Beijing",
  "phonenumber": "914-555-1212",
  "id": 103,
  "updated": "2008-05-21 13:27:57"
  }
]
```

Example 1 Populating the employee phonebook application with a ZRM REST call

[field name][delimiter][operator]

and sMash provides a rich set of operators. For example, `lastname__equals` and `lastname__contains` perform the specified filter based on the "lastname" property value applied to each member of the collection. Operators such as "after" and "between" are provided for properties with date and time values. sMash also enables developers to perform paging through operations such as "start" and "count." The URL syntax uses "=" to specify the value of the filter parameters, and "&" to chain filter conditions together. Thus, if the client sends this URL to the server:

GET http://localhost/resources/employees?location__equals=Beijing&count=5

the server responds with the first five employees located in Beijing.

The other REST verbs are supported in the usual fashion. If the user clicks the "Create" button, the application constructs and transmits this type of HTTP request:

PUT http://localhost:8080/resources/employees/103

If the user clicks the "Delete" button, the application constructs and transmits this type of HTTP request:

DELETE http://localhost:8080/resources/employees/102

ZRM's REST API has the benefit of being a well-understood approach for client access to Web services. Its disadvantage lies in that, from the perspective of a Web developer, it requires some effort to translate the high-level request for data into the correct REST call. sMash therefore provides an implementation of dojo.data— called ZRMStore (packaged as "zero.resource.DataStore")—which provides a client-side cache of items whose master version exists on a sMash server. dojo.data functions that must access the server such as `fetch` and `save` are implemented by mapping the function's semantics to the corresponding ZRM REST URL. This mapping is simplified by the fact that dojo.read "does not specify the syntax or semantics of the query itself": these are supplied with the *query* parameter. The ZRMStore constructor is supplied with the context root of a sMash application (e.g., `http://mycompany.com:8080`). Subsequent invocations of `fetch` specify a valid ZRM URI such as `/resources/employees/` or `/resources/employees/?lastname__contains=Smith`. ZRMStore transmits the full URL to the server, storing the results (if any) in a cache. If no metadata has yet been cached about the ZRM resource, ZRMStore will transmit a metadata URL (e.g., http://mycompany.com:8080/resources/types/employees), and cache the metadata (such as the names and types of the resource's items) for later use.

The bulk of the dojo.read implementation is a thin wrapper that manipulates the "eval'ed" JavaScript object returned by the server. Internally, each item in the cache is a JavaScript object (associative array) such that *item*[*x*] represents "the value of the *x* attribute for the specified item." `store.getAttributes(someItem)` returns the property names of the metadata JSON; `store.getValue(someAttribute, someItem)` returns the item's value for the specified attribute. Implementing the `save` operation is a bit more complicated than `fetch`. ZRMStore must track the set of CUD operations over the course of a "session" (i.e., the period of time since the last `save`) and map the "net" effect (e.g., factoring in calls to `revert`) to a set of ZRM GET, PUT, POST, and DELETE calls. Figure 4 shows the overall architecture.

In summary, ZRMStore provides an implementation of dojo.data, a Web 2.0 data-access API, that is coupled with ZRM, an ODBC-CRUD(REST) data-access API on the server. The analysis of Section 2 shows that this architecture is a good fit for Web 2.0 situational applications. In its current form, however, the schema information exposed by ZRM makes it unsuitable for view-constrainable applications (although nothing in principle prevents ZRM from incorporating "updateable views" function). More importantly, as explained in Section 2, enterprise applications are incompatible with an ODBC-CRUD data-access model—requiring instead an ODBC-SP model. sMash addresses this concern with the use of "custom handlers," essentially a piece of server-side code that is specifically written for a given application.

Zazen [23] resembles ZRM in many ways. It too implements dojo.data with a mapping to a REST API on the server. However, we designed the server-side API to give Zazen aspects of a data-service SOA in order to make Zazen more suitable for view-constrainable and enterprise applications. The key idea is that Zazen uses a

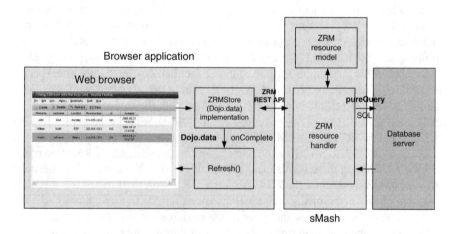

FIG. 4. Client (ZRMStore) and server (ZRM) application architecture.

stored-procedure API, but allows the stored procedures to be implemented using SQL in addition to the standard stored-procedure approach [18].

In contrast to the ODBC-SP approach, Zazen uses a *labeled* SQL approach. The idea is to label an SQL statement such that:

- In the REST call, Web developers supply the SQL statement's label. The data returned by the server are the result set generated by executing the corresponding SQL statement.

- Database administrators optimize the SQL for their particular environment, and validate it using their enterprise's security policies.

- As shown in Fig. 4, the Zazen server mediates between Web client requests (which specify a given label) and the database server (which executes the SQL associated with the Web client's label).

Since labeled SQL is a higher-level abstraction than SQL itself, Zazen addresses an enterprise concern that schema information be encapsulated. The label—for example, "all employees in my department"—in effect names a data service, with the associated SQL providing the service implementation. The SQL statements are not limited to providing rows from a single database table; they can provide JOIN results from multiple tables or from operations of arbitrary complexity. The result set sent by Zazen to the Web client can be cached locally in the browser, so Web developers exploit the benefits of the Ajax approach. Zazen addresses an enterprise's security concerns because Web developers do not even see the SQL that they are executing; database administrators continue to be solely responsible for constructing and validating all SQL that executes in their system. Clients can be prevented from knowing even the column names through SQL that maps real names to virtual names.

By "black-boxing" a chunk of server-side relational database logic as a function that can be called by applications, a labeled SQL statement is, in effect, a stored procedure. Stored procedures have advantages compared to ODBC-CRUD APIs, and database administrators often prefer that they be used even in a desktop application environment. Stored procedures integrate data validation and access control into the database, and allow multiple SQL statements, together with business logic, to be combined in a single package. Zazen must therefore provide an API for Web clients to parameterize a labeled SQL statement. For example, if the invoked SQL is SELECT * FROM EMPLOYEES WHERE SALARY < :MIN_SALARY, the API must allow clients to specify a value for the labeled parameter MIN_SALARY. In Zazen's REST protocol, the *query* parameters include the database name, user name, password, and a label that specifies a Zazen labeled SQL statement. If the labeled SQL includes named parameters, the *query* parameter includes two arrays that specify the *i*th parameter name and value. More generally, every Zazen URL has the form:

```
https://.../statement_label?parameter1=value1[&...&]
parameterN=valueN
```

Other optional URL parameters allow the client to specify filter parameters that subset the contents of the result set in various ways. This ability addresses a major weakness of the labeled SQL approach, namely that it is too inflexible for environments with rapidly changing application requirements. For example, assume that an enterprise has determined that clients with suitable credentials may see the set of employees in a given department via a labeled SQL statement that invokes SELECT * FROM DEPARTMENT. What if an application needs only manager *Smith's* employees rather than the *entire* department's employees? Requiring the enterprise to create a new labeled SQL statement to match such application-specific needs is unrealistic. The alternative forces Web developers to invoke the more general statement, and then filter "by hand" to get the desired subset of data. Doing this correctly and efficiently is hard. The Zazen solution exploits the fact that—assuming that a more general SQL statement is secure—security is not compromised by allowing clients to issue a query that returns a subset of the more general query. We do this with filter operations that reduce the number of rows returned by the query, and/or subset the number of columns returned in each row.

In the Zazen API, therefore, a Web client specifies a "base" query (via the labeled SQL), and can also specify a set of filters that Zazen applies to the result set of the base query. Importantly, the base query is combined with the filters to form a composite query that Zazen delegates to the database server. Instead of being done by Zazen directly, the filter operations are efficiently done by an optimized database server.

Continuing the previous example, the client might choose to specify these filters:

- WHERE MANAGER = "SMITH", to reduce the number of rows returned by the base query for the entire department
- COLUMNS DEPTNO and DEPTNAME, to eliminate the MANAGER column which is already known to be *Smith*

Receiving this input, Zazen constructs this composite query: SELECT DEPTNO, DEPTNAME FROM (SELECT * FROM DEPARTMENT) AS RESULT WHERE MANAGER = "SMITH". Importantly, Zazen does not rewrite the original SQL by, for example, rewriting the WHERE clause. Such an approach makes database administrators uncomfortable, is fragile, and requires run-time analysis of both the original SQL and that provided by the client to ensure that they make sense when combined. In contrast, the composite query leaves the original SQL intact, and uses the filter clauses to successively reduce the scope of the base query. Then, as shown in Fig. 5, the Zazen server uses the JDBC API to ask the database server to execute the constructed SQL.

Zazen uses a similar approach to enable clients to specify that certain columns be used to perform an ascending or descending sort of the result set. Thus, to specify that values of the department number be used to sort the results in ascending order, the client inserts sortAttribute0=deptno and orderAttribute0=ASC into the URI. Zazen implements other filters, such as COUNT, instructing Zazen to return only "count" rows from the result set; and START, instructing Zazen to discard a preliminary set of rows.

Importantly, Zazen's approach of packaging a data service as labeled SQL statements works for data services other than query. The semantics of the service are determined by the SQL itself. As part of the process of validating the SQL, database administrators determine which REST "verb" (or HTTP method [20]) will be associated with a given labeled SQL statement. Our SELECT * FROM DEPART-MENT example is associated with a GET method; SQL such as UPDATE EMPLOYEES SET DEPT = "R56", WHERE LAST_NAME = "SMITH" would be associated with a POST method. Similarly, DELETE FROM EMPLOYEES WHERE SSN = "012-34-5679" is invoked with a DELETE method, and INSERT INTO EMPLOYEES(NAME, SSN) VALUES("JOHN DOE", "012-34-5678") is associated with a PUT method.

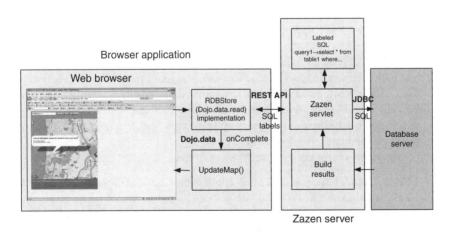

Fig. 5. Zazen's client and server application architecture.

The labeled SQL approach addresses some enterprise concerns since it hides schema information from the Web client. In combination with the use of views on the server, Zazen is suitable for implementing view-constrainable applications. However, this form of Zazen is *not* suitable for enterprise applications because—fundamentally—the server still presents an ODBC-CRUD data-access method. Note that Zazen can be used—using exactly the same configuration— to invoke a stored procedure via standard APIs such as JDBC. This implies that the server can present an ODBC-SP data-access method that encapsulates arbitrary amounts of business logic, written in a high-level programming language, and interleaved with any number of SQL statements. That said, the mismatch between the "direct-to-relational" Web 2.0 style preferred by Web developers (e.g., the dojo.data API) still exists, making it difficult for Web 2.0 applications to perform updates in enterprise applications with the Web 2.0 API. As recommended in Section 2, a more practical Web 2.0 approach for enterprise applications is a partition between function that only reads data and function that updates the data.

4.   Conclusion

In this chapter, we have shown how—from a technology perspective—Web 2.0 applications are best understood as client/server applications in which the client platform (the Web browser) can interact with the server in a more flexible way than Web 1.0 applications. Applications can use asynchronous client/server communication (provided by *XmlHttpRequest* and IFRAME) to modify a Web page without having to request that the server refresh the *entire* Web page. Rather than use the Web browser only as an HTML-rendering engine, the Web browser is used to execute code written in powerful client-side languages such as JavaScript. By encoding data in XML and JSON data structures, data can be efficiently transmitted between client and server. Even more importantly, such data can be fetched as part of an application's background processing (e.g., with *XmlHttpRequest* or IFRAME technologies), and cached for subsequent use.

From an architectural perspective, the use of these Web 2.0 technologies:

- Enable a much larger portion of an application's business logic to reside on the client as compared to Web 1.0 applications.
- Enable the client to cache a much larger portion of an application's data as compared to Web 1.0 applications.

From a user's perspective, the overall effect of these Web 2.0 technologies is that Web applications behave much more responsively than Web 1.0 applications. This will occur if applications are programmed to:

- Reduce the number of costly—because they increase response time—client/server interactions that Web 1.0 applications require to execute business logic
- Reduce the number of costly—because they increase response time—client/server interactions that Web 1.0 applications require to fetch necessary data

Within this context, the chapter focused on the issues related to Web 2.0 access to enterprise data. We showed that the willingness of enterprises to allow Web 2.0 applications access to enterprise data depends on where the application fits in a spectrum of application types and on the difficulty of mapping between the Web 2.0 client-side data-access model and the available server-side data-access APIs. In our analysis, in many cases, enterprises may well choose to forbid naive Web 2.0 data-access techniques to enterprise data. More sophisticated deployment strategies for Web 2.0 applications can address such enterprise concerns.

ACKNOWLEDGMENTS

We thank Judah Diament and Thomas Mikalsen for sharing their insights in many conversations about these topics, and for providing Fig. 1. We also thank Brandon Smith for his careful review of the chapter and important feedback.

REFERENCES

[1] ADO.NET Data Services API Client Reference, 2008. (http://quickstarts.asp.net/3-5-extensions/reference/adoref/default.aspx).

[2] ADO.NET Data Services (formerly known as Project "Astoria"), 2008. (http://msdn.microsoft.com/en-us/data/bb931106.aspx).

[3] Bennett B. T., Hahm B., Leff A., Mikalsen T. A., Rasmus K., Rayfield J. T., and Rouvellou I., 2000. A distributed object oriented framework to offer transactional support for long running business processes. In *ACM Middleware*, pp. 331–348.

[4] Betz K., Leff A., and Rayfield J. T., 2000. Developing highly-responsive user interfaces with DHTML and Servlets. In *Proceedings of the IEEE International Performance, Computing, and Communications Conference, 2000 (IPCCC'00)*, February 2000, pp. 437–443.

[5] Cerami E., 2002. Web Services Essentials Distributed Applications with XML-RPC, SOAP, UDDI & WSDL. O'Reilly, Sebastopol, CA.

[6] Database Connectivity for JavaScript, 2007. (http://w3.alphaworks.ibm.com/techs/overview.jsp?tech=dbcjs).

[7] Date C. J., 2005. Database in Depth: Relational Theory for Practitioners. O'Reilly Media, Sebastopol, CA.

[8] Del.icio.us. 2008. Social bookmarking. (http://del.icio.us/).

[9] Document Object Model (DOM), 2006. (http://www.w3.org/TR/DOM-Level-2-Core/).

[10] Dojo, the JavaScript Toolkit, 2007. (http://dojotoolkit.org/).

[11] Erl T., 2005. Service-Oriented Architecture (SOA): Concepts, Technology, and Design. Prentice-Hall, Englewood Cliffs, NJ.

[12] Flanagan D., 2006. JavaScript: The Definitive Guide, 5th Edn. O'Reilly, Sebastopol, CA.

[13] Flickr, 2008. (http://www.flickr.com/).

[14] Garrett J. J., 2005. Ajax: A new approach to Web applications. (http://www.adaptivepath.com/publications/essays/archives/000385.php).

[15] Gehtland J., Almaer D., and Galbraith B., 2006. Pragmatic Ajax: A Web 2.0 Primer. Pragmatic Bookshelf, Raleigh, NC.

[16] Geiger K., 1995. Inside ODBC. Microsoft Press, Redmond, WA.

[17] Gmail: Google's Approach to Email, 2008. (http://mail.google.com/mail/help/intl/en/about.html).

[18] Harrison G., and Feuerstein S., 2006. MySQL Stored Procedure Programming. O'Reilly, Sebastopol, CA.

[19] IBM System/370, 2008. (http://en.wikipedia.org/wiki/System/370).

[20] Joe Gregorio, 2004. How to create a rest protocol. (http://www.xml.com/pub/a/2004/12/01/restful-web.html).

[21] JSON in JavaScript, 2007. (http://json.org/js.html).

[22] Krasner G. E., and Pope S. T., 1988. A description of the model-view-controller user interface paradigm in the smalltalk-80 system. *Journal of Object-Oriented Programming*, **1**(3): 26–49.

[23] Leff A., and Rayfield J., 2008. Zazen: A mediating SOA between Ajax applications and enterprise data. In *Proceedings of the 2008 IEEE International Conference on Services Computing (SCC 2008)*, pp. 85–92. IEEE Computer Society, Washington, DC.

[24] Leff A., Prokopek P., Rayfield J. T., and Silva-Lepe I., 2001. Enterprise JavaBeans and Microsoft transaction server: Frameworks for distributed enterprise components. *Advances in Computers*, **54**, 99–152.

[25] Leuf B., and Cunningham W., 2001. The Wiki Way: Quick Collaboration on the Web. Addison-Wesley, Boston, MA.

[26] Markstein V., and Cocke J., January 1990. The evolution of RISC technology at IBM. *IBM Journal of Research and Development*, **34**(1): 4–11.

[27] McFarland D. S., 2006. CSS: The Missing Manual. O'Reilly, Sebastopol, CA.

[28] Niemeyer P., and Knudsen J., 2005. Learning Java, 3rd Edn. O'Reilly, Sebastopol, CA.

[29] Norton R. L., and Abraham J. A., 1982. Using write back cache to improve performance of multi-user multi-processors. In *IEEE Proceedings of the 1982 International Conference on Parallel Processing*, August 1982 pp. 326–331.

[30] O'Reilly T., 2005. Web 2.0: Compact definition? (http://radar.oreilly.com/archives/2005/10/web-20-compact-definition.html).

[31] O'Reilly T., September 2005. What is Web 2.0. (http://www.oreilly.com/go/web2).

[32] OAT: OpenAjax Alliance Compliant Toolkit, 2007. (http://ajaxian.com/archives/oat-openajax-alliance-compliant-toolkit).

[33] Opentoro: Database Publishing for the Web, 2007. (http://opentoro.sourceforge.net/).

[34] Ray E. T., 2003. Learning XML, 2nd Edn. O'Reilly, Sebastopol, CA.

[35] Roy Fielding, 2007. Representational state transfer (REST). (http://www.ics.uci.edu/~fielding/pubs/dissertation/rest_arch_style.htm).

[36] Shirky C., 2004. Situated software. (http://www.shirky.com/writings/situated_software.html).

[37] SQL Injection, 2008. (http://en.wikipedia.org/wiki/SQL_injection).

[38] The Yahoo! User Interface Library (YUI), 2008. (http://developer.yahoo.com/yui/).

[39] Transaction Processing Performance Council (TPC), 1994. TPC Benchmark A, Revision 2.0. (http://www.tpc.org/tpca/spec/tpca_current.pdf).

[40] Using dojo.data, 2007. (http://dojotoolkit.org/book/dojo-book-0-9/part-3-programmatic-dijit-and-dojo/data-retrieval-dojo-data-0).

[41] WebSphere sMash, 2008. (http://www.ibm.com/websphere/smash).

[42] Wikipedia, 2008. Representational state transfer. (http://en.wikipedia.org/w/index.php?title=Representational_State_Transfer&oldid=216768839).

[43] XMLHttpRequest, 2008. (http://en.wikipedia.org/wiki/XMLHttpRequest).

Web Content Filtering

JOSÉ MARÍA GÓMEZ HIDALGO

Optenet, Departamento de I+D, C/José Echegaray 8, edificio 3, Parque Empresarial Alvia, Las Rozas, 28230 Madrid, Spain

ENRIQUE PUERTAS SANZ

Universidad Europea de Madrid, Villaviciosa de Odón, 28670 Madrid, Spain

FRANCISCO CARRERO GARCÍA

Universidad Europea de Madrid, Villaviciosa de Odón, 28670 Madrid, Spain

MANUEL DE BUENAGA RODRÍGUEZ

Universidad Europea de Madrid, Villaviciosa de Odón, 28670 Madrid, Spain

Abstract

Across the years, Internet has evolved from an academic network to a truly communication medium, reaching impressive levels of audience and becoming a billionaire business. Many of our working, studying, and entertainment activities are nowadays overwhelmingly limited if we get disconnected from the net of networks. And of course, with the use comes abuse. The World Wide Web features a wide variety of content that are harmful for children or just inappropriate in the workplace.

Web filtering and monitoring systems have emerged as valuable tools for the enforcement of suitable usage policies. These systems are routinely deployed in

corporate, library, and school networks, and contribute to detect and limit
Internet abuse. Their techniques are increasingly sophisticated and effective,
and their development is contributing to the advance of the state of the art in a
number of research fields, like text analysis and image processing.

In this chapter, we review the main issues regarding Web content filtering,
including its motivation, the main operational concerns and techniques used in
filtering tools' development, their evaluation and security, and a number of
singular projects in this field.

1. Introduction

Internet emerged as an important tool of communication for researchers in the academic world, but since the emergence of the World Wide Web, it has quickly evolved into an extremely valuable too in work and business, study and entertainment. Many workers are actively engaged with tasks that involved Web access, including marketing research and customer care, dealing with providers, buying and selling products, and even traditional tasks including human resource management and enterprise resource planning can be performed through Web applications. Students often use the Web as a primary research tool, stay connected to their teachers and other students, and use online learning applications. And in general, the Web is a first-order tool that allows its users to keep in touch with their family, friends, and colleagues through social networks like MySpace, to find and buy products like music or movies, to book travels, to find for new jobs, to play online games, etc. [57].

The popularity of the World Wide Web, and the democratic nature of the Internet (as any user can post their own content to it), makes it prone to abuse. The Web can mainly be abused in two ways: through posting inappropriate content, or through accessing inappropriate content. This chapter primary deals with the second type of abuse.

Most Internet users in democratic countries should agree that accessing to some types of Web content is inappropriate depending on the time and place. A foremost example is the workplace. Often, workers employ at their workplace Internet access to visit inappropriate sites: porn, gambling, job search, online games, entertainment, etc., producing important economic losses for their corporations [40, 62]. Leaving the legality of some types of content apart, it is clear that accessing them at the workplace is an abuse, as the employer is providing Internet access to workers as a work tool. Access to these sites may be legitimate when done at home or cybercafés, but not at the workplace.

Additionally, Web site visitors are rarely identified, and most often, the age of the visitor is simply ignored. Some of the Web contents may be suitable for adults, but they are served without control to children and youngsters. Examples of these contents include pornography, online gambling, dating systems, etc. While legal (depending on the country), these contents are simply not appropriate for children. Moreover, there are evidences of pathologic addiction to these contents even among adults [5].

Internet has also emerged as a means of distributing illegal (or barely legal) content, like child pornography, violence, racism and sects, Web pages promoting anorexia and bulimia, software cracks, etc. All Web users should be protected against these kinds of content, but special attention must be paid to children.

There are regulatory efforts that aim at protecting children in public institutions like schools and libraries, enforcing the utilization of tools for preventing children access to inappropriate content. However, any regulatory approach to children protection and the limitation of illegal content is doomed by the international nature of Internet, and it is limited by the necessity of protecting free speech on the media.

As a consequence, Internet filters and monitoring software has emerged as a tool for avoiding Internet abuse at the workplace, and for aiding parents and public institutions to prevent children access to unsuitable contents. The goal of these software tools is to disallow the access to some kinds of Web content, and to monitor the browsing activity of Internet user for further inspection if needed. Today, Internet filters are a part of many Internet security tools, for perimeter protection, as antivirus, antispam or firewall software, and routinely deployed at corporations and educational institutions by system administrators. Most often, their deployment is enforced by the law, or just accepted by the workers as a part of an agreed acceptable Internet usage policy [55].

Web filters have started as simple tools able to detect and forbid or monitor access to listed Web sites in URL databases, or to Web pages containing a limited number of keywords. As the number of Web pages and sites is always increasing, and the lists and keywords must be manually managed, the URL and keyword-matching approaches are of limited effectiveness.

So, Web filters have evolved to include more sophisticate and effective techniques ranging from to intelligent text analysis to image processing, to cover not only incoming information (e.g., Web content), but also outgoing information (business secrets, credit card numbers, etc.), and to check a wider range of content types and protocols (instant messaging, peer to peer, specific online games, etc.) [28]. With this evolution, filters have even promoted important developments and innovations in some research fields like image processing (running from [19] to more recent works like [36]).

This chapter aims at covering most issues regarding Web content-filtering software, from applications to techniques (with focus on intelligent content analysis), implementation details, and attacks and countermeasures.

2. Motivation and Applications

The increasing availability of inappropriate, dangerous and illegal content in the Web has motivated the emergence of Internet filters and monitor as a protection and enforcement tool. In this section, we discuss the main scenarios of application of this kind of tools, along with the risks regarding privacy and information censorship.

2.1   Controlling Internet Abuse at the Workplace

Internet services are essential in modern corporations, with email as a dominant communication channel between workers and with providers and customers, and the Web routinely used for market research and marketing, as a business to business and to consumer platform, etc. But as the Internet contains much entertainment information (from the pornography and gambling industry, to news, travels, etc.), it is being used by employers to waste time and resources in nonwork tasks. When ethically used, access to recreational Web sites can make employees more informed, happy, satisfied and possibly more productive [58].

The words *cyberslacking* and *cyberloafing* are being used to make reference to Internet abuse, defined in Lim *et al.* [40] as "any voluntary act of employees using their companies' Internet access during office hours to surf nonwork-related Web sites for nonwork purposes, and access (including receiving and sending) nonwork-related email" (p. 67). In Siau *et al.* [55], a number of Internet-related abuses are described, including:

- *Copyright infringement, plagiarism.* Using illegal or pirated software that cost organizations millions of dollars because of copyright infringements. Copying of Web sites and copyrighted logos
- *Transmission of confidential data.* Using the Internet to display or transmit trade secrets
- *Pornography.* Accessing sexually explicit sites from workplace as well as the display, distribution, and surfing of these offensive sites
- *Nonwork-related download or upload.* Propagation of software that ties up office bandwidth. Programs such as Emule and BitTorrent allow the transmission of movies, music, and graphical materials
- *Leisure use of the Internet.* Loafing around the Internet, which includes shopping, sending e-cards and personal email, gambling online, chatting, game playing, auctioning, stock trading, and doing other personal activities
- *Usage of external Internet service providers.* Using an external Internet service provider (ISP) to connect to the Internet to avoid detection
- *Moonlighting.* Using office resources such as networks and computers to organize and conduct personal business (side jobs)

Of course, not all these kinds of abuse are related to Web content, and more importantly, not all employees are guilty of Internet abuse. In Websense, Inc., [62], the results of a survey of Internet activities are presented. The results of 286 workers' answers to the question: "Do you ever access each of the following types of Web sites from work?" are presented in Fig. 1. As it can be seen, a high proportion

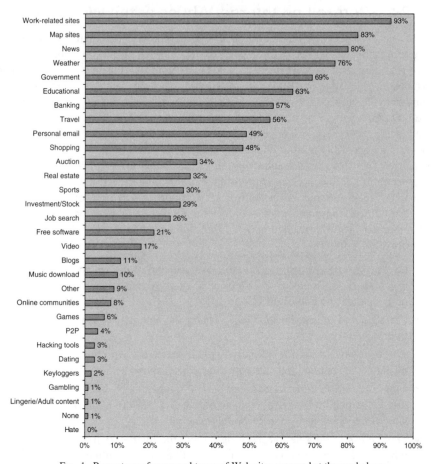

Fig. 1. Percentage of users and types of Web sites accessed at the workplace.

of employees admit using map, news, and weather sites, which are most often nonwork sites. In fact, of those employees who access nonwork-related Web sites, the average time accessing the Internet at work is 12.81 h, and the average time accessing nonwork-related Web sites at work is 3.06 h. Remarkably, the study was performed before the explosion of social networks like MySpace or Facebook, which have attracted many users in the latest 2 years.

A number of the types of content accessed may be legitimate under several circumstances:

- The existence of an acceptable Internet usage policy that states the time in which employees can make a personal use of Internet access (e.g., at lunch time).
- The work needs of the employee involve accessing some of the types of content, like *online banking* in a Financial Department, *job search* in a Human Resources Department, travel for a secretary in charge of travel planning, etc.

Moreover, letting the workers accessing some types of content (online banking or shopping) may make them more productive, as some regulations allow employees to ask for time for personal administrative tasks (e.g., once a week or month). In consequence, workers may not ask for this personal time if they can do their administrative tasks online at the workplace.

The access of workers to inappropriate Web content can have an important impact on the corporation [63]:

- *Productivity loss.* The time invested in personal use of the Web can dramatically decrease employee's productivity. Several studies report different figures to estimate the economic consequences, but the actual cost depends on the size of the company, the salary of the workers and the importance of the abuse. Regarding this, we are not aware of truly reliable statistics, but as a example, a corporation with 100 employees wasting an average 10% of their time in personal use of the Web, and an average salary of $30,000 a year, may be wasting $300,000 a year because of this reason.
- *Bandwidth waste.* As a limited resource, positive Internet access of some workers can be very slow, or just impossible, if other less ethical users are wasting it in: downloading big files like movies, music, or software programs; connecting to audio and video streaming Web sites; playing online games or visiting virtual worlds; visiting rich media (e.g., map) sites; etc. In short, let us think about the Internet access as having a single telephone set in an office, and a worker permanently making personal phone calls; the consequence is that the other workers will not be able to use it to communicate to customers.
- *Legal liability.* For a number of illegal infringements, a corporation may be liable on behalf of the worker that has actually committed the offence. This may include, depending of the country regulation, a number of crimes that are a consequence of Web downloads, including software piracy, possession and/or distribution of pedophilic material, possession and/or distribution of offensive material (running from sexual harassment to Nazi or sects publicity), copyright infringement, and several others. Also, the Web can be used to several illegal activities like hacking, defamation, fraud, etc., that may be done by an employee at the workplace.

- *Security breaches.* On one side, the corporation workstations can be infected by a number of malware programs that are currently distributed through dangerous Web sites. Also, the infected workstations can become "zombies" used to send spam, host illegal Web sites, make distributed denial of service attacks, etc. On the other side, unethical workers can reveal sensitive information or just corporate secrets through the Web.

Corporations have to address Web access control in order to make it productive and avoid these risks. While legally having the right to run Web filtering and monitoring software, several researchers have performed studies that demonstrate that these software programs should be used to enforce agreed acceptable Internet usage policies. In general, Internet abuse and even addiction must be approached as a Human Resources issue [21]:

- Educating managers and employees on the signs of Internet abuse
- Creating better policies regarding what employers expect from employees' use of the Internet at work
- Offering resources to employees who get caught in the Web
- In extreme cases, taking disciplinary actions

An Internet usage policy defines appropriate behavior when using company Internet resources and outlines the ramifications for violations [56]. In particular, the employer should be sure of covering all the abuses sketched above: copyright infringement and plagiarism, transmission of confidential data, pornography, nonwork-related download or upload, leisure use of the Internet, usage of external ISPs, moonlighting, etc. There are some guidelines for defining a good Internet usage policy [55]:

- State the company's values. These values may include profit making, professionalism, and cost-saving endeavors.
- The policy should complement the code for ethical computer use, and other codes and policies of the company.
- Make it clear the company's system should be used only for business purposes.
- Emphasize that the company reserves the right to monitor all forms of Internet and email use, and list all types of monitoring carried out.
- Stress that transmission, display, or storage of sexually explicit, defamatory, or offensive materials is strictly prohibited at all times.
- Enforce policy in a consistent and uniform manner, and assure disciplinary action will follow if there is a violation of policy.
- Involve employees in the AIUP development process and ensure that employees understand and agree with the policy.

As Internet and the behavior of workers evolve, the Internet usage policy must be suitably managed with Simmers [56]:

- Periodic (weekly, monthly, and bimonthly) generation of Internet usage reports to allow feedback on policy compliance
- Discussion of these reports at appropriate levels of the organization
- Actions taken against those who violate policy, per action steps established in the policy
- Addition of Web sites identified in usage reports as inappropriate to the filtering feature of the monitoring tool
- Periodic review and update of the policy

However, although the necessity for acceptable usage policies has been recognized by more and more institutions, these are still quite inconsistent. In an study performed by Palo Alto Networks on 20 large institutions covering around 350,000 users, it has been found that existing policies ran from completely absent, to existing several-year-old policies, to a fairly detailed policy that outlined specific applications and use cases [41]. Most often, the existing policies were not able to cover the ever-increasing range of Web-related applications used by the employees, and a number of them were present in a majority of the institutions, including circumventors (proxies and anonymizers), Web-based file sharing applications, instant messaging and Web mail, and many others.

Web filtering and monitoring tools play a key role in the enforcement of these policies, as their filtering and reporting abilities may be used to limit Internet abuse. Also, these tools can be used to prevent the usage of emerging applications, which can be the source of more abuse. Moreover, the overwhelming majority of employees (92%) believe that their company has the right to install Web-filtering technology [62].

2.2   Children Protection

Internet and the Web have quickly become extremely useful tools for children and youngsters, either as a source of information and recreation, or as a communication tool that links them to their friends and family. Moreover, kids are especially active in Internet, as many of them have born after the emergence of the Web and they are more technology-friendly than many adults.

However, children are a very sensitive Internet user group, since they are in the phase of shaping their mind, and they must be especially protected. Children face a number of risks in Internet, including [31]:

- Being exposed to inappropriate or even illegal contents, like Web pages promoting food disorders (anorexia and bulimia), pornography, drugs promotion, bomb making and terrorism, hate speech and racism, sects, hacking, gambling sites, etc.

- Contact and abuse by online sexual predators, who take advantage of anonymity to get in touch with children, seduce them and even physically engaging them to do sexual acts

- Cyber-bullying and loss of reputation that includes sending hateful messages or even death threats to children, spreading lies about them online, making nasty comments on their social-networking profiles, or creating a Web site to bash their looks or reputation

- Illegal activities, which include the full range from being victims of online fraud to actively taking part into activities like hacking, sharing illegal content, and others

- Online addiction, especially to online gaming and sometimes to very damaging activities like gambling

For instance, children and teens often employ their Internet time to keep in touch with friends and other students by using instant messaging and social networks. In a survey conducted in 2004 for the Pew Internet and American Life Project [43], based on 1100 teens aged between 12 and 17, 75% of children that go online (971) do send or receive instant messages (736), and most of them (60%) do it daily or from three to five times a week. Moreover, 56% of the teens that use instant messaging have created a public profile, being exposed not only to already known people but to strangers. In another survey conducted for the same organization in 2006 [37], some 32% of online teenagers (and 43% of social-networking teens) report having been contacted online by complete strangers and 17% of online teens (31% of social-networking teens) have "friends" on their social network profile who they have never personally met.

The necessity of protecting children has been recognized by governments and social institutions, which have enacted a number of regulations aiming at this goal. Representative regulations are:

- The USA Children's Internet Protection Act [60], which requires schools and libraries that receive federal funds for discounted telecommunications, Internet access, or internal connections services to adopt an Internet safety policy and employ technological protections that block or filter certain visual depictions deemed obscene, pornographic, or harmful to minors.

- The European Union Convention on Cybercrime[1] [11], which precisely defines child pornography-related criminal offences, and that defines a Europe-wide framework regarding this topic. This framework has been extended to racism and xenophobic crimes by the Additional Protocol to the Convention on Cybercrime, Concerning the Criminalization of Acts of a Racist and Xenophobic Nature Committed through Computer Systems [12].

International cooperation with local action is required for protecting children against most of the risks they face online, but apart from general frameworks like the Convention on Cybercrime, there are very limited possibilities due to the transnational nature of the Internet, and the existence of criminal paradises in countries with soft or nonexistent regulations. Most often, individual countries like France and Australia have issued particular laws that address children protection by even demanding the ISPs to provide parental controls and Internet filters to their customers.

Protection of children in the Internet is not only a government issue, but mostly a parental issue. Most parents are concerned about the online risks and they actively face them. For instance, in a survey conducted by the Kaiser Family Foundation [47] on 1008 parents of children ages 2–17, two-thirds say they are very concerned about the amount of inappropriate media[2] content children in this country are exposed to and many believe media is a major contributor to young people's violent or sexual behaviors. In particular, nearly three out of four parents (73%) say they know "a lot" about what their kids are doing online (among all parents with children nine or older who use the Internet at home). Most parents say they check their children's instant messaging "buddy lists," look to see what Web sites they have been to after they go online, and review what their children have posted online. In sum, they seem to be taking advantage of the tools available to them to monitor what their children are doing online.

Of course, children protection is not only a technology issue, and not only includes filters but hotlines, education, good practices, family contracts, and usage policies [9], but still filters have revealed as a major tool for complementing other approaches.

---

[1] This kind of frameworks are to be signed by participating countries, which further have to ratificate them locally and put them into practice. Unfortunately, most often, major countries do not ratificate them.

[2] In this study, "media" makes reference to TV, music, movies, gaming, and the Internet.

2.3   Internet Filtering and Free Speech

The increasing utilization of Web filters raises important concerns regarding free speech and censorship on the Internet. Nearly since their very beginning, the Internet and the Web have been open networks, but the publication of content was limited to technical persons. With the emergence of blogging and social networks, nearly everybody can have a Web presence. So, the Web is essentially democratic nowadays, and most people can find a vehicle in it for expressing their opinions and concerns, in short, a vehicle for the exercise of the First Amendment to the United States Constitution.

The democratic nature of Internet has been protected by traditional organizations like the American Civil Liberties Union, and more specific institutions like the Electronic Frontier Foundation, or projects like the Open Net Initiative (ONI). For instance, ONI's mission is "to identify and document Internet filtering and surveillance, and to promote and inform wider public dialogs about such practices."

In particular, the ONI has edited a book entitled "Access Denied: The Practice and Policy of Global Internet Filtering" [15] that covers political, social, and technical issues regarding Internet filtering, and presents a report on a number of countries that make use of filtering technologies to limit their citizens Internet access. For example, the authors of the book have found evidences that commercial Internet filters are being used in a number of countries: "Saudi Arabia uses SmartFilter as a filtering proxy and displays a block page to users when they try to access a site on the country's block list. (...). United Arab Emirates, Oman, Sudan, and Tunisia also use SmartFilter" (Chapter 1). SmartFilter is an Internet filtering and monitoring tool by the United States-based corporation Secure Computing, which is a leading vendor in the educational United States market.

Filtering and free speech is also an important concern in democratic countries. For instance, the Child Online Protection Act (COPA) [8] is a law in the United States of America, passed in 1998 with the declared purpose of restricting access by minors to any material defined as harmful to such minors on the Internet. The definition of harmful to minors in this regulation is "any communication (...) that is obscene or that

a. the average person, applying contemporary community standards, would find, taking the material as a whole and with respect to minors, is designed to appeal to, or is designed to pander to, the prurient interest;
b. depicts, describes, or represents, in a manner patently offensive with respect to minors, an actual or simulated sexual act or sexual contact, an actual or simulated normal or perverted sexual act, or a lewd exhibition of the genitals or post-pubescent female breast; and
c. taken as a whole, lacks serious literary, artistic, political, or scientific value for minors."

Under this regulation, several cases have been opened against a number of Webmasters and corporations. In most of them, the defendants have argued that COPA is unconstitutional, and some of them have been absolved. Recently, after a succession of appeals, a court decision [2] has stated that "the Child Online Protection Act (. . .) facially violates the First and Fifth Amendments of the Constitution (. . .) (1) COPA is not narrowly tailored to advance the Government's compelling interest in protecting children from harmful material on the World Wide Web ('Web'); (2) there are less restrictive, equally effective alternatives to COPA; and (3) COPA is impermissibly overbroad and vague." In conclusion, the federal courts have ruled that the law violates the constitutional protection of free speech, and therefore have blocked it from taking effect.

There is a very difficult equilibrium between freedom of speech and other freedoms and protections. For instance, the conclusions of the (European) Expert Seminar on Combating Racism While Respecting Freedom of Expression [17] state that "freedom of expression and freedom from racism and racial discrimination are not conflicting, but complementary rights. We should keep in mind that human rights are interdependent and interconnected. This means that (i) there can be no such thing as two conflicting human rights and that, (ii) human rights need to be interpreted in light of each other."

Considering all these opinions and facts, our main conclusions are:

- Filtering at corporations is out of the freedom of speech versus censorship debate. The Internet connection is provided as a work tool, under the policies of a private company. Still, privacy is a concern.
- There are many evidences that filters are being used as censorship tools in undemocratic countries.
- Any regulation regarding children protection must balance its enforcement with free speech, and must not only rely on technical measures, but also on other as proposed by the COPA Commission.

In other words, filters are policy enforcement tools. If the policies are wrong, their usage can lead to censorship. If the policies are correct, they can be very useful.

3. Web Filters Operation and Techniques

As Web filters have many possible scenarios, depending on the target users, institution organization, networks and carriers, etc., there are a number of operational issues to consider that we address in this section. Also, we also review the main techniques used in currently available filtering tools.

3.1   Operational Issues

The main operation issues we discuss are the dilemma between filtering and monitoring, available filtering categories, profiles and personalization, and network deployment.

3.1.1   Filtering Versus Monitoring

A fundamental dilemma that organizations and parents have to address is whether to filter inappropriate contents, or just monitor Internet access. Moreover, both approaches can be combined as certain types of contents may be just blocked, while others can be monitored. The difference between filtering and monitoring is the following one:

- Filtering involves detecting a Web request, taking the decision about the suitability of the requested content (according to the defined policies), and sending the user the desired content, or blocking it by resetting the connection or sending an alternative content (a stop page).
- Monitoring consists of storing Web requests, always serving the desired content. The stored logs of activity can be later analyzed, to detect unacceptable patterns of behavior.

Both approaches can be combined to enforce policy compliance. For instance, a corporation may decide to block access to peer-to-peer (P2P) networks,[3] as they are bandwidth-consuming applications rarely related to work; however, the corporation may just monitor the rest of Web access. In another example, a corporation may decide to filter out job search engines for all employees except for Human Resources workers, who may be monitored to avoid a personal use of these engines.

Filtering is an intrusive and disrupting approach, as the users often perceive that the content is blocked (although the stop page may be simulating a network error). Also, the filtering tool may incur into false positives, which are appropriate contents classified as inappropriate, and blocked in consequence. For instance, many Web filters tend to classify sexual education sites as pornographic, and this may be an important concern for schools and libraries, or even a disaster for a health-related corporation.

---

[3] Most P2P networks are usually blocked at the firewall level (discarding connections to specific ports). However, there is an increasing number of P2P and other applications that send their traffic through the port 80 (reserved to Web), and can be blocked by protocol analysis and detection.

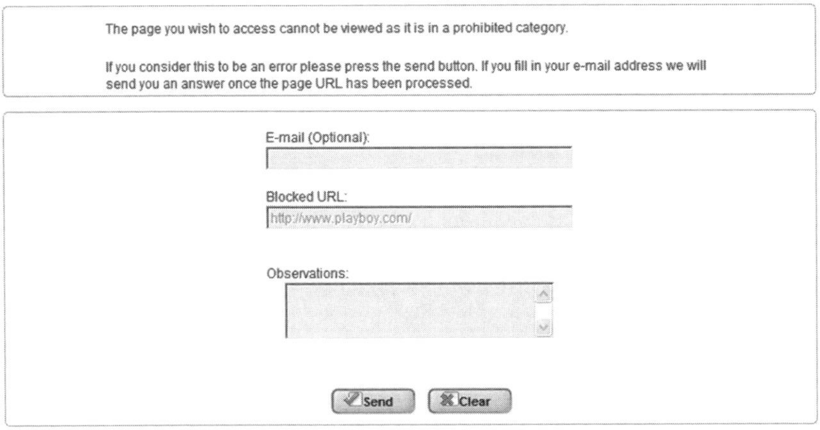

> The page you wish to access cannot be viewed as it is in a prohibited category.
>
> If you consider this to be an error please press the send button. If you fill in your e-mail address we will send you an answer once the page URL has been processed.

E-mail (Optional):

Blocked URL:
http://www.playboy.com/

Observations:

[✓ Send]   [✗ Clear]

FIG. 2. An example of stop page that allows requesting for the review of the requested content.

So, filters often send a block page that allows sending a request for the review of the blocked Web page, either to the filter manufacturer or to the system administrator. Figure 2 shows a typical stop page with this functionality. Obviously, false negatives (inappropriate Web pages that are not detected by the filter) are rarely reported by the end users, but supervisors and administrators can periodically screen logs and reports to detect these abuses, and ask for the review if needed.

Monitors are less intrusive than filters, but they must be supported with very powerful analysis tools, which may allow detecting inappropriate behavior. Most often, these systems are used as research tools used to collect exhibits when there other evidences (as complaints by other users, as, e.g., the colleagues of a worker that disturbs them by abusing of online pornography). Monitors are dual to filters, and many security tools can perform both tasks at the same time, just by configuration.

3.1.2   Filtering Categories and Personalization

An important question is: What is an inappropriate content? The kinds of inappropriate content may vary from organization to organization, and even from user to user in the same organization. For instance, blocking job search engines may be very sensible in a corporation, but not appropriate for a school. Or, some users may be allowed to see some contents (like teachers reviewing pro-Nazi Web pages), while others possibly should get the same requests blocked (like the students).

Personalization requirements in Web-filtering tools are increasing. Institutions specify Internet usage policies that define not only the contents to be blocked or monitored, but the user profiles and their privileges. These user profiles can depend, for example, on the position or the department in corporations. To define these profiles and enforce the appropriate policies, there are at least two requirements:

1. Filter policies and profiles must be easily deployed in multisite institutions. Many organizations are geographically distributed, like international corporations or networks of schools or libraries. In those cases, the departments or types of users may also be distributed, but policies ruling their privileges should be easily managed by system administrators and policy makers. In an optimal situation, multiple instances of a filter (one per site or station) would be collectively managed in a centralized fashion, from just one administration post. This does not imply that the policies and profiles are centralized, as current technologies allow spreading configuration changes in distributed systems.
2. Profile definition must be very flexible in terms of contents to be supervised. This problem is usually addressed by the definition of a wide number of categories that cover many types of content. For instance, the Optenet Web filter currently includes more than 50 categories, ranging from pornography, violence or sects to financial institutions, job search and directory, and street maps. This wide range of categories makes possible to deliver sophisticate profiles that can meet the needs of schools, libraries, the government, or corporations. Moreover, filters even include the definition of new categories by the system administrator, usually as lists of URLs pointing to user-defined sites. In Fig. 3, we show a typical category administration interface that allows to define new categories, to test URLs against current categories, or even to synchronize the categories with respect to the provider ones.

Current Internet-filtering tools often address these topics and provide effective approaches to deal with them.

3.1.3 Network Deployment

Filtering systems must currently face a number of challenges: organization locations can be distributed, filtering services can be provided at the carrier, users can demand station local filters, etc. In consequence, Web-filtering tools can be deployed in a wide variety of network scenarios, what dramatically affects their customization, performance, and security requirements.

In Fig. 4, we present a number of scenarios and network points in which Internet filters can be deployed. These points are tagged with numbers, which correspond to network general locations. We discuss these scenarios and their properties in the next paragraphs.

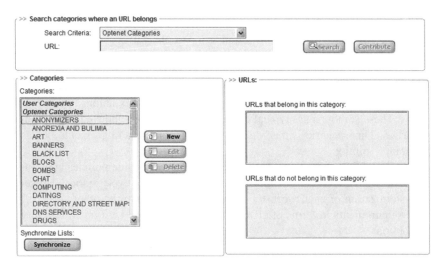

Fig. 3. An example of category administration interface.

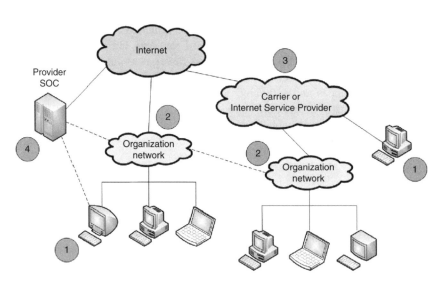

Fig. 4. Network points of filter deployment.

3.1.3.1 *Filtering at the Workstation.* Filters and monitors can be deployed at final user workstations, often as a part of a full security suite including antivirus, firewall, etc. Some vendors that offer these suites are Symantec, Trend Micro, Optenet, and others. Another flavor is safe browsers, tools that include filtering as the main functionality, like Nippy[4] or KidSplorer.[5] Even more, nearly all traditional Web browsers supply filtering functionalities among their security options. These solutions are typical choices for home users, and small and medium enterprises. This scenario is marked as 1 in Fig. 4, and it is often mentioned as an "endpoint" solution.

This kind of deployment can hardly accommodate site-wide policies applying to all the computers, and requires individual configuration of every station. However, full customization of each workstation can be achieved. On the other side, performance requirements in terms of efficiency (processing time) are much less than in other options.

Perhaps, the main weakness of this approach is its security. As filtering is performed in the local workstation, technology-savvy employees and kids often find ways to hack the system and access the blocked content. Also, they can even find the hack in the Web itself.

3.1.3.2 *Filtering at the Institution Network.* The filtering system can be deployed at the institution network. The system can be installed at a consumer (usually dedicated) server, or may be provided as appliance Modes of operation include bridging (the filtering server is put between the access point and the rest of the network), routing, and proxying (the server is put at the same level of other workstations, but it acts as a router or as a proxy server), among others. Vendors of appliances and software packages for network-level filtering include Optenet,[6] WebSense,[7] or IronPort,[8] and open-source packages like DansGuardian[9] or POESIA.[10] This is a suitable choice for distributed organizations, which most often are big corporations or federations of schools. This operation point is marked as 2 in Fig. 4.

---

[4] http://www.mynippy.net/.
[5] http://www.devicode.com/kidsplorer/.
[6] http://www.optenet.com/.
[7] http://www.websense.com/.
[8] http://www.ironport.com/.
[9] http://dansguardian.org/.
[10] http://www.poesia-filter.org/.

Regarding customization, many filter vendors provide nowadays coordination mechanisms among servers installed in distributed locations. A number of providers offer unified administration consoles that allow the administrator to specify profiles and policies that apply to the whole "virtual" corporate network. This the reason why we draw a discontinuous line between two organization networks, as they may be located at different offices, possibly linked to different ISPs.

Performance requirements for these filtering servers are stronger, as the system must be able to monitor the traffic of hundreds or thousands of concurrent users. In consequence, this mode of deployment requires dedicated high performance servers or appliances (typically with special network hardware).

The filtering system is usually much less vulnerable in this scenario. Probably, the most dangerous attacks are physical (disconnecting the machine that hosts the filter) or of social engineering (getting the administration password by fooling the administrator).

3.1.3.3 *Filtering at the ISP.* ISPs or carriers are always improving their commercial services to their customers. In particular, many current ISPs offer security services to their clients, including parental controls for home users, and full security services (firewalling, antivirus and antispam, Web filtering). In this case, the filters and other software products are installed at servers in the carrier operation centers, possibly as appliances. Quite frequently, the service is provided by the carrier using its own brand, being the filter vendor a private brand. Vendor of carrier-level filtering technology includes Optenet and Fortinet.[11] This scenario is suitable for all kinds of institutions, and even for home users. The service is most often billed by subscription. This scenario is marked as 3 in Fig. 4.

When services are provided in this way, they are typically regarded as "software as a service" (SaaS) [18]. No equipment or software installation is needed at the customer premises. It is often believed that SaaS does not allow much configuration by the user, but this belief is incorrect. For instance, a combination of a firewall and a Web filter can be managed remotely by the end user administrator, to implement the full suite of policies defined by the corporation or kid tutor. The possibilities of configuration only depend on the quality of the filtering solution and the kind of service that the ISP wants to offer.[12]

---

[11] http://www.fortinet.com/.

[12] For instance, the carrier can offer a "silver" low-cost service that allows less configuration options than a "gold," more expensive one, which enables the administrator to configure port blocking, categories, profiles, policies, etc.

Regarding performance, no doubt this is a very hard and challenging scenario. The servers that supports the service have to deal with even millions of concurrent users, with nearly no delay. This kind of filters are extremely optimized in terms of processing time, they are typically deployed in server farms, and have grid-like abilities including high scalability, redundancy, etc.

From the point of view of security, these filters are far stronger than the previous ones. Carrier physical and software security measures are extreme, as the whole of their service depends on it.

3.1.3.4 *Filtering as a Third-Party Service.* An alternative deployment scenario is that in which the service is provided at a their-party network, commonly regarded as service "in the cloud." In this case, a vendor distributes a network of (security) operation centers (SOCs) across even the world, and the customers send their Web traffic though these SOCs (for instance, by proxying). This operation mode can also be considered SaaS, as the customer gets the service without hardware or software licensing. An example of vendors is ScanSafe[13] and WebSense. This scenario is suitable for all kind of organizations, including home users, but is most often targeted to small and medium enterprises. Filtering as a third-party service is pointed as 4 in Fig. 4. The discontinuous lines represent the fact that filtering can be performed at any level of an organization. All concerns about configuration, performance, and security are the same as carrier-level filtering, except perhaps for the fact that these services are weaker against distributed denial of service attacks.

3.2 Filtering Techniques

In this section, we describe the main techniques used in filtering and monitoring tools. We explicitly exclude port blocking, because it is usually implemented as a firewall-level service.

3.2.1 Self-Regulation

Self-regulation consists on good practices that are implemented by content providers, and generally involve:

---

[13] http://www.scansafe.com/.

1. A self-labeling system and policy used to describe the content in terms of its explicit nature, suitability for children, etc., and that is used by the content provider to tag their stuff.
2. A filter on the client side that recognizes content labels and match them with the own policies of the filter user, delivering or blocking the content as required.

Popular labeling systems include PICS and ICRA. PICS [44] is a set of specifications created by the World Wide Web Consortium (W3C) to define a platform for the creation of content rating systems. It enables Web publishers to associate labels or metadata with Web pages to limit certain Web content with explicit nature targeted at adult audiences from reaching other groups of Internet users. ICRA (formerly the Internet Content Rating Association) is part of the Family Online Safety Institute, an international, nonprofit organization working to develop a safer Internet. The centerpiece of the organization is the descriptive vocabulary, often referred to as "the ICRA questionnaire." Content providers check which of the elements in the questionnaire are present or absent from their Web sites. This then generates a small file containing the labels that is then linked to the content on one or more domains. The broad topics covered by the ICRA vocabulary are:

- The presence or absence of nudity
- The presence or absence of sexual content
- The depiction of violence
- The language used
- The presence or absence of user-generated content and whether this is moderated
- The depiction of other potentially harmful content such as gambling, drugs, and alcohol

Most popular browsers include security options regarding ICRA. For instance, Microsoft Internet Explorer includes a (password-protected) Content Advisor in which is possible to define what kind of content is can be displayed. In Fig. 5, we show the Content Advisor, with the category "Nudity & Sexual Material—Context Variable—Arts" selected. The bottom slider is used to define the privilege level. Also, the ICRA itself has developed an endpoint Web filter named ICRAFilter that makes use of this labeling system.

However, the adoption of PICS and ICRA labels is not regulated and it is possible for some publishers to mislabel their Web content either by intent or by mistake. The existence of a third party reviewing the labeled contents is unfeasible. PICS and ICRA should therefore only be used as a supplementary tool in any Web-filtering system, as it is many commercial and open-source systems.

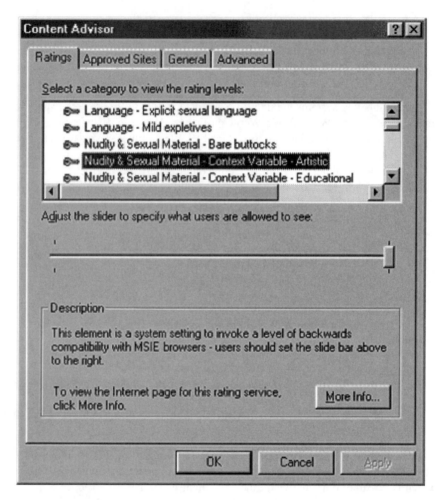

Fig. 5. Microsoft Internet Explorer Content Advisor with ICRA labels.

3.2.2 Listings

This technique restricts or allows access by comparing the requested Web page's URL (and equivalent IP address) with URLs in a stored list. Two types of lists can be maintained. A black list contains URLs of objectionable Web sites to block; a white list contains URLs of permissible Web sites. Most Web-filtering systems that employ URL blocking use black lists.

This approach's chief advantages are speed and efficiency. A system can make a filtering decision by matching the requested Web page's URL with one in the list even before a network connection to the remote Web server is made. However, this approach requires implementing a URL list, and it can identify only the sites on the list. Also, unless the list is updated constantly, the system's accuracy will decrease over time owing to the explosive growth of new Web sites.

Most Web-filtering systems that use URL blocking employ teams of human reviewers to actively search for objectionable Web sites to add to the black list. They then make this list available for downloading as an update to the list's local copy. This is both time consuming and resource intensive. However:

- Filter vendors have defined internal protocols and deployed suitable tools that make the list updating process fast and effective. For instance, some filter provider make use of Web spiders (bots that recursively download Web pages by following their links) that automatically tag a number of heavily connected to other objectionable Web sites using the tags of these latter sites; after, the pages are sent to review by manual experts that are able to correct the tags in case of mistakes, but most often just have to validate the automatic classification.

- Efficacy not only depends on the list, but on the Web usage. As in many other domains, most popular Web sites accumulate a vast majority of visits, following a Zipf's law distribution [6]. It is possible to achieve high performance with relatively small lists by closely studying users' behavior and focusing on most popular URLs.

Another advantage of this approach is its fast and efficient operation, highly desirable in a Web-filtering system. Using sophisticated content analysis techniques during classification, the system can first identify the nature of a Web page's content. If the system determines that the content is objectionable, it can add the page's URL to the black list. Later, if a user tries to access the Web page, the system can immediately make a filtering decision by matching the URL. Dynamically updating the black list achieves speed and efficiency, and accuracy is maintained provided that content analysis is accurate.

Because of these pros, nearly all commercial and open-source Web filters make use of this technology as their primary filtering technique. Current commercial URL lists include from 3 to 15 million items.

3.2.3   Keyword Matching

The most primitive form of content analysis is keyword matching. This intuitively simple approach blocks access to Web sites on the basis of the occurrence of offensive words and phrases on those sites. It compares every word or phrase on a retrieved Web page against those in a keyword dictionary of prohibited words and phrases. Blocking occurs if the number of matches reaches a predefined threshold.

This fast content analysis method can quickly determine if a Web page contains potentially harmful material. However, it is well known for overblocking—that is, blocking many Web sites that do not contain objectionable content. Because it filters content by matching keywords (or phrases) such as "sex" and "breast," it could accidentally block Web sites about sexual harassment or breast cancer, or even the home page of someone named Sexton. Although the dictionary of objectionable words and phrases does not require frequent updates, the high overblocking rate greatly jeopardizes a Web-filtering system's capability and is often unacceptable. However, a Web-filtering system can use this approach to decide whether to further process a Web page using a more precise content analysis method, which usually requires additional processing time.

3.2.4 Intelligent Content Analysis

Intelligent content analysis is an attempt at achieving semantic understanding of the Web contents. In particular, intelligent classification techniques can be used to categorize Web pages into different groups (e.g., pornographic and nonpornographic) according to the statistical occurrence of sets of features. This categorization if latter used by the system to decide whether to deliver the content or not according to the profiles and policies defined in terms of the available categories.

The two most prominent content analysis technologies are text classification and image processing (discussed below), although there is some work on video processing (e.g., [33]). These techniques are always category dependent, that is, a specialized classifier must be built for each category, most often using machine learning (ML) approaches that learn the most interesting features of Web pages in the category. Moreover, specific techniques used to detect certain types of content (e.g., pornography) may be ineffective with respect to other types of content (hate speech), as it is the case of image processing: techniques used to detect skin areas are just not suited to the detection of Nazi symbols.

The most important drawback of these techniques is their performance. Although it is possible to build quite efficient systems (most often decreasing the effectiveness of the tool), the overall processing time makes them inappropriate for the most demanding situations (like filtering at the carrier). However, if the intelligent content filter is called only when the URL is not in the vendor database, the number of requests that fire this component may be very small, and their results cached or inserted in the URL listings. Many current commercial tools include text analysis techniques, but because of performance, image processing is restricted to endpoint solutions or to offline (e.g., forensic) systems.

Another drawback is that building intelligent analysis tools does require special knowledge and expertise,[14] and that it is difficult to correct system mistakes as the techniques are quite complex.

4. Text-Based Filtering

Amongst the different techniques used for text-based Web content filtering, automated text categorization (TC) is currently the most widely used. The purpose of this task is to assign documents to a set of predefined categories (also named as classes or topics) [53]. Although Automatic Text Categorizers can be build by hand (e.g., by defining a set of heuristic rules), the complexity of Web content requires the automatic construction of these systems using an ML approach. This approach consists on training a text classifier using a set of manually labeled documents, and has proved to be as accurate as human experts.

Complexity of Web content is defined in part by its structure, but a key point is the fact that authors are continuously adapting their contents to avoid filtering systems. From the point of view of machine learning, it can be considered as an Adversarial Classification problem [13], and since contents are mainly textual, it is defined as Adversarial Text Classification.

4.1 Text Classification Tasks

The aim of Text Classification is to provide structure to an unstructured repository of text, thereby easing storage, search, and browsing [54]. This discipline belongs to the broad field of text mining (TM) [26], or, more precisely, to Knowledge Discovery in textual databases.

The first approach used successfully to face the problem of TC was knowledge engineering (KE), in the 1980s. A knowledge engineer had to build an expert system that could automatically classify text, but his lack of knowledge on the domain required the intervention of a domain expert. Moreover, the system had to be maintained by hand over time, making it a high-cost process in terms of human work.

From the 1990s, the KE approach was substituted by the use of statistical techniques, making it a suitable problem for the field of statistical natural language processing (NLP). In this approach the classifier is built using a general inductive

---

[14] These components have to be developed by experts in data mining, text classification, and image processing.

process trained with a set of example documents. The main advantages of NLP over KE are:

- The high degree of automation, since the engineer develops an automatic builder of classifiers
- Reusability, because the automatic builder can be applied to the creation of many different classifiers for many different problems and domains just by changing the training set of documents
- Easiness of maintenance, since changes on the system only require changes on the training set and a new training process
- High availability (current and future) of inductive learning algorithms
- Accuracy of automatic classifiers usually outperforms those built by human experts

The number of Text Classification tasks has increased with the years, and several ways of organizing these tasks can be found on literature. According to Lewis [38], TC tasks can be classified using two axes: type of learning and granularity of text elements. The two types of learning are defined by the training set control:

1. *Supervised learning.* Set of classes is known when building the training set, and there are examples for each of the classes.
2. *Unsupervised learning (clustering).* Set of classes is unknown before training, and the goal is to group textual entities according to similar contents.

Three levels of granularity can be defined, considering terms, phrases, or documents as atomic elements:

1. *Terms.* Ranging from words stems and single words to short expressions
2. *Phrases.* Going from clauses to complex sentences
3. *Documents.* Including short spam emails, medium-sized papers, or even whole books

Table I shows some of the most representative TC tasks categorized according to these two axes. For instance, named entity recognition is the task of detecting proper names, temporal expressions, and quantities inside text documents [4]. It is a supervised task because all the possible entities are known from the beginning (names of persons, organizations, locations, expressions of times, quantities, monetary values, percentages, etc.), and the elements considered are terms composed of one or few words. Text segmentation identifies a sequence of clauses or sentences that display local coherence within a document [34]. It is unsupervised because segments do not correspond to predefined classes, and the process is applied to phrases as text elements.

TABLE I
AN ORGANIZATION OF TEXT CLASSIFICATION TASKS

	Supervised learning	Unsupervised learning
Terms	Disambiguation Part of speech tagging Named entity recognition Partial chunking	New meaning discovery
Phrases	Automatic summarization	Text segmentation
Documents	Documents retrieval Text categorization	Documents clustering

Sometimes, these tasks are not the main goal of a TC system, and can act as a service for other tasks. For instance, part of speech (POS) tagging, named entity recognition, and disambiguation are often used as previous steps to text categorization to improve the quality of the attributes, assigning a suitable meaning to a term.

4.2 Text Categorization Types

Text categorization admits two different taxonomies according to the number of categories defined and the degree of confidence on the decision taken. The first taxonomy differentiates between single-label and multilabel TC: single-label TC assigns only one category to a given document, while in multilabel TC a document may belong to zero, one or more than one category. The second is usually approached as a problem of deciding if a document belongs to each on the categories individually.

The second taxonomy distinguishes between hard and soft categorization. Hard categorization consists of deciding whether a document definitely belongs to a category or not. On the other hand, soft categorization involves giving a numeric score that indicates the degree of confidence of the classifier to ensure that the document belongs to a category. Hard categorization is very useful to create rankings of documents in terms of their proximity to a given category.

4.3 Text Classification Process

According to Sebastiani [54], we can describe the TC process as consisting of four main phases:

1. *Document indexing*. Documents must be mapped to a compact representation of its content that can be directly interpreted both by a classifier-building

algorithm and by a built classifier. The most widely used representation is a vector of attributes that occur in the training set, each one with a value corresponding to the weight that it may have for the document.

The initial set of attributes is usually comprised of the whole set of words that appear within the whole documents set, excluding a series of common words that are defined in what is called a stop list. In many cases these words are reduced to their stems (morphological roots). Weights are assigned using statistical heuristics that represent facts such as the number of times that a term occurs in a document (term frequency), or the number or documents that contain the term (inverse term frequency).

Within the last few years, some research works on document indexing are beginning to use more complex attributes, either by grouping single words into words n-grams, parsing the text to obtain syntactic information, or by extracting concepts to represent the semantics of the text. However, they have not shown to have improved the standard representation of words.

2. *Dimensionality reduction.* The sizes of the vectors obtained after the first phase generally are in the order of tens of thousands or even hundreds of thousands, making efficiency of learners very hard to achieve. The second step involves reducing the length of these vectors to produce a new representation of documents.

Most common techniques to produce dimensionality reduction are grouped either into feature extraction methods, such as latent semantic indexing [39] or term clustering [38]; or feature selection techniques, such as chi-square [64], information gain [38], or mutual information [16]. Feature extraction methods combine several dimensions into what will be a new single attribute in the reduced vector; feature selection techniques attempt to determine and select the best attributes from the original set, instead of generating new attributes.

3. *Classifier learning.* A general inductive process trained with a set of example documents automatically builds a text classifier. The representation for each document is that obtained after the second phase.

Amongst the most popular supervised learners used for text categorization, we can cite probabilistic Bayesian models, Bayesian networks, decision trees, Boolean decision methods, neural networks, classifier ensembles, or support vector machines, but the number of techniques explored is longer [53]. These algorithms highly differ in terms of the type of model created, efficacy and efficiency, and capacity to manage huge amounts of attributes. Currently, support vector machines (SVMs) [29] and boosting [51] stand out from the rest, since they have outperformed competitors in different benchmarks and challenges.

4. *Evaluation.* The most important aspect for evaluation of classifiers is effectiveness, since it is very important to minimize the errors made by the system.

However, sometimes it is convenient to consider other measures related to efficiency, understandability of models, portability and scalability of techniques, etc.

4.4 Web Content Filtering as Text Categorization

Web content filtering can be faced as an adversarial text classification problem, since most content in Web pages is raw text. A critical aspect that must be considered comes from the fact that it is a multiclass problem: each type of content (pornography, racism, gambling games, etc.) corresponds to a category, and the classifier system must be capable of detecting if a Web page belongs to a determined category in order to allow different filtering profiles to system administrators. The most commonly used approach to face this problem is to build an independent classifier for each of the categories.

The four phases for the TC process described above must be adapted to the characteristics of this problem as follows:

1. *Document indexing.* Web pages have a rich HTML format that is usually misused by most research works. However, some approaches make explicit use of it, such as the system described in Agarwal *et al.* [1], which considers seven specific sections for Web documents: URL, hyperlink tags, image tags, title, metadata, body, and tables. Words are separated according to the section, thus building vectors of vectors to represent Web pages.

    The vocabulary set is constructed using diverse approaches depending on both the page language and domain (pornography, violence, etc.). For instance, Lee *et al.* [35] build a vocabulary set of 55 words by hand to classify a Web page as pornographic. In Guermazi *et al.* [24], several dictionaries in several languages are manually constructed, with words that are likely to indicate if a Web page can be categorized within the violence domain.

    The most widely used representation is the vector of words, applying stop lists and stemming when the language supports it (usually occidental languages). Examples of it can be found on [1, 7, 22, 32]. Some approaches use part of speech tags, such as noun, adjective, or verbs [23, 59], as well as punctuation marks [23]. The use of words *n*-grams has also produced positive results [23, 42].

    Weights used for attributes are from diverse nature, ranging from binaries [22, 59] to term frequencies [7, 23, 42] and to the combination of TF and IDF [1, 7, 32].

2. *Dimensionality reduction.* Most works do not make use of dimensionality reduction, although there are some exceptions. For instance in Gómez Hidalgo *et al.* [22], information gain is used to filter those terms that do not seem to be important for pornography detection, and Chou *et al.* [7] compare three quality

measures for three different filtering domains in the workplace (news, buys, and sports).

3. *Classifier learning.* A high number of ML methods have been tested for Web content filtering, but the lack of standard collections or competitive challenges does not allow achieving solid conclusions about the quality of those algorithms. The following can be found amongst the most commonly used algorithms: several versions of Naïve Bayes [7, 22, 42], decision trees [7, 22, 24], lazy learners such as *k-nearest neighbors* [7, 59], neural networks [7, 35], and support vector machines [1, 7, 22, 23, 32, 42].

   References [7] and [22] are the most exhaustive comparative studies, being the first about abuse in the workplace and the second about pornography. In the first study, C4.5 produces the best results, followed by kNN and SVM; in the second study, SVM proves to be clearly the most effective. However, since both domains and data sets are different, it is impossible to establish a comparison between them and extract any kind of conclusions.

4. *Evaluation.* Works presented in this field are totally heterogeneous, which makes it impossible to compare evaluation results. All researches make use of private sets of Web pages in very different domains (pornography, racism, violence, abuse in workplace, etc.), and in multiple languages (English, Spanish, Chinese, Italian, etc.). The lengths of the sets are variable, ranging from few hundred to several thousands. Moreover, evaluation metrics are diverse, including precision and recall, *F*-measure, accuracy and error, and the ROCHH method.

5. Image Processing Techniques

Image processing has been a very active research field in the last 20 years, especially since the emergence and popularization of the Web and the increasing availability of image content on it. Among the domains to be filtered, the most popular one is by far pornography and naked people (see, e.g., [20, 25, 36, 52, 61]), and there is scarce work in other domains like hate speech (e.g., Nazi symbols [65]).

Many existing techniques used for filtering adult content classify Web pages as porn or safe using their text content. However, those approaches have some limitations: they are very dependent on the language; they need pages containing enough text for a reliable classification and usually do not work with obfuscated texts [48].

Images are an essential part of World Wide Web. They are used to make sites more attractive to the visitor. But in adult sites, multimedia content can be the main element of the site. It is possible to find adult Web sites that are mainly composed by text, sites like blogs with content for adults, or Webs with erotic stories, but most adult Web sites usually have a significant amount of images, many of them with explicit content. There are also sites where the percentage of text is very low. Sites like Thumbnail Gallery Posts (TGPs) usually have one or two lines of text and the rest of the Web page is composed of pictures.

Those sites cannot be filtered with traditional texts filters, so effective filtering of images is very desirable in a filtering solution. Unfortunately, there are properties in objectionable images that make the problem very difficult [61]:

- Most images contain nonuniform background.
- Foreground may contain textual noise like phone numbers, URLs, etc.
- Content may range from grayscale to 24-bit color.
- Some images may have a very low resolution.
- Views can be taken from a high variety of angles.
- May contain many people.
- People can have different skin colors.
- May contain both people and animals.
- May contain only some parts of a person.
- People may be partially dressed.

We review some image processing techniques that address pornographic image detection in the next sections.

5.1   Adult Image Recognition Using Skin Detection

One of the first and most popular techniques used for filtering images with naked people is the one proposed by Forsyth [20]. His approach looks for probable skin regions in the image and extracts groups and features from those regions. Those groups feed a geometric filter based on skeletal structure to identify human presence. In Fig. 6, we show an image before and after it has been processed to highlight skin areas.

In Fig. 7, we present a diagram that shows the main processing steps in image analysis and classification. The first step in a system that identifies naked people present in images is to identify areas of skin using the color histograms of the images. The color of human skin in a picture is created by a combination of three factors: blood, melanin, and light conditions. The two first elements involve colors red, yellow, and brown and for that reason, skin colors are between those hues. Light conditions cannot be controlled but we can extract features that do not depend on that parameter.

Fig. 6. A nude picture before and after skin area detection.

5.1.1   Preprocessing Images

For extracting skin areas, 8-bit RGB images are need. Since most images will be in JPG format, the first step is to reduce the number of colors, converting them to RGB format. Some other filters like scaling or noise reduction can also be applied in this step.

5.1.2   Skin Detection

Skin is usually detected in a two step task. First, those pixels whose colors are very likely to be skin are selected. Then, we expand the selection to include those pixels with similar color and texture to pixels selected in the previous step.

Next step is to locate groups of connected skin pixels. When connected components of pixels which are probably skin are over a certain threshold, usually ranging

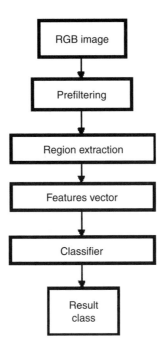

FIG. 7. Main stages in image processing and classification.

from 50% to 60%, they are then extracted and grouped. The number of connected groups can be used as a feature for classification. These connected groups can also feed a geometric filter based on skeletal structure to identify human presence [20].

Other approaches for filtering objectionable images propose to complement the technique proposed above with many other features for detecting pornographic images. Jones and Rehg [30] propose to use the following features for the classification process:

- Percentage of pixels detected as skin
- Average probability of the skin pixels
- Size in pixels of the largest connected component of skin
- Number of connected components of skin
- Percentage of colors with no entries in the skin and nonskin histograms

Rowley *et al.* [48] propose to include another skin-independent features like image attributes (size, shape, etc.), Entropy features for distinguish adult-content images from icons or banners, clutter features (amount of texture in skin regions), and face detection.

This approach can classify 89% of the images with an average processing speed of 11 s per image [3].

5.2 Adult Image Recognition Using Wavelets

Although we can achieve very good results with the techniques commented in the previous section, those systems have a performance problem that make them unusable in real-world systems. The system proposed by Forsyth can take about 6 min to process an image using a workstation.[15] Later refinements decrease the processing time, but they were taking over 1 min per image.

A totally different approach for filtering adult images is the one used in Wang *et al.* [61] that uses a combination of different filters, including an icon filter, a graph photo detector, a color histogram filter, a texture filter, an a wavelet-based shape matching algorithm. That system is practical for a real-world implementation because it takes less than 2 s to process each image and achieves very good results.

This system uses an algorithm that compares the semantic content of images containing human bodies. Using moment analysis, textures, histograms, and statistics, the algorithm produces a features vector that provides a high accuracy in recognition of nude human bodies in a picture.

For the wavelet analysis, the approach uses Daubechies' wavelets [14] that separates the image into clean distinct low-frequency and high-frequency parts. Daubechies' wavelets are not as easy to implement as other, simpler wavelets (like Haar ones), but they are highly suitable for general-purpose images. In Fig. 8, we show an example of 2D Daubechies' wavelet.

6. Evaluation of Web Filters

The evaluation of Web filters is a prominent issue, given their increasing necessities of improvement. As user navigation patterns change over time, and the number of users is always growing, the only way to keep the filters effective is routinely performing tests to check their actual performance.

---

[15] At the time of his writing, current workstations are thousand of times faster.

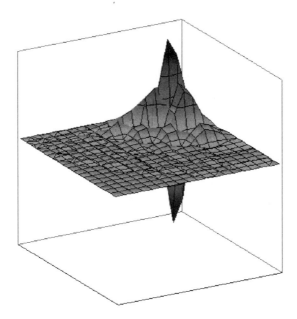

Fig. 8. Daubechies 20 2D wavelet.

We classify the evaluation of Web-filtering tools into two categories:

1. Industrial evaluations, quite often performed by analysts on demand of a commercial vendor, or by software magazines
2. Scientific evaluations, performed in the context of scientific works like those presented in previous sections covering intelligent content analysis

We discuss the procedures, advantages, and drawbacks of both types of evaluations in the next sections.

6.1 Industrial Evaluation

An industrial evaluation is a test performed by a magazine or a third-party laboratory, which reviews a number of products and determines the strengths and weaknesses of the tested tools.

The main advantage of industrial evaluations is that they usually cover the full range of features of the tools, to provide their readers a trustable opinion that may be used to take decisions about which tool to purchase. Examples of such reviews are:

- In [49], a group of 12 endpoint Internet filters for kids are reviewed by PC magazine analysts, focusing on the ability to block and monitor the coverage of instant messaging, the existence of connection time control, and the power of remote notification and management.

- SC magazine periodically reviews enterprise market Web content filter. On its 2007 review,[16] the features covered are ease of use, performance, documentation, support, and value for money.

Of course, the evaluation is much targeted to certain types of customers and solutions. For instance, in an endpoint solution for parental control, the following features should be covered:

- Filtering algorithms (object analysis, URL based, keyword based, and dynamic categorization)
- Filtering capabilities (filter categories, editable filter lists, chat filtering, chat monitoring, chat blocking, newsgroup blocking, IM port blocking, peer-to-peer blocking, FTP blocking, customizable port blocking, email filtering, email blocking, popup blocking, predator blocking, and personal information blocking)
- Reporting capabilities (remote reporting, notification alerts by email, log reports sent by email, summary history reporting, detailed history reporting, graphical reporting, and logging of security violations)
- Management capabilities (individual user profiles, password controls, remote management, and stealth options)
- Other functionality features (immediate overriding of blocks, warning/not just blocking, daily time limits, negligible surfing time impacts, updated URL/ filtering rules, and blocking sensitivity settings)
- Help/support options (help, product documentation, and technical support available)
- Supported browsers (Internet Explorer, Netscape, FireFox, Opera, and Chrome)
- Supported platforms (Vista, XP, 2000, NT, Mac, and Linux)

The main drawbacks of industrial tests are their subjectivity and lack of rigor. For instance:

- Performance evaluation is reported in unknown conditions, including from the test set size and composition, to the hosting machines setup. Moreover, testing conditions may be favorable to a specific vendor. Performance measures are never supported with statistical tests.
- Criteria regarding a number of features (usability, scalability, etc.) are not under public review, and are rarely supported by real scenarios.
- Procedures are also private, and may also be unfair.

---

[16] http://www.scmagazineus.com/Web-content-filtering-2007/GroupTest/10/.

However, these evaluations can be very helpful to make an initial screening of vendors, in order to take a purchase decision.

6.2   Scientific Evaluation

Scientific evaluations are those developed in the context of well-defined experiments supported by rigorous procedures and metrics, as usually in scientific papers. These evaluations are usually performed by personnel with scientific training, in laboratory conditions, and more importantly, the experiments are reproducible and the results comparable.

We have reviewed above a number of papers covering a number of technical approaches to Web filtering. With respect to the evaluation reported in these papers, we conclude that:

- The only quality feature tested in the scientific literature regarding Web filtering is effectiveness or accuracy, or in other words, the degree of success that the system has when blocking inappropriate contents and allowing appropriate contents. The efficiency is only occasionally considered (most often in the case of image processing), although it plays a critical role in real-world conditions. Other features like scalability, portability, usability, etc., are vastly ignored.

- In the case of effectiveness, there is a lack of common data sets, procedures, and metrics. These features must be agreed by the scientific community, and the main vehicle to achieve this goal is the organization of rigorous competitive evaluations, as those performed in other domains like spam filtering. In this domain, the Text Retrieval Conferences have featured a track devoted to spam filtering [10], which has established common procedures and metrics, and disseminated standard data sets, which have promoted a considerable development of current techniques.

6.2.1   Performance Evaluation

In any scientific evaluation of the effectiveness of a classification system like a Web filter, three main issues must be considered:

- Test sets, which are collections of URLs, Web pages, images, client requests, etc., correctly classified by human experts. The systems are feed with the contents of the test set, and their decisions compared to those of human beings. Collections should be public and standard.

- Procedures that define, for example, if the contents (e.g., URLs) are served to the classifier one by one or in batches, etc. The procedures must be defined with the goal of resembling real-world scenarios.

- Performance metrics that fairly allow the comparison of several technical approaches or systems.

Unfortunately, nearly all the collections used in the papers reviewed in this chapter are private, and rarely shared with other researchers. Moreover, they hardly represent real-world situations, as they are composed of sets of items (URLs, HTML files, images, etc.) without user frequency information. As user requests are highly biased to a relatively small set of popular sites, these collections do not represent real-user behavior.

Regarding procedures, all the studies reviewed make use of batch testing, consisting of presenting the full set of items to classify to the system, but not allowing it to learn from previous mistakes or hits. As in spam filtering, online methods that do allow learning while testing may better resemble operational environments [10].

Metrics of evaluation used in the literature are not standard either. The evaluation of effectiveness is aimed to estimate the quality of the classifier in terms of success and failure rates over a set of classified items. The metrics used have been adopted from the fields of information retrieval and machine learning.

Table II shows a confusion matrix, representing possible outcomes of a binary (two categories) classification system when comparing its classification results to the correct ones (gold standard). Compared to that gold standard, retrieved items can be true positive (TP) if the classifier has identified a positive document as positive, false positive (FP) if the classifier has assigned positive to a negative document, false negative (FN) when a positive document is categorized as negative, and true negative (TN) if a negative document has been classified as negative. Related to these values, the most commonly used measures are [50]:

- Precision (P): proportion of items classified as positive that are really positives
- Recall (R): proportion of items classified as positive from the whole set of positive items
- Accuracy (A): proportion of items that have been well classified
- Error (E): proportion of items that have been classified incorrectly

TABLE II
CONFUSION MATRIX FOR TWO CLASSES

	Real $\to C^+$	Real $\to C^-$
Classifier $\to C^+$	TP	FP
Classifier $\to C^-$	FN	TN

These metrics are defined by the following formulas:

$$R = \frac{TP}{TP + FN}, \quad P = \frac{TP}{TP + FP}, \quad A = \frac{TP + TN}{N}, \quad E = \frac{FP + FN}{N}.$$

One of the challenges when interpreting precision and recall is that there is usually a tradeoff between them: if a system tries to increase precision, recall will decrease, and vice versa. This has led to several ways to combine both factors, being the most widely used the F-measure [50], which can be calculated according to the following expression:

$$F_\beta = \frac{(1 + \beta^2)RP}{(\beta^2 P) + R}.$$

The parameter β represents the relative value of precision: lower values represent more emphasis on precision, whereas higher values indicate more emphasis on recall. A value of $\beta = 1$ is often used, giving the same weight to precision and recall. F_1 is computed with the following formula:

$$F_1 = \frac{2RP}{R + P}.$$

When multiple categories are defined (e.g., pornography, violence, gambling, etc.), these measures must be averaged to some extent. It can be done in two ways: calculating the arithmetic average for all categories (macroaveraging), thus giving the same weight to all categories; or averaging by assigning a weight to each category in terms of the number of instances that it contains (microaveraging).

Other alternative measures often employed in the context of Web page filtering are:

- Overblocking: proportion of safe items that are blocked by the classifier
- Underblocking: proportion of unsafe items that incorrectly allowed by the classifier

The reader can easily discover that overblocking and underblocking can be computed as $1 - P$ and $1 - R$, respectively.

Some researchers have made the effort of trying to resemble some of the procedures in more standardized fields like spam filtering (e.g., [22]), by using, for example, the Receiver Operating Characteristic Convex Hull method, which provides a better understanding of the behavior of a classifier under imprecise conditions.

6.2.2 The Kaiser–Resnick Study

Perhaps, the most influential and serious study regarding Web-filtering evaluation is that developed by Resnick and others [45, 46]. Under the deployment of the Children Internet Protection Act, the Kaiser Family Foundation commissioned a team leaded by Resnick to perform a test of the effectiveness of commercial filters with respect to pornography versus health information.

In a simulation of adolescent Internet searching, these researchers compiled the search results from 24 health information searches and six pornography searches. They manually classified the content of each site as pornography (516 sites), health information (2467 sites), or other (1004 sites). After, they tested six filtering tools commonly used in libraries and schools and one home product, each at 2 or 3 levels of blocking restrictiveness. At the least restrictive blocking setting, configured to block only pornography, the products tested blocked a mean of 1.4% of health information sites. However, the 10% of health sites found using some search terms related to sexuality (e.g., safe sex, condoms) and homosexuality (e.g., gay) were blocked. The mean pornography blocking rate was 87%. At moderate settings, the mean blocking rate was 5% for health information sites, and 90% for pornography. At the most restrictive settings, the mean blocking rate was 24% for health information sites, and 91% for pornography sites.

The main positive issues of this experiment are:

- The test collection tries to resemble an operational environment that is young- sters searching the Internet for health information. Moreover, the test collection is public and available for researchers.
- The researchers made good and effective effort toward evaluating the tradeoff between overblocking and underblocking, by defining configuration scenarios with different levels of restrictiveness.

Unfortunately, the study is narrow (young people, health vs pornography) and the URLs used in it are outdated. However, this study represents by far the best practice in filtering effectiveness evaluation.

7. Attacks and Countermeasures

In this section, we discuss a number of approaches that have been used to avoid filtering without detection. We do not cover physical attacks or hacking, as these are easily detected.

7.1 Disguising and Wrong Self-Labeling

Many Web filters block sites using a black list with URLs of adult sites. Some of those filters use only the domain name and not the IP address, so an easy way to bypass that kind of filters is to use the IP address instead of the usual URL address.

An attacker (i.e., a person that wants to visit a blocked adult Web site) can open a command prompt and make a ping to the blocked domain. When making ping, the IP address of the site is shown, so now he could go to the browser and type the IP address instead of the normal URL.

Even if the Web filter blocked the IP address of the site, attackers can obfuscate the URLs. For example, they can take each number in the IP address and convert it to a hexadecimal format. Then in the browser enter:

"http://0x(hex1).0x(hex2).0x(hex3).0x(hex4)"

There are many scripts in the Web that will do this conversion. To avoid attackers to use these techniques to bypass the filters, content filters and/or deobfuscators for URLS must be implemented.

Content publishers can also avoid Web content filters by disguising the content, using JavaScript and dynamically generated content. The content filter does not receive html text but JavaScript obfuscated code. Many filters cannot parse and interpret JavaScript code so they cannot classify the page as harmful so they are passed to the client.

Another common practice used by Web adult publishers is to use safe labels to tag the content of their pages instead of the right ones. By this reason, filters based on labels are not very reliable.

7.2 Proxies

A circumventor is a method of defeating blocking policies implemented using proxy servers. Ironically, most circumventors are also proxy servers, of varying degrees of sophistication, which effectively implement "bypass policies." By using an external proxy server, we could bypass a local filter. There are also several Web services that allow you browse anonymously, bypassing some network restrictions. By using those services, local clients make connections only to the server where the service is hosted, so any filters which block particular URLs can be bypassed because clients never have to communicate directly with the target server.

There are many public proxies servers that can be used for browsing the net. To use those proxies for browsing, the attacker has to change the network properties of the Web browser specifying the proxy server address and the port. Because of this reason, many system administrators do not allow to change the connection properties of the browsers, so users without administrative privileges will not be available to use an external proxy.

Unfortunately, there are versions of some browsers that can be taken in a pen drive (portable applications) that can be used without installing them in the computer, just running the directly from the pen drive. Users can change properties of those browsers, using external proxies without problems.

Even if an attacker cannot use an external proxy, there are still "home-made" techniques to simulate a proxy by using legitimate Web services like search engines or translation Web sites. When Google bots crawl the Web they store a copy of the content visited in Google's servers. Then, those cached copies can be consulted using Google's "cache:" operator. Since big search engines like Google are usually in white listings to avoid filtering them, an attacker can view objectionable content by viewing the cached versions of the Web sites. A similar strategy can be used with online translators that allow translating any Web page from one language to another, because an attacker would be visiting the translation service Web server instead of the original one. Translators can also be used to confuse content filters, just translating the Web site to a language not supported by the filter.

7.3 Anonymization Networks

Most Web content filters work analyzing the content transmitted to the hosts so they will not work if the traffic is encrypted or obfuscated.

TOR[17] is a software project aiming to protect its users against traffic analysis attacks. TOR operates an overlay network of onion routers that enable anonymous outgoing connections and anonymous "hidden" services. It also encrypts the data transmitted over the net, so content filters cannot analyze it. TOR uses a series of three proxies—computers (or nodes) which communicate on your behalf using their own identifying information, in such a way that none of them know both your identifying information and your destination.

Luckily, TOR requires administrative privileges to be installed and configured properly for a safer navigation, so normal users will not be able to use this kind of software in school or workplace networks.

8. Review of Singular Projects

There are many projects and solutions oriented to provide effective Web content-filtering solutions. As we have previously seen, a relevant amount of research has been focused on designing algorithms and techniques able to process textual or graphic elements of Web content to classify it accordingly. We synthesize in this section aspects of three representative cases of research projects of increasing dimension.

---

[17] http://www.torproject.org/.

8.1 Wavelet Image Pornography Elimination

The wavelet image pornography elimination (WIPE) system [61] developed by Wang, Li, and Wiederhold was motivated in the situation we have already depicted, in which families for instance have broader access to Internet and access of objectionable graphics by children is increasingly a problem that many parents are concerned about. WIPE was designed to classify an image as objectionable or benign.

The system compares the semantic content of images mainly consisting of objects such as the human body. It uses a combination of an icon filter, a graph photo detector, a color histogram filter, a texture filter, and a wavelet-based shape matching algorithm to provide a decision about online objectionable pornographic images. Semantically meaningful feature vector matching is carried out so that comparisons between a given online image and images in a premarked trained data set can be performed efficiently and effectively.

The combination of techniques used allows the system to face problems such us low quality of images, images containing more than one person, or only some parts of a person, and the different skin colors of the persons in one or several images. The system was used and evaluated with a training database of about 500 objectionable images and about 8000 benign images, and a test set of 1076 objectionable images and 10,809 benign images, demonstrating results of 96% sensitivity and 9% of wrongly classified benign photographs.

This project has become the top reference regarding pornographic image processing techniques, and it is probably one of the most influential ones in the short history of Web filtering.

8.2 Public Open-Source Environment for Safer Internet Access

Public Open-Source Environment for Safer Internet Access[18] (POESIA) [27] was a multisite project funded under the EU Internet Action Plan. The project included actions to develop, test, evaluate, and promote a fully open-source and extensible filtering software solution. POESIA provides an advanced Internet-filtering system, intended primarily for use in schools and other educational establishments, with the aim of providing safe and educationally appropriate Internet access for young people.

---

[18] http://www.poesia-filter.org/.

POESIA's approach is to use multiple filters each of which addresses some source of evidence that is of potential use in identifying harmful pages. The evidence detected can then be combined by a decision mechanism component to produce an overall decision for each page. In this way, the system can best exploit whatever information is available to determine which pages should be filtered. The POESIA filters include some that implement widely used filtering methods based on listed Web sites, but it promotes automatic content-based analysis of Web pages to achieve a broader coverage. The system includes filters addressing both image and textual content. The multiple filters of the system operate in combination. For example, a page from a site which is not in the URL lists will be analyzed for the content. If the page contains a reasonable quantity of text, this alone might allow a reject decision, but if there is limited text, it might require the combination of image and text evidence for a decision to be made. The decision mechanism plays an important role in weighting the available evidence to produce an overall judgment.

For image-based filtering, POESIA includes the implementation of a detector to identify pornographic images exploiting a range of learning and image processing methods. It includes a maximum entropy model for skin detection. The output of skin detection is a grayscale skin map with the gray indicating the belief of skin. Some simple features are then calculated from the skin map and fit ellipses, and used to train a multilayer perceptron classifier with back propagation [65]. The detector is able to cope difficulties as variations of the skin colors and of the capturing conditions (illumination, camera, compression, noise, etc.), resulting specially practical compared with those existing systems in terms of processing speed.

For textual content the system includes specific filters for different languages. The system includes filters for English, Spanish, and Italian. The filters differ in some methods they employ, partly reflecting an attempt to optimize over the different aspects of the languages. However, the filters are alike in offering both "light" and "heavy" filtering modes. Light filtering, which uses little NLP, provides rapid assessment of content for straightforwardly classifiable pages. For other pages, heavy filtering, making greater use of NLP is invoked to provide more sensitive detection of content indicators. Light filtering includes conventional statistical text classification techniques, using bag-of-words representation, with stop list and stemming, according to the vector space model (VSM) and linear support vector machine (SVM) classifiers. Heavy filtering makes a deeper analysis of the content including different linguistic features such as noun phrases recognized using POS, named entities, and some specific aspects depending of the language and different additional machine learning techniques [27].

The system was tested and evaluated by an end user team: Telefonica R&D and FCR (Spain), the software firm PIXEL (Italy), and the Liverpool Hope University (United Kingdom). There were considered different end user cases and educational contexts.

Some aspects were reaffirmed such as POESIA software should not be limited to filtering one language, filter a variety of content and allow flexibility for users to define the content that must be rejected. For the categories of contents filtered, pornography high, gross language medium and racism and violence low.

The POESIA architecture readily allows for the inclusion of additional or substitute filters, and so the open-source character of the project allows for the continuing development of the system.

We consider this project very important because it proposes an agent-like architecture, and a two-level filtering operation, that are still quite advanced. Also, its open-source nature makes an important difference.

8.3   NetProtect I and II

NetProtect[19] and NetProtect II are projects partially funded by the European Commission under the Safer Internet Action Plan and related to the development of rating and filtering systems for Internet content.

The NetProtect project (2001–2002) aimed at building a prototype of a third-party filtering solution able to filter out pornographic material found on Web pages expressed in either English, French, German, Greek, or Spanish. NetProtect II (2002–2003) was the follow-up project of NetProtect I. The overall objective of the NetProtect II project was to focus on improving and industrializing the NetProtect prototype in order to have a commercially available product by the end of this new project. Surf-mate was the final software solution commercialized based on the NetProtect components.

NetProtect provides a solution for Internet access filtering dealing with pornography, and also violence, bomb-making, and drugs found on Web sites expressed in eight languages: Dutch, English, French, German, Greek, Italian, Portuguese, and Spanish. The NetProtect project also investigated tools able to filter not only Web pages, but also discussion while chatting on the Web or reading newsgroups or email. It follows a similar scheme to the previous POESIA project integrating white and black lists and assessing textual and graphic content of each page individually.

Surf-mate is a resulting software tool from NetProtect. It finally combines all state-of-the-art techniques for classification of multimedia documents:

- Black/white list of URLs and keywords pattern detection mechanism to analyze URLs (thanks to Optenet[20])

---

[19] http://www.net-protect.org/.
[20] http://www.optenet.com/

- Machine learning based on the fly text (thanks to the text classifier that was especially developed for the NetProtect II project and the topic classifier that has been developed for the previous NetProtect project)
- Real-time images classification (based on the F4i's ICA component).

Perhaps, the first serious study of the effectiveness of existent filters that after guided the development of a commercial effective tool, makes this project a must know in the Web-filtering field.

9. Conclusions and Future Trends

In this chapter, we have presented a review of state-of-the-art Web content-filtering tools and techniques. The review is preceded by a motivation section that defines sensible usage scenarios of these tools, and discusses censorship and free speech issues. Also, we cover some attacks to filtering tools.

After this review, we reach the following conclusions:

- From the point of view of usage, Web content filters are a support tool. They must be used to enforce suitable Internet usage policies that must be agreed between decision makers and the users, and supported by a wide variety of other measures including education and information. Filters can only be as bad as the policies, and on the other side, they can be very valuable and contribute to children protection in the Internet.
- Technically, Web filters have reached a very good degree of complexity and effectiveness, and they are routinely deployed in a variety of scenarios. However, they are not perfect and still make mistakes. Further improvement is required.
- To foster the required technical improvement, the research community has to agree with respect to evaluation procedures and metrics. Moreover, we believe that the best approach to deal with this is following the good practice in the spam filtering domain, which is setting up a competitive evaluation framework similar to the spam filtering one.

As a final note, we must remind the ever-changing nature of the Web and its users. This covers especially content creators and sexual predators. On one side, everyone can easily publish a Web page (e.g., a blog), and this freedom must be encompassed with the need of children protection. On the other side, the emergence of new interaction tools (like, e.g., social networks like MySpace[21] or Facebook,[22] online games like World of Warcraft,[23] virtual worlds like Second Life[24] and Lively,[25] or content streaming sites like YouTube) must be supervised closely; kids and adolescents are easily attracted by these tools, where they get exposed to sexual predators. Next-generation Web filters must be able to deal with these evolving hazards.

REFERENCES

[1] Agarwal N., Liu H., and Zhang J., June 2006. Blocking objectionable Web content by leveraging multiple information sources. *SIGKDD Explorations Newsletter*, **8**(1): 17–26.

[2] American Civil Liberties Union, 2008. United States Court of Appeals for the Third Circuit, No. 07-2539, American Civil Liberties Union and others vs. Michael B. Musakey. Available at: http://www.ca3.uscourts.gov/opinarch/072539p.pdf.

[3] Arentz W. A., and Olstad B., 2004. Classifying offensive sites based on image content. *Computer Vision and Image Understanding*, **94**(1–3): 295–310.

[4] Bikel D., Schwartz R., and Weischedel R., 1999. An algorithm that learns what's in a name. *Machine Learning*, **34**(1–3): 211–231.

[5] Block J., 2008. Editorial: Issues for DSM-V: Internet addiction. *American Journal of Psychiatry*, **165**: 306–307.

[6] Breslau L., Cao P., Fan L., Phillips G., and Shenker S., 1999. Web caching and Zipf-like distributions: Evidence and implications. In *Proceedings of Infocom'99*, IEEE Press, New York, NY.

[7] Chou C., Sinha A., and Zhao H., 2008. A text mining approach to Internet abuse detection. *Information Systems and E-Business Management*, **6**: 419–439.

[8] Commission on Child Online Protection, 2000. Report to Congress. Available at: http://www.copacommission.org/report/COPAreport.pdf.

[9] Consortium for School Networking, 2001. Safeguarding the Wired Schoolhouse: A Briefing Paper on School District Options for Providing Access to Appropriate Internet Content. White Paper available at: http://www.safewiredschools.org/pubs_and_tools/white_paper.pdf.

[10] Cormack G., 2007. TREC 2007 spam track overview. In *Proceedings of the 16th Text Retrieval Conference (TREC 2007)*, NIST Special Publication: SP 500–274.

[11] Council of Europe, 2001. Convention of Cybercrime. ETS No. 185, available at: http://conventions.coe.int/Treaty/EN/Treaties/Html/185.htm.

[12] Council of Europe, 2003. Additional Protocol to the Convention on cybercrime, concerning the criminalisation of acts of a racist and xenophobic nature committed through computer systems. ETS No. 189, available at: http://conventions.coe.int/Treaty/en/Treaties/Html/189.htm.

[13] Dalvi N., Domingos P., Mausam S., Sanghai S., and Verma D., 2004. Adversarial classification. In *Proceedings of the 10th International Conference on Knowledge Discovery and Data Mining*, pp. 99–108. ACM Press, Seattle, WA.

[14] Daubechies I., 1992. Ten lectures on wavelets. In *Proceedings of SIAM'92*.

---

[21] http://www.myspace.com/.
[22] http://www.facebook.com/.
[23] http://www.worldofwarcraft.com/.
[24] http://secondlife.com/.
[25] http://www.lively.com/.

[15] Deibert R., Palfrey J., Rohozinski R., and Zittrain J., (Eds.) 2008. Access Denied: The Practice and Policy of Global Internet Filtering. MIT Press, Cambridge, MA.

[16] Dumais S. T., Platt J., Heckerman D., and Sahami M., 1998. Inductive learning algorithms and representations for text categorization. In *Proceedings of CIKM-98, 7th ACM International Conference on Information and Knowledge Management*, (G. Gardarin, J. C. French, N. Pissinou, K. Makki, and L. Bouganim, Eds.) pp. 148–155. ACM Press, New York, NY.

[17] European Commission Against Racism and Intolerance, 2006. Expert Seminar: Combating Racism while respecting Freedom of Expression Proceedings, Strasbourg, 16–17 November 2006, available at: http://www.coe.int/t/dghl/monitoring/ecri/activities/22-Freedom_of_expression_Seminar_2006/NSBR2006_proceedings_en.pdf.

[18] Firstbrook P., 2007. Pros and Cons of SaaS Secure Web Gateway Solutions, Gartner Research, ID No. G00145299.

[19] Fleck M., Forsyth D., and Bregler C., 1996. Finding naked people. In *Proceedings of the 4th European Conference on Computer Vision*, Cambridge, UK, pp. 593–602.

[20] Forsyth D. A., and Fleck M. M., 1996. Identifying nude pictures. In *Applications of Computer Vision, 1996, Proceedings 3rd IEEE Workshop on WACV*, pp. 103–108.

[21] Fox A., 2007. Caught in the Web. *HR Magazine*, **52**(12): 35–39.

[22] Gómez Hidalgo J. M., Puertas Sanz E., Carrero García F., and de Buenaga Rodríguez M., 2003. Categorización de texto sensible al coste para el filtrado de contenidos inapropiados en Internet. *Procesamiento del Lenguaje Natural*, **31:** 13–20 (in Spanish).

[23] Greevy E., and Smeaton A. F., 2004. Text categorisation of racist texts using a support vector machine. In *Proceedings of JADT*.

[24] Guermazi R., Hammami M., and Hamadou A., 2007. Combining Classifiers for Web Violent Content Detection and Filtering Computational Science—ICCS 2007, pp. 773–780.

[25] Hammami M., Chahir Y., and Chen L., February 2006. Webguard: A Web filtering engine combining textual, structural, and visual content-based analysis. *IEEE Transactions on Knowledge and Data Engineering*, **18**(2): 272–284.

[26] Hearst M., 1999. Untangling text data mining. In *Proceedings of ACL'99: The 37th Annual Meeting of the Association for Computational Linguistics*.

[27] Hepple M., Ireson N., Allegrini P., Marchi S., Montemagni S., and Gomez Hidalgo J. M., 2004. NLP-enhanced content filtering within the POESIA project. In *Proceedings of LREC*.

[28] Internet Security Systems, 2006. Proventia content analysis technology: An ISS whitepaper. Document No. PM-PROCONA-0506.

[29] Joachims T., 1998. Text categorization with support vector machines: Learning with many relevant features. In *Proceedings of the European Conference on Machine Learning*, (C. Nédellec and C. Rouveirol, Eds.), pp. 137–142. Springer-Verlag, Berlin.

[30] Jones M. J., and Rehg J. M., 1998. *Statistical color models with applications to skin detection*, Technical Report CRL 98/11.

[31] Kam K., 2007. 4 Dangers of the Internet. WebMD, available at: http://www.webmd.com/parenting/features/4-dangers-internet.

[32] Kim Y., Nam T., and Won D., 2006. 2-way text classification for harmful Web documents. In *Computational Science and Its Applications—ICCSA 2006*, pp. 545–551.

[33] Kim C., Kwon O., Kim W., and Choi S., 2008. Automatic system for filtering obscene video. In *ICACT 2008. 10th International Conference on Advanced Communication Technology*, vol. 2, pp. 1435–1438.

[34] Kozima H., 1993. Text segmentation based on similarity between words. In *Proceedings of the 31st Annual Meeting on Association for Computational Linguistics*, 22–26 June 1993, Columbus, OH.

[35] Lee P., Hui S., and Fong A., 2002. Neural networks for Web content filtering. In *Intelligent Systems*, IEEE, vol. 17(5): pp. 48–57.

[36] Lefebvre G., Zheng H., and Laurent C., 2006. Objectionable image detection by ASSOM competition. In *Proceedings of the International Conference on Image and Video Retrieval*, July 2006, (A. Z. Tempe and H. Sundaram *et al.*, Eds.), Lecture Notes in Computer Science, **4071**: pp. 201–210. Springer-Verlag, Berlin.

[37] Lenhart A., and Madden M., 2007. Teens, Privacy & Online Social Networks. Pew Internet & American Life Project report, available at: http://www.pewinternet.org/pdfs/PIP_Teens_Privacy_SNS_Report_Final.pdf.

[38] Lewis D. D., 1992. Representation and learning in information retrieval. Ph.D. Thesis, Department of Computer Science. University of Massachusetts, Amherst, MA.

[39] Li Y. H., and Jain A. K., 1998. Classification of text documents. *The Computer Journal*, **41**(8): 537–546.

[40] Lim V., Thompson S., and Loo G., 2002. How do I loaf here? Let me count the ways. *Communications of the ACM*, **45**(1): 66–70.

[41] Palo Alto Networks, 2008. The Application Usage and Risk Report. An Analysis of End User Application Trends in the Enterprise. White Paper available at: http://www.paloaltonetworks.com/literature/whitepapers/Application_Usage_Risk_Report_April08.pdf.

[42] Polpinij J., Chotthanom A., Sibunruang C., Chamchong R., and Puangpronpitag S., 2006. Content-based text classifiers for pornographic Web filtering. In *IEEE International Conference on Systems, Man and Cybernetics, 2006 (SMC'06)*, vol. 2, pp. 1481–1485.

[43] Princeton Survey Research Associates International, 2004. Parents & Teens 2004 Survey. A survey conducted for the Pew Internet & American Life Project, available at: http://www.pewinternet.org/pdfs/PIP_Teens_04_Questionnaire.pdf.

[44] Resnick P., and Miller J., 1996. PICS: Internet access controls without censorship. *Communications of the ACM*, **39**(10): 87–93.

[45] Resnick P., Hansen D., and Richardson C., September 2004. Calculating error rates for filtering software. *Communications of the ACM*, **47**(9): 67–71.

[46] Richardson C., Resnick P., Hansen D., and Rideout V., 2002. Does pornography-blocking software block access to health information on the Internet? *Journal of the American Medical Association*, **288**(22): 2887–2894.

[47] Rideout V., 2007. Parents, Children & Media. A Kaiser Family Foundation Survey, available at: http://kaiserfamilyfoundation.org/entmedia/upload/7638.pdf.

[48] Rowley H. A., Jing Y., and Baluja S., 2006. Large scale image-based adult-content filtering. In *International Conference on Computer Vision Theory and Applications*.

[49] Rubenking N., 2008. 12 Tools to Keep Kids Safe Online. PC Magazine Security Product Guide, available at: http://www.pcmag.com/article2/0,2817,2272565,00.asp.

[50] Salton G., and McGill M. J., 1983. Introduction to Modern Information Retrieval. McGraw-Hill Computer SeriesNew York, NY.

[51] Schapire R., and Singer Y., 2000. BoosTexter: A boosting-based system for text categorization. *Machine Learning*, **39**(2–3): 135–168.

[52] Schettini R., Brambilla C., Cusano C., and Cixocca G., 2003. On the detection of pornographic digital images. In *Visual Communications and Image Processing 2003. Proceedings of the SPIE*, (T. Ebrahimi and T. Sikora, Eds.), vol. 5150, pp. 2105–2113.

[53] Sebastiani F., 2002. Machine learning in automated text categorization. *ACM Computing Surveys*, **34**(1): 1–47.

[54] Sebastiani F., 2006. Classification of text, automatic. In *The Encyclopaedia of Language and Linguistics*, (K. Brown, Ed.), 2nd edn, vol. 14, pp. 457–462. Elsevier Science Publishers, Amsterdam, Netherlands.

[55] Siau K., Fui-Hoon F., and Teng L., 2002. Acceptable Internet use policy. *Communications of the ACM*, **45**(1): 75–79.

[56] Simmers C., 2002. Aligning Internet usage with business priorities. *Communications of the ACM*, **45**(1): 71–74.

[57] Spink A., Jansen B. J., Wolfram D., and Saracevic T., 2002. From e-sex to e-commerce: Web search changes. *IEEE Computer*, **35**(3): 133–135.

[58] Stanton J., 2002. Company profile of the frequent Internet user. *Communications of the ACM*, **45**(1): 55–59.

[59] Su G., Li J., Ma Y., and Li S., 2004. Improving the precision of the keyword-matching pornographic text filtering method using a hybrid model. *Journal of Zhejiang University Science*, **5**(9): 1106–1113.

[60] Victory N., 2003. Children's Internet Protection Act. Pub. L. 106–554, Study of Technology Protection Measures in Section 1703, Report to Congress, available at: http://www.ntia.doc.gov/ntiahome/ntiageneral/cipa2003/cipareport_08142003.htm.

[61] Wang J., Li J., Wiederhold G., and Firschein O., 1998. System for screening objectionable images. In Computer Communications vol. 21(15), pp. 1355–1360. Elsevier Science Publishers, Amsterdam, Netherlands.

[62] Websense, Inc., 2006. Web@Work Survey 2006. Conducted by Harris Interactive (available at http://www.websense.com/).

[63] Wynn A., and Trudeau P., 2001. Internet abuse at work: Corporate networks are paying the price. SurfControl White Paper.

[64] Yang Y., and Pedersen J. O., 1997. A comparative study on feature selection in text categorization. In *Proceedings of ICML-97, 14th International Conference on Machine Learning*, (D. H. Fisher, Ed.), pp. 412–420. Morgan Kaufmann Publishers, San Francisco, CA.

[65] Zheng H., Liu H., and Daoudi M., 2004. Blocking objectionable images: Adult images and harmful symbols. In 2004 *IEEE International Conference on Multimedia and Expo*, vol. 2, pp. 1223–1226.

Author Index

Numbers in *italics* indicate the pages on which complete references are given.

Subject Index

Contents of Volumes in This Series

339